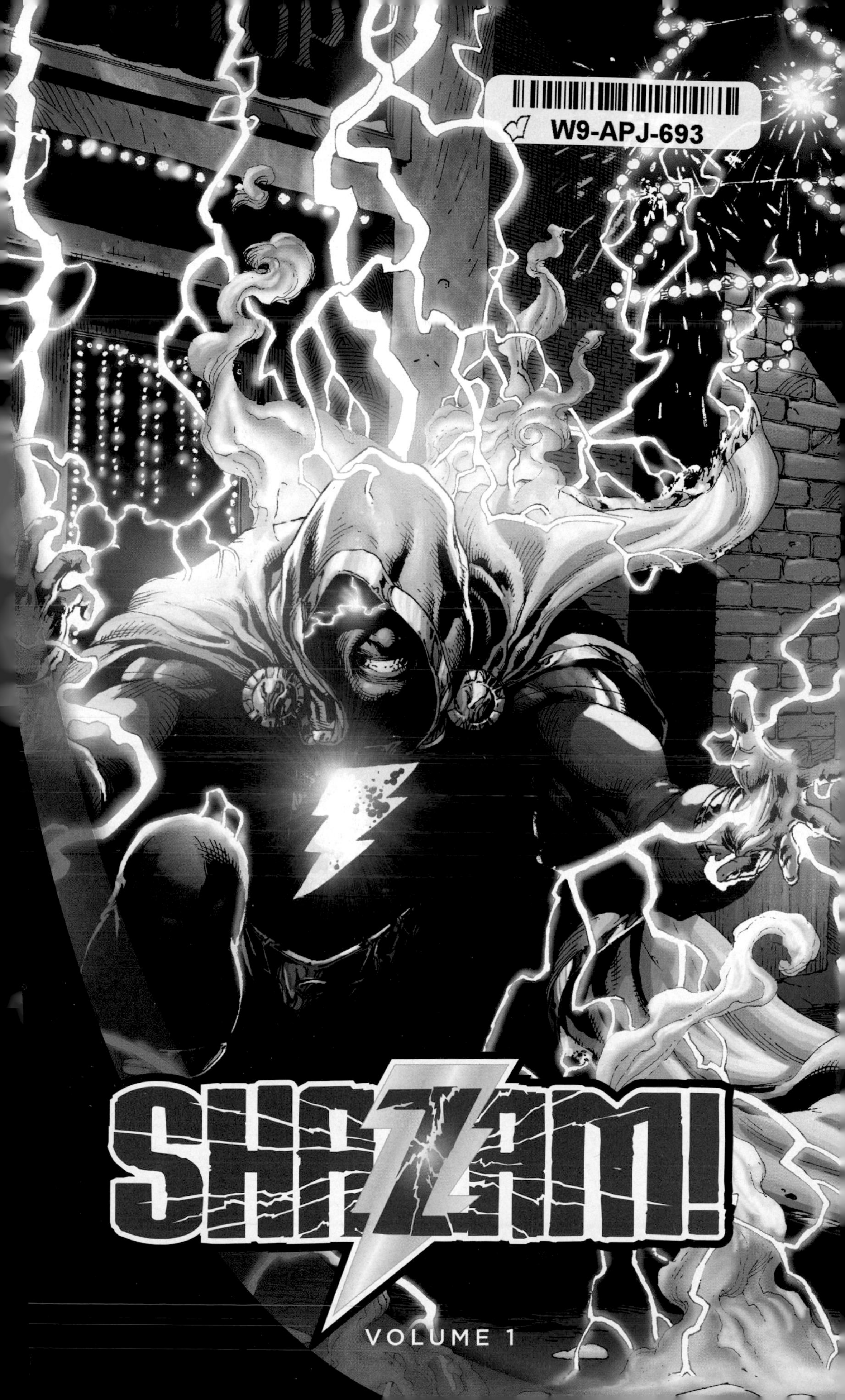

SHAZAM!

VOLUME 1

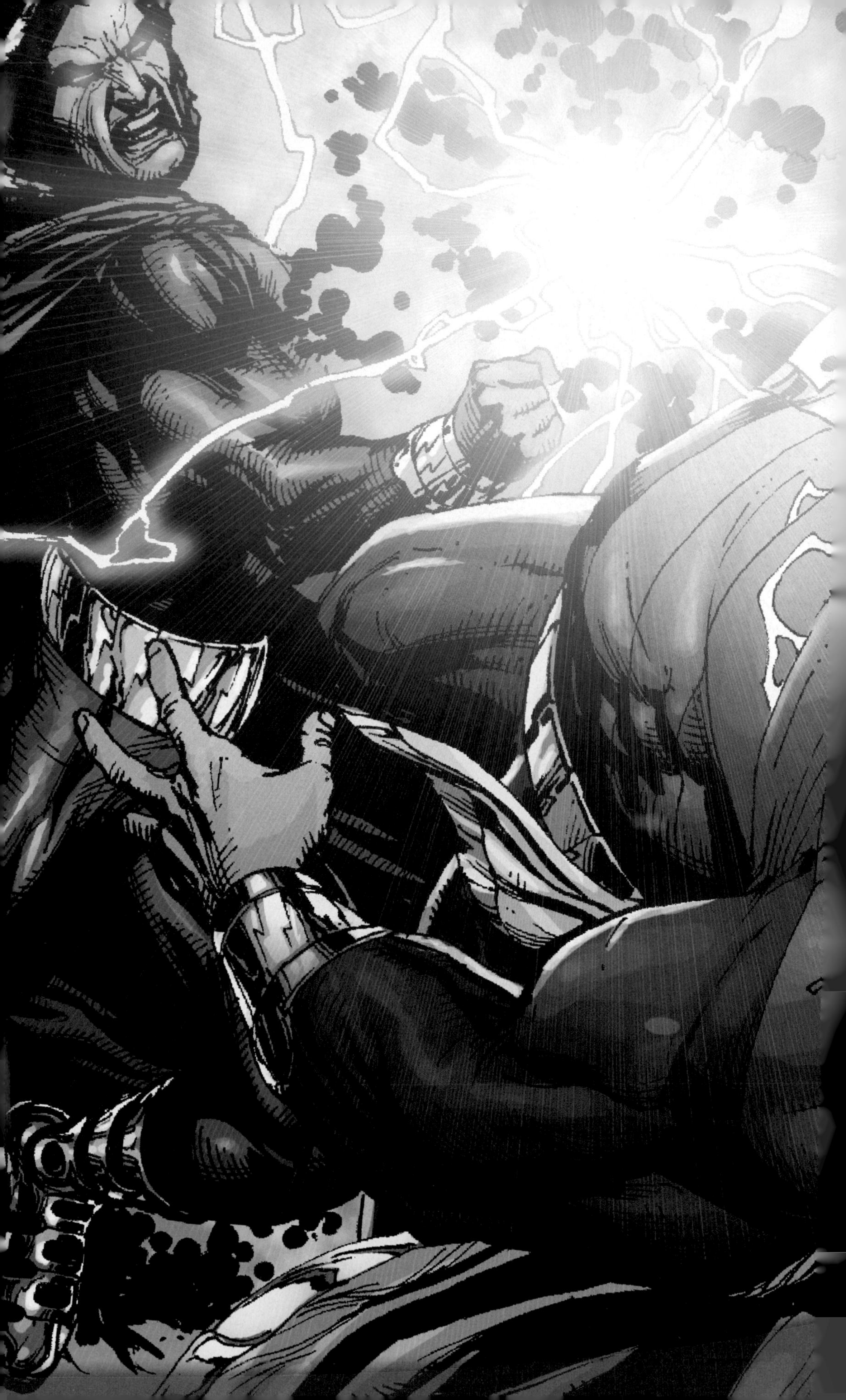

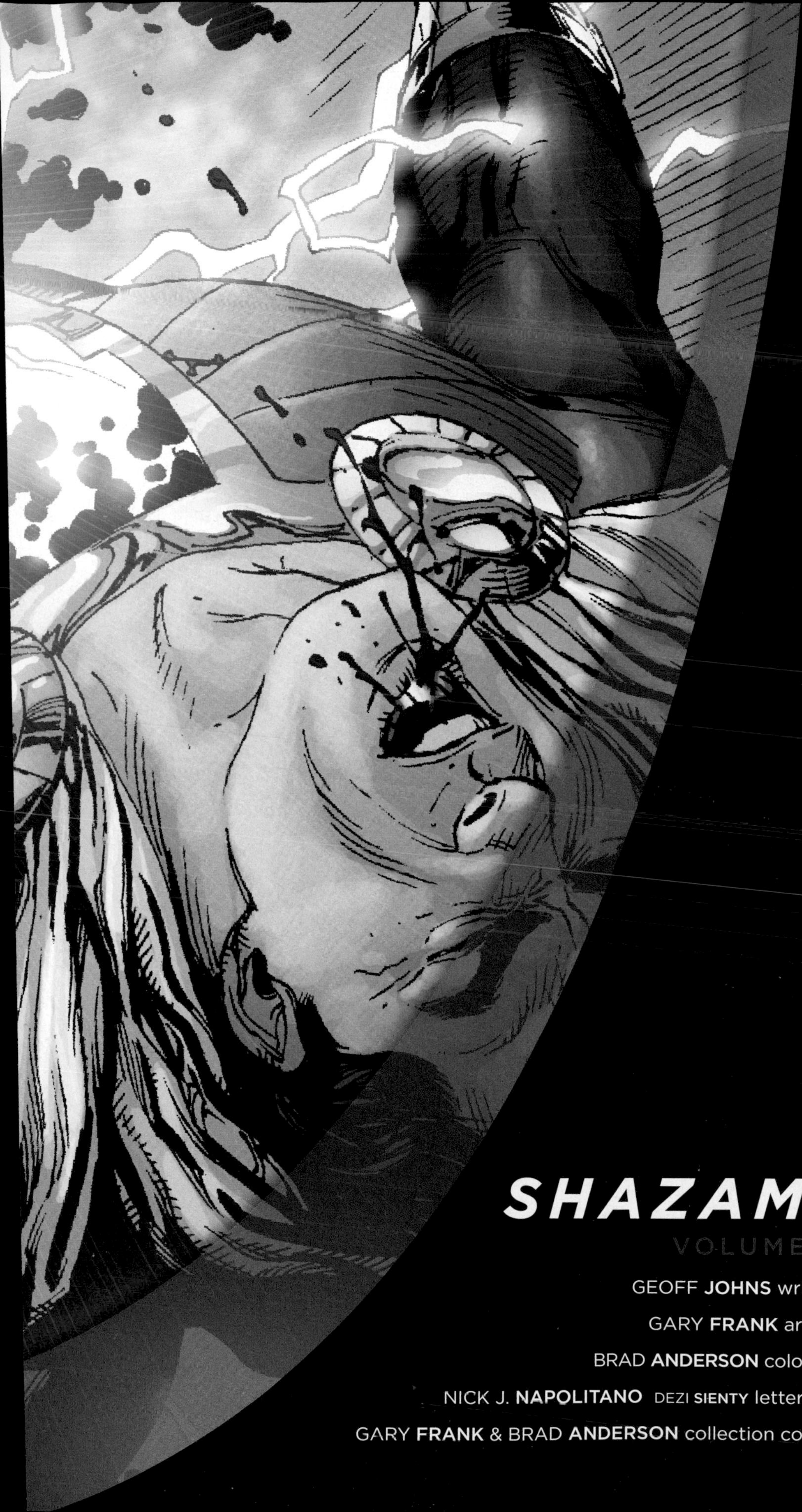

SHAZAM!

VOLUME 1

GEOFF **JOHNS** writer

GARY **FRANK** artist

BRAD **ANDERSON** colorist

NICK J. **NAPOLITANO** DEZI **SIENTY** letterers

GARY **FRANK** & BRAD **ANDERSON** collection cover

BRIAN CUNNINGHAM Editor - Original Series KATIE KUBERT Associate Editor - Original Series
DARREN SHAN KATE STEWART Assistant Editors - Original Series
JEB WOODARD Group Editor - Collected Editions PETER HAMBOUSSI Editor - Collected Edition
STEVE COOK Design Director - Books ROBBIE BIEDERMAN Publication Design

BOB HARRAS Senior VP - Editor-in-Chief, DC Comics
PAT McCALLUM Executive Editor, DC Comics

DAN DiDIO Publisher JIM LEE Publisher & Chief Creative Officer
BOBBIE CHASE VP - New Publishing Initiatives & Talent Development
DON FALLETTI VP - Manufacturing Operations & Workflow Management LAWRENCE GANEM VP - Talent Services
ALISON GILL Senior VP - Manufacturing & Operations HANK KANALZ Senior VP - Publishing Strategy & Support Services
DAN MIRON VP - Publishing Operations NICK J. NAPOLITANO VP - Manufacturing Administration & Design NANCY SPEARS VP - S
MICHELE R. WELLS VP & Executive Editor, Young Reader

SHAZAM! VOLUME 1

DC Comics, 2900 West Alameda Avenue, Burbank, CA 91505
DC - a WarnerMedia Company.
Printed by LSC Communications, Kendallville, IN, USA. 6/21/19. Fourth Printing.

SC ISBN: 978-1-4012-4699-0

PEFC Certified
This product is from sustainably managed forests and controlled sources
PEFC
PEFC/29-31-337
www.pefc.org

Library of Congress Cataloging-in-Publication Data

Johns, Geoff, 1973- author.
Shazam! volume 1 / Geoff Johns, Gary Frank.
pages cm
"Originally published in single magazine form as Justice League 7-11, 0, 14-16, 18-21."
ISBN 978-1-4012-4699-0
1. Graphic novels. I. Frank, Gary, 1969- illustrator. II. Title.
PN6728.S46J64 2013
741.5'973—dc23
2013020543

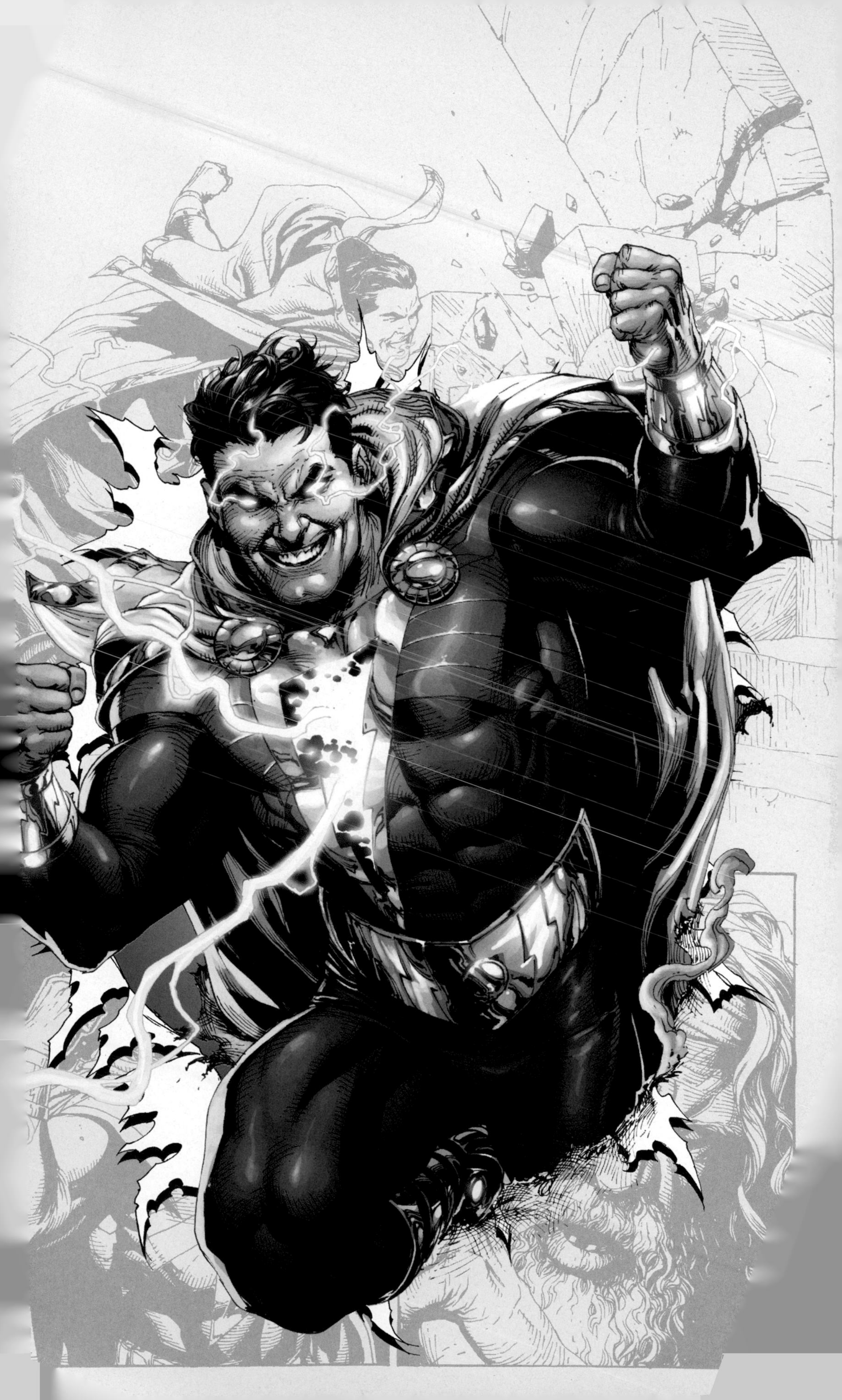

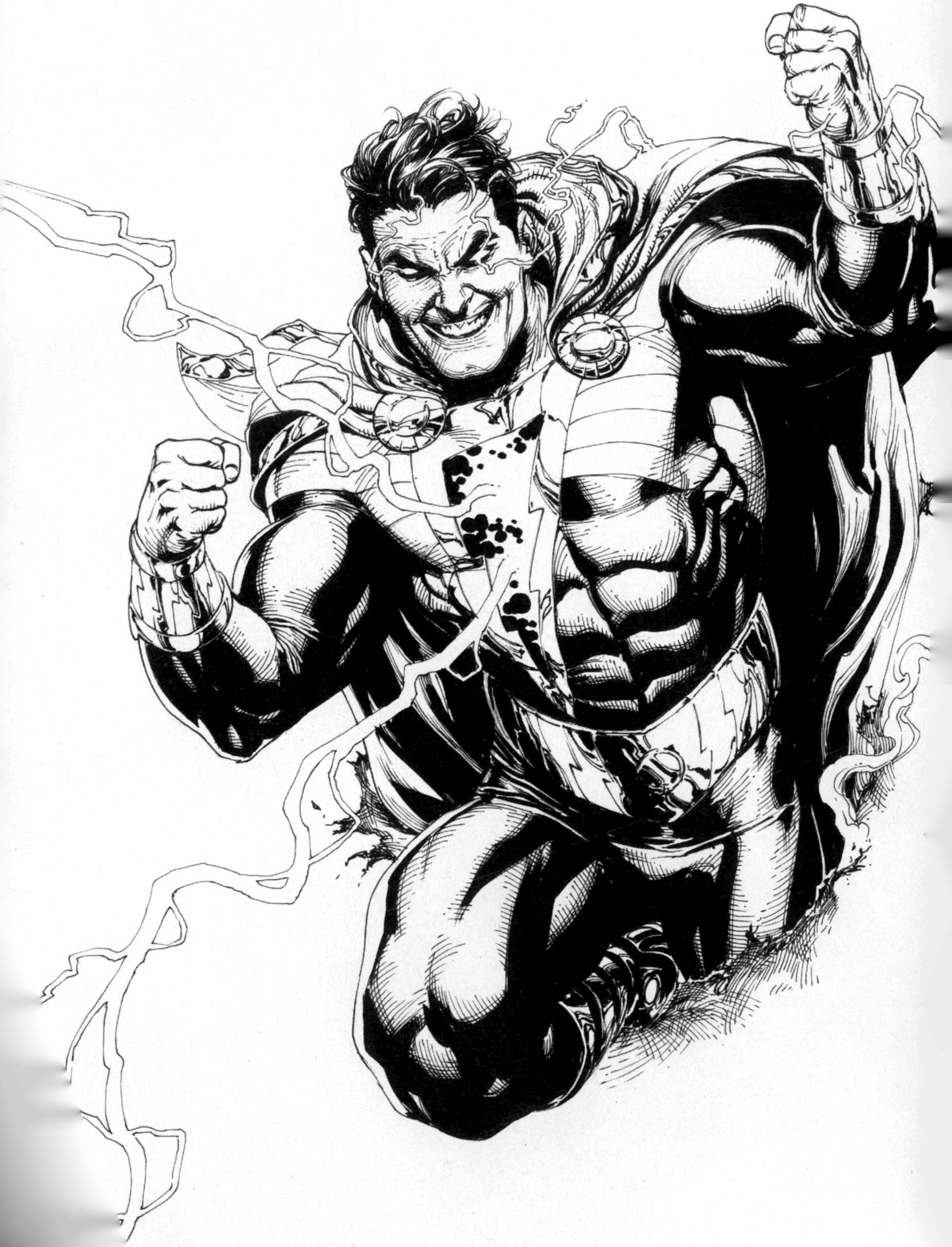

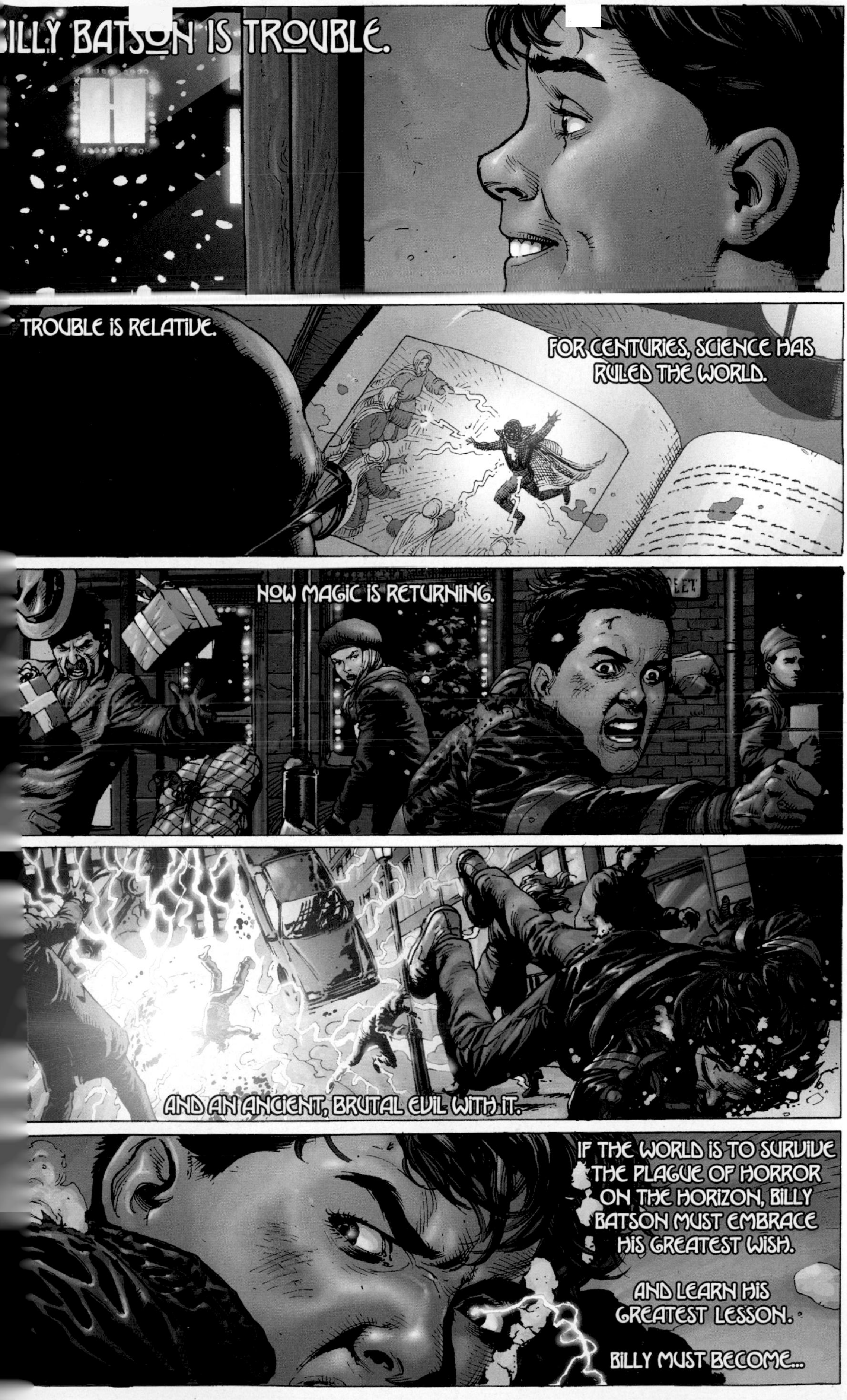
ILLY BATSON IS TROUBLE.
TROUBLE IS RELATIVE.
FOR CENTURIES, SCIENCE HAS RULED THE WORLD.
NOW MAGIC IS RETURNING.
AND AN ANCIENT, BRUTAL EVIL WITH IT.
IF THE WORLD IS TO SURVIVE THE PLAGUE OF HORROR ON THE HORIZON, BILLY BATSON MUST EMBRACE HIS GREATEST WISH.
AND LEARN HIS GREATEST LESSON.
BILLY MUST BECOME...

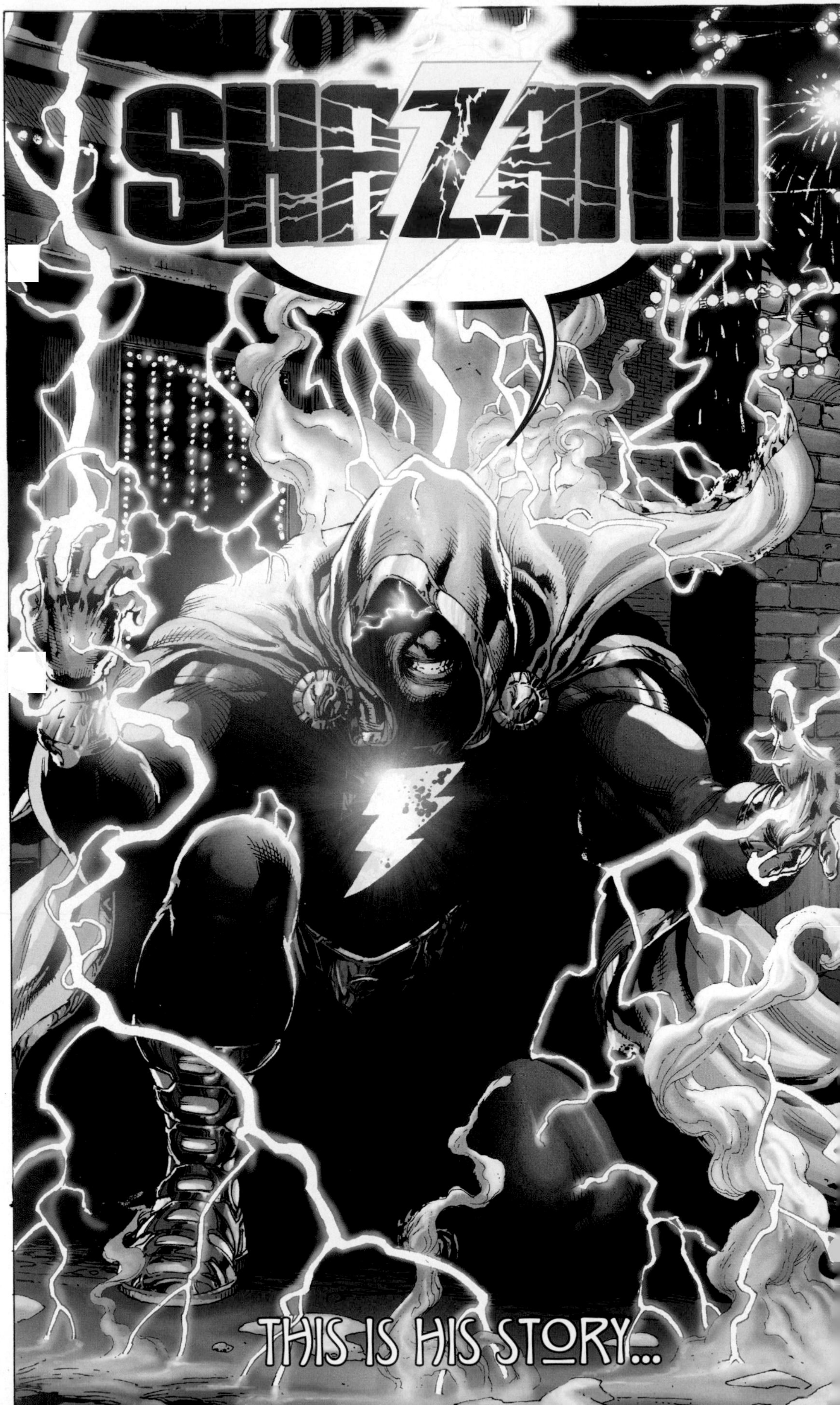
SHAZAM!
THIS IS HIS STORY...

"IT HAPPENED ON A NORMAL DAY."

"I WAS ON MY WAY TO WORK LIKE ALWAYS."

"I DON'T REMEMBER DOING ANYTHING SPECIAL."

NO HOME
NO MONEY
NO FOOD.

WALKED INTO THE BUILDING.

"I GOT IN THE ELEVATOR WITH EVERYONE.

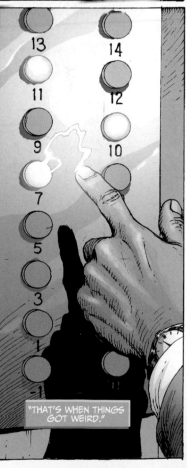

"THAT'S WHEN THINGS GOT WEIRD."

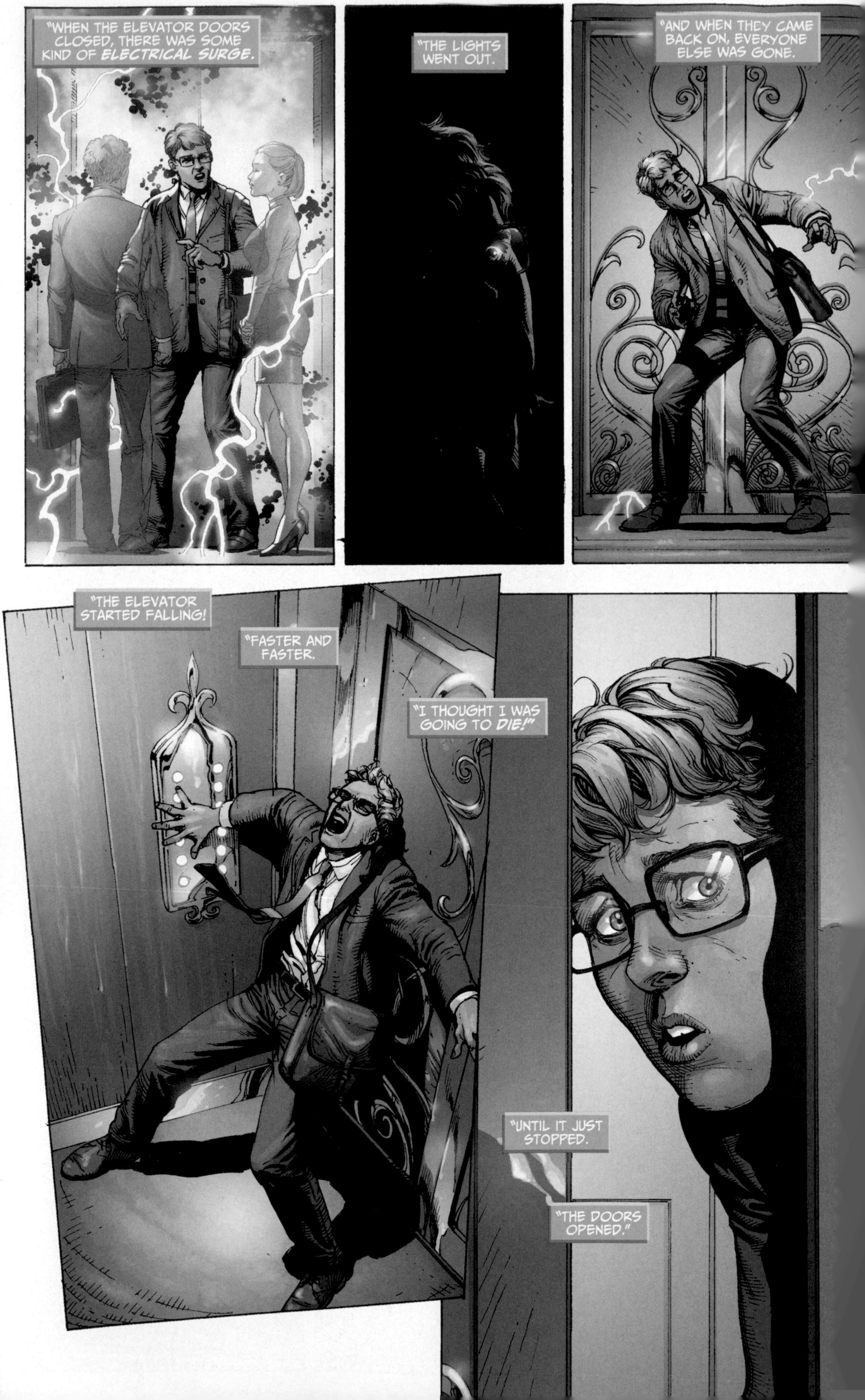
"WHEN THE ELEVATOR DOORS CLOSED, THERE WAS SOME KIND OF *ELECTRICAL SURGE*.
"THE LIGHTS WENT OUT.
"AND WHEN THEY CAME BACK ON, EVERYONE ELSE WAS GONE.
"THE ELEVATOR STARTED FALLING!
"FASTER AND FASTER.
"I THOUGHT I WAS GOING TO *DIE!*"
"UNTIL IT JUST STOPPED.
"THE DOORS OPENED."

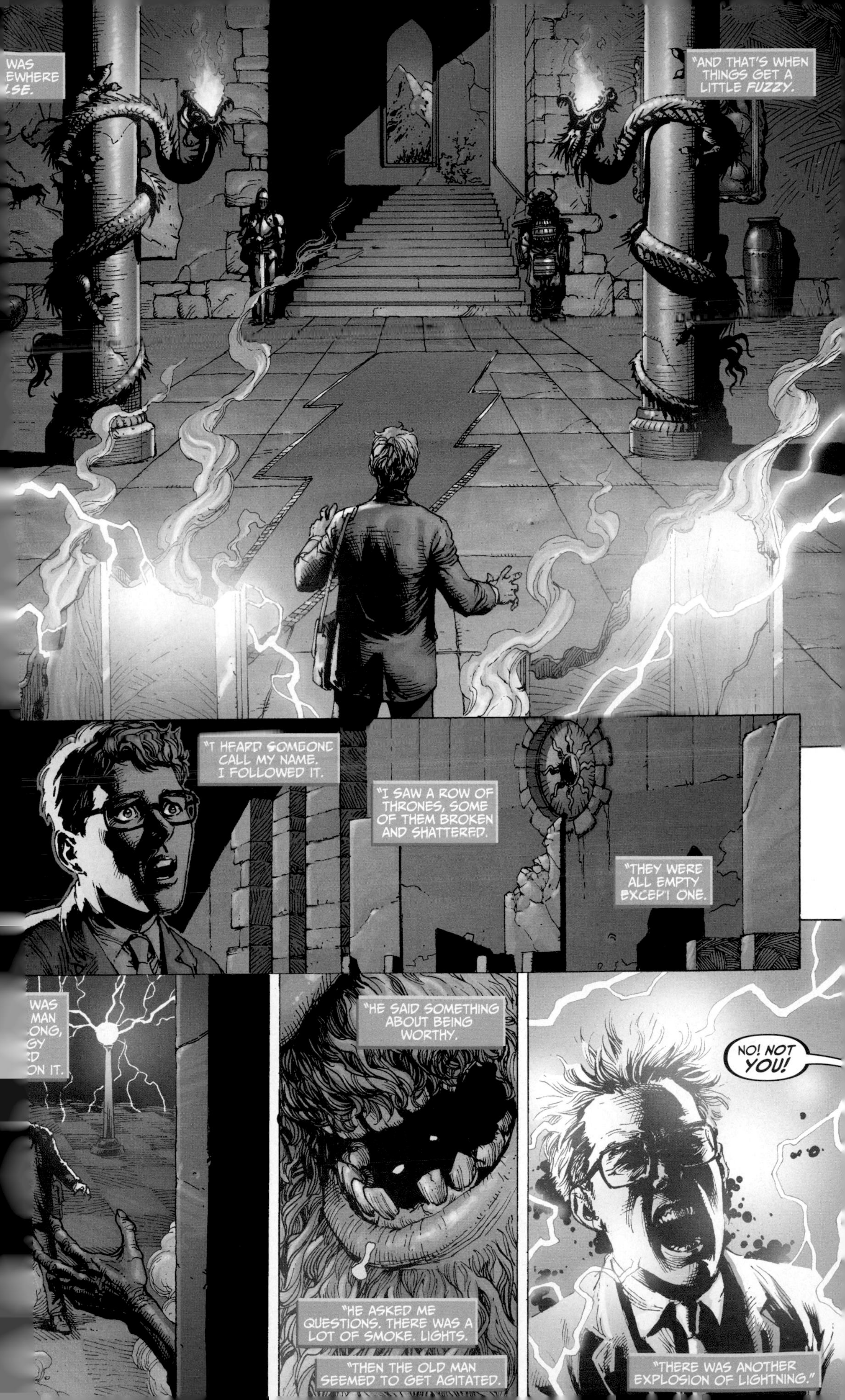
WAS
EWHERE
LSE.
"AND THAT'S WHEN THINGS GET A LITTLE FUZZY.
"I HEARD SOMEONE CALL MY NAME. I FOLLOWED IT.
"I SAW A ROW OF THRONES, SOME OF THEM BROKEN AND SHATTERED.
"THEY WERE ALL EMPTY EXCEPT ONE.
WAS
MAN
ONG,
GY
D
ON IT.
"HE SAID SOMETHING ABOUT BEING WORTHY.
"HE ASKED ME QUESTIONS. THERE WAS A LOT OF SMOKE. LIGHTS.
"THEN THE OLD MAN SEEMED TO GET AGITATED.
NO! NOT YOU!
"THERE WAS ANOTHER EXPLOSION OF LIGHTNING."

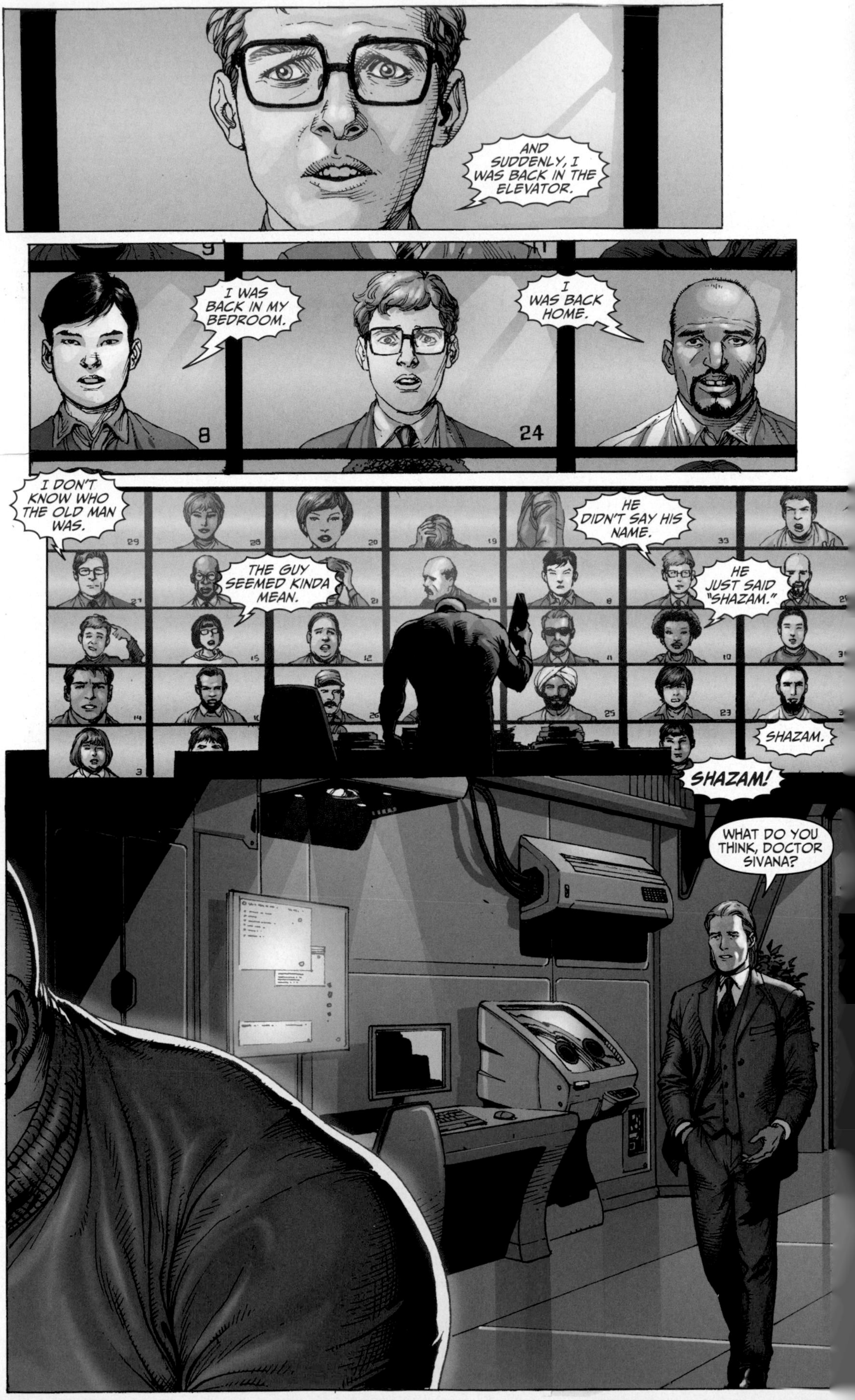
AND SUDDENLY, I WAS BACK IN THE ELEVATOR.
I WAS BACK IN MY BEDROOM.
I WAS BACK HOME.
I DON'T KNOW WHO THE OLD MAN WAS.
THE GUY SEEMED KINDA MEAN.
HE DIDN'T SAY HIS NAME.
HE JUST SAID "SHAZAM."
SHAZAM.
SHAZAM!
WHAT DO YOU THINK, DOCTOR SIVANA?

I THINK THIRTY-SEVEN PEOPLE FROM *ACROSS* THE *WORLD* WITH NO CONNECTION WHATSOEVER ALL SEEM TO SHARE A *SIMILAR EXPERIENCE.*

THEY WALKED INTO AN ELEVATOR OR OUT OF A TENT OR ONTO A BUS AND IN A *BURST OF LIGHTNING*--

--ENDED UP *SOMEWHERE* ELSE.

SOMEWHERE *STRANGE.*

THIS ISN'T THE FIRST CLAIM OF *"MYSTICAL ABDUCTION,"* GREGORY.

WHEN THESE ACCOUNTS ARE TAKEN AS A *WHOLE,* THE DETAILS START TO TELL A TALE THAT CORRELATES ALMOST EXACTLY TO THE LEGEND OF *BLACK ADAM.*

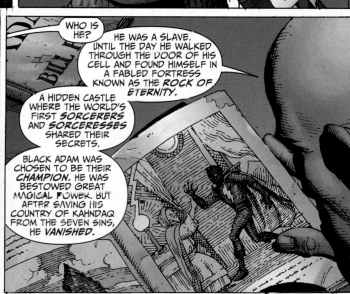

WHO IS HE?

HE WAS A SLAVE. UNTIL THE DAY HE WALKED THROUGH THE DOOR OF HIS CELL AND FOUND HIMSELF IN A FABLED FORTRESS KNOWN AS THE *ROCK OF ETERNITY.*

A HIDDEN CASTLE WHERE THE WORLD'S FIRST *SORCERERS* AND *SORCERESSES* SHARED THEIR SECRETS.

BLACK ADAM WAS CHOSEN TO BE THEIR *CHAMPION.* HE WAS BESTOWED GREAT *MAGICAL POWER.* BUT AFTER SAVING HIS COUNTRY OF KAHNDAQ FROM THE SEVEN SINS, HE *VANISHED.*

THE TALE OF *BLACK ADAM* IS MORE THAN A SIMPLE STORY.

IT *HAS* TO BE!

I SPENT MY *LIFE* TRYING TO UNLOCK THE *SECRETS* OF *SCIENCE* TO SAVE MY FAMILY.

BUT SCIENCE *FAILED.* THEY NEED A *MIRACLE.*

THEY NEED *MAGIC.*

MAGIC *EXISTS.*

AND AT LAST I KNOW HOW TO *FIND* IT.

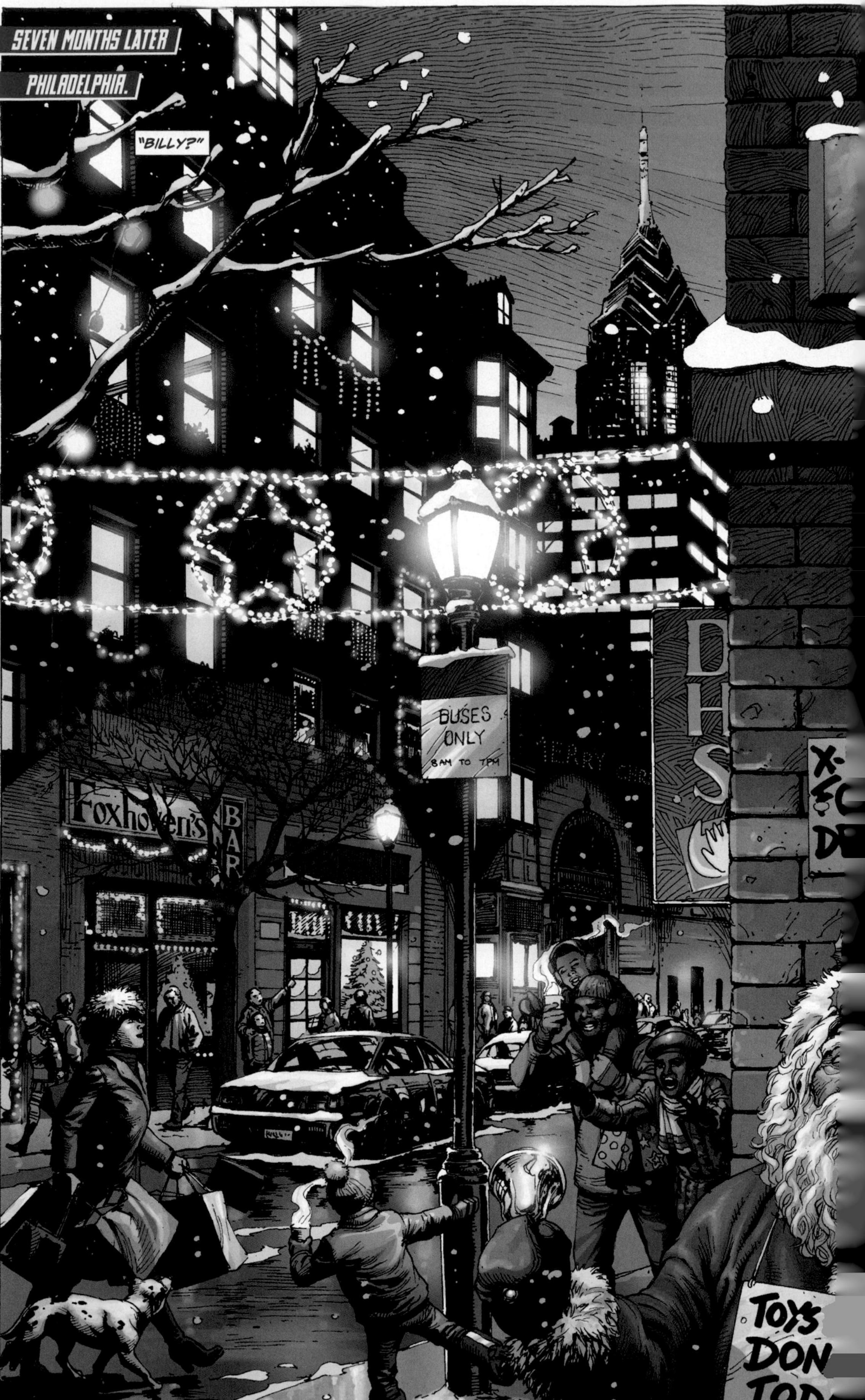
SEVEN MONTHS LATER
PHILADELPHIA.
"BILLY?"
BUSES ONLY
8AM TO 7PM
Foxhoven's
BAR

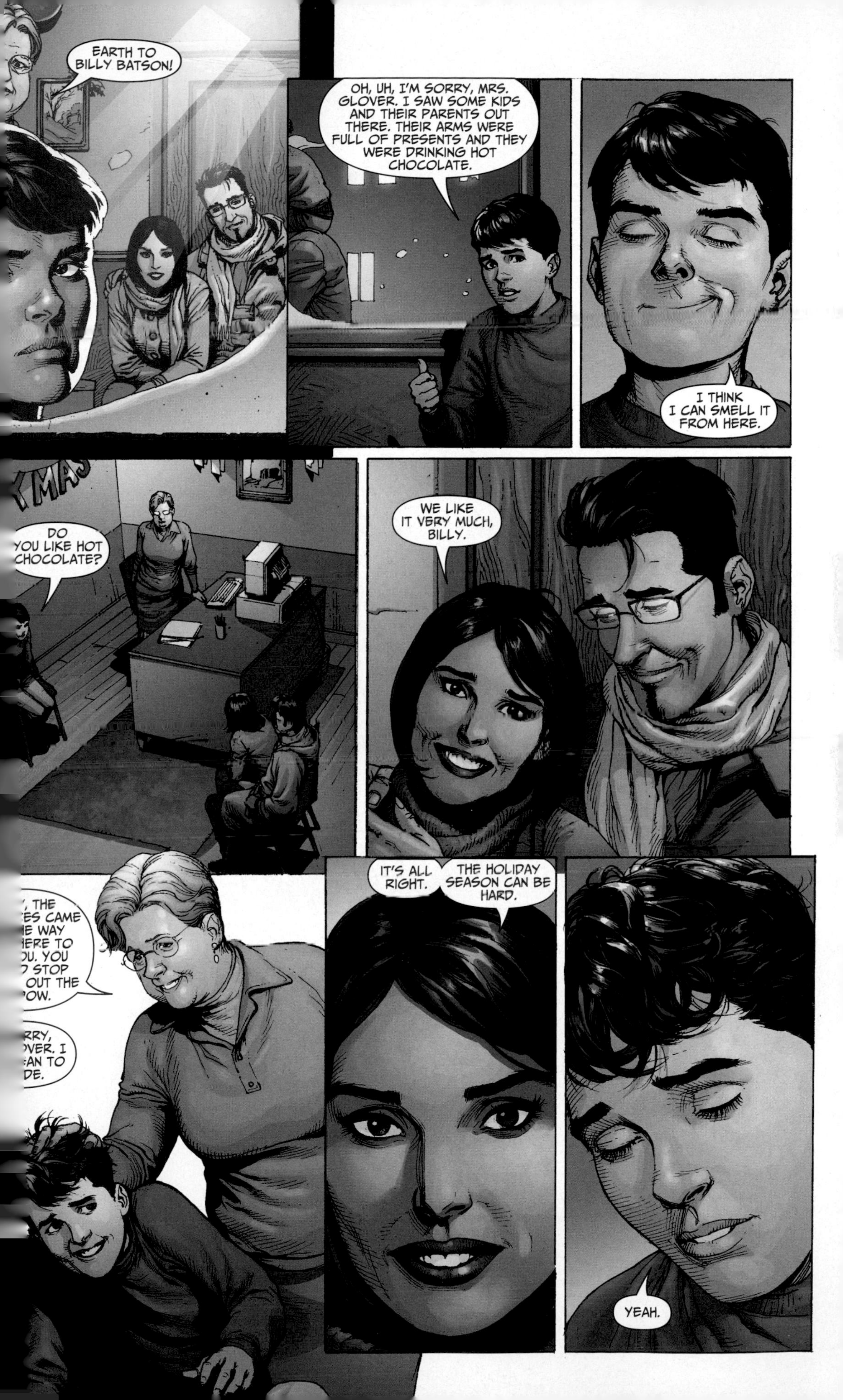
EARTH TO BILLY BATSON!
OH, UH, I'M SORRY, MRS. GLOVER. I SAW SOME KIDS AND THEIR PARENTS OUT THERE. THEIR ARMS WERE FULL OF PRESENTS AND THEY WERE DRINKING HOT CHOCOLATE.
I THINK I CAN SMELL IT FROM HERE.
DO YOU LIKE HOT CHOCOLATE?
WE LIKE IT VERY MUCH, BILLY.
IT'S ALL RIGHT.
THE HOLIDAY SEASON CAN BE HARD.
YEAH.

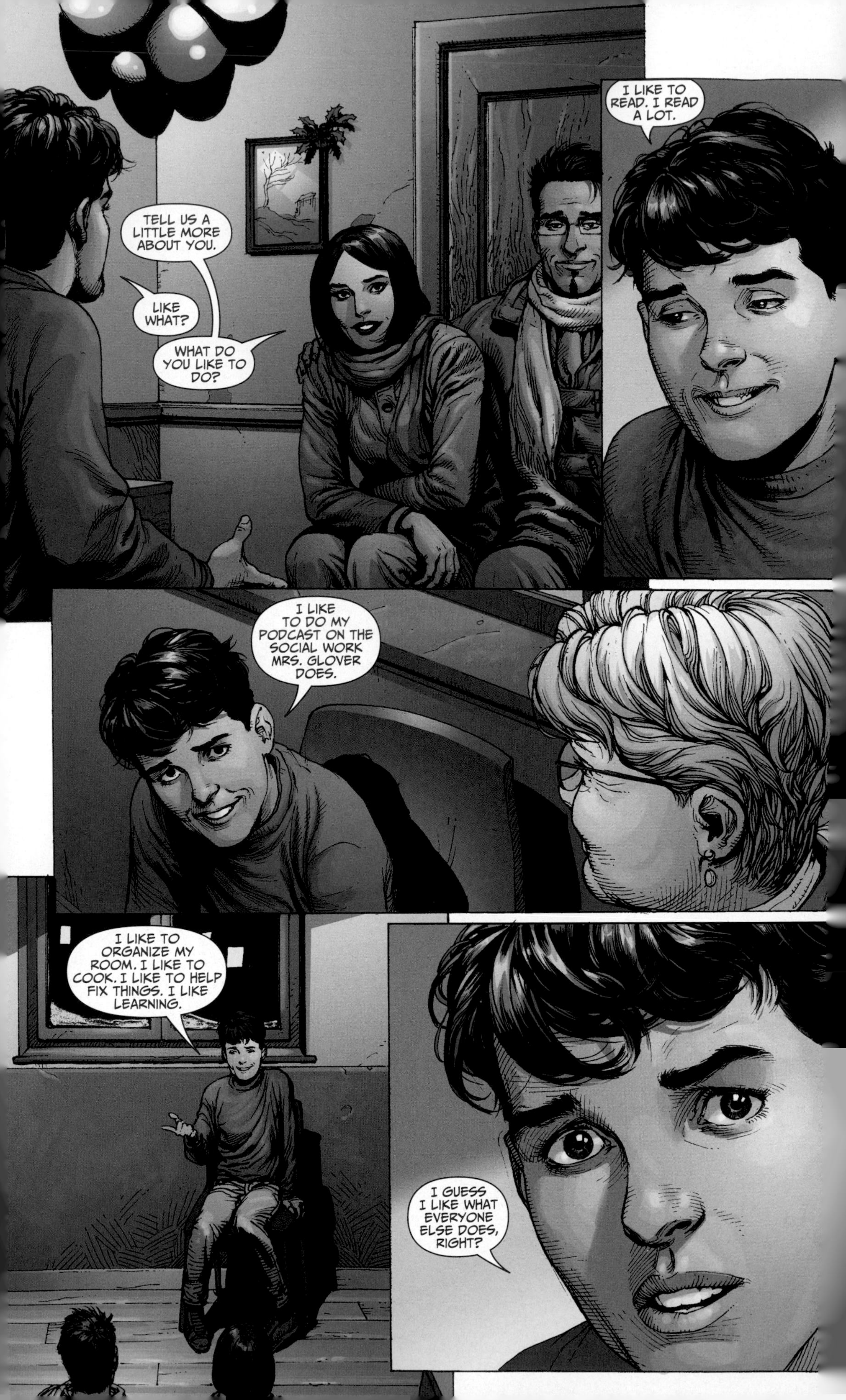
TELL US A LITTLE MORE ABOUT YOU.
LIKE WHAT?
WHAT DO YOU LIKE TO DO?
I LIKE TO READ. I READ A LOT.
I LIKE TO DO MY PODCAST ON THE SOCIAL WORK MRS. GLOVER DOES.
I LIKE TO ORGANIZE MY ROOM. I LIKE TO COOK. I LIKE TO HELP FIX THINGS. I LIKE LEARNING.
I GUESS I LIKE WHAT EVERYONE ELSE DOES, RIGHT?

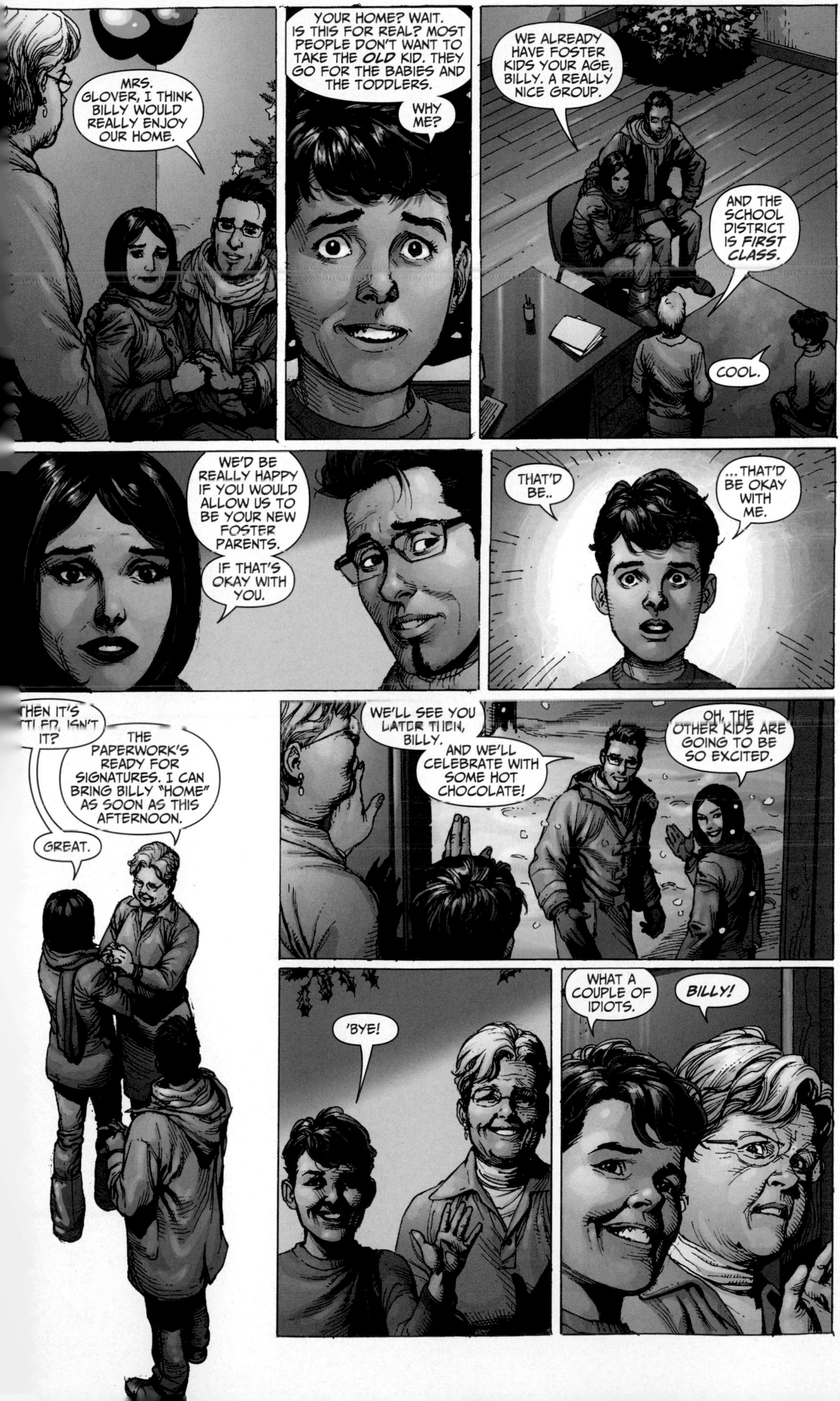
MRS. GLOVER, I THINK BILLY WOULD REALLY ENJOY OUR HOME.
YOUR HOME? WAIT. IS THIS FOR REAL? MOST PEOPLE DON'T WANT TO TAKE THE OLD KID. THEY GO FOR THE BABIES AND THE TODDLERS.
WHY ME?
WE ALREADY HAVE FOSTER KIDS YOUR AGE, BILLY. A REALLY NICE GROUP.
AND THE SCHOOL DISTRICT IS FIRST CLASS.
COOL.
WE'D BE REALLY HAPPY IF YOU WOULD ALLOW US TO BE YOUR NEW FOSTER PARENTS.
IF THAT'S OKAY WITH YOU.
THAT'D BE..
...THAT'D BE OKAY WITH ME.
THEN IT'S TTLED, ISN'T IT?
THE PAPERWORK'S READY FOR SIGNATURES. I CAN BRING BILLY "HOME" AS SOON AS THIS AFTERNOON.
GREAT.
WE'LL SEE YOU LATER THEN, BILLY.
AND WE'LL CELEBRATE WITH SOME HOT CHOCOLATE!
OH, THE OTHER KIDS ARE GOING TO BE SO EXCITED.
'BYE!
WHAT A COUPLE OF IDIOTS.
BILLY!

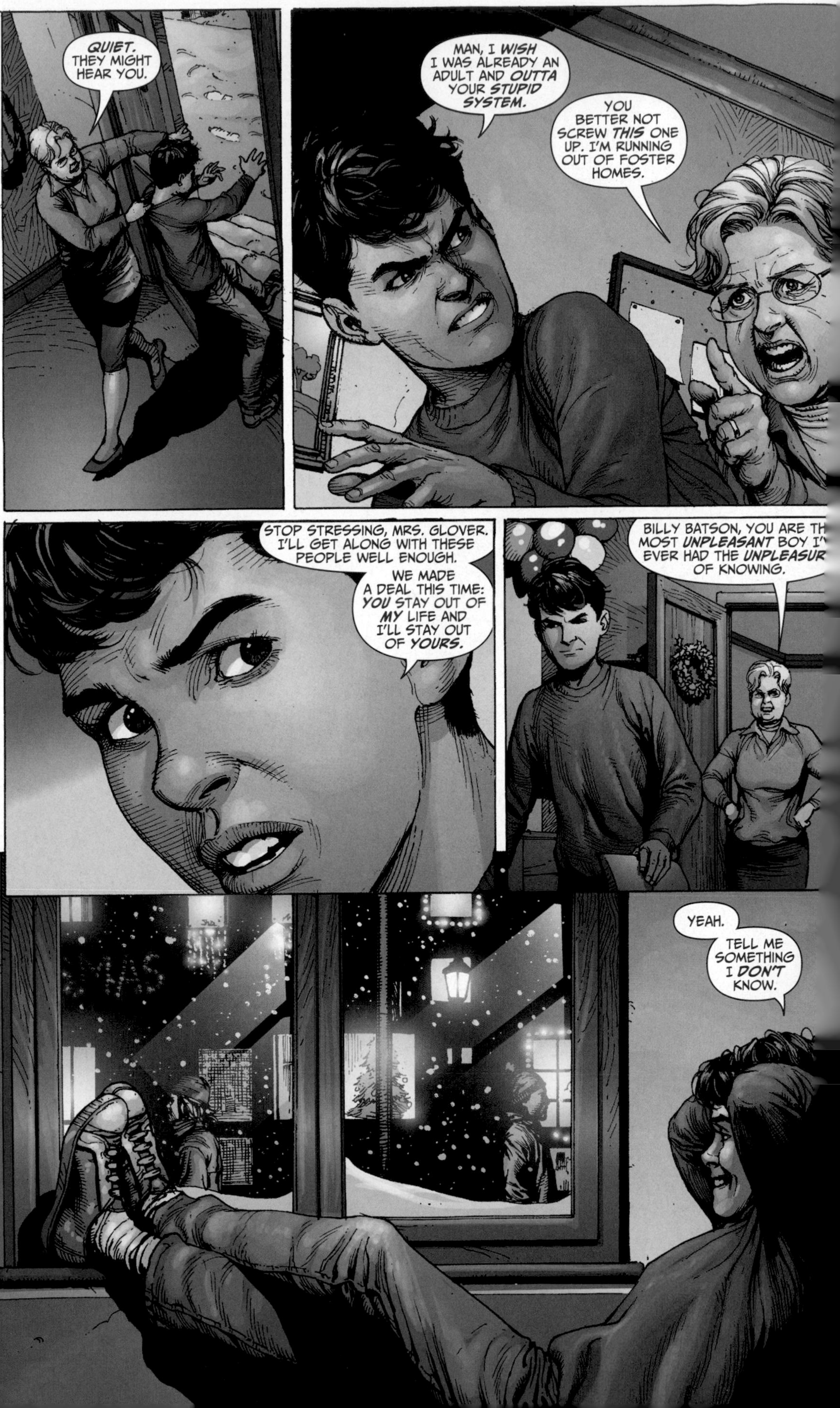
QUIET. THEY MIGHT HEAR YOU.
MAN, I WISH I WAS ALREADY AN ADULT AND OUTTA YOUR STUPID SYSTEM.
YOU BETTER NOT SCREW THIS ONE UP. I'M RUNNING OUT OF FOSTER HOMES.
STOP STRESSING, MRS. GLOVER. I'LL GET ALONG WITH THESE PEOPLE WELL ENOUGH.
WE MADE A DEAL THIS TIME: YOU STAY OUT OF MY LIFE AND I'LL STAY OUT OF YOURS.
BILLY BATSON, YOU ARE TH MOST UNPLEASANT BOY I' EVER HAD THE UNPLEASUR OF KNOWING.
YEAH.
TELL ME SOMETHING I DON'T KNOW.

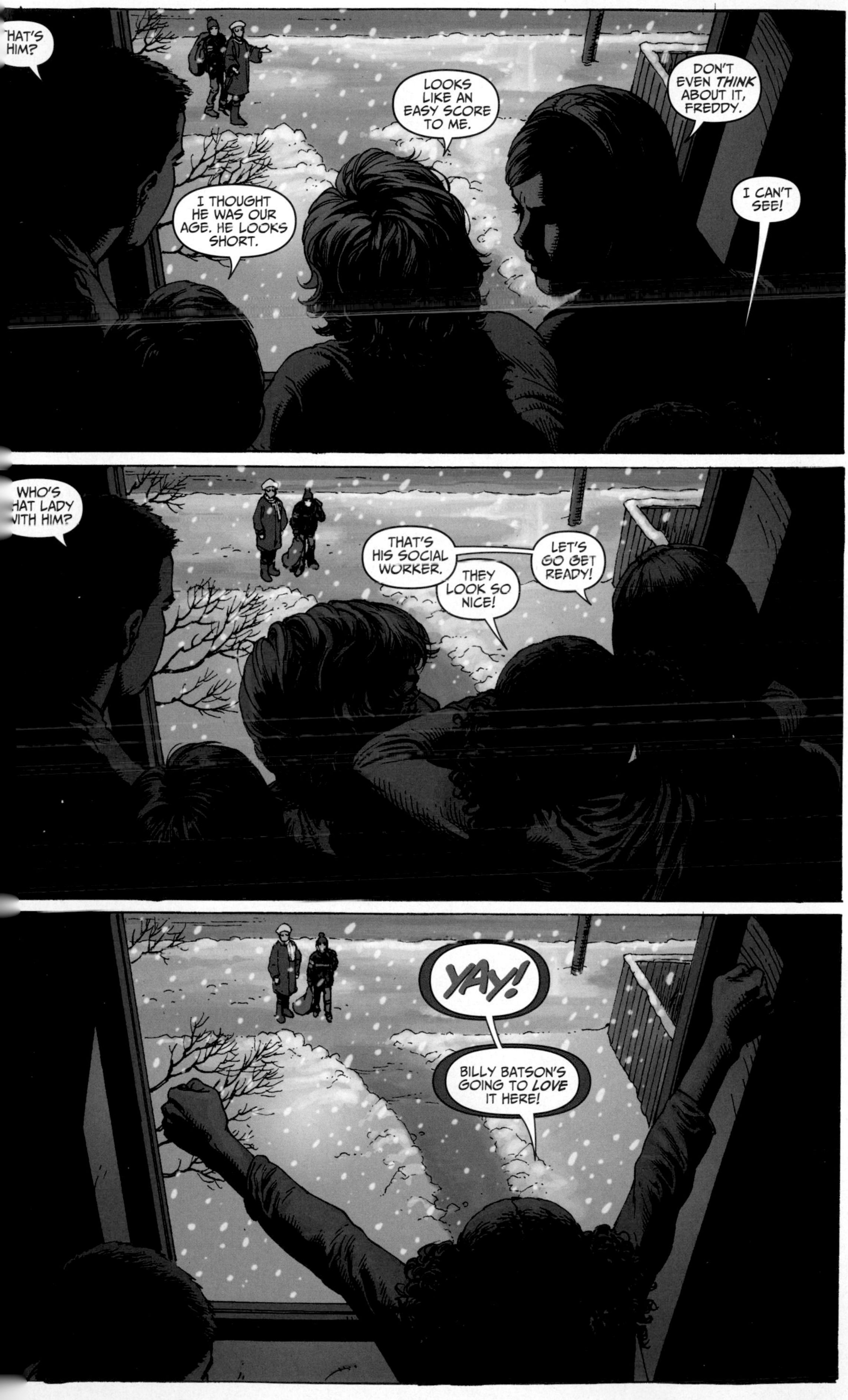
HAT'S HIM?
LOOKS LIKE AN EASY SCORE TO ME.
DON'T EVEN THINK ABOUT IT, FREDDY.
I THOUGHT HE WAS OUR AGE. HE LOOKS SHORT.
I CAN'T SEE!
WHO'S HAT LADY WITH HIM?
THAT'S HIS SOCIAL WORKER.
LET'S GO GET READY!
THEY LOOK SO NICE!
YAY!
BILLY BATSON'S GOING TO LOVE IT HERE!

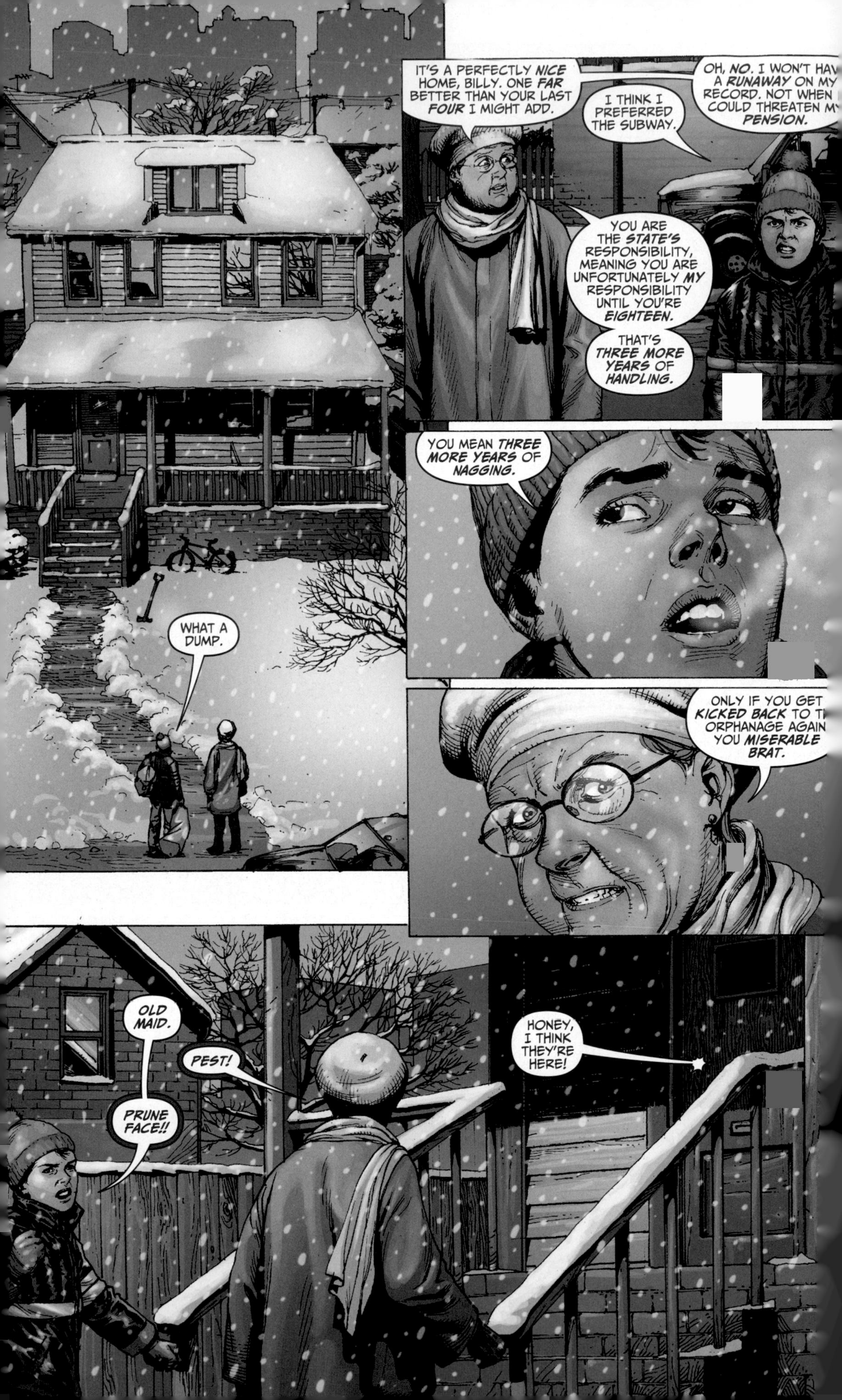

IT'S A PERFECTLY NICE HOME, BILLY. ONE FAR BETTER THAN YOUR LAST FOUR I MIGHT ADD.
I THINK I PREFERRED THE SUBWAY.
OH, NO. I WON'T HAV A RUNAWAY ON MY RECORD. NOT WHEN COULD THREATEN M PENSION.
YOU ARE THE STATE'S RESPONSIBILITY, MEANING YOU ARE UNFORTUNATELY MY RESPONSIBILITY UNTIL YOU'RE EIGHTEEN.
THAT'S THREE MORE YEARS OF HANDLING.
WHAT A DUMP.
YOU MEAN THREE MORE YEARS OF NAGGING.
ONLY IF YOU GET KICKED BACK TO T ORPHANAGE AGAIN YOU MISERABLE BRAT.
OLD MAID.
PEST!
PRUNE FACE!!
HONEY, I THINK THEY'RE HERE!

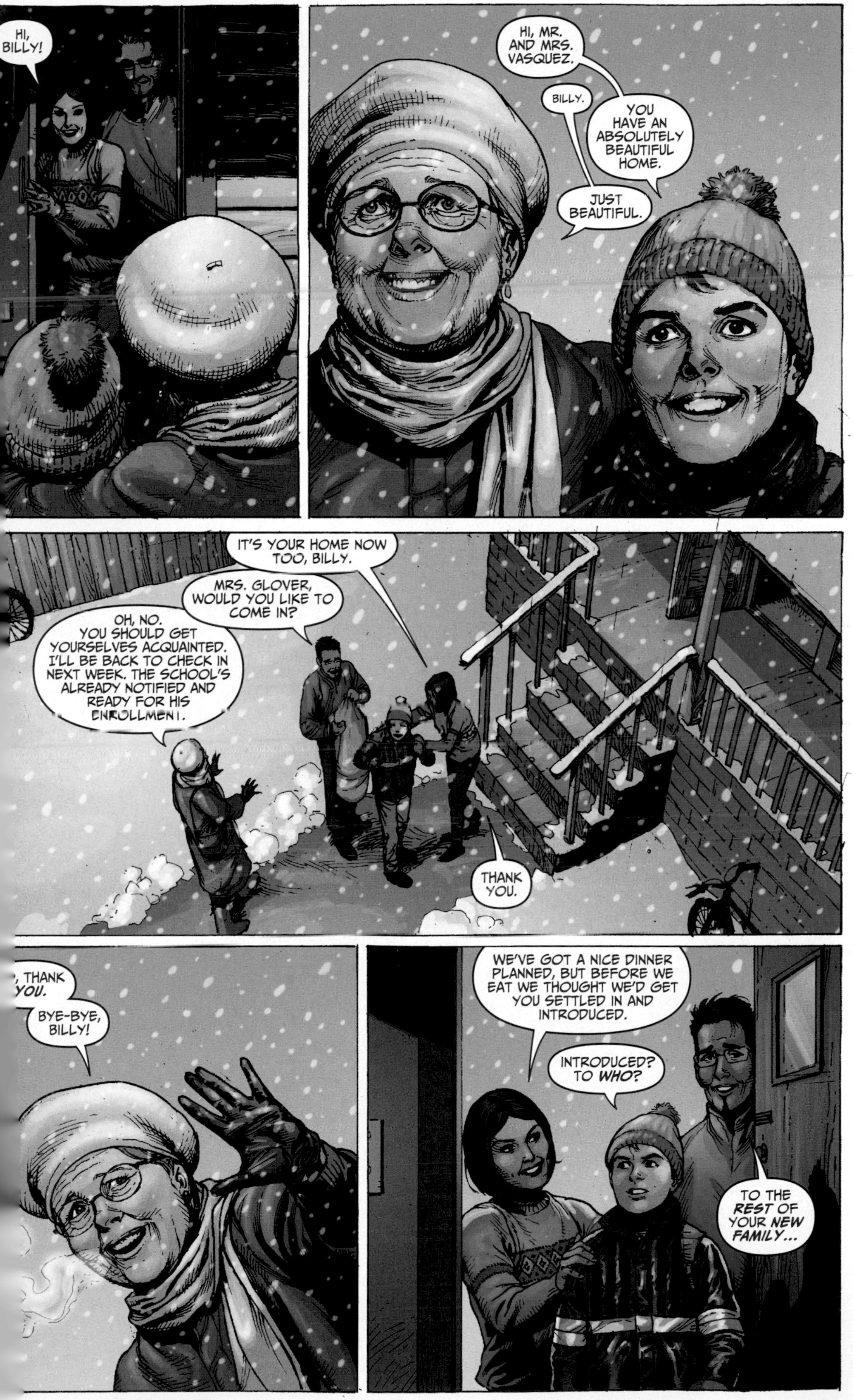

HI, BILLY!
HI, MR. AND MRS. VASQUEZ.
BILLY.
YOU HAVE AN ABSOLUTELY BEAUTIFUL HOME.
JUST BEAUTIFUL.
IT'S YOUR HOME NOW TOO, BILLY.
MRS. GLOVER, WOULD YOU LIKE TO COME IN?
OH, NO. YOU SHOULD GET YOURSELVES ACQUAINTED. I'LL BE BACK TO CHECK IN NEXT WEEK. THE SCHOOL'S ALREADY NOTIFIED AND READY FOR HIS ENROLLMENT.
THANK YOU.
THANK YOU.
BYE-BYE, BILLY!
WE'VE GOT A NICE DINNER PLANNED, BUT BEFORE WE EAT WE THOUGHT WE'D GET YOU SETTLED IN AND INTRODUCED.
INTRODUCED? TO WHO?
TO THE REST OF YOUR NEW FAMILY...

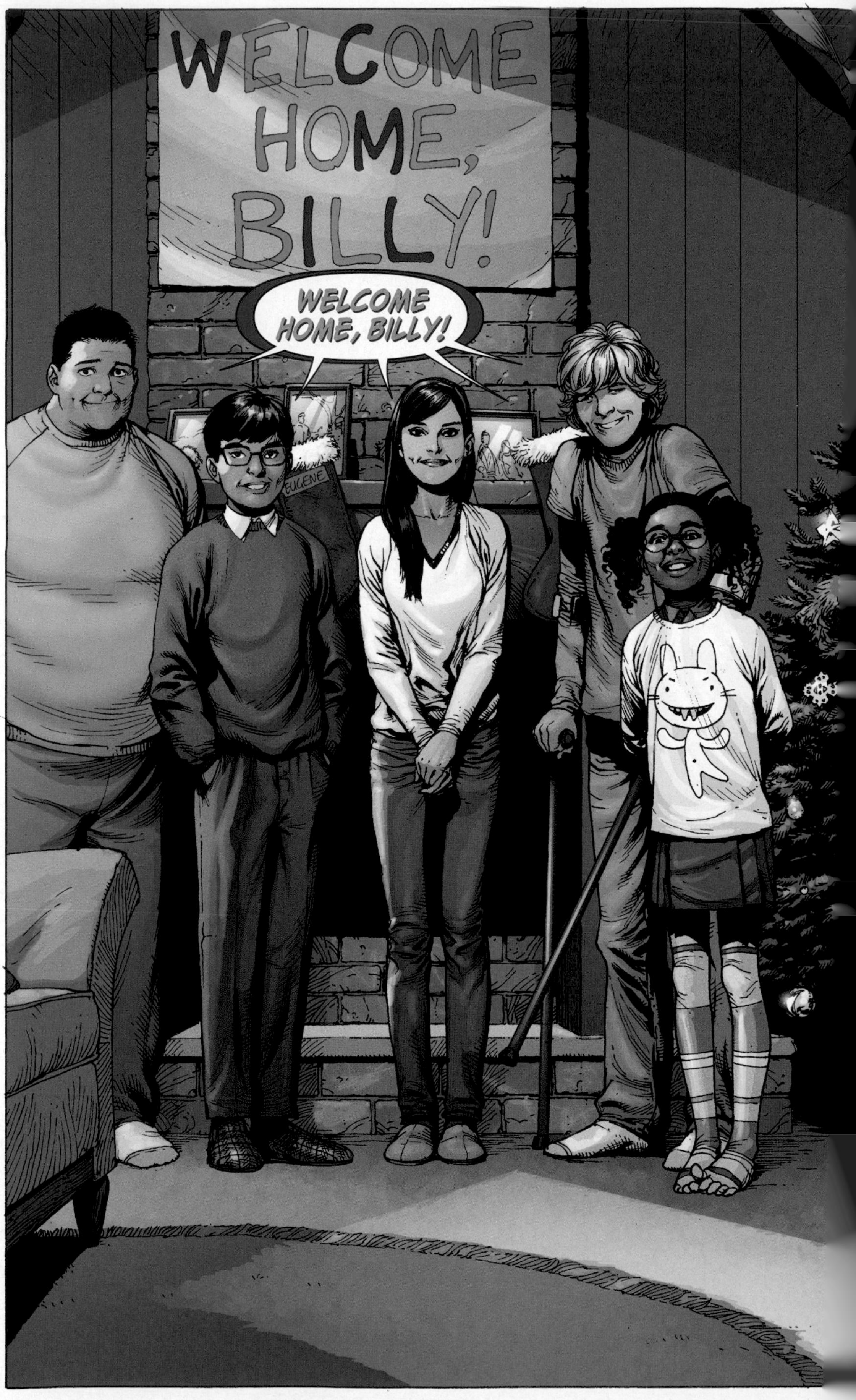
WELCOME HOME, BILLY!
WELCOME HOME, BILLY!
EUGENE

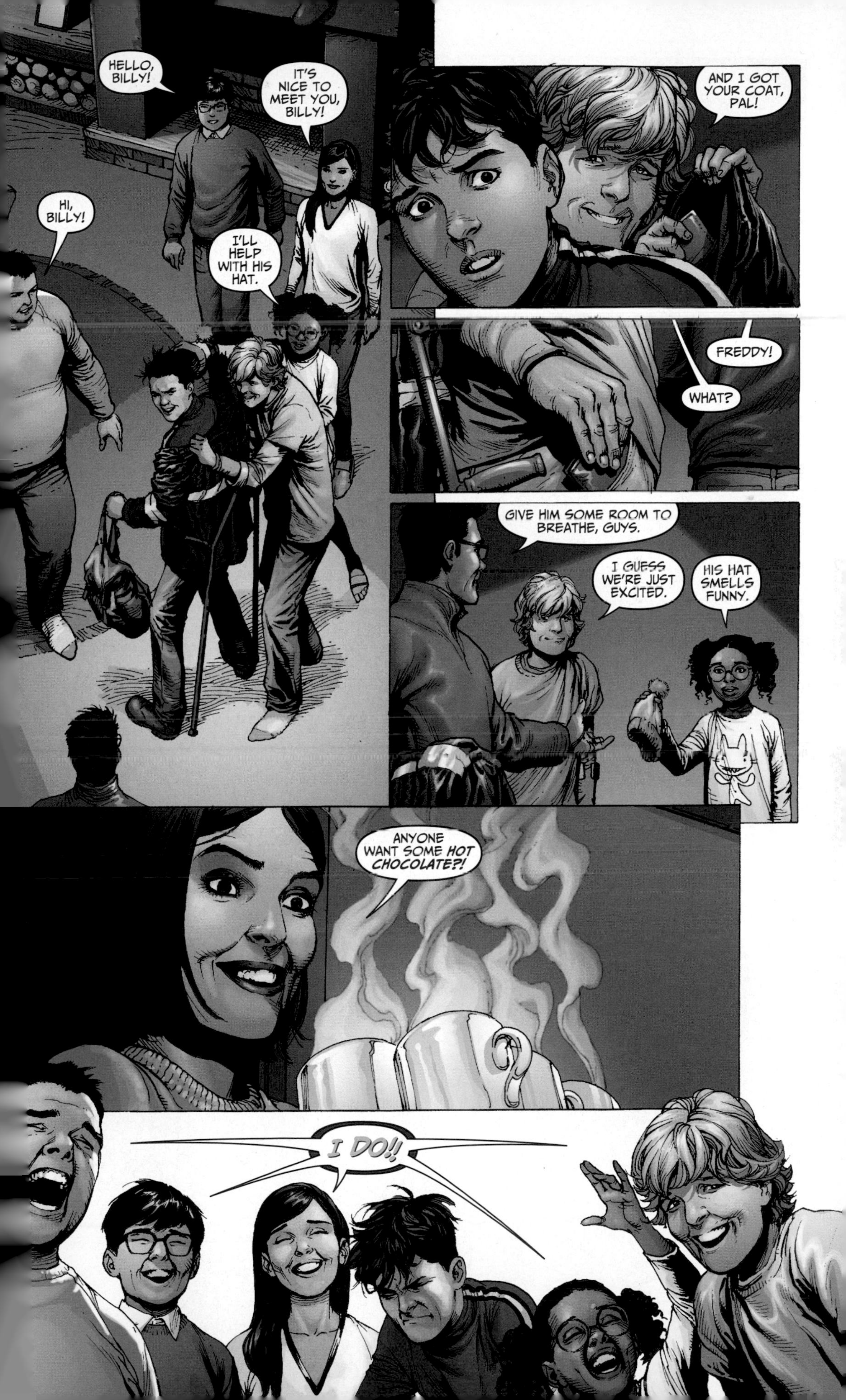
HELLO, BILLY!
IT'S NICE TO MEET YOU, BILLY!
HI, BILLY!
I'LL HELP WITH HIS HAT.
AND I GOT YOUR COAT, PAL!
FREDDY!
WHAT?
GIVE HIM SOME ROOM TO BREATHE, GUYS.
I GUESS WE'RE JUST EXCITED.
HIS HAT SMELLS FUNNY.
ANYONE WANT SOME HOT CHOCOLATE?!
I DO!!

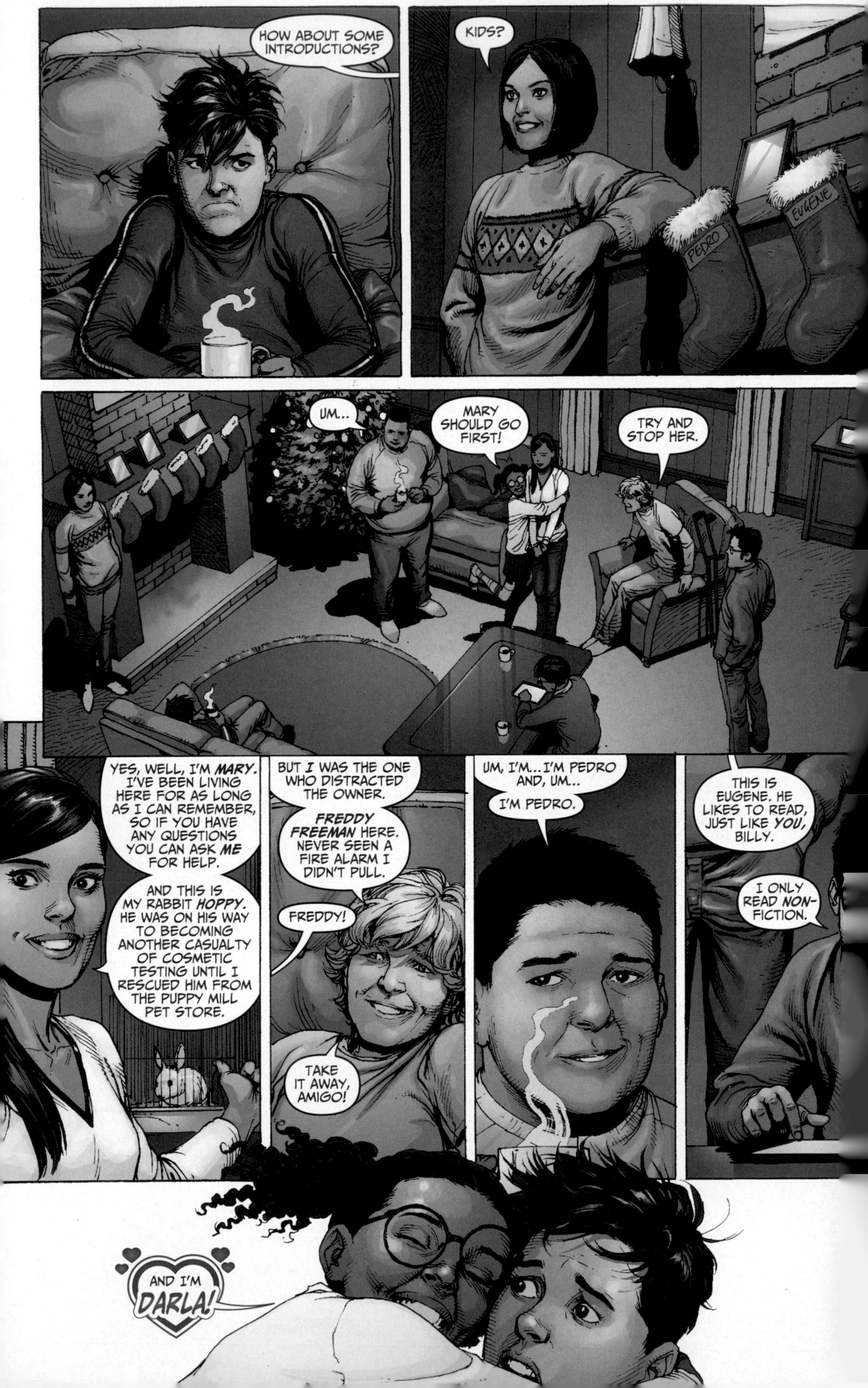

HOW ABOUT SOME INTRODUCTIONS?
KIDS?
PEDRO
EUGENE
UM...
MARY SHOULD GO FIRST!
TRY AND STOP HER.
YES, WELL, I'M MARY. I'VE BEEN LIVING HERE FOR AS LONG AS I CAN REMEMBER, SO IF YOU HAVE ANY QUESTIONS YOU CAN ASK ME FOR HELP.
AND THIS IS MY RABBIT HOPPY. HE WAS ON HIS WAY TO BECOMING ANOTHER CASUALTY OF COSMETIC TESTING UNTIL I RESCUED HIM FROM THE PUPPY MILL PET STORE.
BUT I WAS THE ONE WHO DISTRACTED THE OWNER.
FREDDY FREEMAN HERE. NEVER SEEN A FIRE ALARM I DIDN'T PULL.
FREDDY!
TAKE IT AWAY, AMIGO!
UM, I'M...I'M PEDRO AND, UM...
I'M PEDRO.
THIS IS EUGENE. HE LIKES TO READ, JUST LIKE YOU, BILLY.
I ONLY READ NON-FICTION.
AND I'M DARLA!

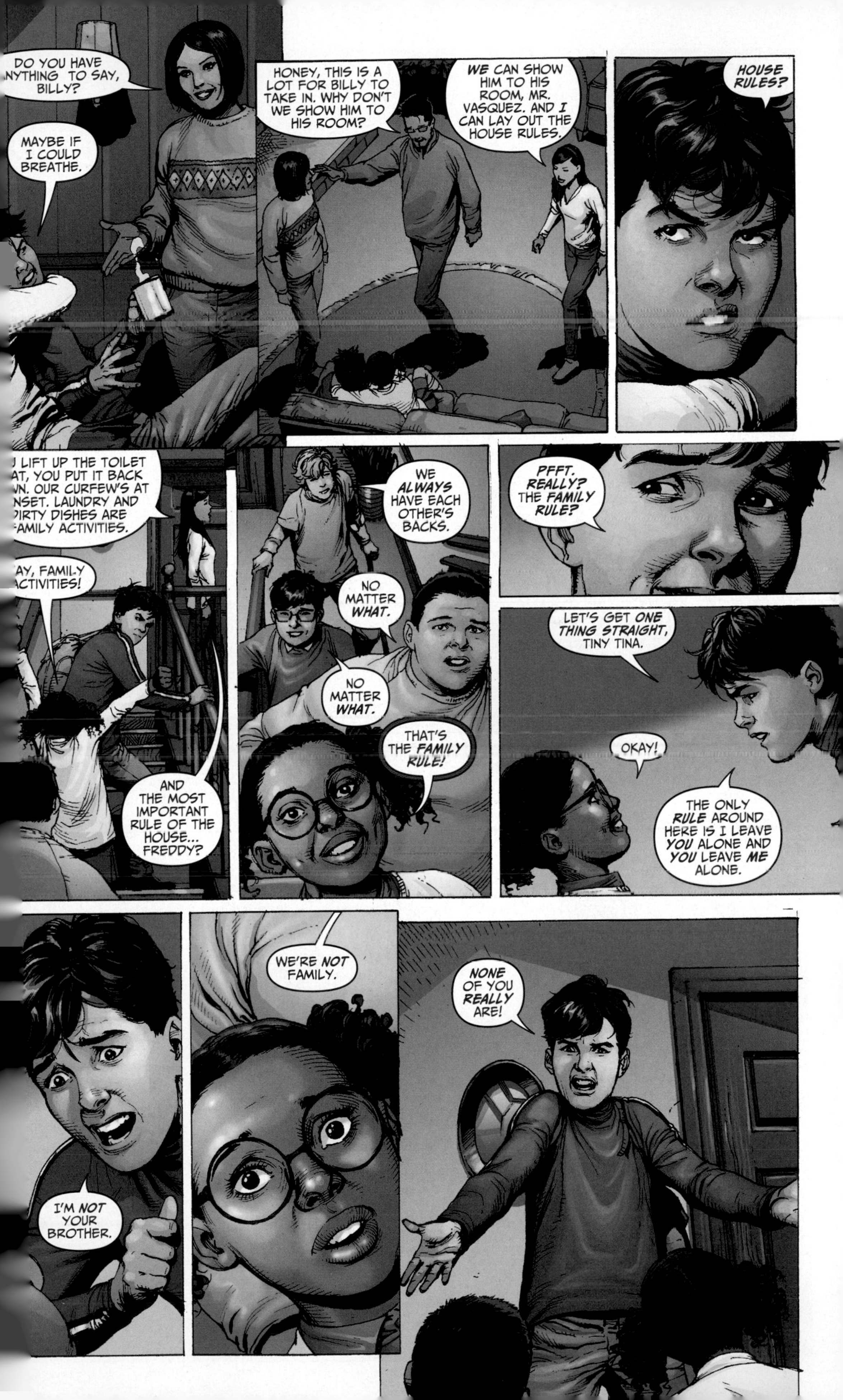
DO YOU HAVE
NYTHING TO SAY,
BILLY?
MAYBE IF
I COULD
BREATHE.
HONEY, THIS IS A
LOT FOR BILLY TO
TAKE IN. WHY DON'T
WE SHOW HIM TO
HIS ROOM?
WE CAN SHOW
HIM TO HIS
ROOM, MR.
VASQUEZ. AND I
CAN LAY OUT THE
HOUSE RULES.
HOUSE
RULES?
U LIFT UP THE TOILET
AT, YOU PUT IT BACK
WN. OUR CURFEW'S AT
NSET. LAUNDRY AND
DIRTY DISHES ARE
FAMILY ACTIVITIES.
AY, FAMILY
ACTIVITIES!
AND
THE MOST
IMPORTANT
RULE OF THE
HOUSE...
FREDDY?
WE
ALWAYS
HAVE EACH
OTHER'S
BACKS.
NO
MATTER
WHAT.
NO
MATTER
WHAT.
THAT'S
THE FAMILY
RULE!
PFFT.
REALLY?
THE FAMILY
RULE?
LET'S GET ONE
THING STRAIGHT,
TINY TINA.
OKAY!
THE ONLY
RULE AROUND
HERE IS I LEAVE
YOU ALONE AND
YOU LEAVE ME
ALONE.
I'M NOT
YOUR
BROTHER.
WE'RE NOT
FAMILY.
NONE
OF YOU
REALLY
ARE!

WHAT?

DARLA?

DARLA, WAIT!

SMOOTH, DUDE.

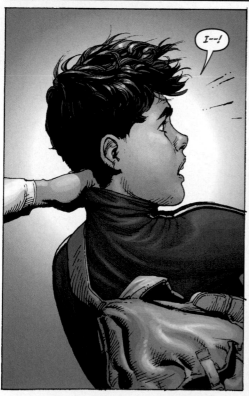

I--!

NFFF!

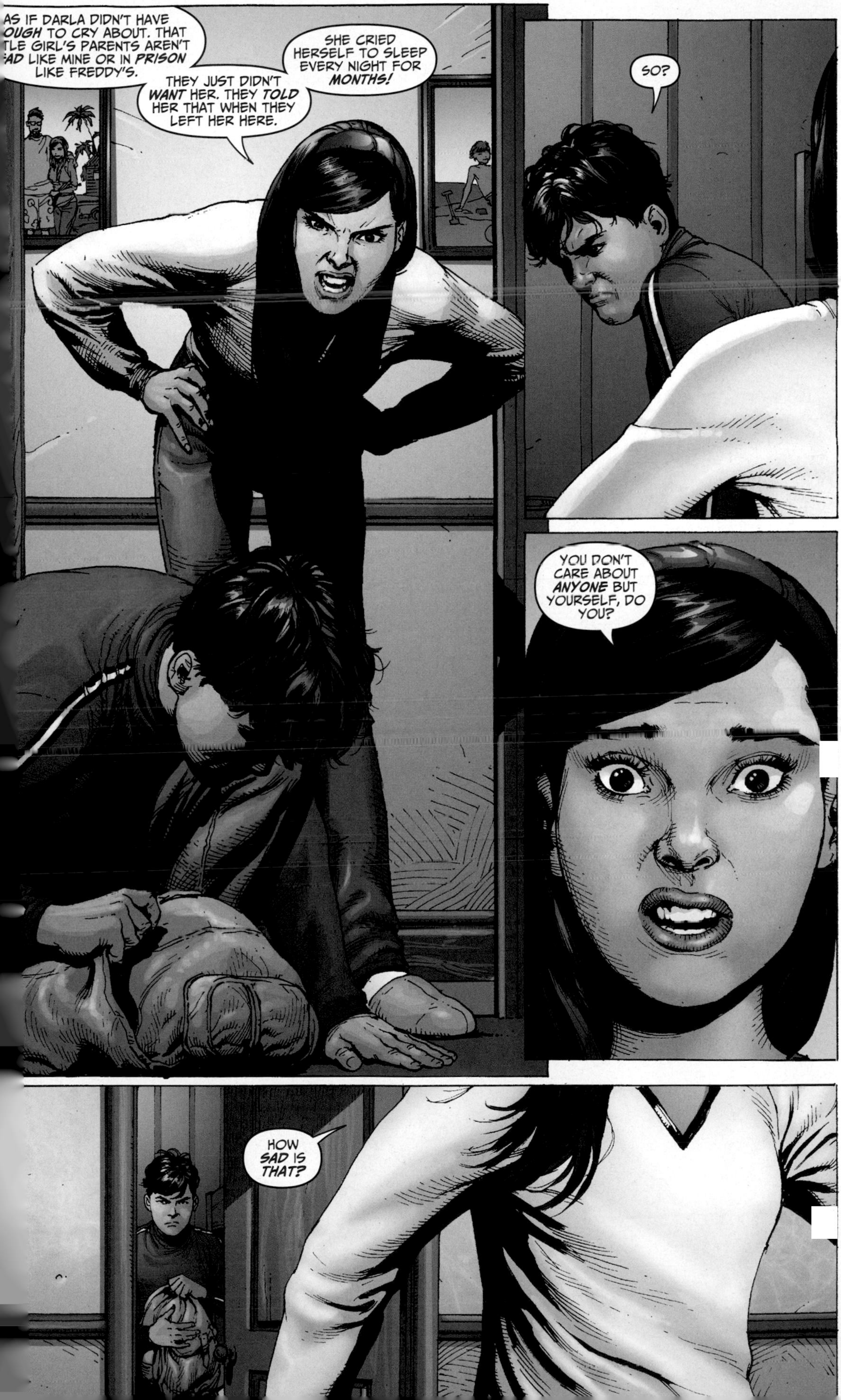
AS IF DARLA DIDN'T HAVE OUGH TO CRY ABOUT. THAT TLE GIRL'S PARENTS AREN'T AD LIKE MINE OR IN PRISON LIKE FREDDY'S.
THEY JUST DIDN'T WANT HER. THEY TOLD HER THAT WHEN THEY LEFT HER HERE.
SHE CRIED HERSELF TO SLEEP EVERY NIGHT FOR MONTHS!
SO?
YOU DON'T CARE ABOUT ANYONE BUT YOURSELF, DO YOU?
HOW SAD IS THAT?

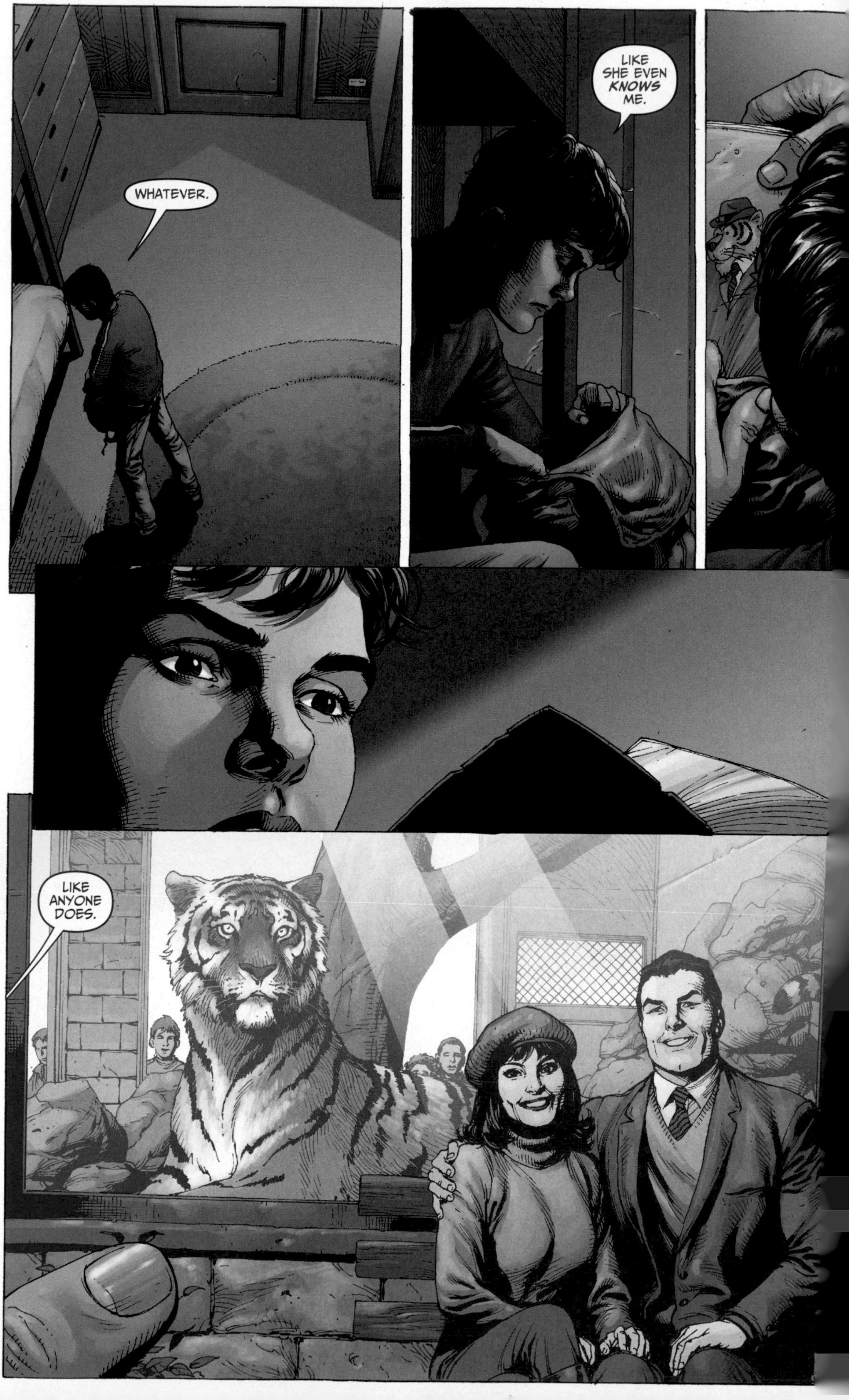
WHATEVER.
LIKE SHE EVEN KNOWS ME.
LIKE ANYONE DOES.

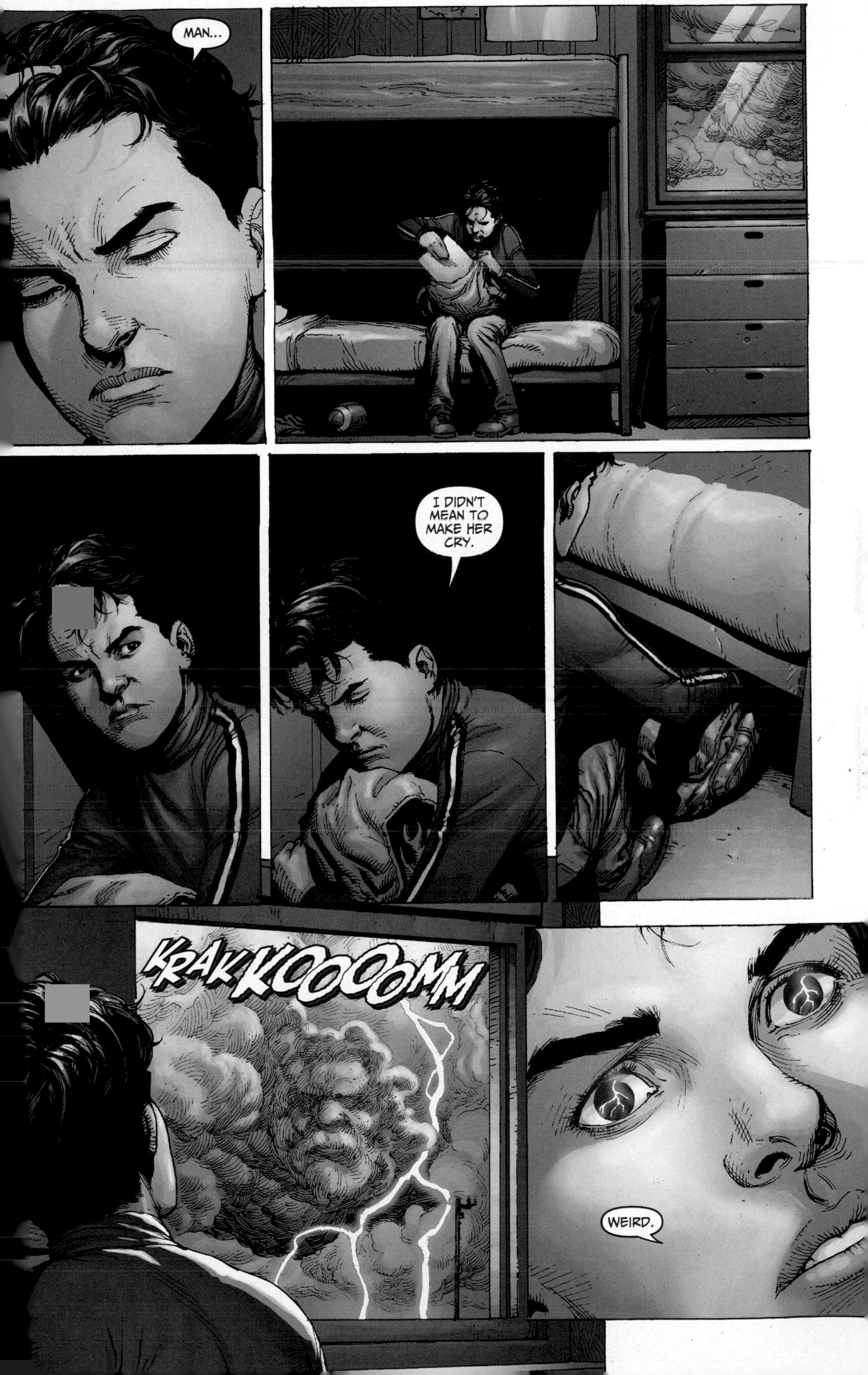
MAN...
I DIDN'T MEAN TO MAKE HER CRY.
KRAKKOOOOOMM
WEIRD.

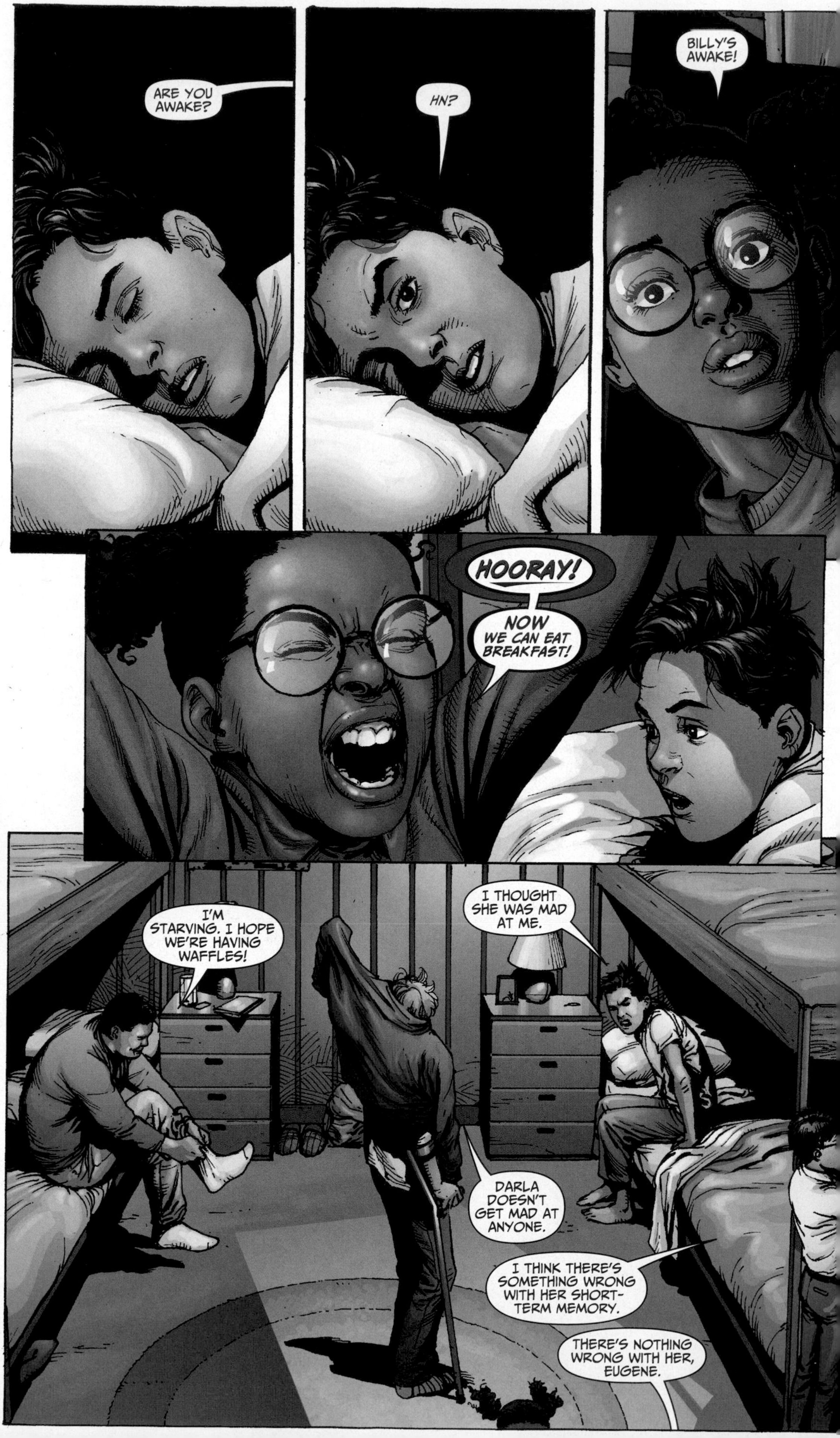

ARE YOU AWAKE?
HN?
BILLY'S AWAKE!
HOORAY!
NOW WE CAN EAT BREAKFAST!
I'M STARVING. I HOPE WE'RE HAVING WAFFLES!
I THOUGHT SHE WAS MAD AT ME.
DARLA DOESN'T GET MAD AT ANYONE.
I THINK THERE'S SOMETHING WRONG WITH HER SHORT-TERM MEMORY.
THERE'S NOTHING WRONG WITH HER, EUGENE.

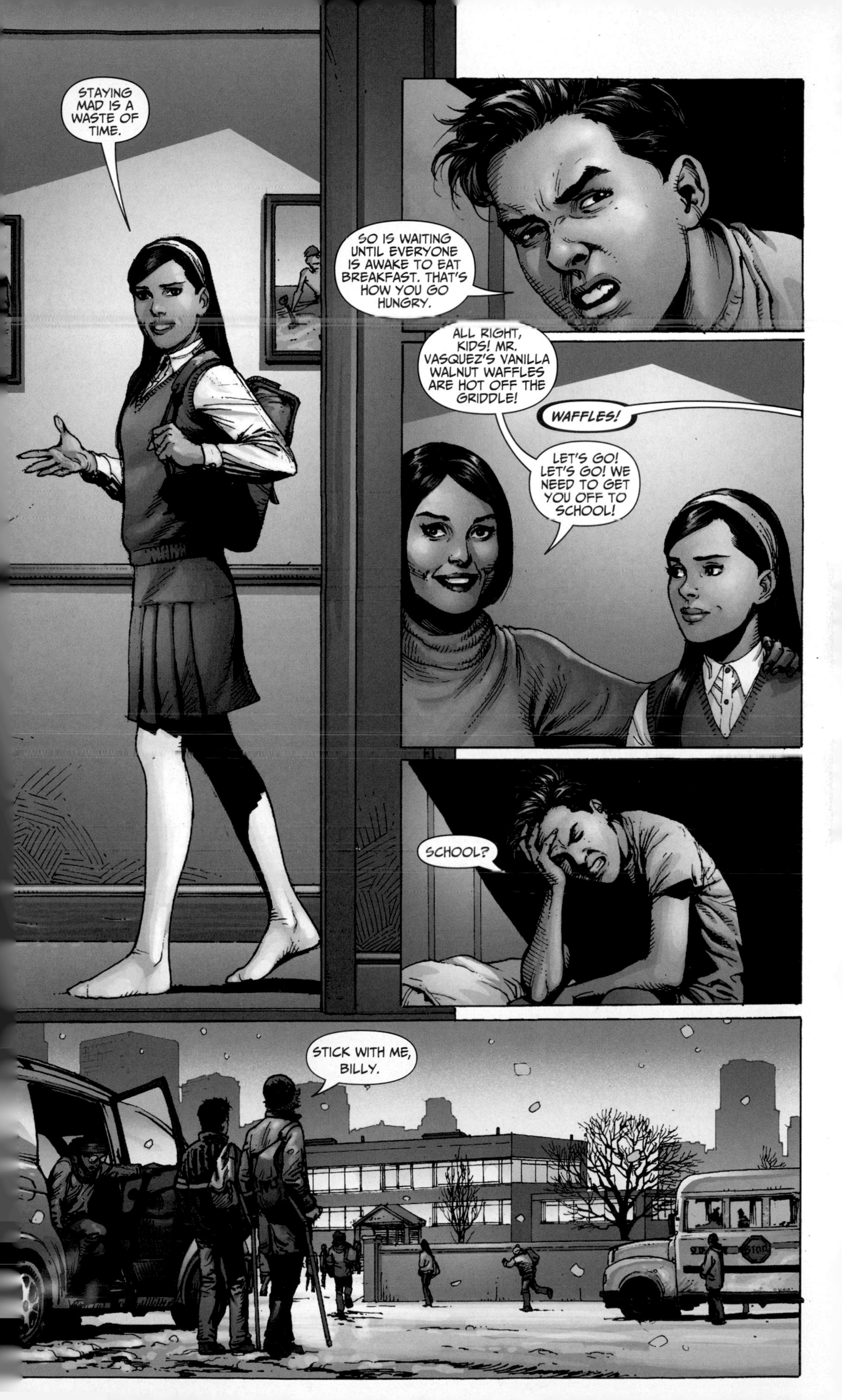
STAYING MAD IS A WASTE OF TIME.
SO IS WAITING UNTIL EVERYONE IS AWAKE TO EAT BREAKFAST. THAT'S HOW YOU GO HUNGRY.
ALL RIGHT, KIDS! MR. VASQUEZ'S VANILLA WALNUT WAFFLES ARE HOT OFF THE GRIDDLE!
WAFFLES!
LET'S GO! LET'S GO! WE NEED TO GET YOU OFF TO SCHOOL!
SCHOOL?
STICK WITH ME, BILLY.

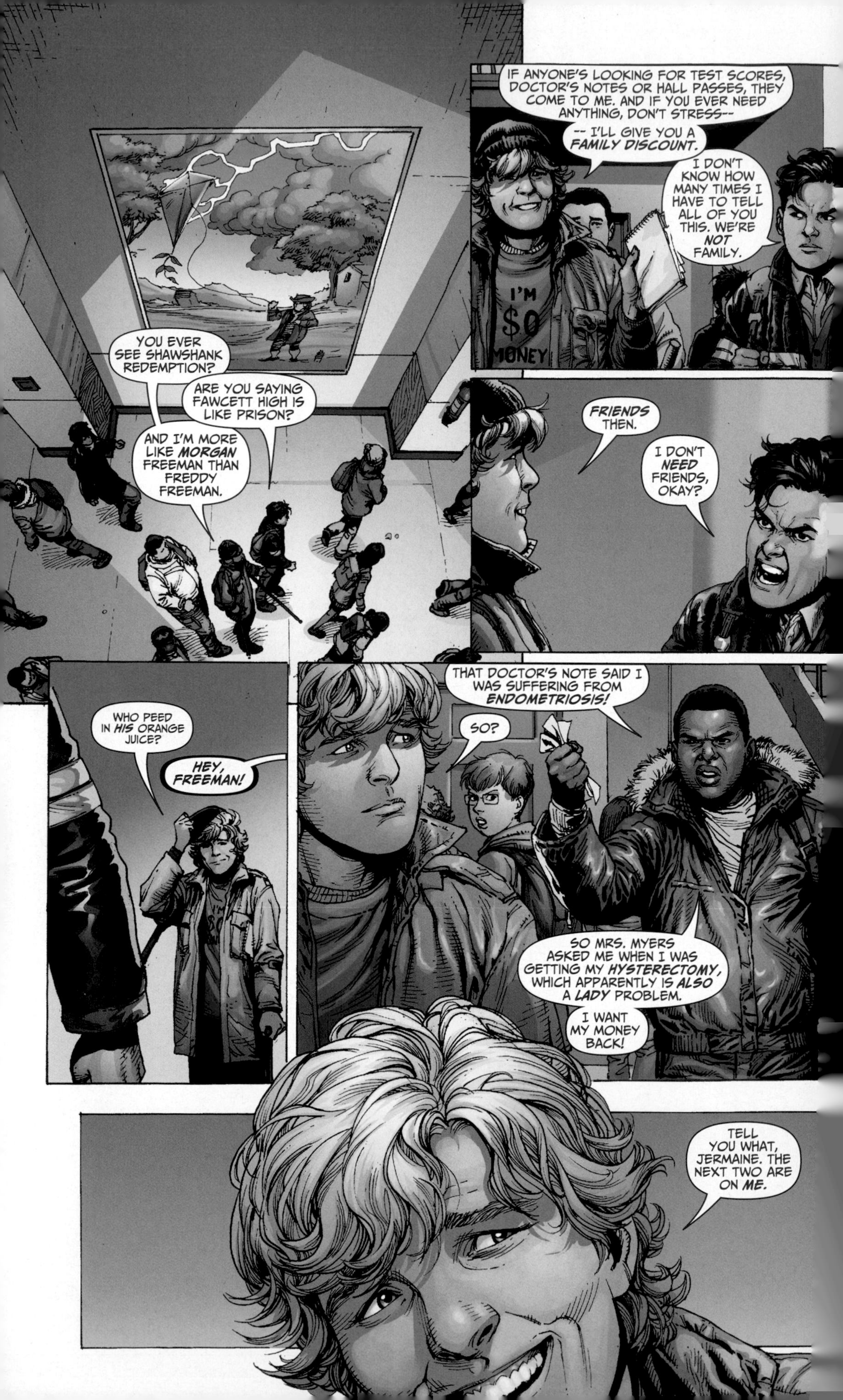

IF ANYONE'S LOOKING FOR TEST SCORES, DOCTOR'S NOTES OR HALL PASSES, THEY COME TO ME. AND IF YOU EVER NEED ANYTHING, DON'T STRESS--
-- I'LL GIVE YOU A FAMILY DISCOUNT.
I DON'T KNOW HOW MANY TIMES I HAVE TO TELL ALL OF YOU THIS. WE'RE NOT FAMILY.
I'M $0 MONEY
YOU EVER SEE SHAWSHANK REDEMPTION?
ARE YOU SAYING FAWCETT HIGH IS LIKE PRISON?
AND I'M MORE LIKE MORGAN FREEMAN THAN FREDDY FREEMAN.
FRIENDS THEN.
I DON'T NEED FRIENDS, OKAY?
WHO PEED IN HIS ORANGE JUICE?
HEY, FREEMAN!
THAT DOCTOR'S NOTE SAID I WAS SUFFERING FROM ENDOMETRIOSIS!
SO?
SO MRS. MYERS ASKED ME WHEN I WAS GETTING MY HYSTERECTOMY, WHICH APPARENTLY IS ALSO A LADY PROBLEM.
I WANT MY MONEY BACK!
TELL YOU WHAT, JERMAINE. THE NEXT TWO ARE ON ME.

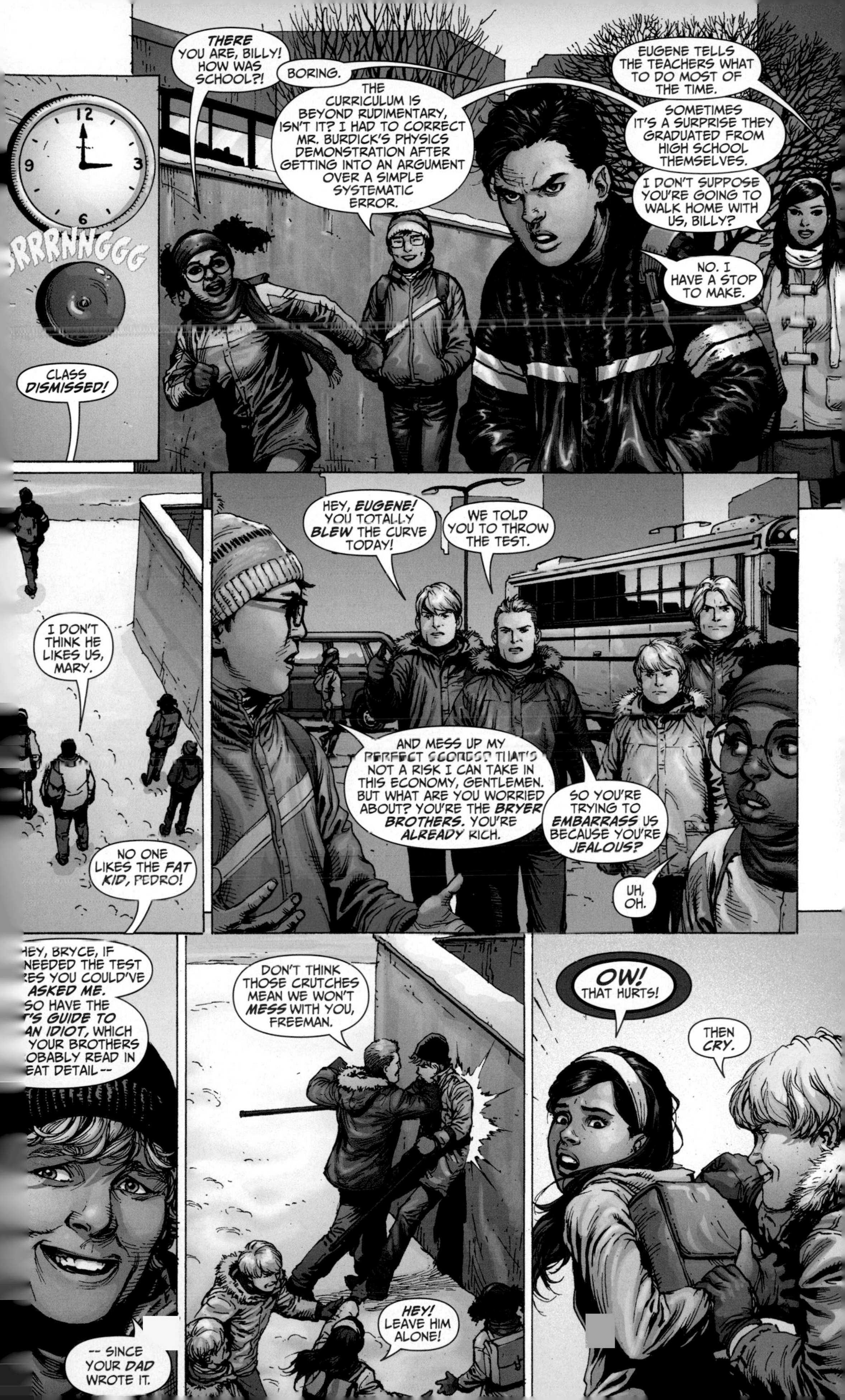

SRRRNNGGG
CLASS DISMISSED!
THERE YOU ARE, BILLY! HOW WAS SCHOOL?!
BORING.
THE CURRICULUM IS BEYOND RUDIMENTARY, ISN'T IT? I HAD TO CORRECT MR. BURDICK'S PHYSICS DEMONSTRATION AFTER GETTING INTO AN ARGUMENT OVER A SIMPLE SYSTEMATIC ERROR.
EUGENE TELLS THE TEACHERS WHAT TO DO MOST OF THE TIME.
SOMETIMES IT'S A SURPRISE THEY GRADUATED FROM HIGH SCHOOL THEMSELVES.
I DON'T SUPPOSE YOU'RE GOING TO WALK HOME WITH US, BILLY?
NO. I HAVE A STOP TO MAKE.
I DON'T THINK HE LIKES US, MARY.
NO ONE LIKES THE FAT KID, PEDRO!
HEY, EUGENE! YOU TOTALLY BLEW THE CURVE TODAY!
WE TOLD YOU TO THROW THE TEST.
AND MESS UP MY PERFECT SCORES? THAT'S NOT A RISK I CAN TAKE IN THIS ECONOMY, GENTLEMEN. BUT WHAT ARE YOU WORRIED ABOUT? YOU'RE THE BRYER BROTHERS. YOU'RE ALREADY RICH.
SO YOU'RE TRYING TO EMBARRASS US BECAUSE YOU'RE JEALOUS?
UH, OH.
EY, BRYCE, IF NEEDED THE TEST ES YOU COULD'VE ASKED ME. SO HAVE THE 'S GUIDE TO AN IDIOT, WHICH YOUR BROTHERS OBABLY READ IN EAT DETAIL --
-- SINCE YOUR DAD WROTE IT.
DON'T THINK THOSE CRUTCHES MEAN WE WON'T MESS WITH YOU, FREEMAN.
HEY! LEAVE HIM ALONE!
OW! THAT HURTS!
THEN CRY.

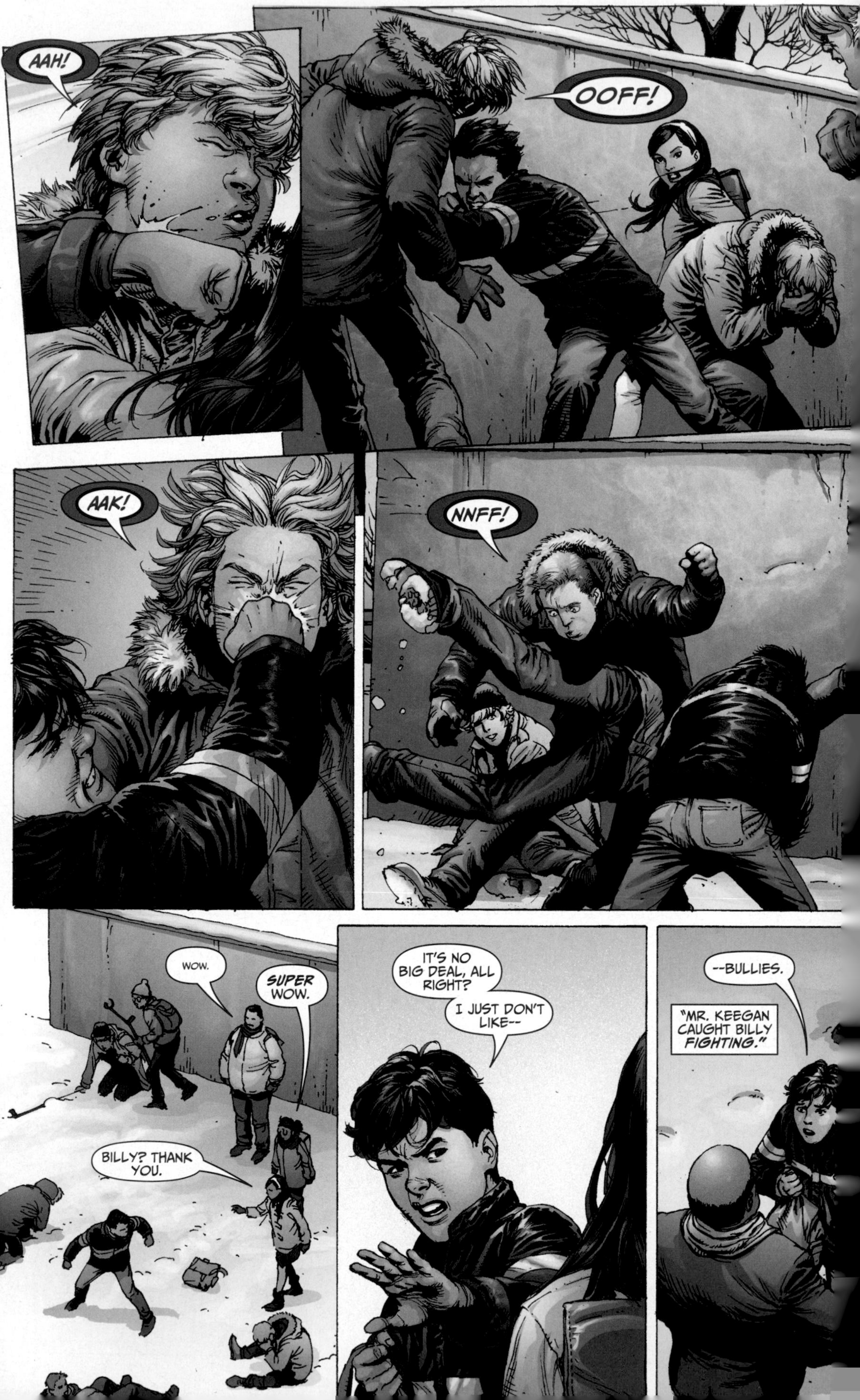
AAH!
OOFF!
AAK!
NNFF!
WOW.
SUPER WOW.
BILLY? THANK YOU.
IT'S NO BIG DEAL, ALL RIGHT?
I JUST DON'T LIKE--
--BULLIES.
"MR. KEEGAN CAUGHT BILLY FIGHTING."

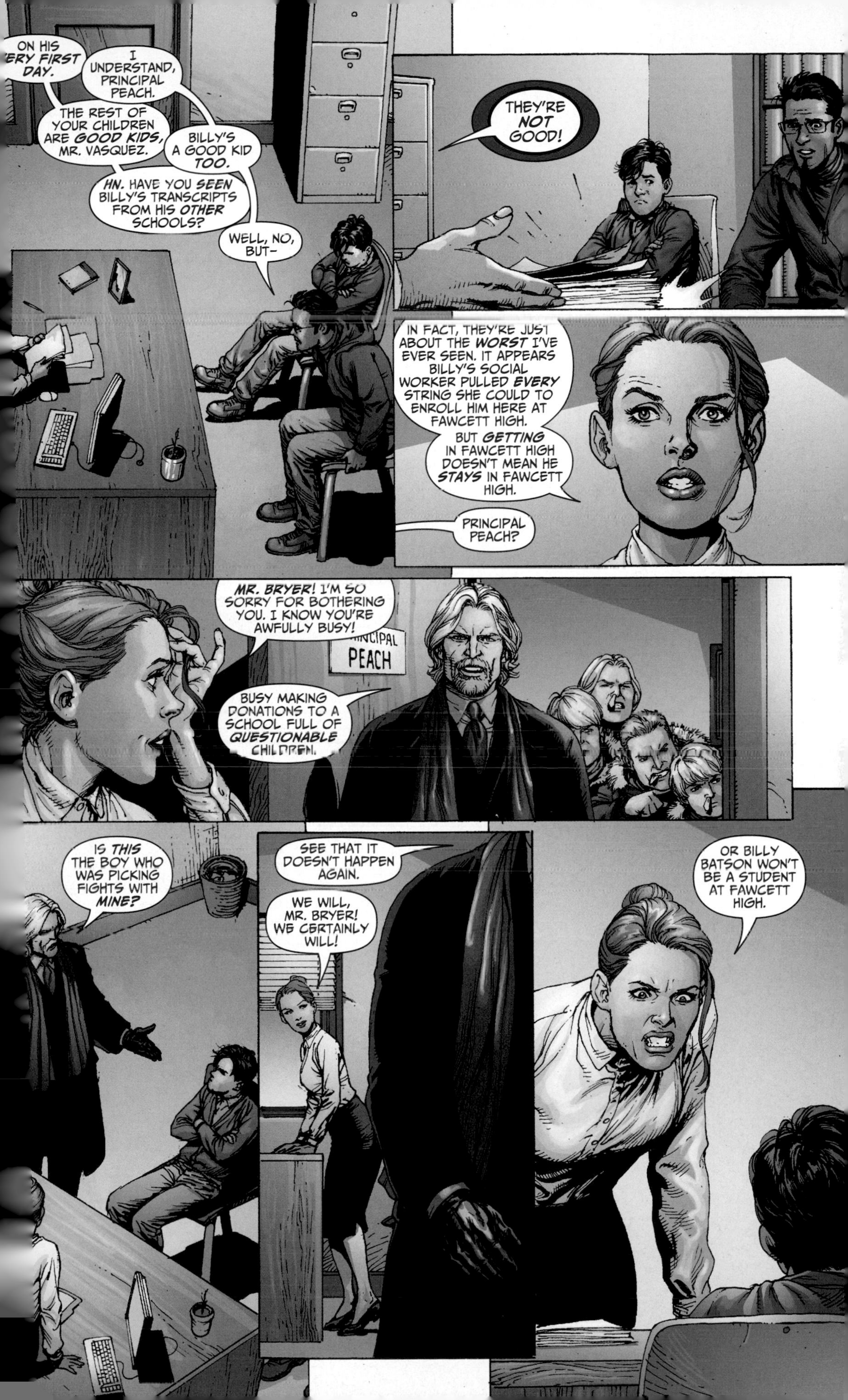
ON HIS ...ERY FIRST DAY.
I UNDERSTAND, PRINCIPAL PEACH.
THE REST OF YOUR CHILDREN ARE GOOD KIDS, MR. VASQUEZ.
BILLY'S A GOOD KID TOO.
HN. HAVE YOU SEEN BILLY'S TRANSCRIPTS FROM HIS OTHER SCHOOLS?
WELL, NO, BUT–
THEY'RE NOT GOOD!
IN FACT, THEY'RE JUST ABOUT THE WORST I'VE EVER SEEN. IT APPEARS BILLY'S SOCIAL WORKER PULLED EVERY STRING SHE COULD TO ENROLL HIM HERE AT FAWCETT HIGH.
BUT GETTING IN FAWCETT HIGH DOESN'T MEAN HE STAYS IN FAWCETT HIGH.
PRINCIPAL PEACH?
MR. BRYER! I'M SO SORRY FOR BOTHERING YOU. I KNOW YOU'RE AWFULLY BUSY!
PEACH
BUSY MAKING DONATIONS TO A SCHOOL FULL OF QUESTIONABLE CHILDREN.
IS THIS THE BOY WHO WAS PICKING FIGHTS WITH MINE?
SEE THAT IT DOESN'T HAPPEN AGAIN.
WE WILL, MR. BRYER! WE CERTAINLY WILL!
OR BILLY BATSON WON'T BE A STUDENT AT FAWCETT HIGH.

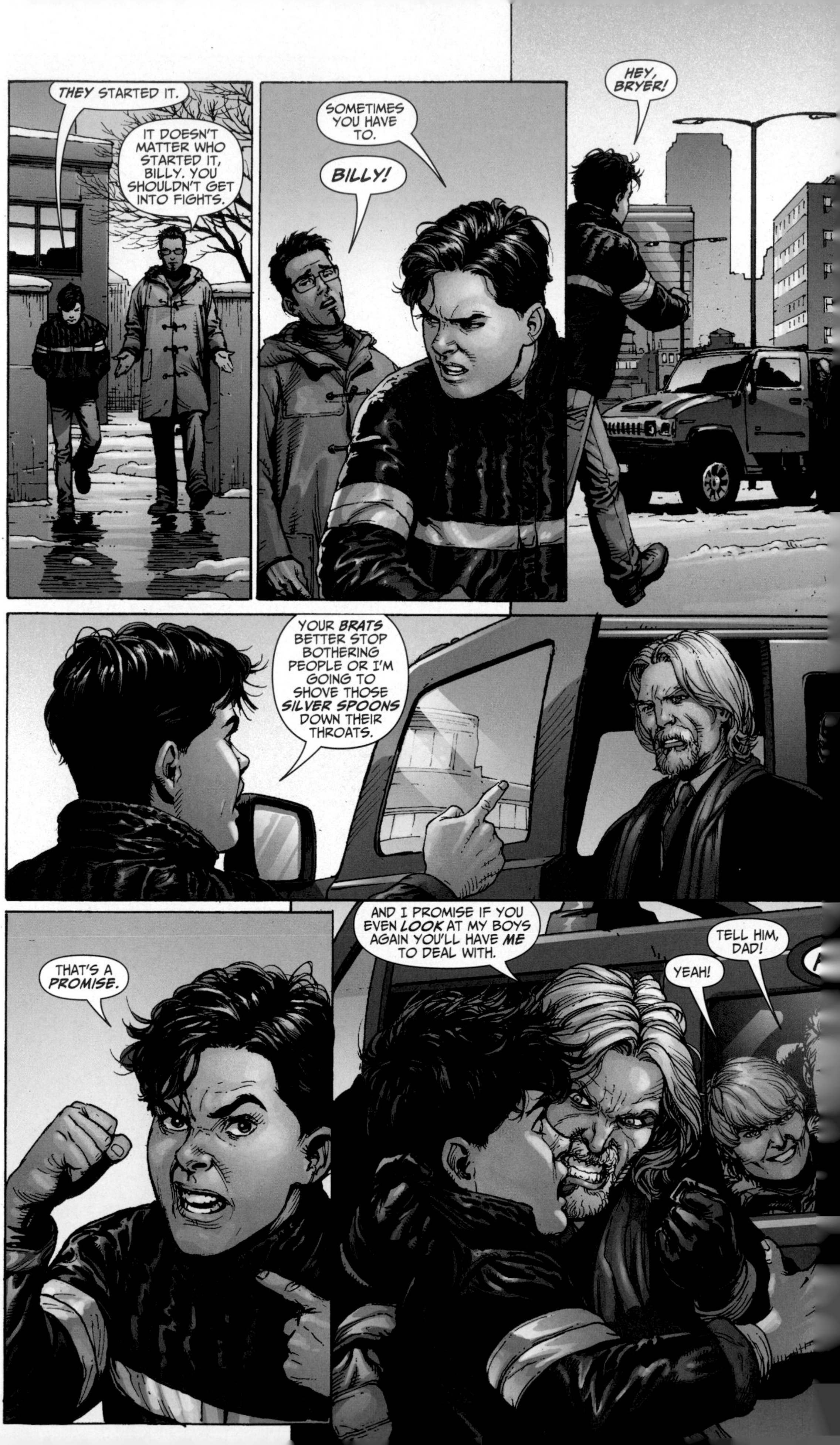

THEY STARTED IT.
IT DOESN'T MATTER WHO STARTED IT, BILLY. YOU SHOULDN'T GET INTO FIGHTS.
SOMETIMES YOU HAVE TO.
BILLY!
HEY, BRYER!
YOUR BRATS BETTER STOP BOTHERING PEOPLE OR I'M GOING TO SHOVE THOSE SILVER SPOONS DOWN THEIR THROATS.
THAT'S A PROMISE.
AND I PROMISE IF YOU EVEN LOOK AT MY BOYS AGAIN YOU'LL HAVE ME TO DEAL WITH.
YEAH!
TELL HIM, DAD!

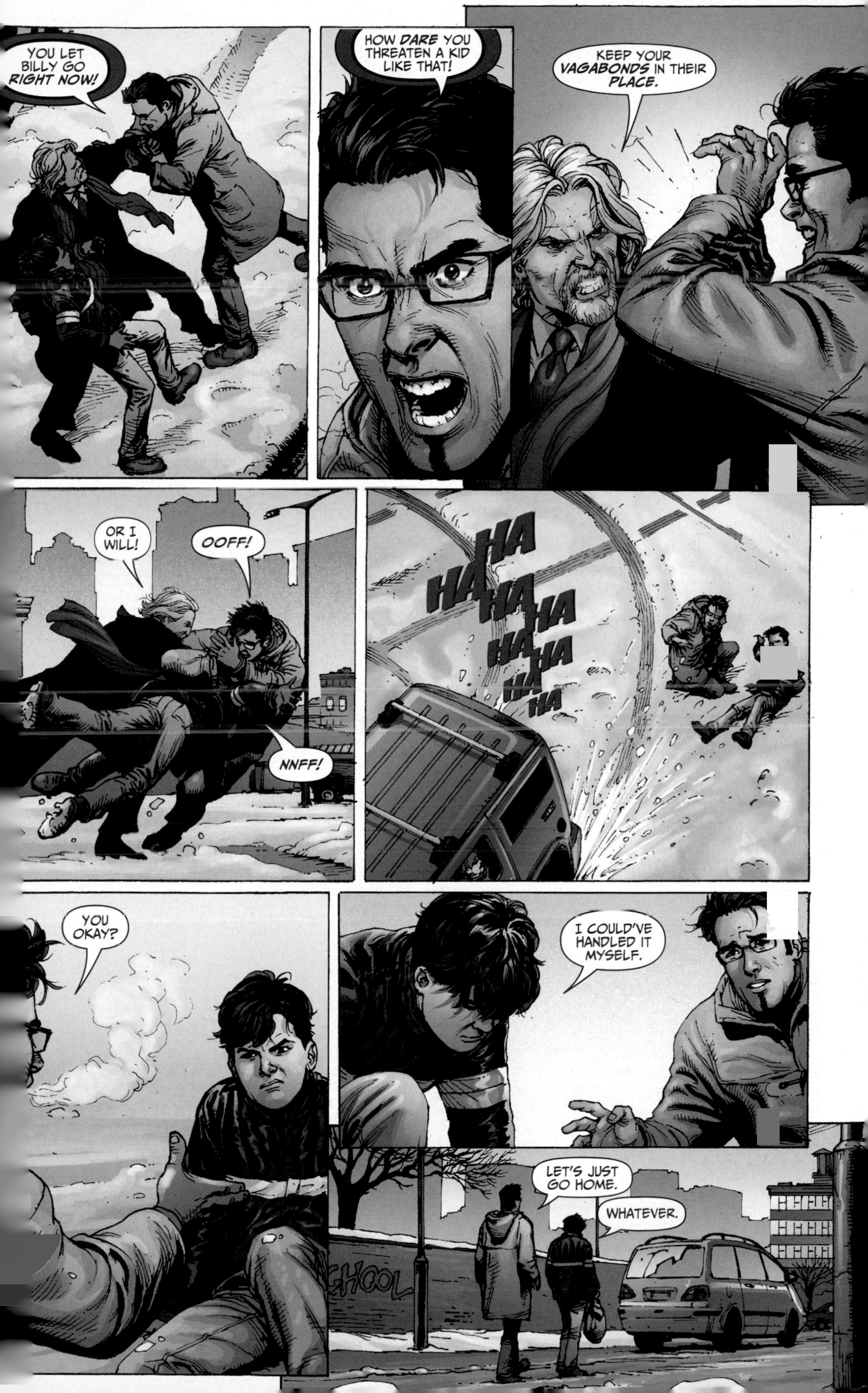
YOU LET BILLY GO RIGHT NOW!
HOW DARE YOU THREATEN A KID LIKE THAT!
KEEP YOUR VAGABONDS IN THEIR PLACE.
OR I WILL!
OOFF!
NNFF!
HA HA HA HA HA HA HA HA HA
YOU OKAY?
I COULD'VE HANDLED IT MYSELF.
LET'S JUST GO HOME.
WHATEVER.

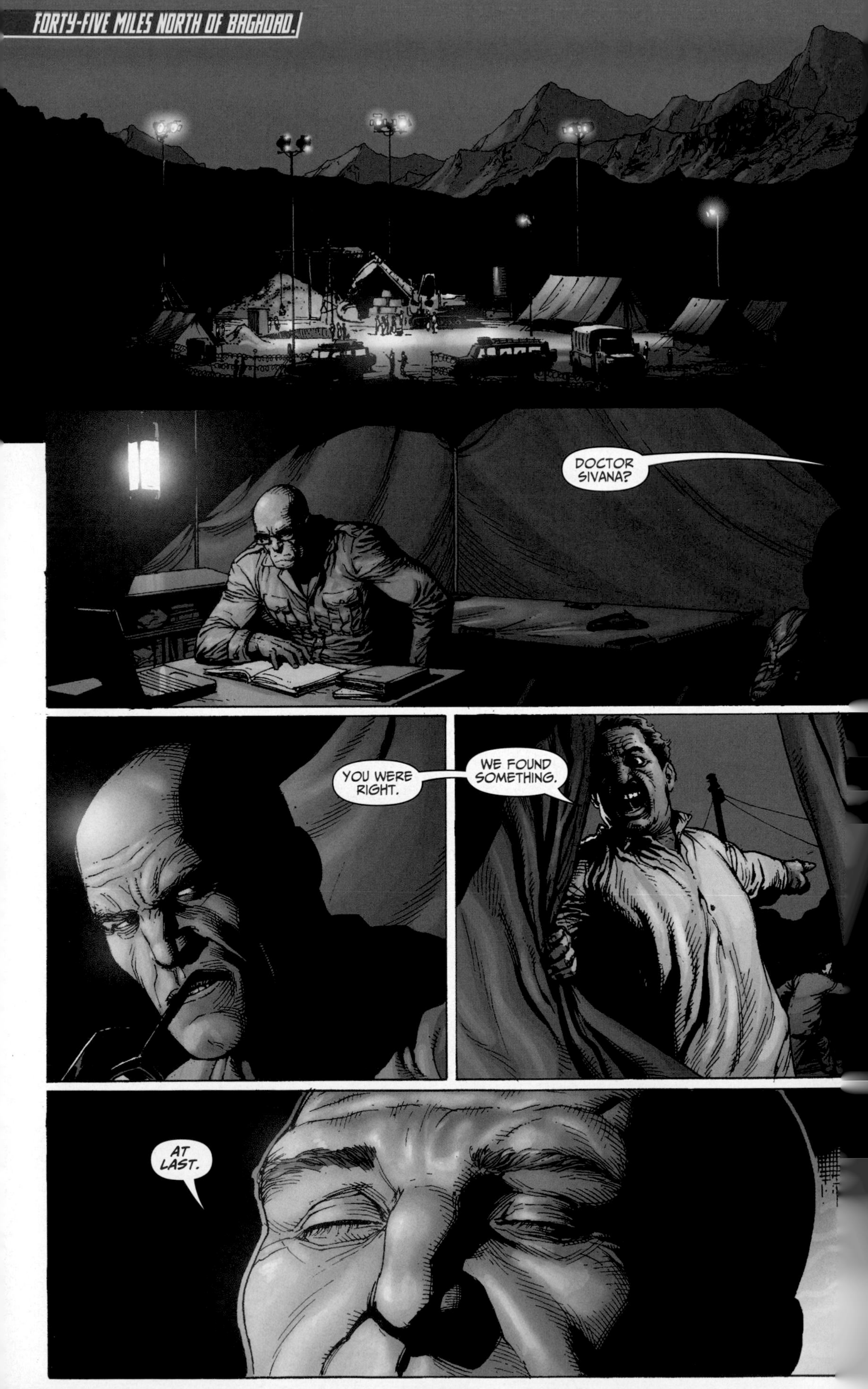
FORTY-FIVE MILES NORTH OF BAGHDAD.
DOCTOR SIVANA?
YOU WERE RIGHT.
WE FOUND SOMETHING.
AT LAST.

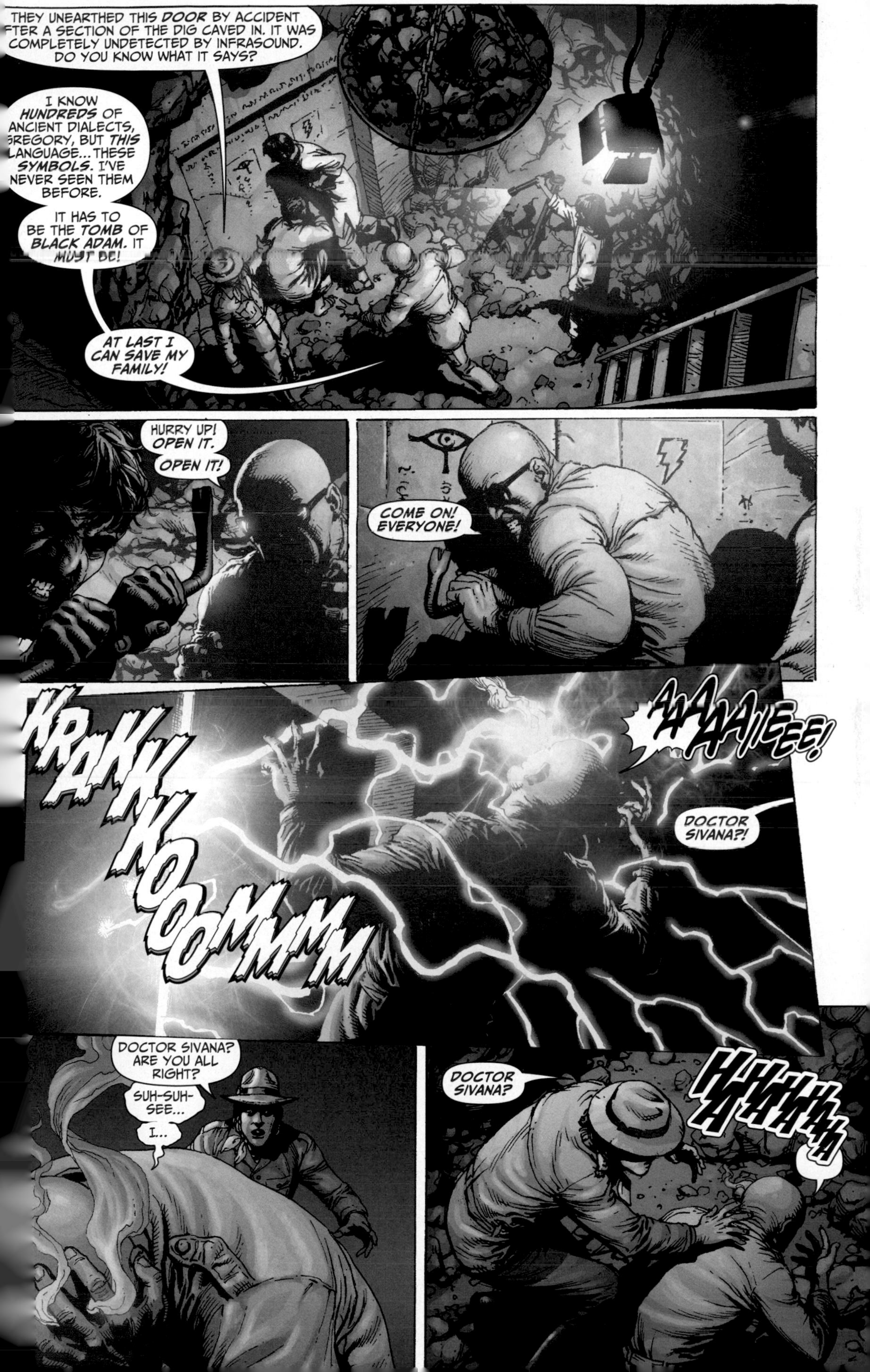

THEY UNEARTHED THIS DOOR BY ACCIDENT AFTER A SECTION OF THE DIG CAVED IN. IT WAS COMPLETELY UNDETECTED BY INFRASOUND. DO YOU KNOW WHAT IT SAYS?
I KNOW HUNDREDS OF ANCIENT DIALECTS, GREGORY, BUT THIS LANGUAGE... THESE SYMBOLS. I'VE NEVER SEEN THEM BEFORE.
IT HAS TO BE THE TOMB OF BLACK ADAM. IT MUST BE!
AT LAST I CAN SAVE MY FAMILY!
HURRY UP! OPEN IT.
OPEN IT!
COME ON! EVERYONE!
KRAKKKOOOMMMM
AAAAAIIEEE!
DOCTOR SIVANA?!
DOCTOR SIVANA? ARE YOU ALL RIGHT?
SUH-SUH-SEE...
I...
DOCTOR SIVANA?
HAHAHAHA

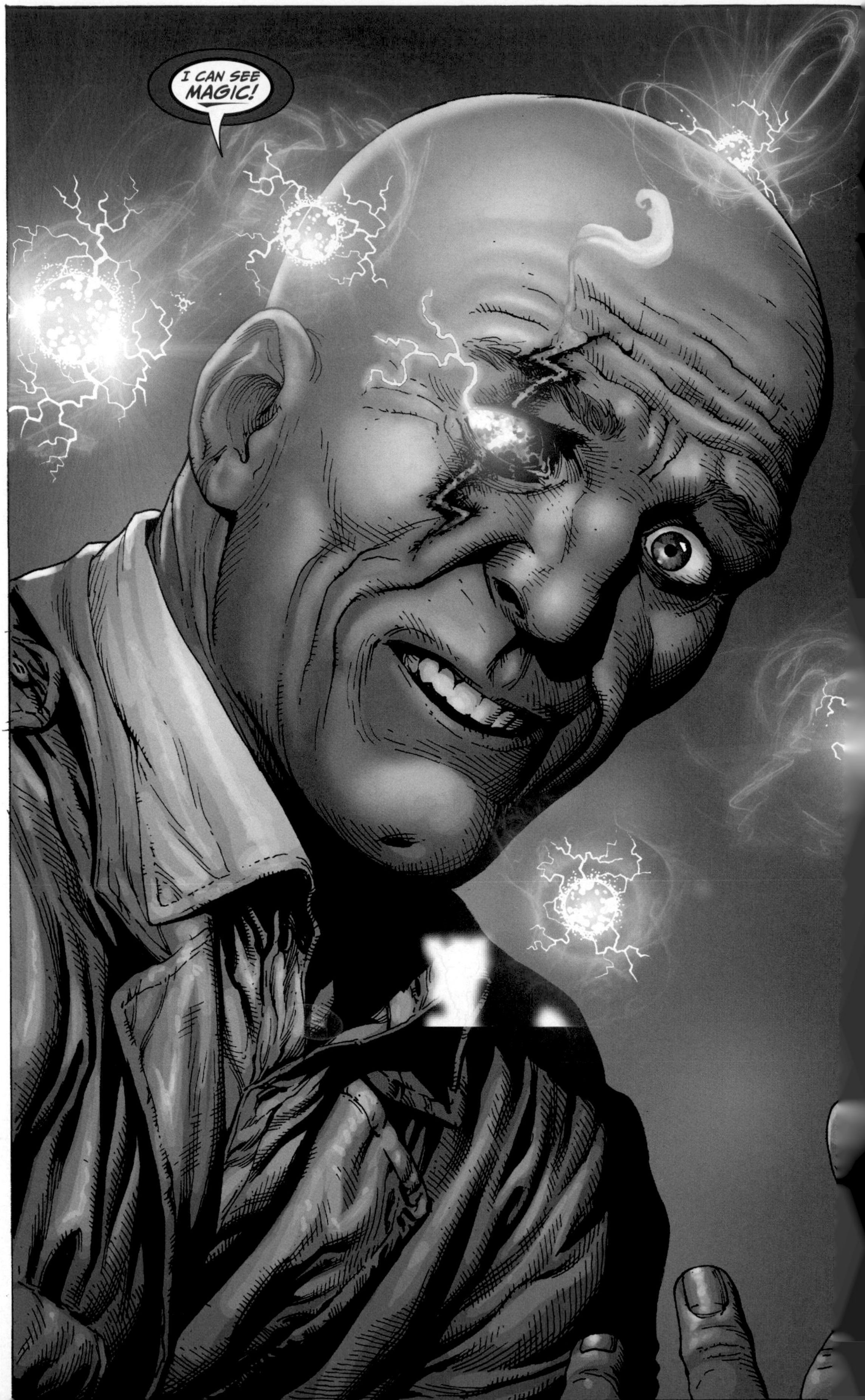
I CAN SEE MAGIC!

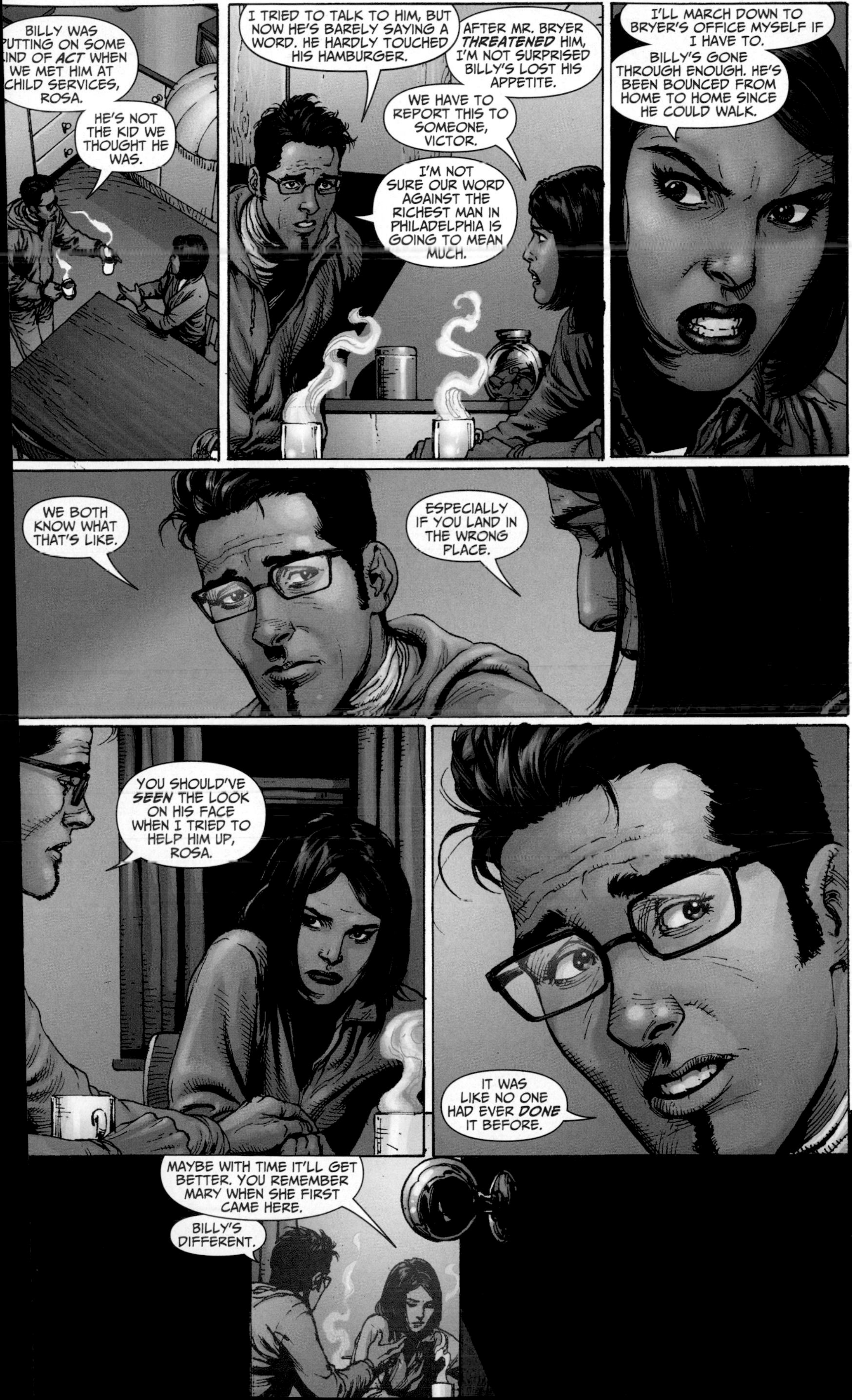

BILLY WAS PUTTING ON SOME KIND OF ACT WHEN WE MET HIM AT CHILD SERVICES, ROSA.
HE'S NOT THE KID WE THOUGHT HE WAS.
I TRIED TO TALK TO HIM, BUT NOW HE'S BARELY SAYING A WORD. HE HARDLY TOUCHED HIS HAMBURGER.
AFTER MR. BRYER THREATENED HIM, I'M NOT SURPRISED BILLY'S LOST HIS APPETITE.
WE HAVE TO REPORT THIS TO SOMEONE, VICTOR.
I'M NOT SURE OUR WORD AGAINST THE RICHEST MAN IN PHILADELPHIA IS GOING TO MEAN MUCH.
I'LL MARCH DOWN TO BRYER'S OFFICE MYSELF IF I HAVE TO.
BILLY'S GONE THROUGH ENOUGH. HE'S BEEN BOUNCED FROM HOME TO HOME SINCE HE COULD WALK.
WE BOTH KNOW WHAT THAT'S LIKE.
ESPECIALLY IF YOU LAND IN THE WRONG PLACE.
YOU SHOULD'VE SEEN THE LOOK ON HIS FACE WHEN I TRIED TO HELP HIM UP, ROSA.
IT WAS LIKE NO ONE HAD EVER DONE IT BEFORE.
MAYBE WITH TIME IT'LL GET BETTER. YOU REMEMBER MARY WHEN SHE FIRST CAME HERE.
BILLY'S DIFFERENT.

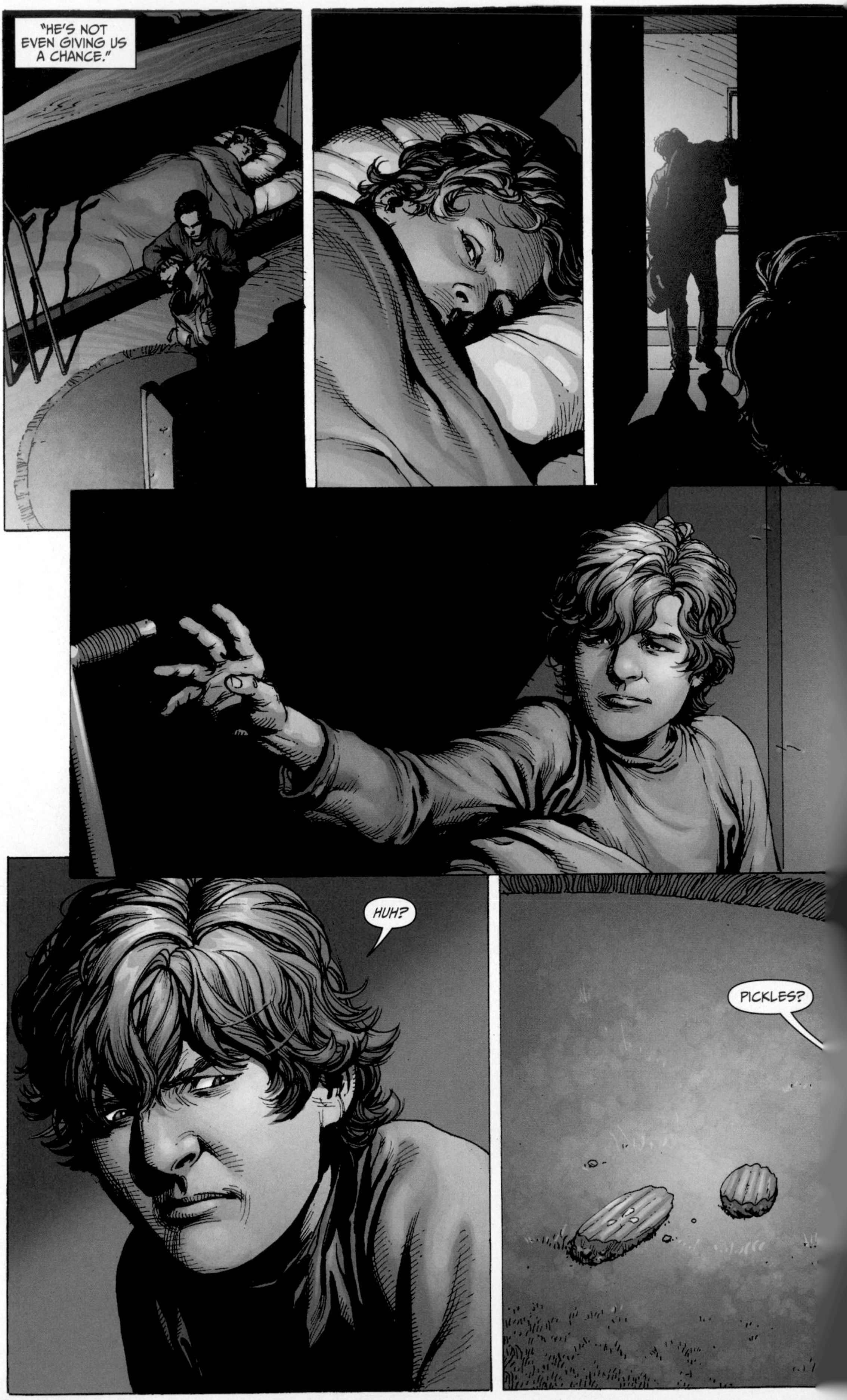
"HE'S NOT EVEN GIVING US A CHANCE."
HUH?
PICKLES?

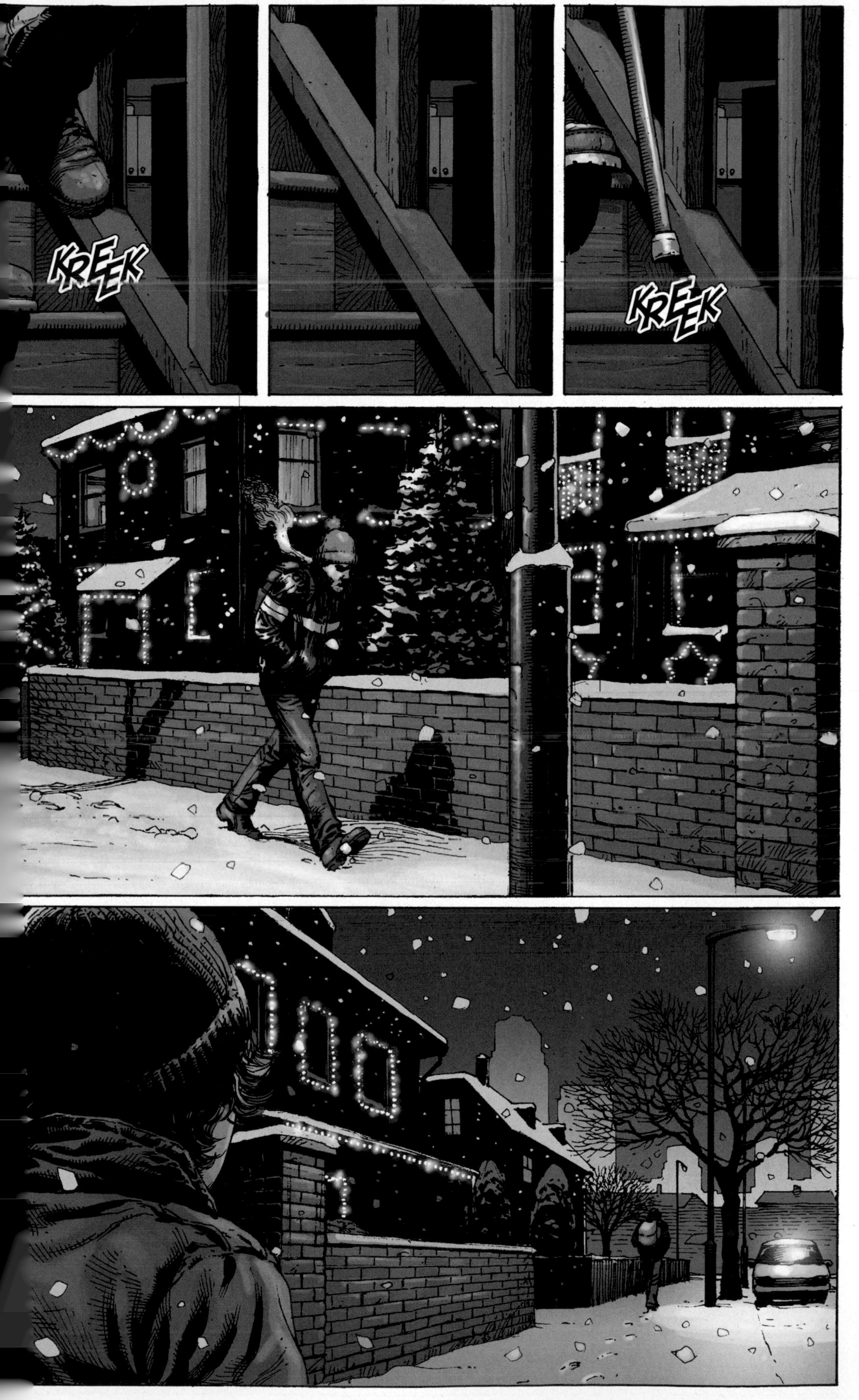
KREEK
KREEK

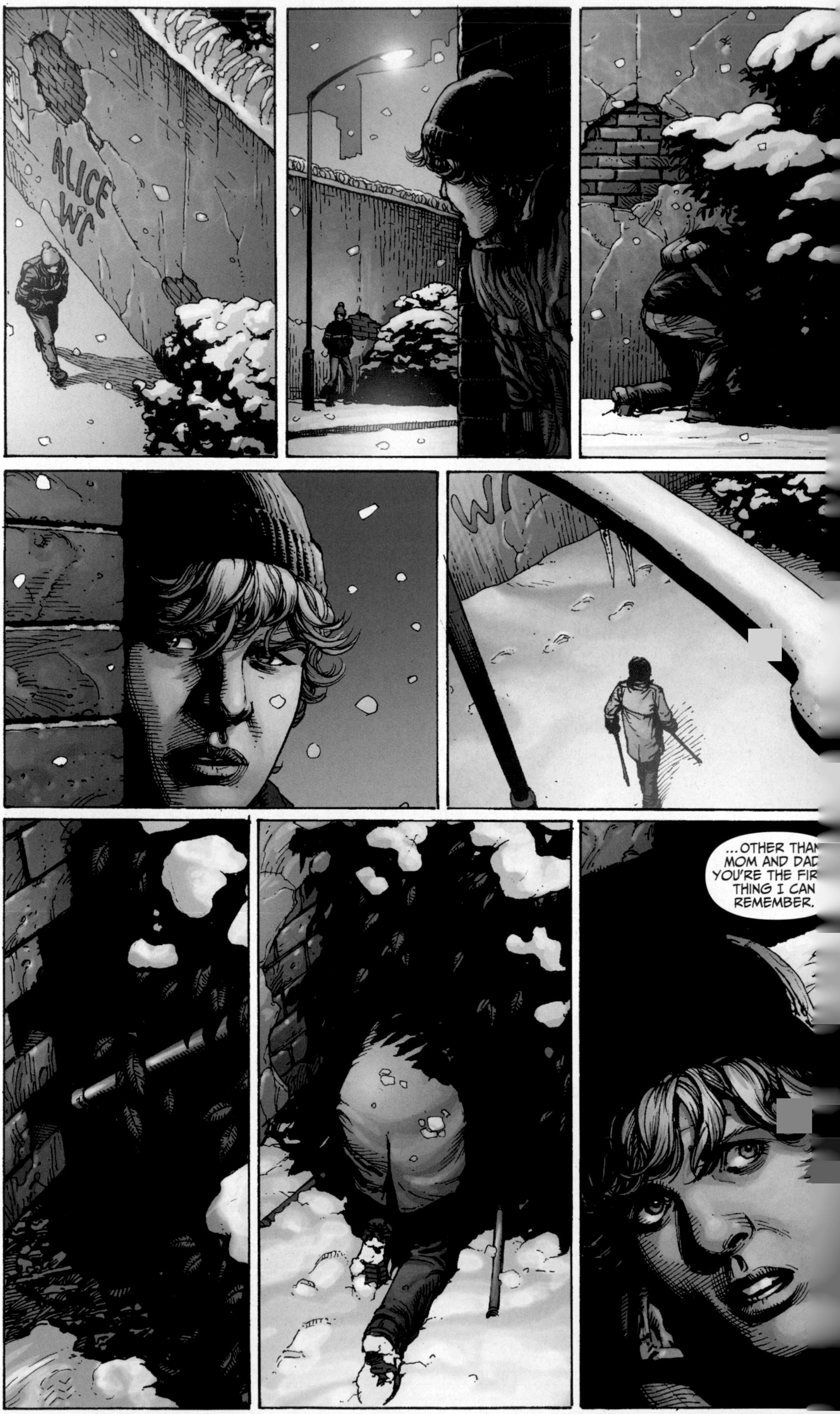
ALICE
WC
...OTHER THA
MOM AND DAD
YOU'RE THE FIR
THING I CAN
REMEMBER.

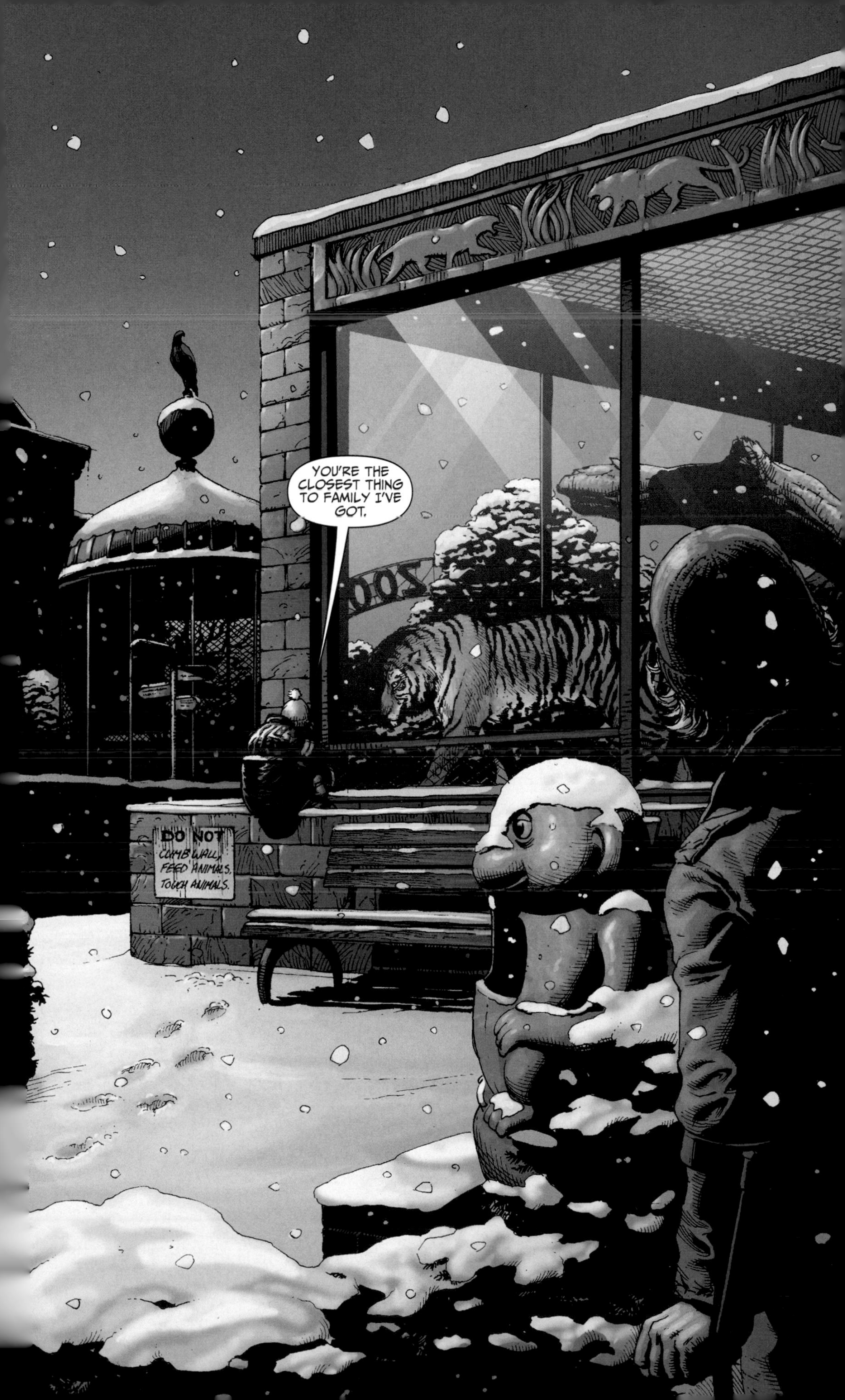
YOU'RE THE CLOSEST THING TO FAMILY I'VE GOT.
DO NOT
CLIMB WALL,
FEED ANIMALS,
TOUCH ANIMALS.

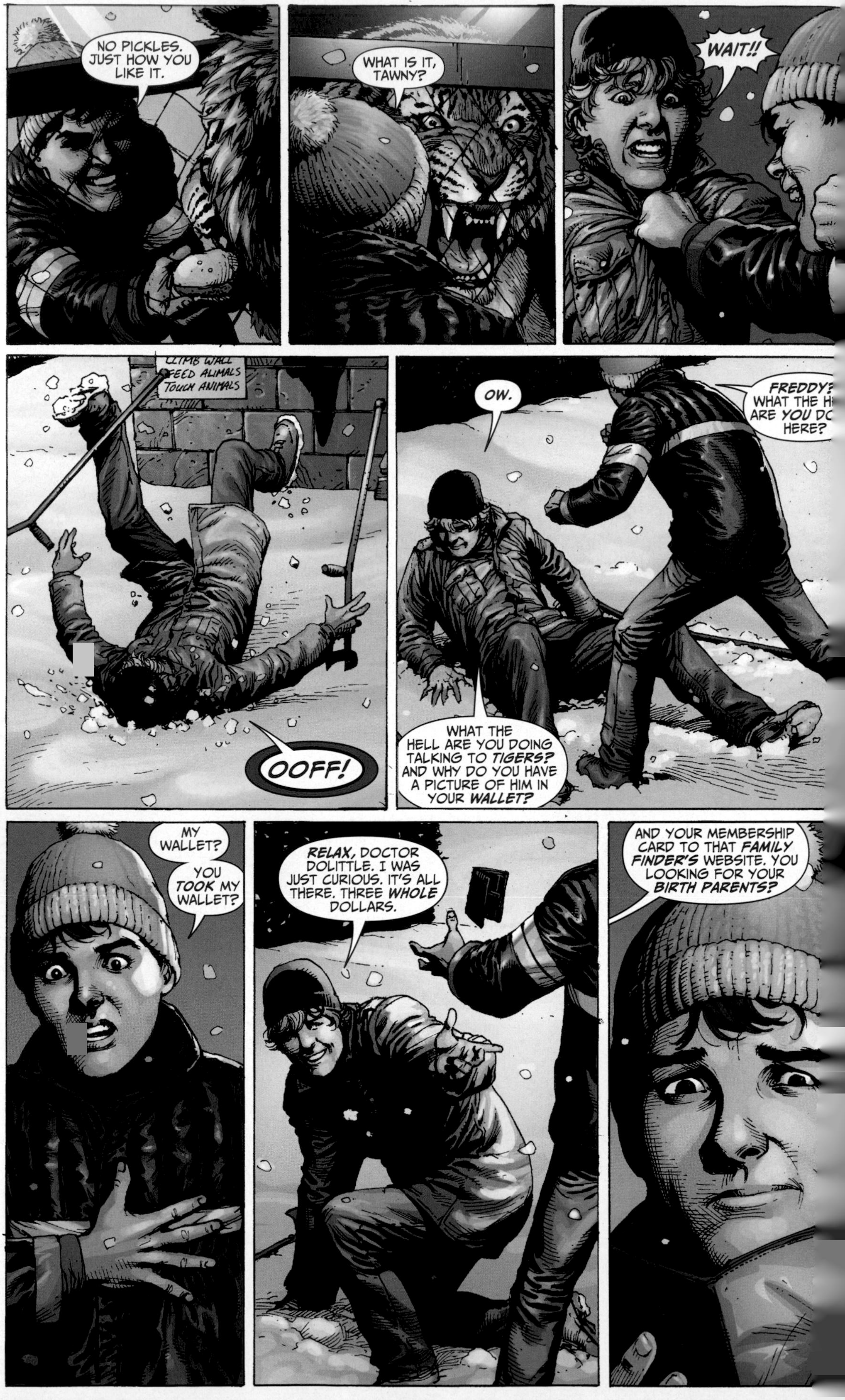
NO PICKLES. JUST HOW YOU LIKE IT.
WHAT IS IT, TAWNY?
WAIT!!
CLIMB WALL
FEED ALIMALS
TOUCH ANIMALS
OOFF!
OW.
FREDDY? WHAT THE H ARE YOU DO HERE?
WHAT THE HELL ARE YOU DOING TALKING TO TIGERS? AND WHY DO YOU HAVE A PICTURE OF HIM IN YOUR WALLET?
MY WALLET?
YOU TOOK MY WALLET?
RELAX, DOCTOR DOLITTLE. I WAS JUST CURIOUS. IT'S ALL THERE. THREE WHOLE DOLLARS.
AND YOUR MEMBERSHIP CARD TO THAT FAMILY FINDER'S WEBSITE. YOU LOOKING FOR YOUR BIRTH PARENTS?

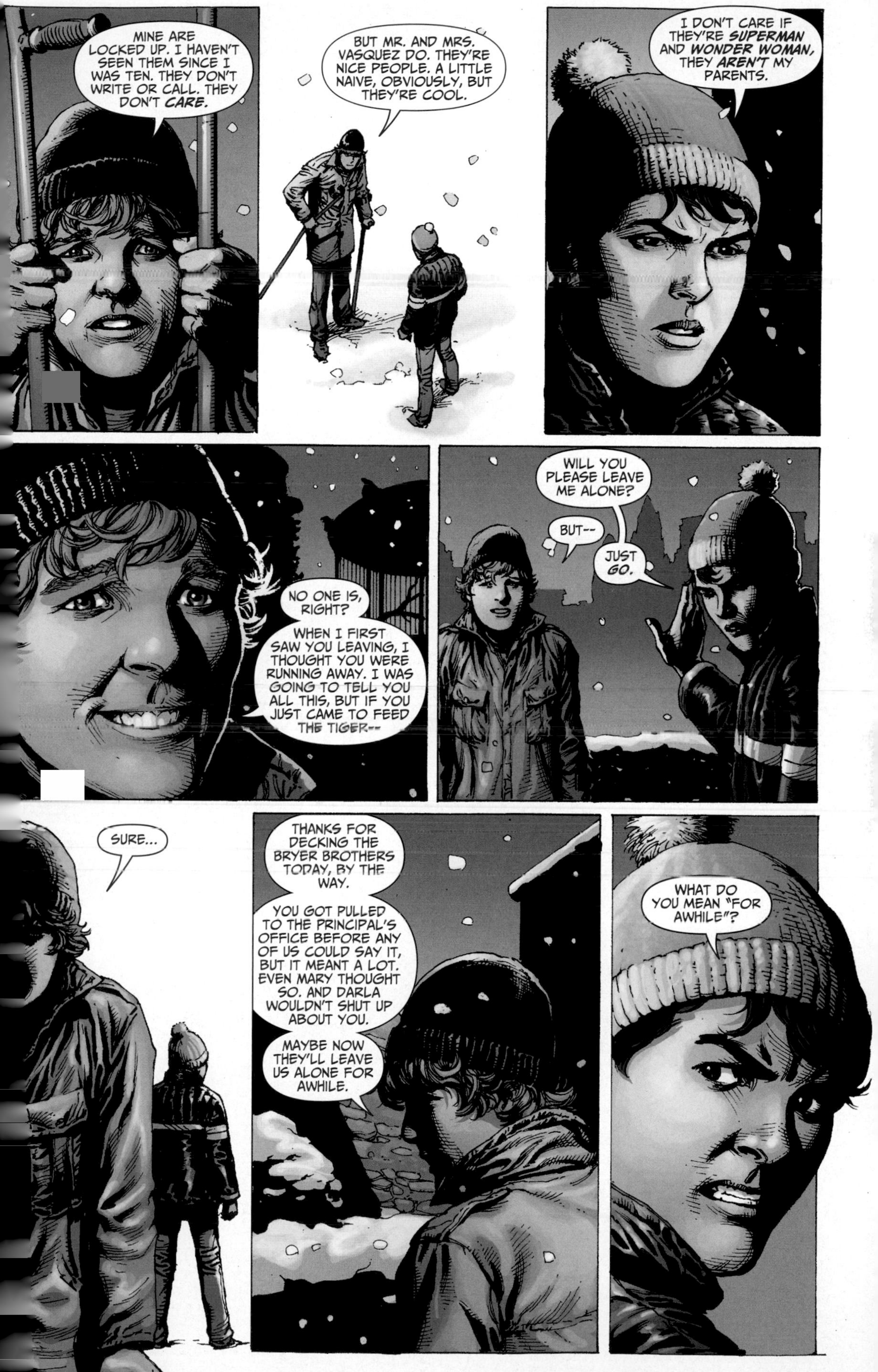
MINE ARE LOCKED UP. I HAVEN'T SEEN THEM SINCE I WAS TEN. THEY DON'T WRITE OR CALL. THEY DON'T CARE.
BUT MR. AND MRS. VASQUEZ DO. THEY'RE NICE PEOPLE. A LITTLE NAIVE, OBVIOUSLY, BUT THEY'RE COOL.
I DON'T CARE IF THEY'RE SUPERMAN AND WONDER WOMAN, THEY AREN'T MY PARENTS.
NO ONE IS, RIGHT?
WHEN I FIRST SAW YOU LEAVING, I THOUGHT YOU WERE RUNNING AWAY. I WAS GOING TO TELL YOU ALL THIS, BUT IF YOU JUST CAME TO FEED THE TIGER--
WILL YOU PLEASE LEAVE ME ALONE?
BUT--
JUST GO.
SURE...
THANKS FOR DECKING THE BRYER BROTHERS TODAY, BY THE WAY.
YOU GOT PULLED TO THE PRINCIPAL'S OFFICE BEFORE ANY OF US COULD SAY IT, BUT IT MEANT A LOT. EVEN MARY THOUGHT SO. AND DARLA WOULDN'T SHUT UP ABOUT YOU.
MAYBE NOW THEY'LL LEAVE US ALONE FOR AWHILE.
WHAT DO YOU MEAN "FOR AWHILE"?

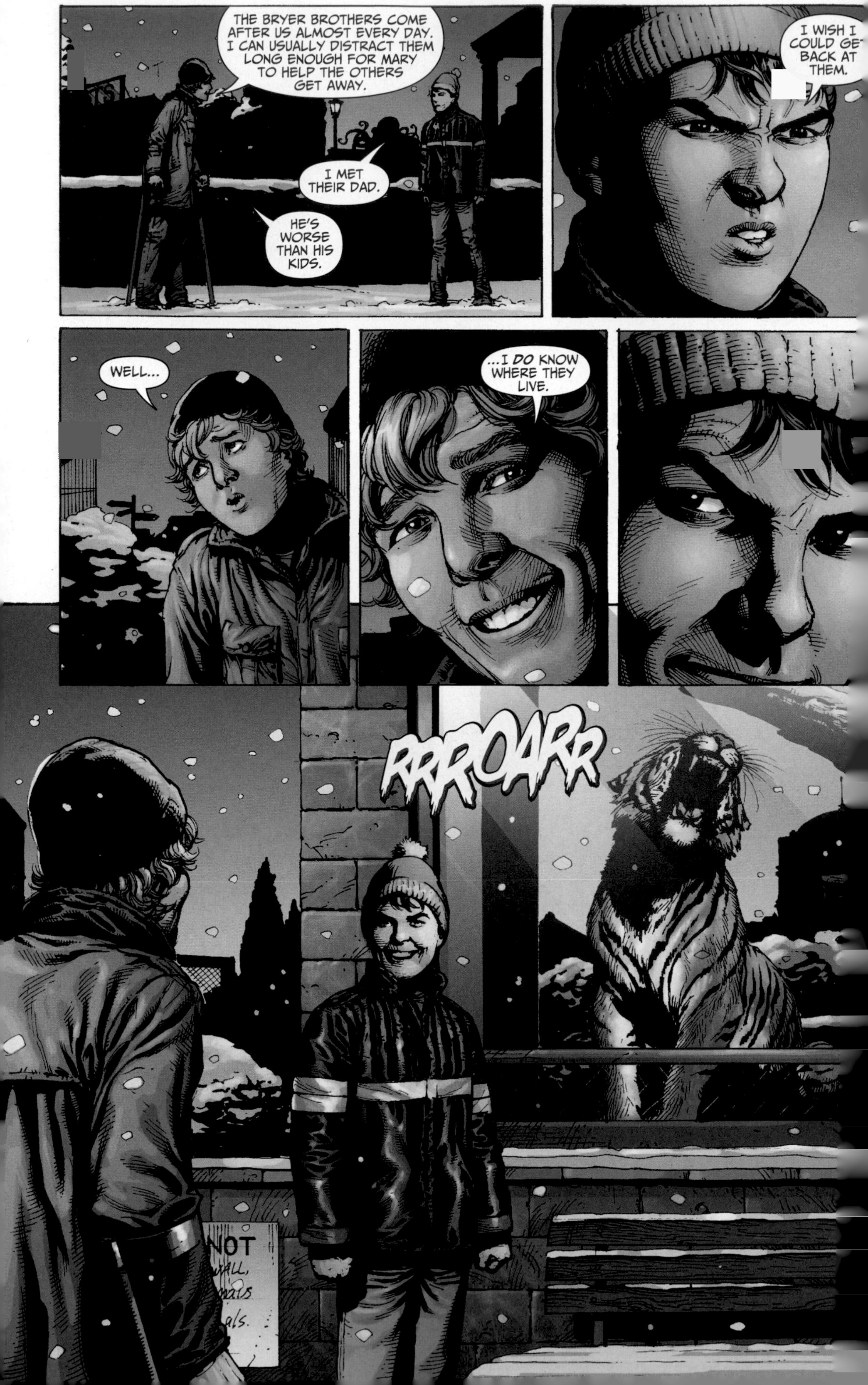
THE BRYER BROTHERS COME AFTER US ALMOST EVERY DAY. I CAN USUALLY DISTRACT THEM LONG ENOUGH FOR MARY TO HELP THE OTHERS GET AWAY.
I MET THEIR DAD.
HE'S WORSE THAN HIS KIDS.
I WISH I COULD GET BACK AT THEM.
WELL...
...I DO KNOW WHERE THEY LIVE.
RRROARR
NOT

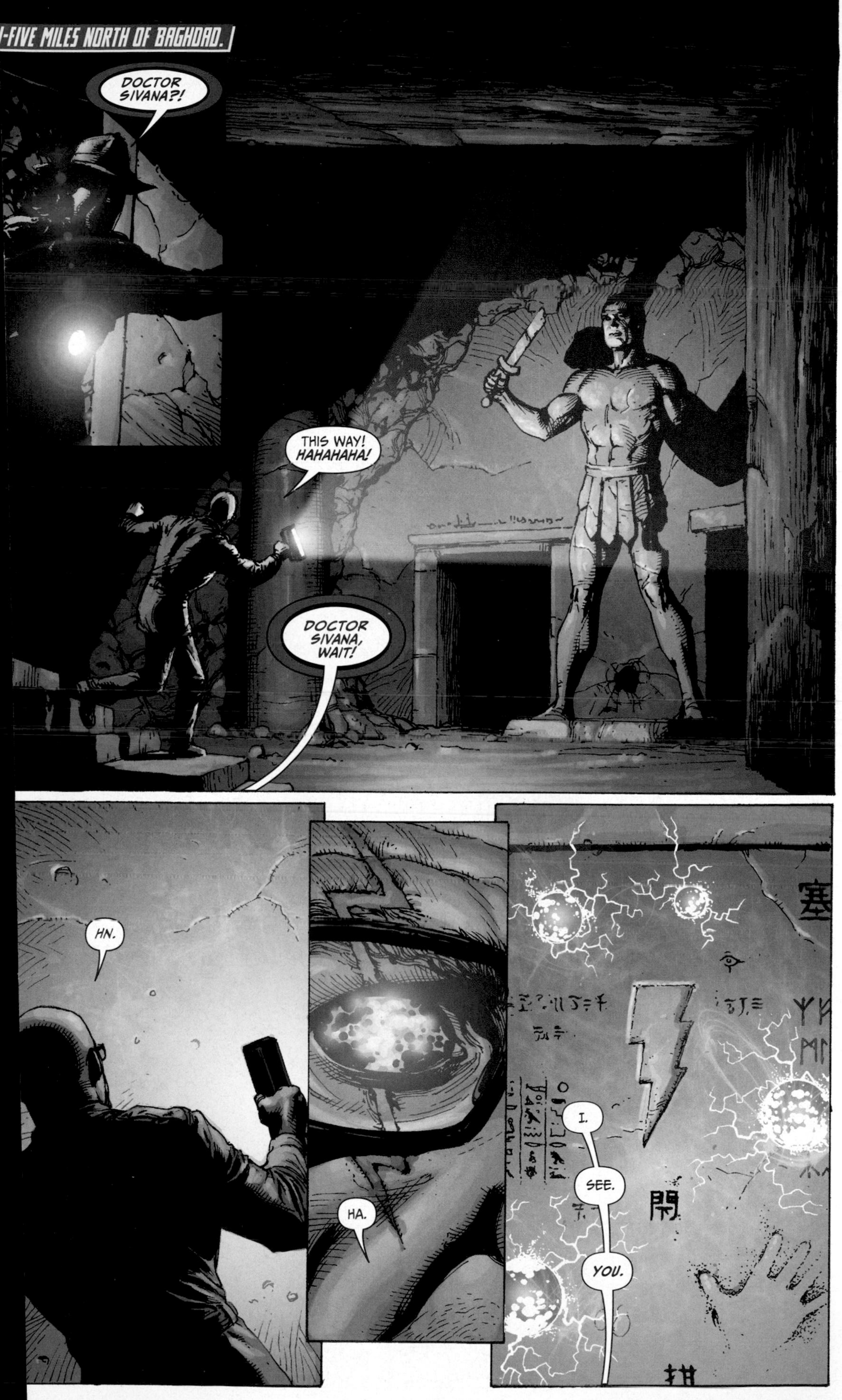
-FIVE MILES NORTH OF BAGHDAD.
DOCTOR SIVANA?!
THIS WAY! HAHAHAHA!
DOCTOR SIVANA, WAIT!
HN.
HA.
I.
SEE.
YOU.

DOCTOR SIVANA? THERE'S NOTHING THERE. IT'S JUST A WALL.

BUT THE ROOM AHEAD, WE CAN SEE A *GLITTER-ING.*

< TREASURE! >

TREASURE, GABIR SAYS. WE'VE FOUND SOMETHING!

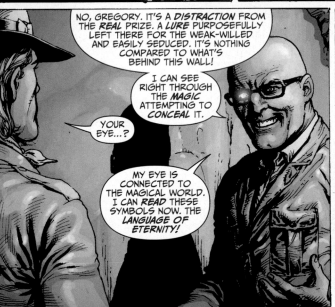

NO, GREGORY. IT'S A *DISTRACTION* FROM THE *REAL* PRIZE. A *LURE* PURPOSEFULLY LEFT THERE FOR THE WEAK-WILLED AND EASILY SEDUCED. IT'S NOTHING COMPARED TO WHAT'S BEHIND THIS WALL!

I CAN SEE RIGHT THROUGH THE *MAGIC* ATTEMPTING TO *CONCEAL* IT.

YOUR EYE...?

MY EYE IS CONNECTED TO THE *MAGICAL* WORLD. I CAN *READ* THESE SYMBOLS NOW. THE *LANGUAGE OF ETERNITY!*

IT SAYS HERE THAT *BLACK ADAM* WILL BE IMPRISONED UNTIL A BEING WHO CAN *DESTROY* HIM IS FOUND!

HIS ENEMIES *PUT* HIM HERE, BUT *WE* CAN *RELEASE* HIM--

--AND BRING *MAGIC* BACK TO THE WORLD!

IT SAYS THIS TOMB CANNOT BE OPENED BUT WITH *ONE WORD...*

SHA

KZZATT   KZZATT

...SHAZAM!

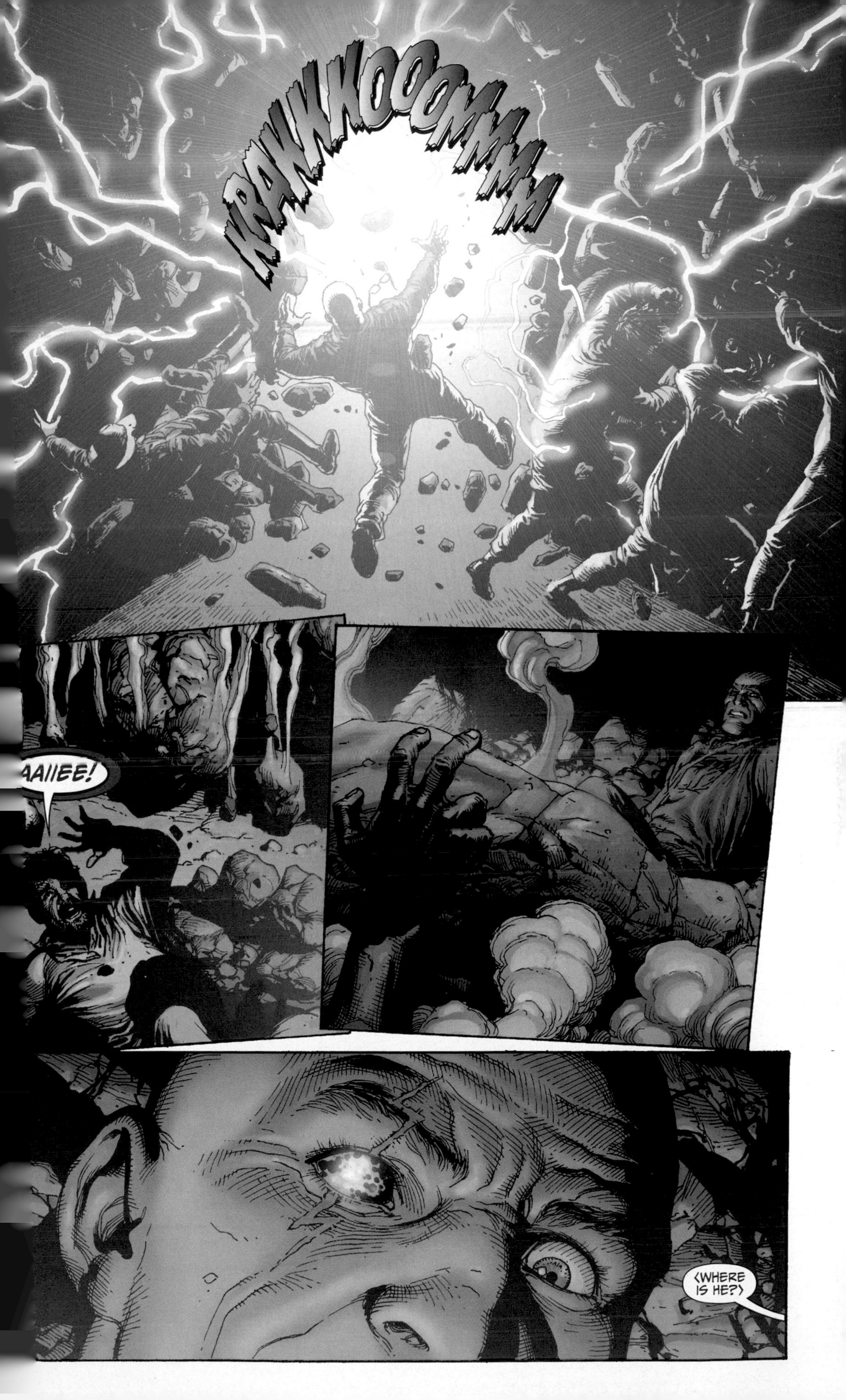
KRAKKOOOMMM
AAIIEE!
‹WHERE IS HE?›

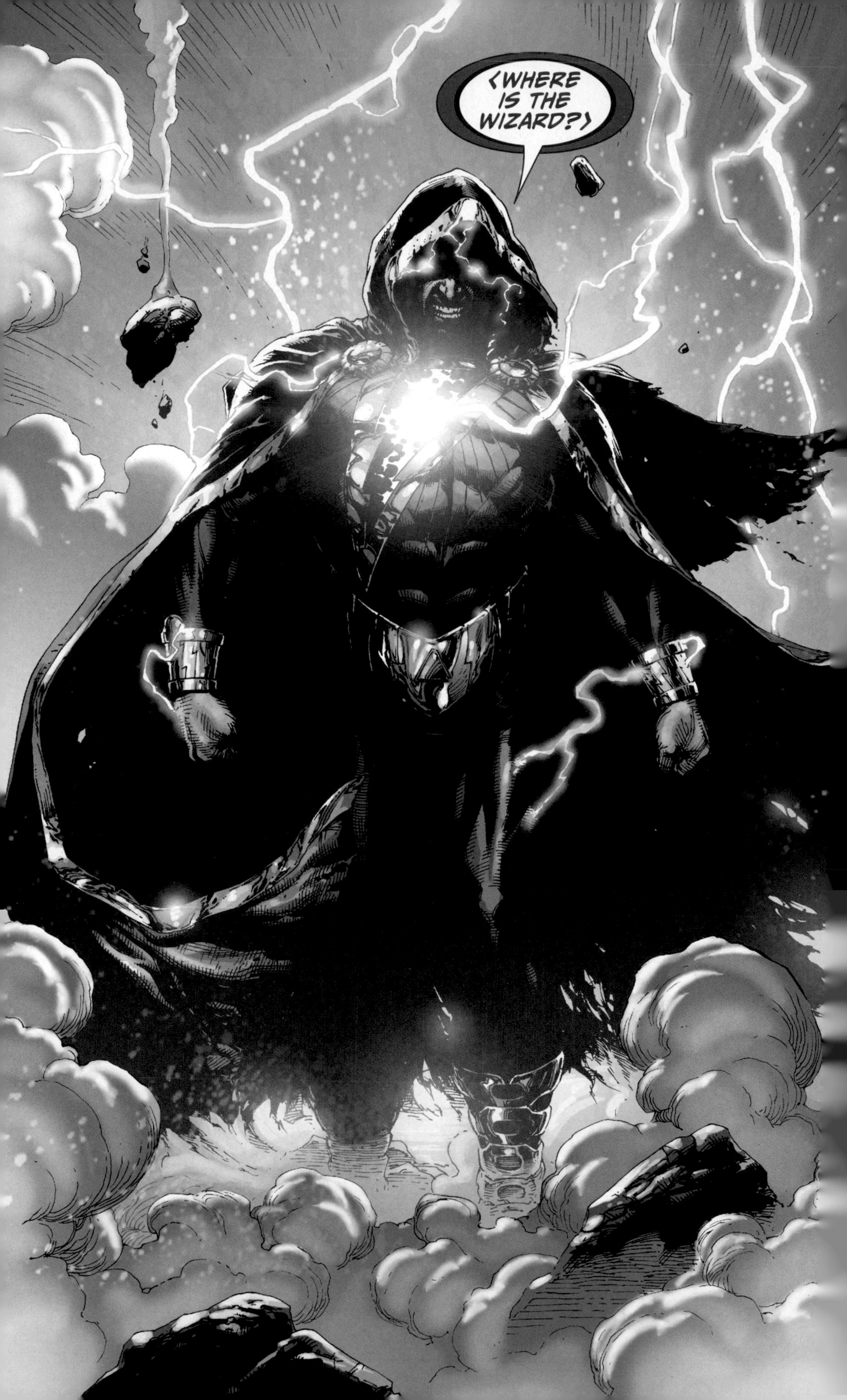
<WHERE IS THE WIZARD?>

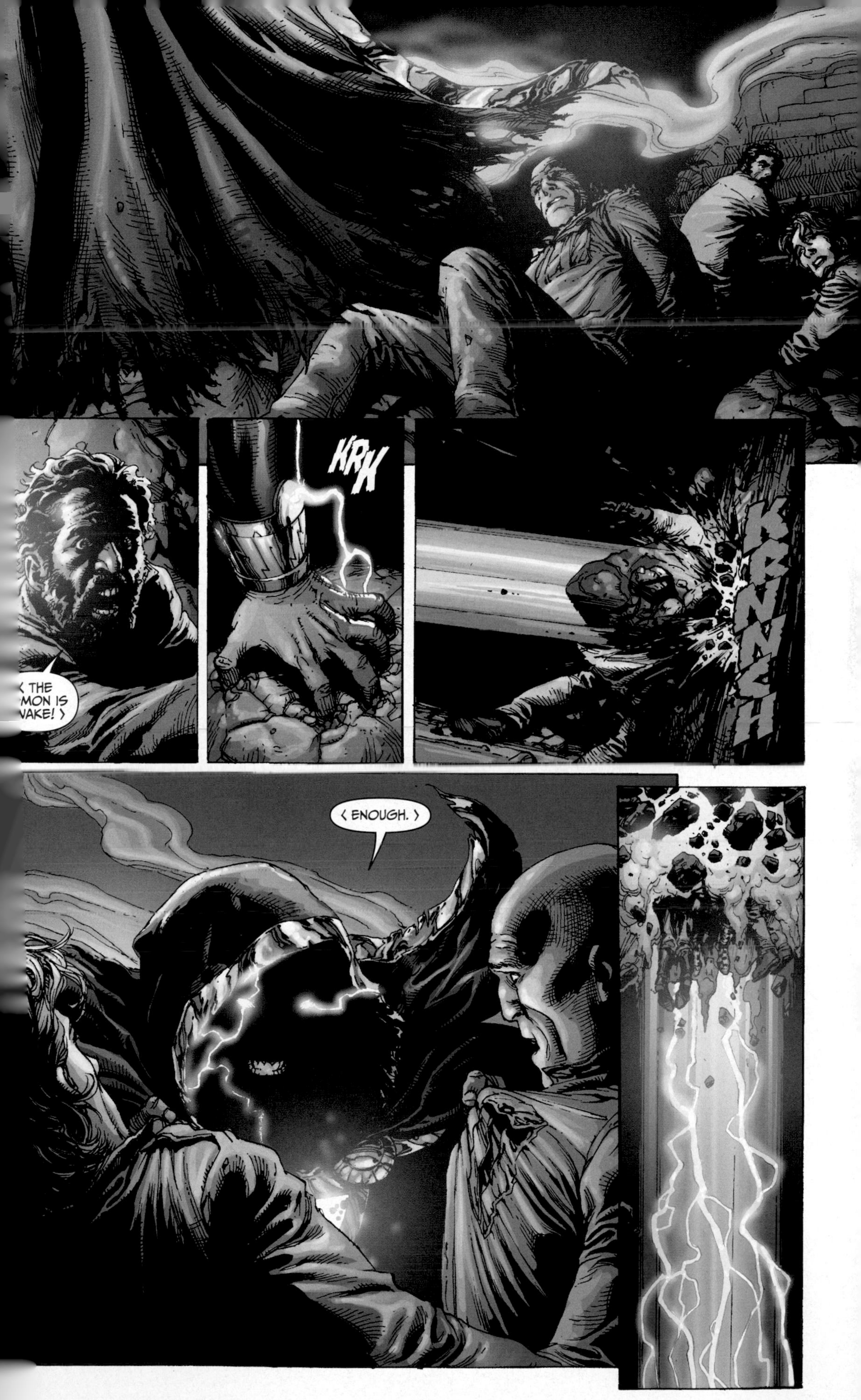
THE
MON IS
WAKE! ›
KRK
KRNNCH
‹ ENOUGH. ›

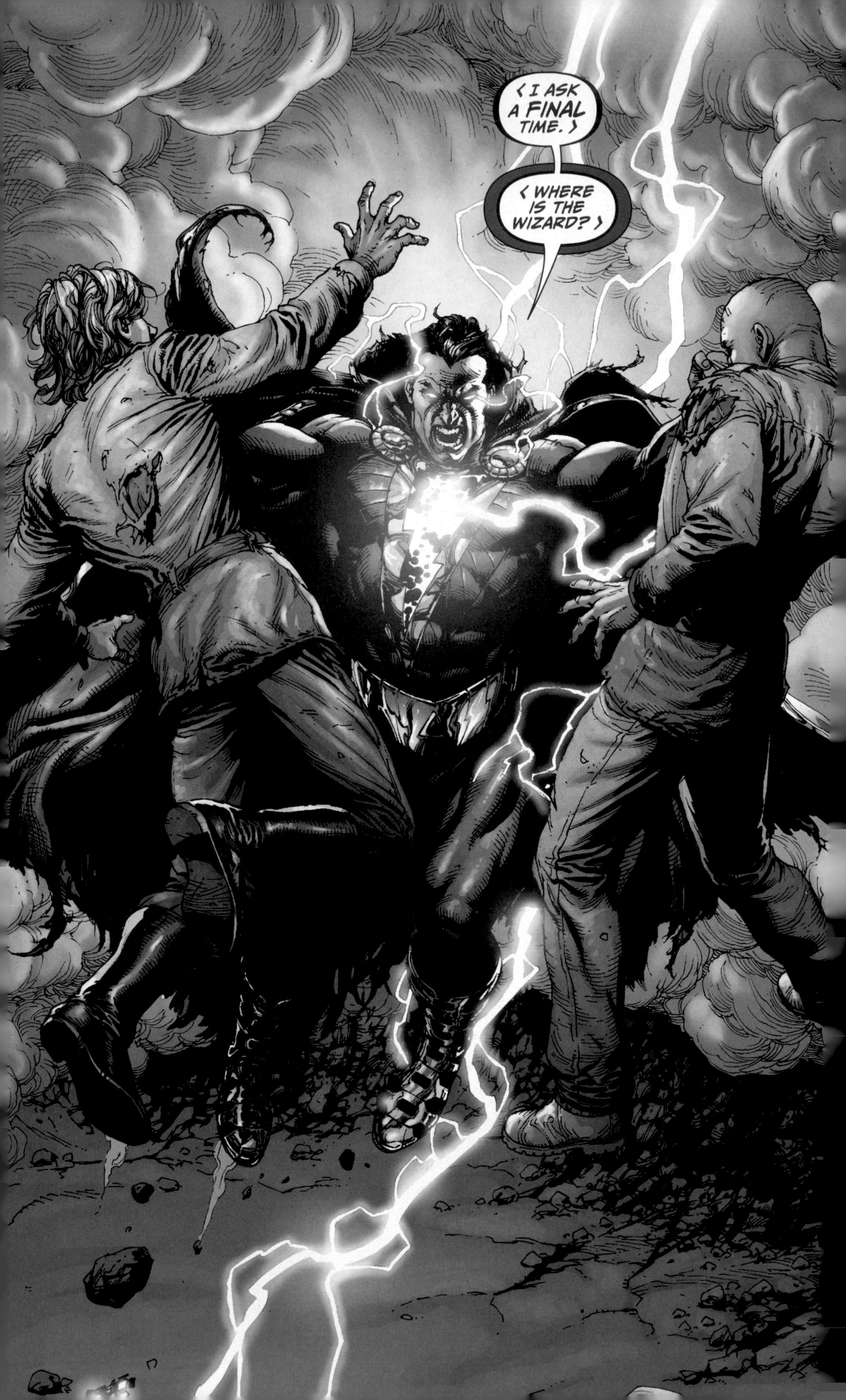

‹ I ASK A FINAL TIME. ›
‹ WHERE IS THE WIZARD? ›

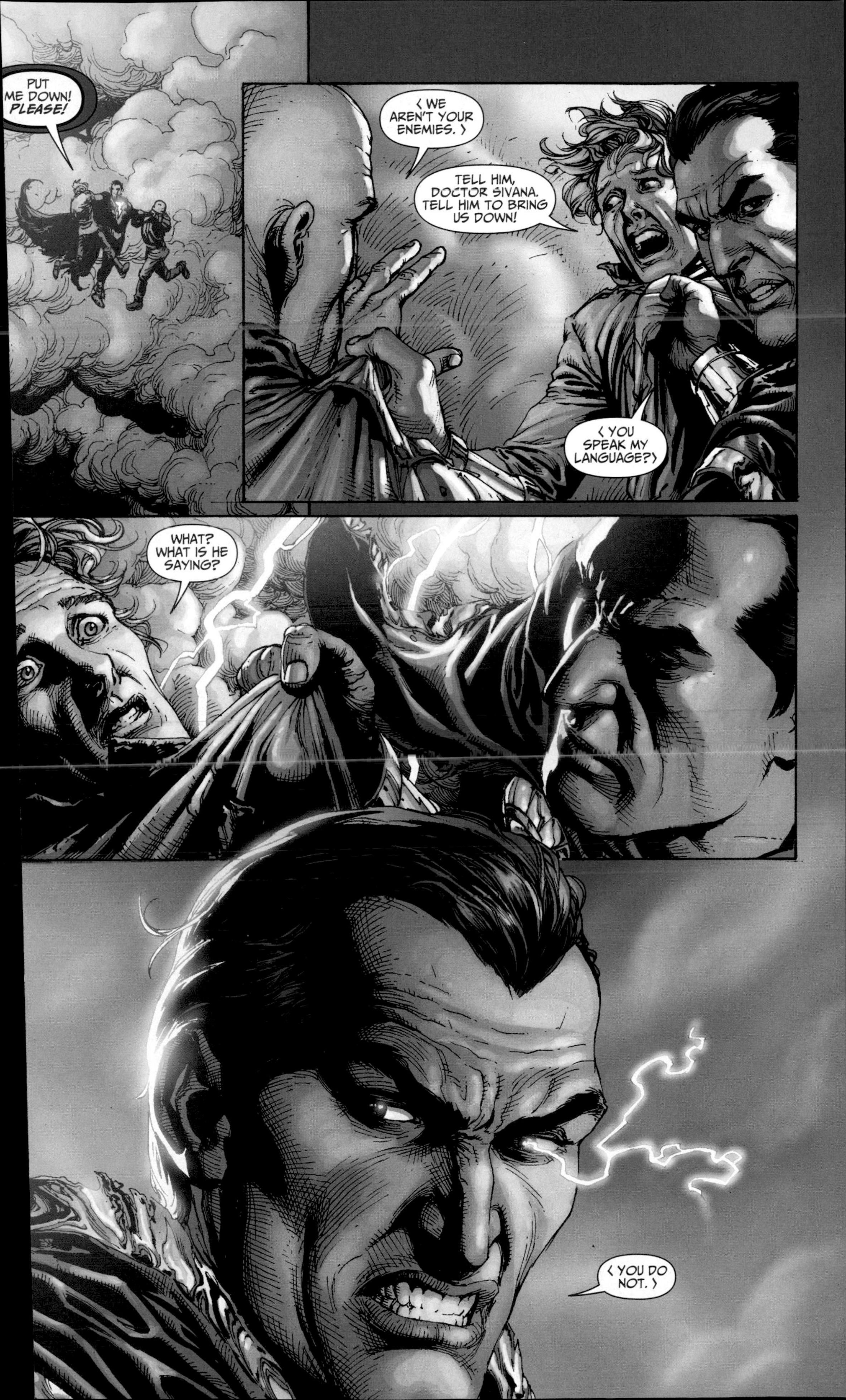
PUT ME DOWN! *PLEASE!*
‹ WE AREN'T YOUR ENEMIES. ›
TELL HIM, DOCTOR SIVANA. TELL HIM TO BRING US DOWN!
‹ YOU SPEAK MY LANGUAGE?›
WHAT? WHAT IS HE SAYING?
‹ YOU DO NOT. ›

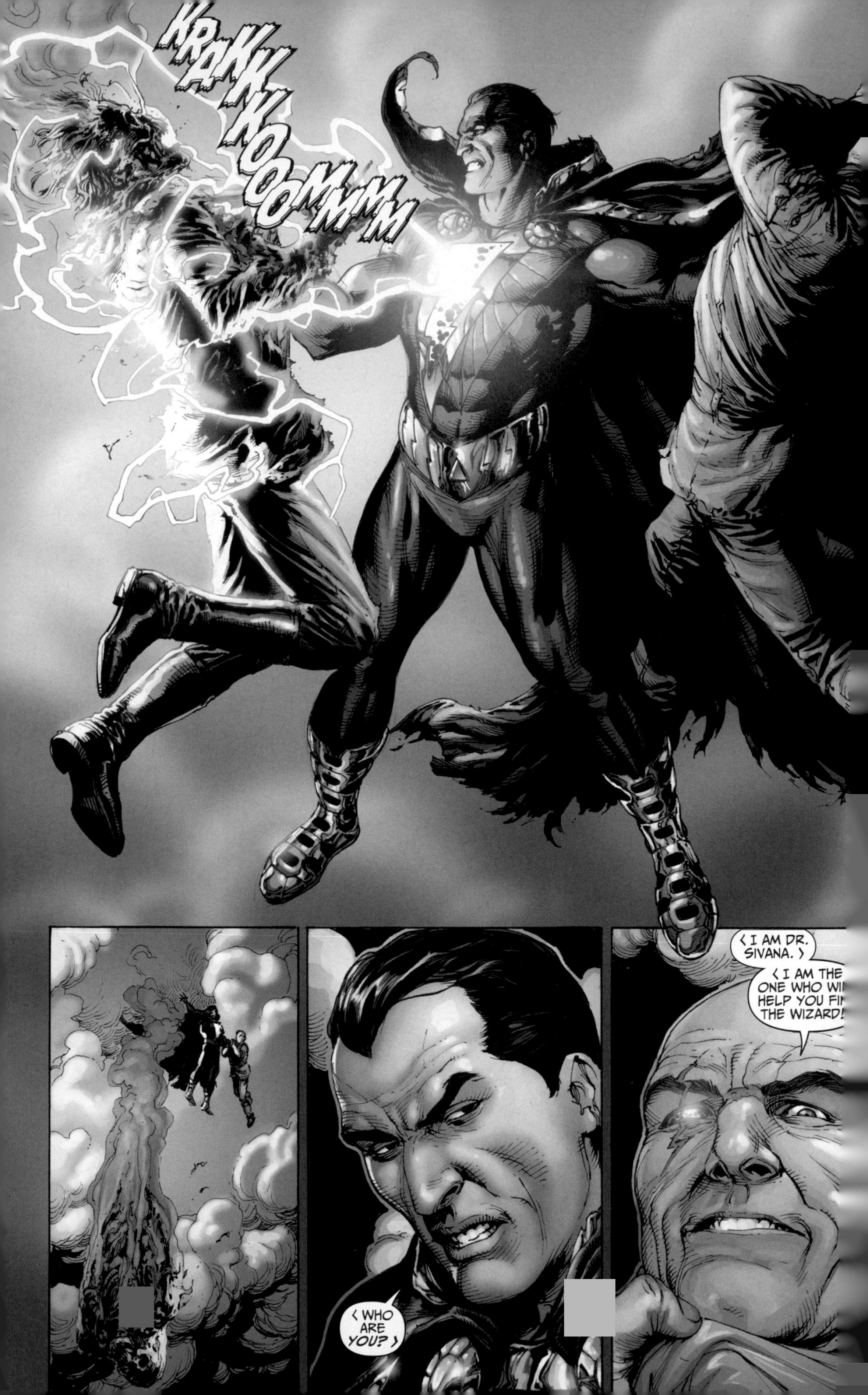
KRAKKOOOMMMM
‹ WHO ARE YOU? ›
‹ I AM DR. SIVANA. ›
‹ I AM THE ONE WHO WI HELP YOU FI THE WIZARD!

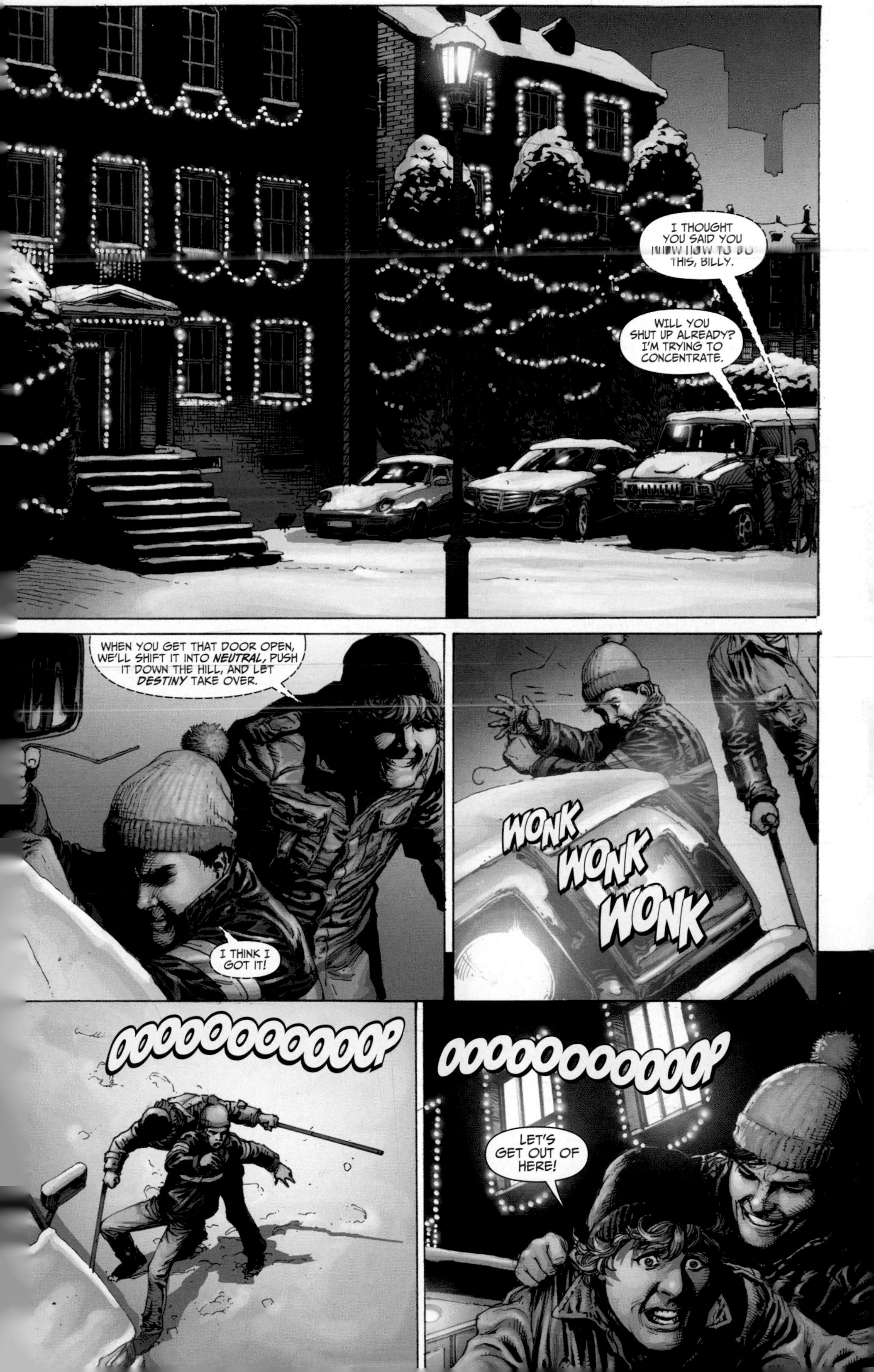
I THOUGHT YOU SAID YOU KNOW HOW TO DO THIS, BILLY.
WILL YOU SHUT UP ALREADY? I'M TRYING TO CONCENTRATE.
WHEN YOU GET THAT DOOR OPEN, WE'LL SHIFT IT INTO NEUTRAL, PUSH IT DOWN THE HILL, AND LET DESTINY TAKE OVER.
I THINK I GOT IT!
WONK
WONK
WONK
OOOOOOOOOOOP
OOOOOOOOOOOP
LET'S GET OUT OF HERE!

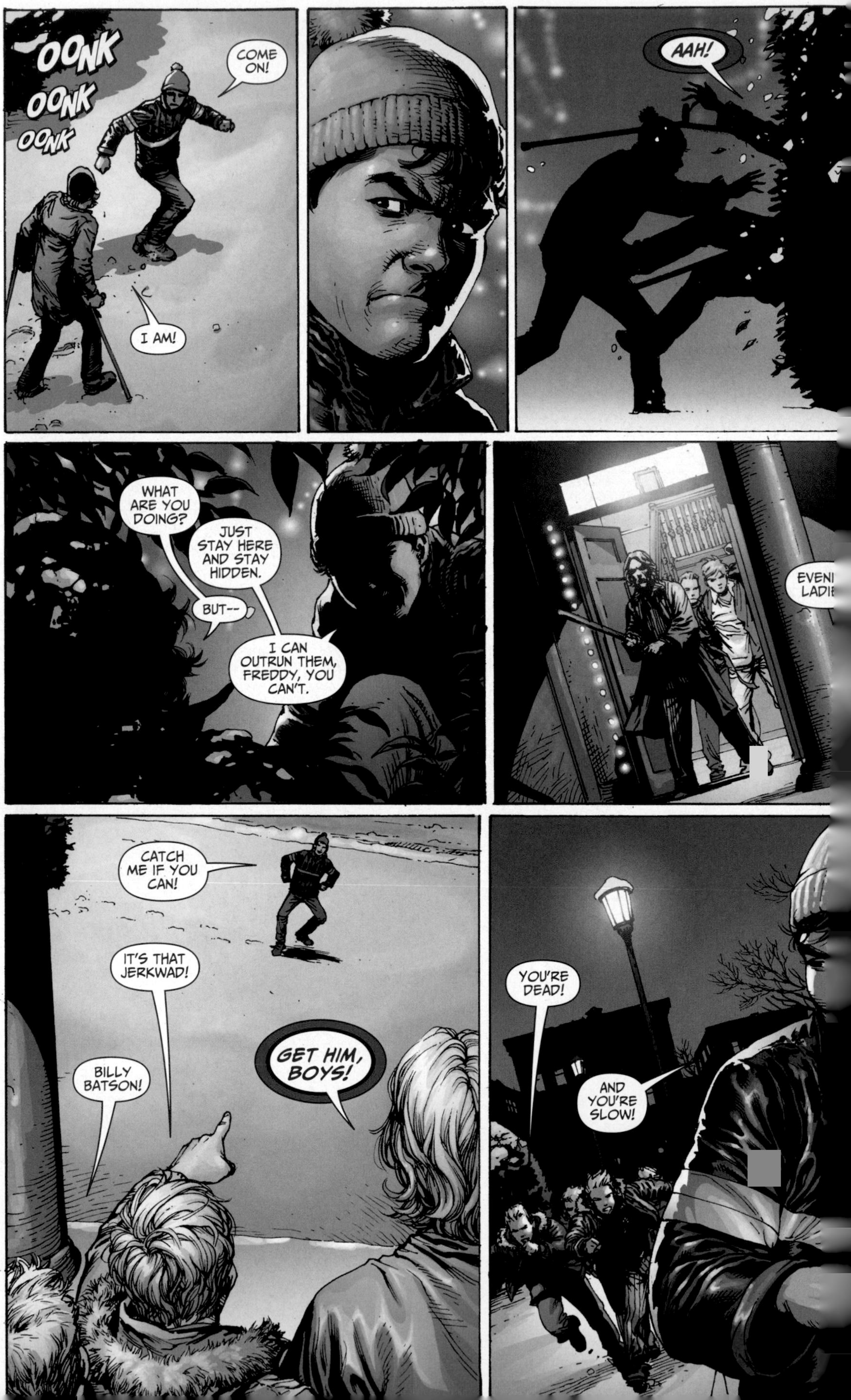
OONK
OONK
OONK
COME ON!
I AM!
AAH!
WHAT ARE YOU DOING?
JUST STAY HERE AND STAY HIDDEN.
BUT--
I CAN OUTRUN THEM, FREDDY, YOU CAN'T.
CATCH ME IF YOU CAN!
IT'S THAT JERKWAD!
BILLY BATSON!
GET HIM, BOYS!
YOU'RE DEAD!
AND YOU'RE SLOW!

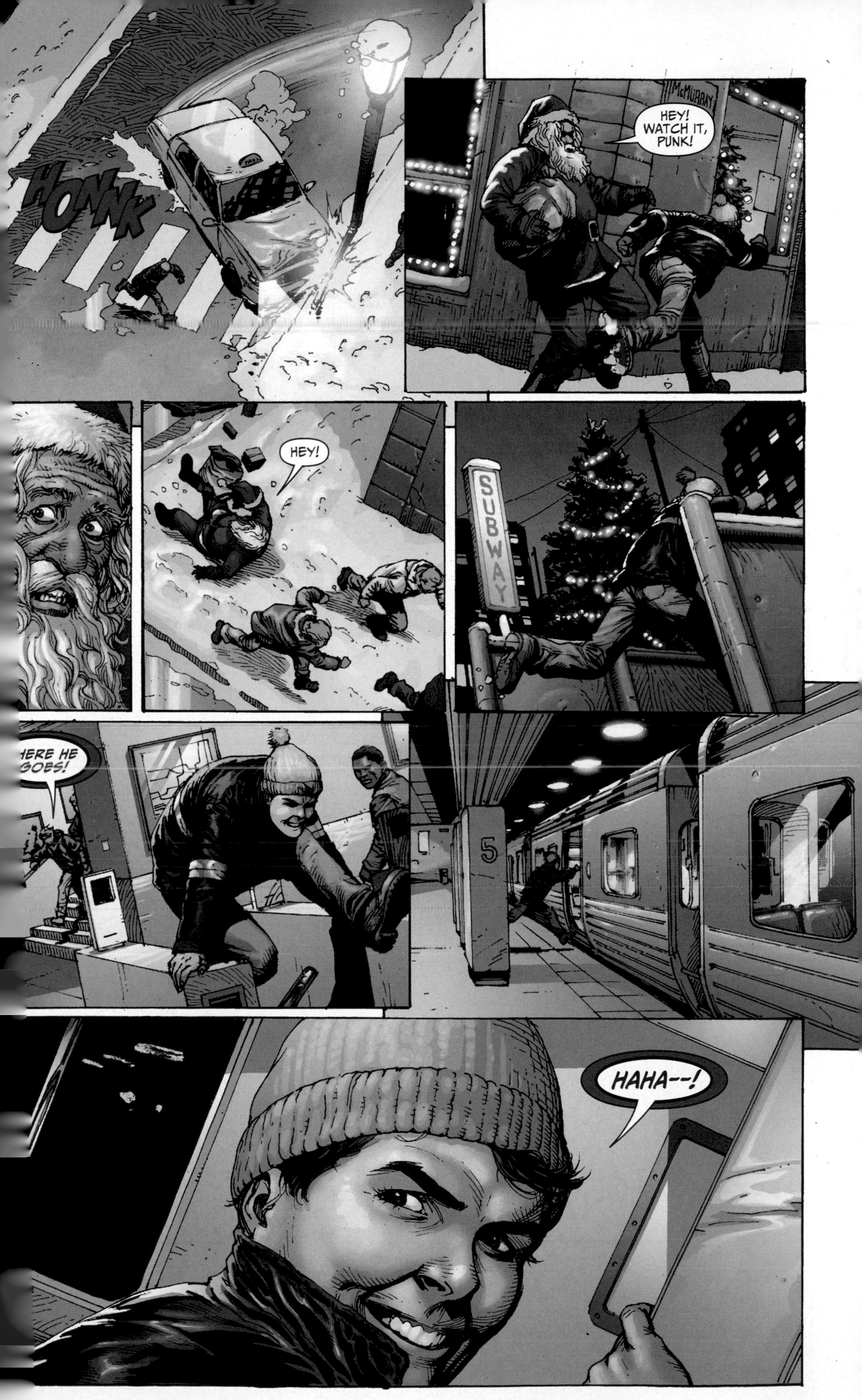
HONNK
McMURRAY
HEY! WATCH IT, PUNK!
HEY!
SUBWAY
HERE HE GOES!
5
HAHA--!

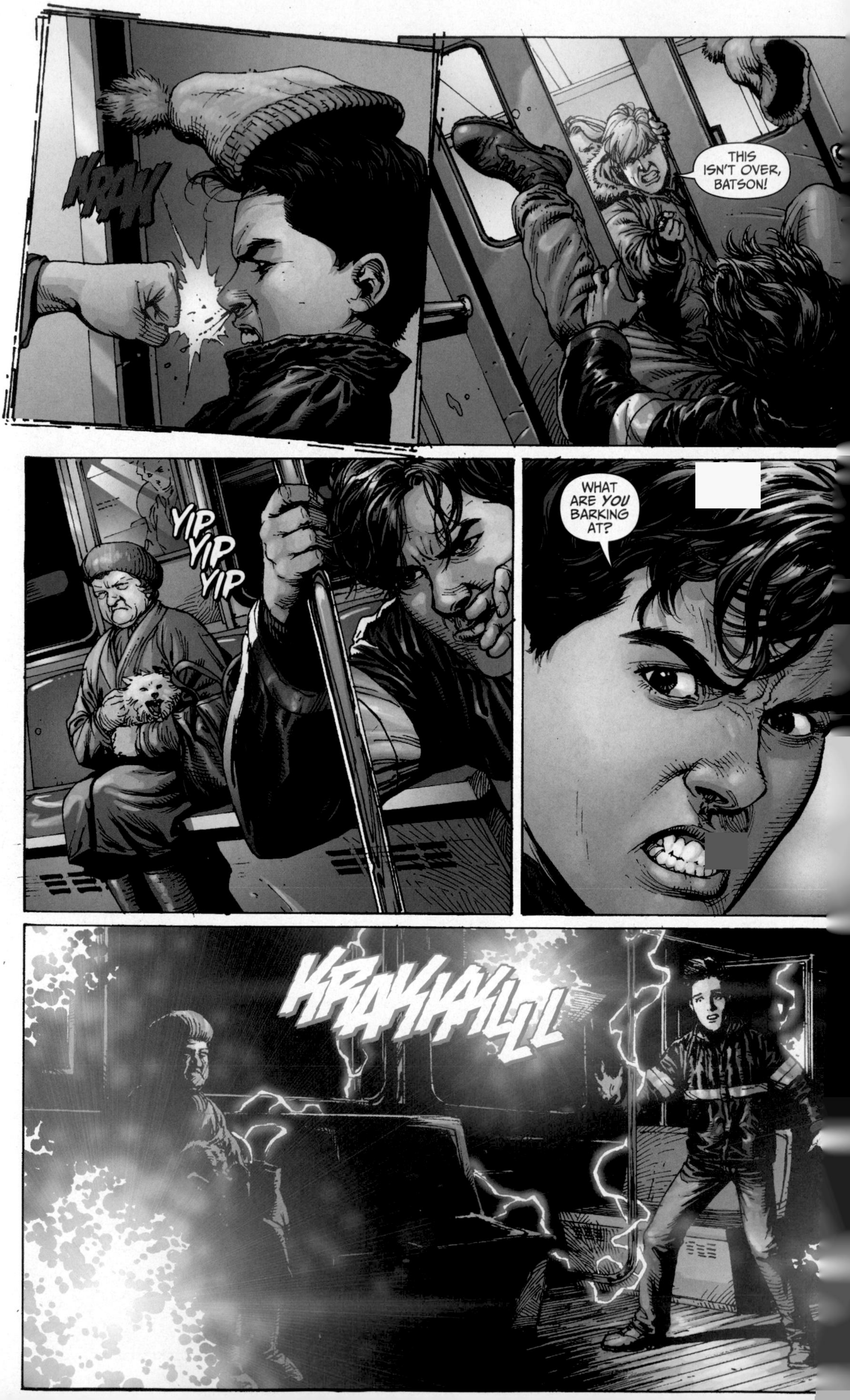
KRAK
THIS ISN'T OVER, BATSON!
YIP YIP YIP
WHAT ARE YOU BARKING AT?
KRAKKALL

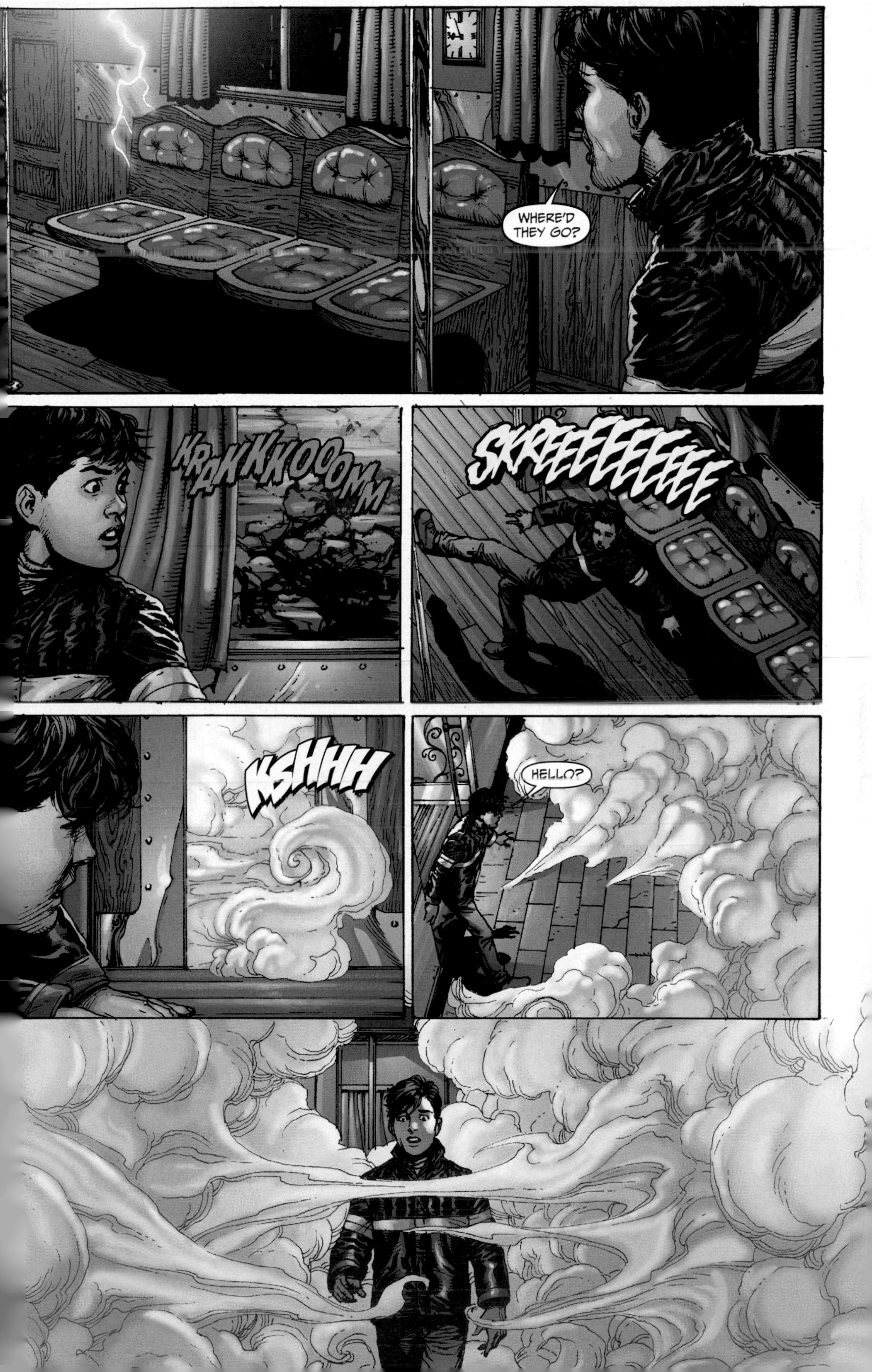
WHERE'D THEY GO?
KRAKKKOOOMM
SKREEEEEEEEEE
KSHHH
HELLO?

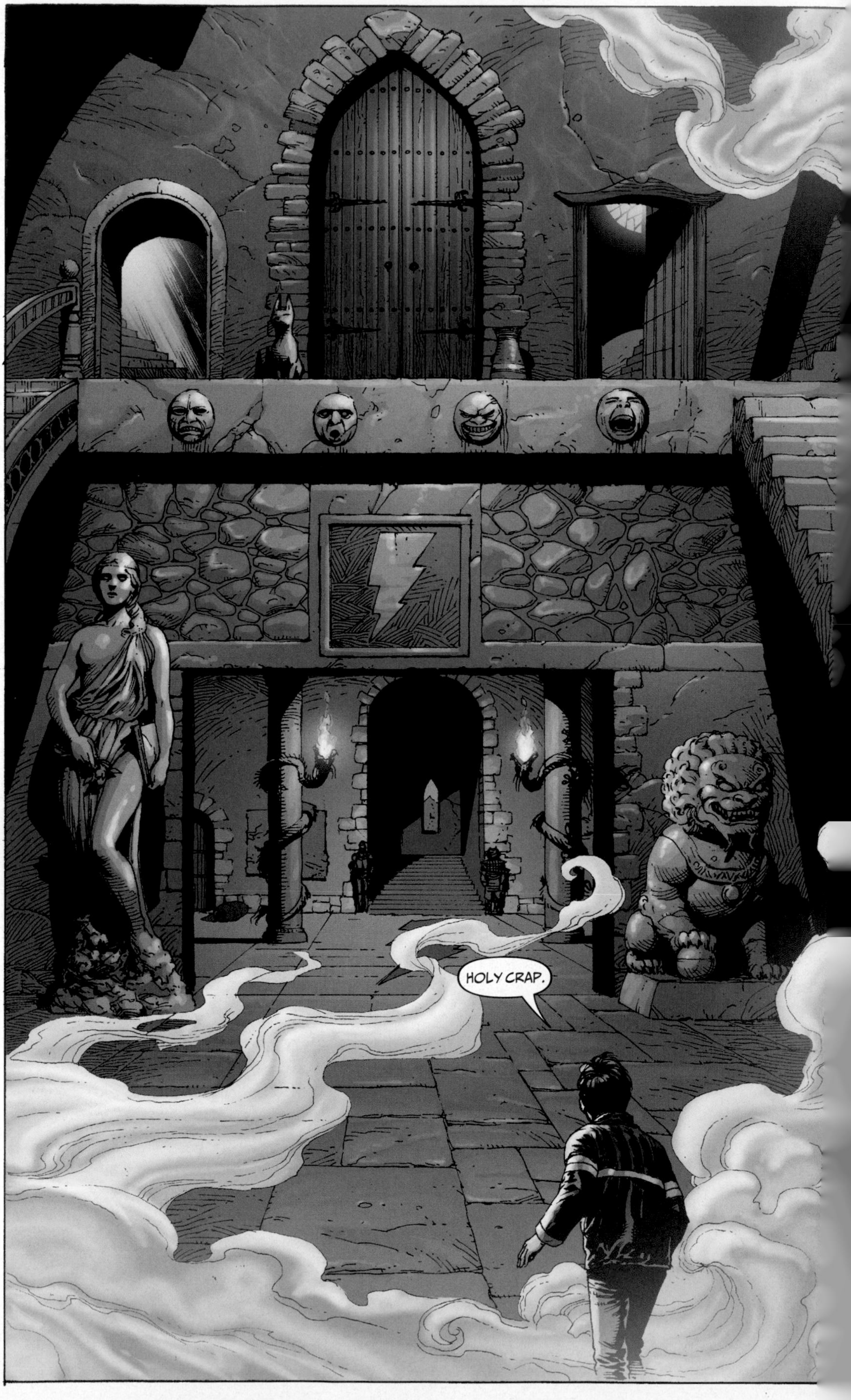
HOLY CRAP.

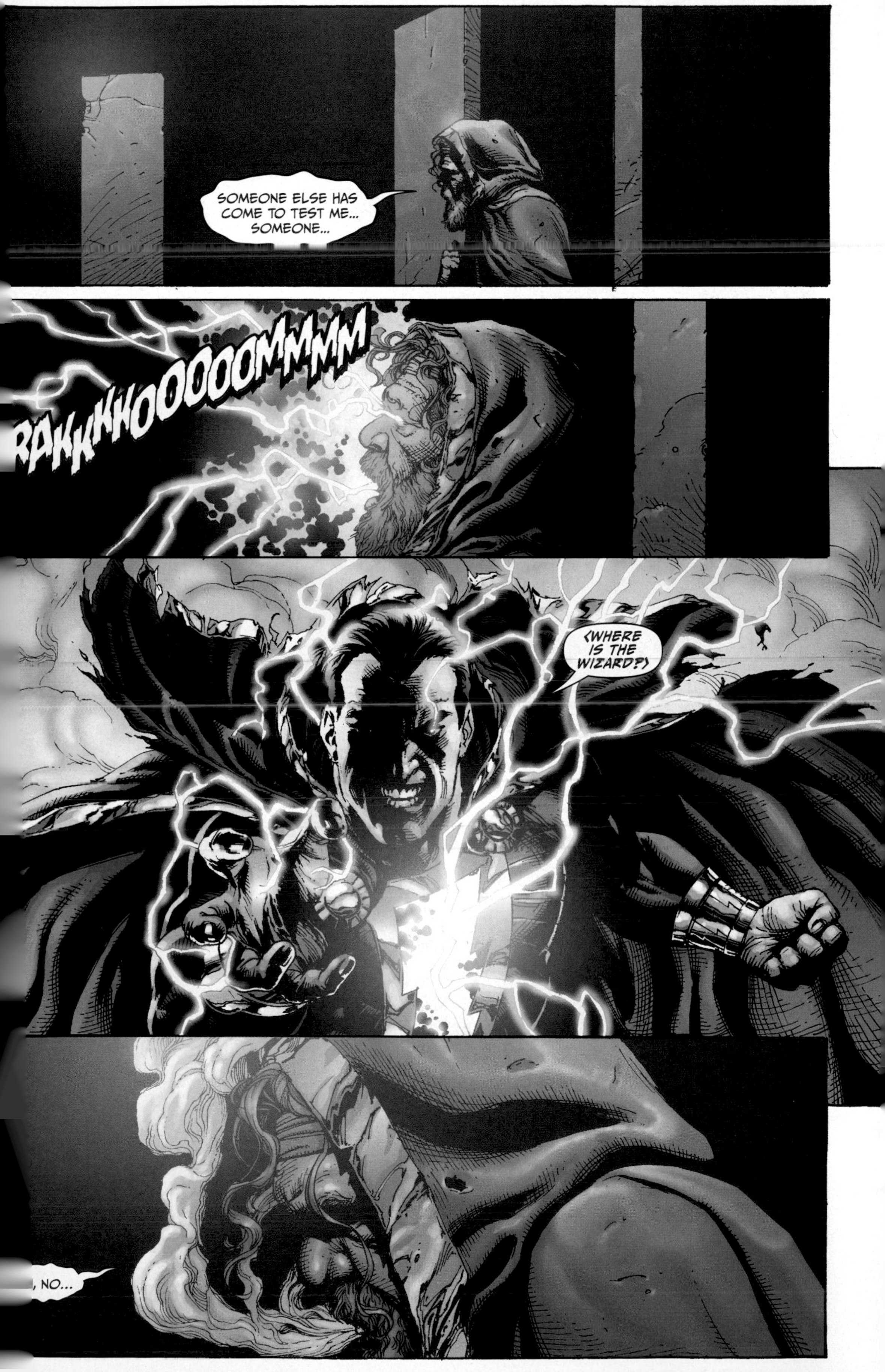
SOMEONE ELSE HAS COME TO TEST ME... SOMEONE...
RAKKKKOOOOOOMMMM
<WHERE IS THE WIZARD?>
, NO...

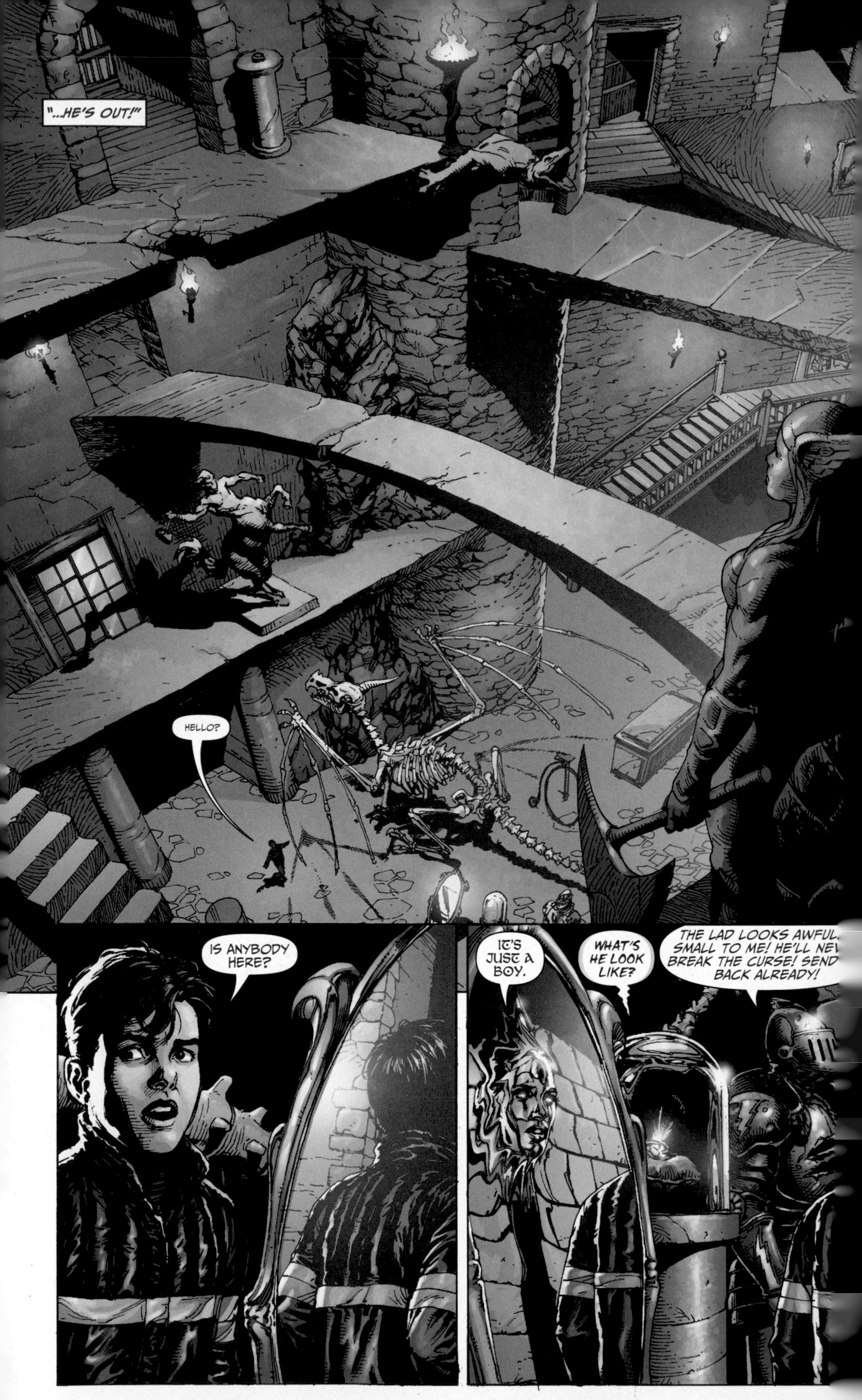
"...HE'S OUT!"
HELLO?
IS ANYBODY HERE?
IT'S JUST A BOY.
WHAT'S HE LOOK LIKE?
THE LAD LOOKS AWFUL SMALL TO ME! HE'LL NEV BREAK THE CURSE! SEND BACK ALREADY!

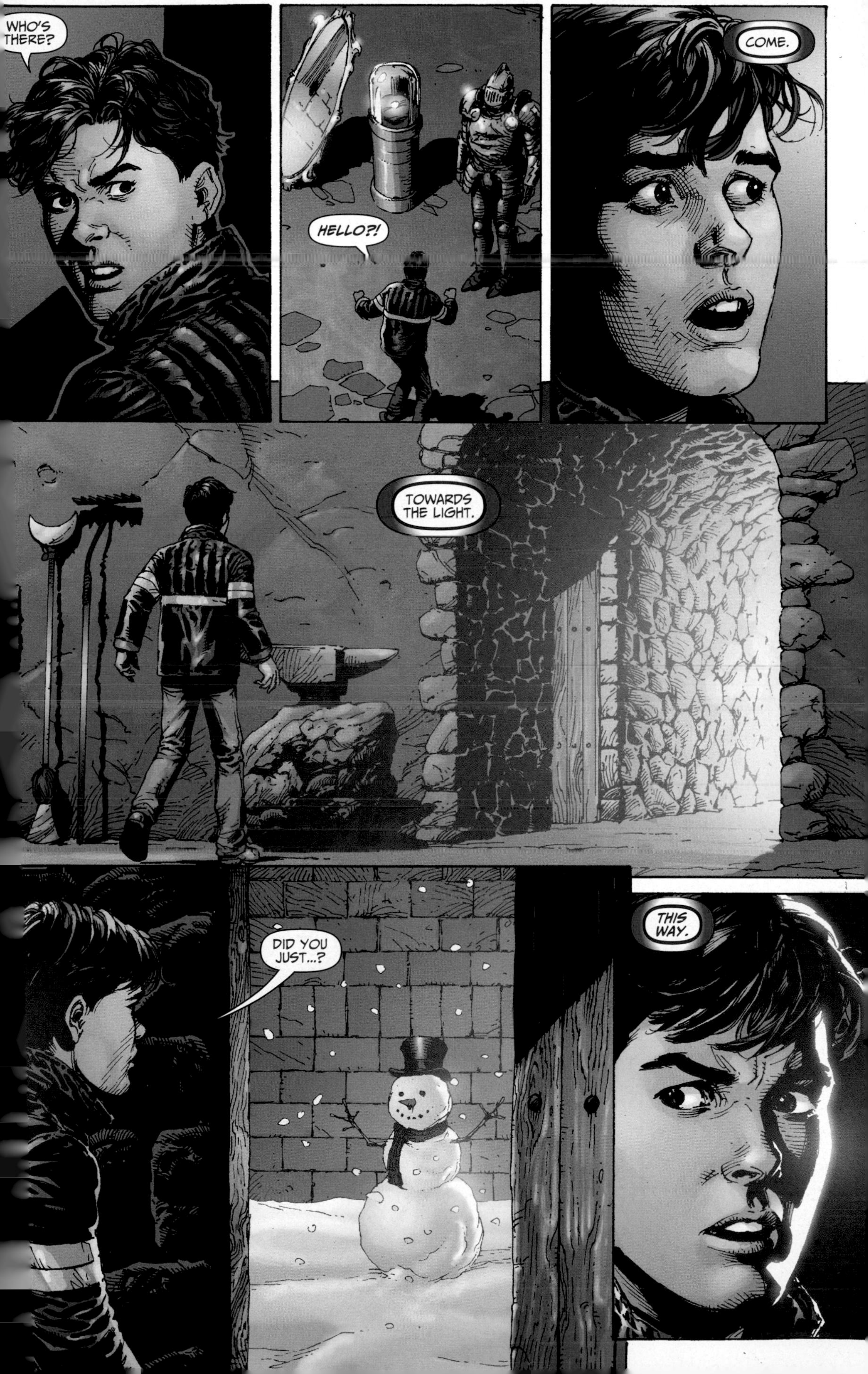
WHO'S THERE?
HELLO?!
COME.
TOWARDS THE LIGHT.
DID YOU JUST...?
THIS WAY.

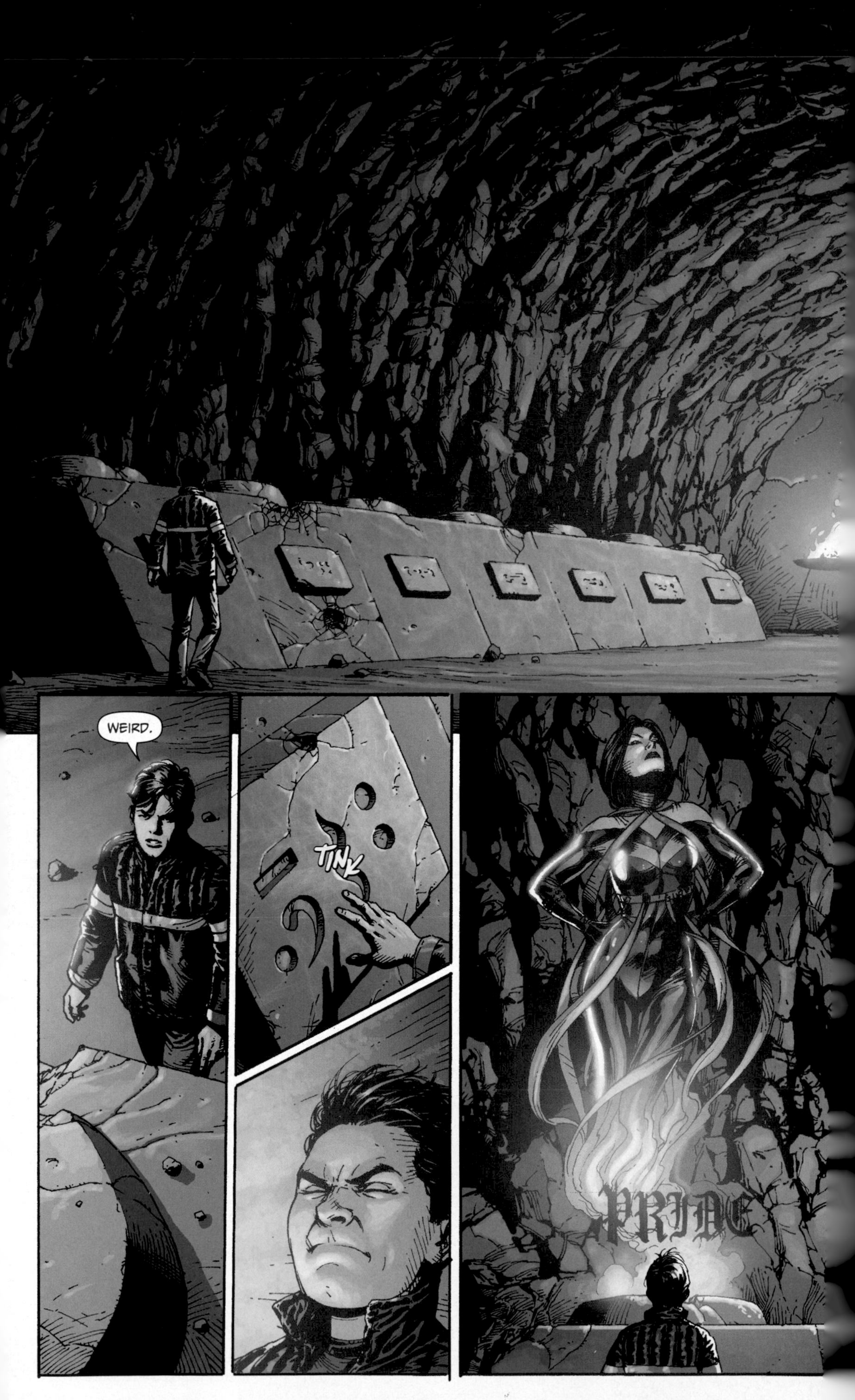

WEIRD.
TINK
PRIDE

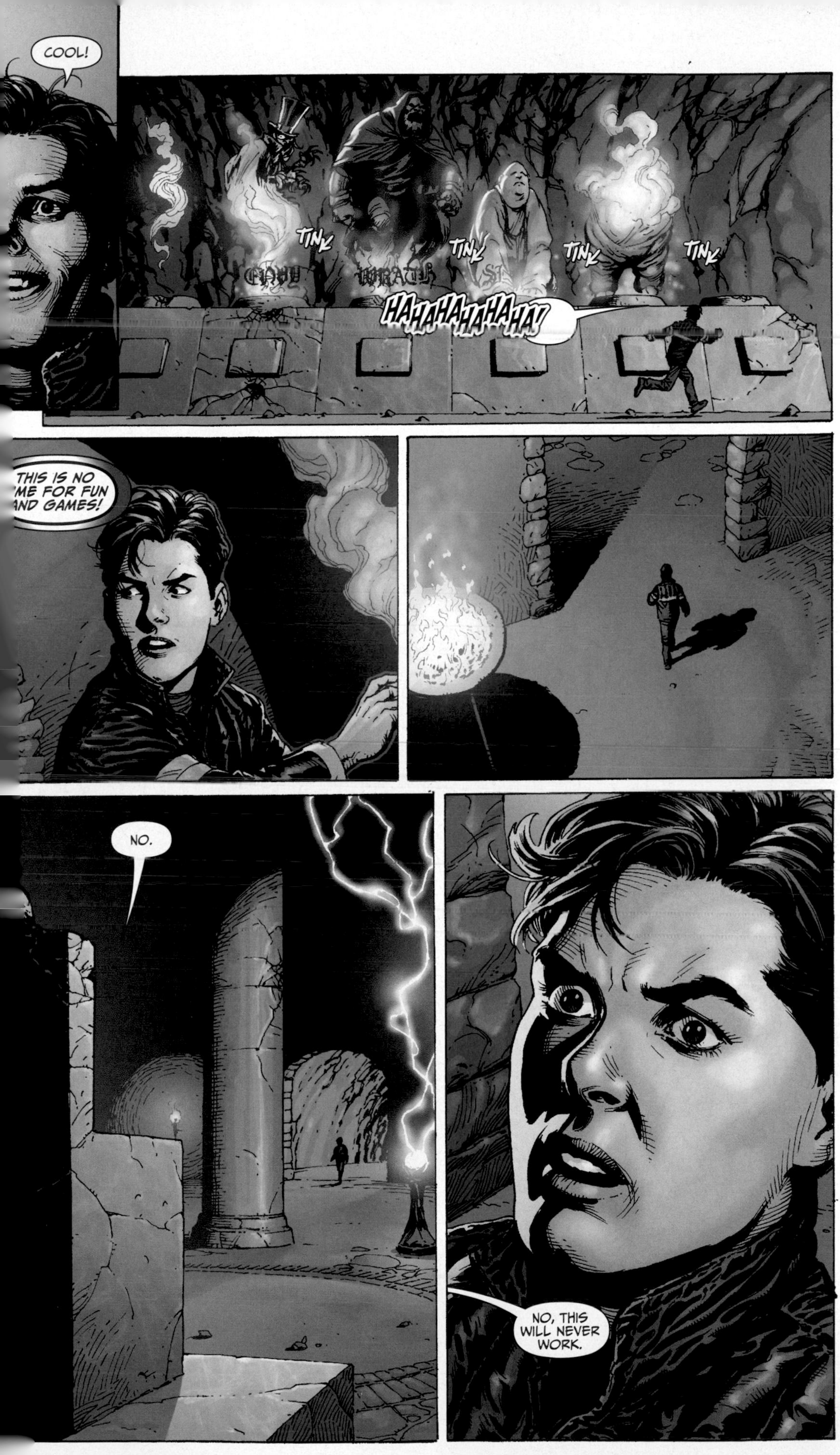
COOL!
ENVY
WRATH
TINK
TINK
TINK
TINK
HAHAHAHAHAHA!
THIS IS NO
ME FOR FUN
AND GAMES!
NO.
NO, THIS WILL NEVER WORK.

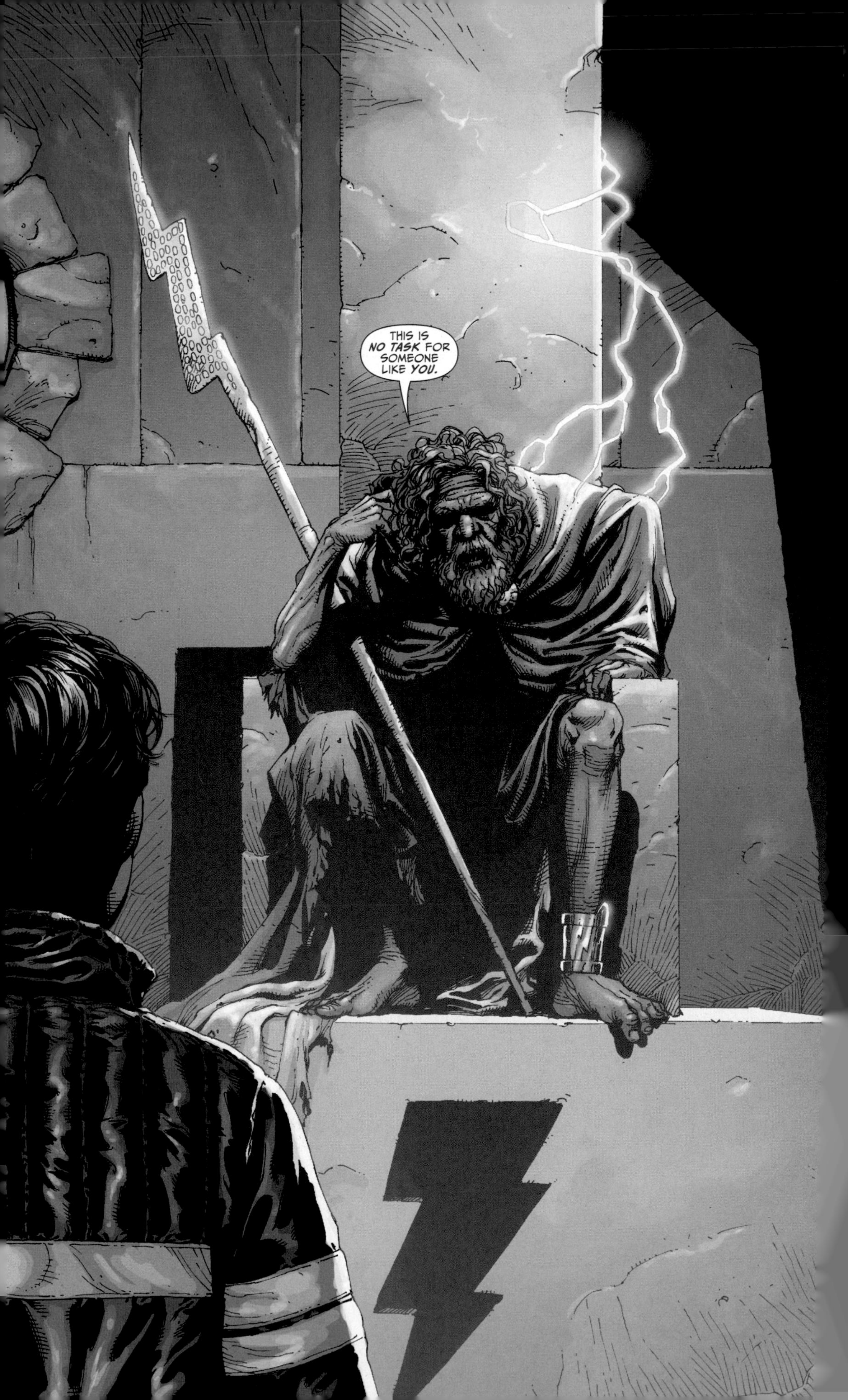
THIS IS NO TASK FOR SOMEONE LIKE YOU.

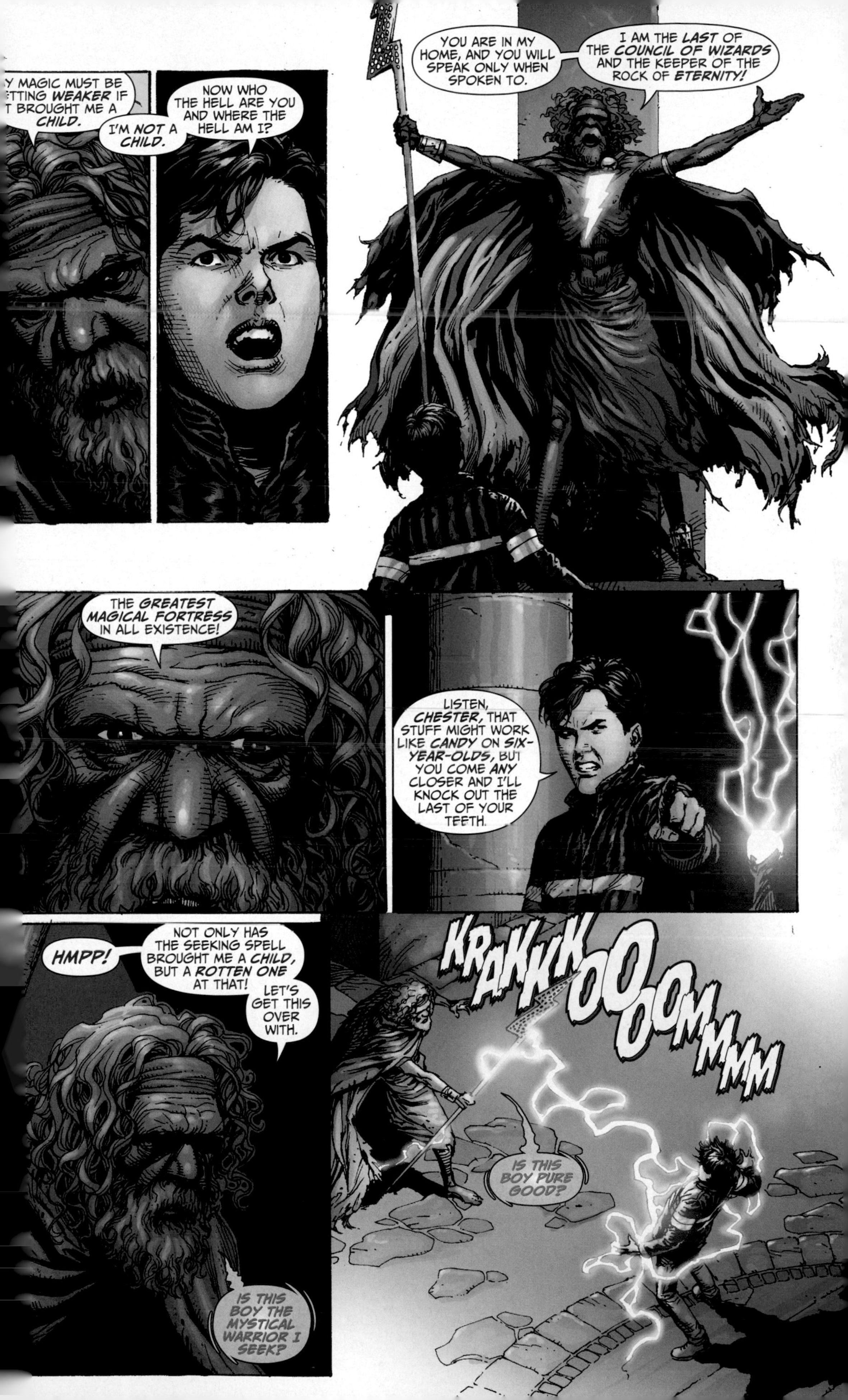
Y MAGIC MUST BE
ETTING WEAKER IF
T BROUGHT ME A
CHILD.
I'M NOT A CHILD.
NOW WHO THE HELL ARE YOU AND WHERE THE HELL AM I?
YOU ARE IN MY HOME, AND YOU WILL SPEAK ONLY WHEN SPOKEN TO.
I AM THE LAST OF THE COUNCIL OF WIZARDS AND THE KEEPER OF THE ROCK OF ETERNITY!
THE GREATEST MAGICAL FORTRESS IN ALL EXISTENCE!
LISTEN, CHESTER, THAT STUFF MIGHT WORK LIKE CANDY ON SIX-YEAR-OLDS, BUT YOU COME ANY CLOSER AND I'LL KNOCK OUT THE LAST OF YOUR TEETH.
HMPP!
NOT ONLY HAS THE SEEKING SPELL BROUGHT ME A CHILD, BUT A ROTTEN ONE AT THAT!
LET'S GET THIS OVER WITH.
IS THIS BOY THE MYSTICAL WARRIOR I SEEK?
KRAKKKOOOOMMMM
IS THIS BOY PURE GOOD?

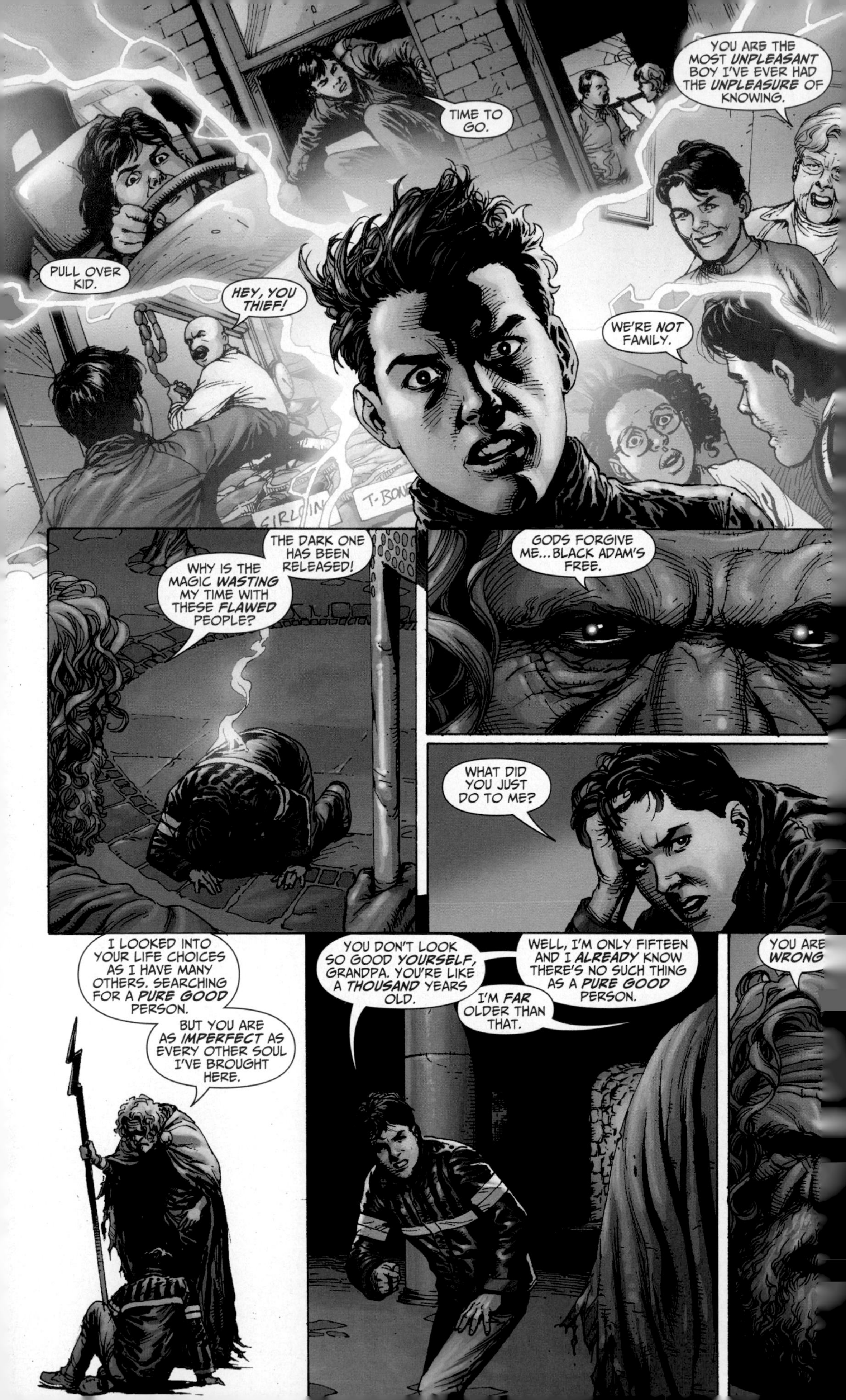
TIME TO GO.
YOU ARE THE MOST UNPLEASANT BOY I'VE EVER HAD THE UNPLEASURE OF KNOWING.
PULL OVER KID.
HEY, YOU THIEF!
WE'RE NOT FAMILY.
SIRLOIN
T-BONE
THE DARK ONE HAS BEEN RELEASED!
WHY IS THE MAGIC WASTING MY TIME WITH THESE FLAWED PEOPLE?
GODS FORGIVE ME...BLACK ADAM'S FREE.
WHAT DID YOU JUST DO TO ME?
I LOOKED INTO YOUR LIFE CHOICES AS I HAVE MANY OTHERS. SEARCHING FOR A PURE GOOD PERSON.
BUT YOU ARE AS IMPERFECT AS EVERY OTHER SOUL I'VE BROUGHT HERE.
YOU DON'T LOOK SO GOOD YOURSELF, GRANDPA. YOU'RE LIKE A THOUSAND YEARS OLD.
I'M FAR OLDER THAN THAT.
WELL, I'M ONLY FIFTEEN AND I ALREADY KNOW THERE'S NO SUCH THING AS A PURE GOOD PERSON.
YOU ARE WRONG

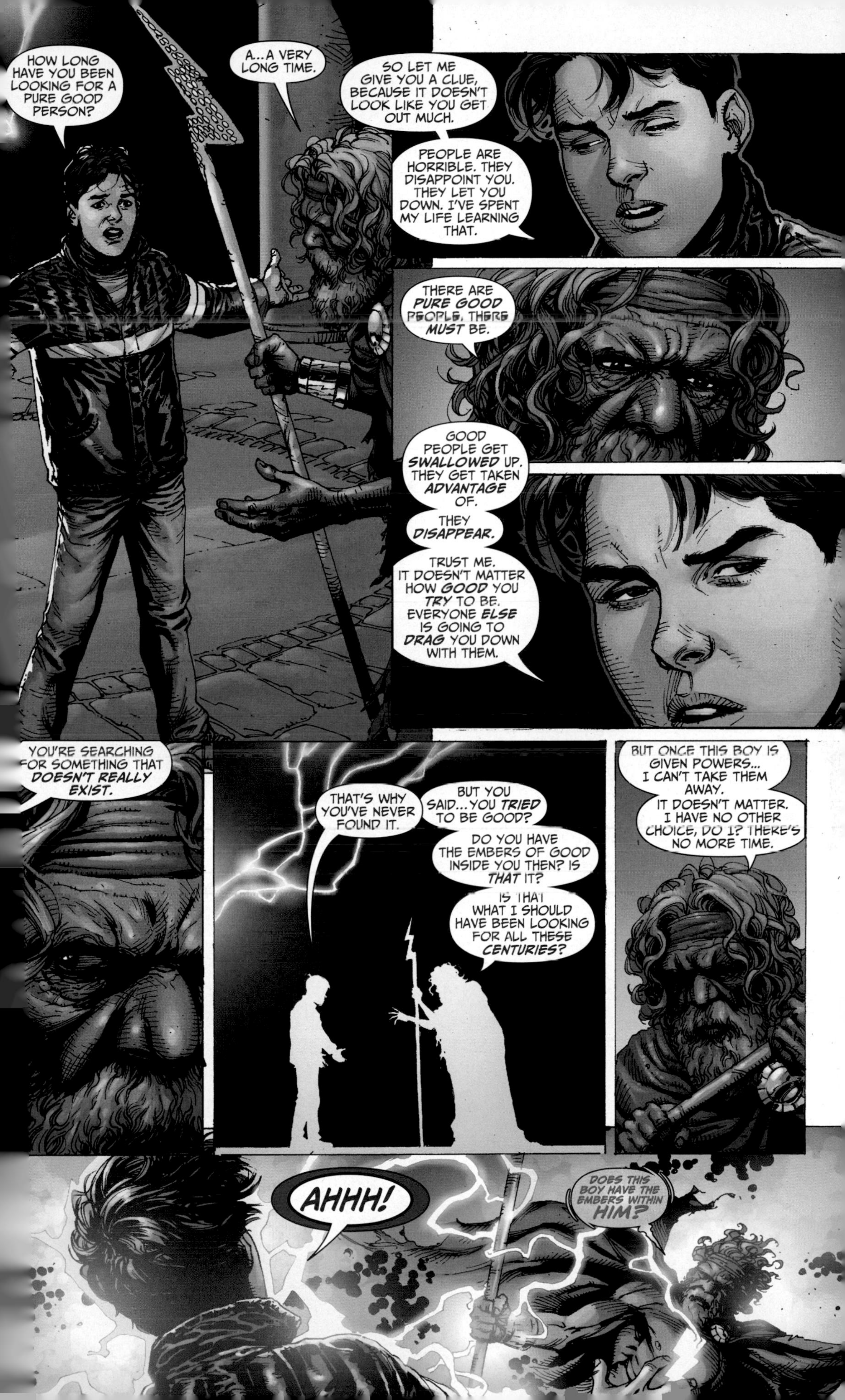
HOW LONG HAVE YOU BEEN LOOKING FOR A PURE GOOD PERSON?
A...A VERY LONG TIME.
SO LET ME GIVE YOU A CLUE, BECAUSE IT DOESN'T LOOK LIKE YOU GET OUT MUCH.
PEOPLE ARE HORRIBLE. THEY DISAPPOINT YOU. THEY LET YOU DOWN. I'VE SPENT MY LIFE LEARNING THAT.
THERE ARE PURE GOOD PEOPLE. THERE MUST BE.
GOOD PEOPLE GET SWALLOWED UP. THEY GET TAKEN ADVANTAGE OF.
THEY DISAPPEAR.
TRUST ME. IT DOESN'T MATTER HOW GOOD YOU TRY TO BE. EVERYONE ELSE IS GOING TO DRAG YOU DOWN WITH THEM.
YOU'RE SEARCHING FOR SOMETHING THAT DOESN'T REALLY EXIST.
THAT'S WHY YOU'VE NEVER FOUND IT.
BUT YOU SAID...YOU TRIED TO BE GOOD?
DO YOU HAVE THE EMBERS OF GOOD INSIDE YOU THEN? IS THAT IT?
IS THAT WHAT I SHOULD HAVE BEEN LOOKING FOR ALL THESE CENTURIES?
BUT ONCE THIS BOY IS GIVEN POWERS... I CAN'T TAKE THEM AWAY.
IT DOESN'T MATTER. I HAVE NO OTHER CHOICE, DO I? THERE'S NO MORE TIME.
AHHH!
DOES THIS BOY HAVE THE EMBERS WITHIN HIM?

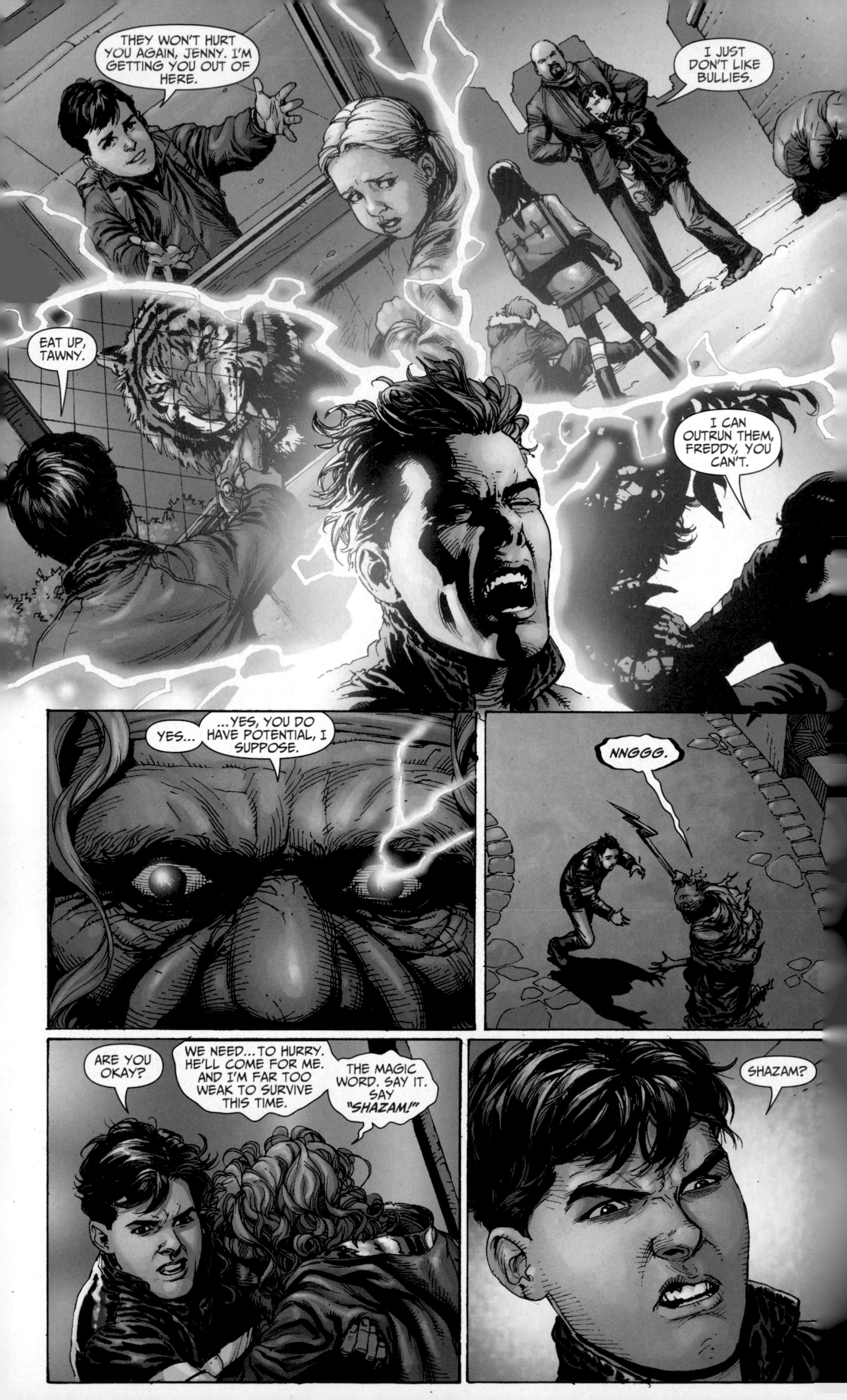

THEY WON'T HURT YOU AGAIN, JENNY. I'M GETTING YOU OUT OF HERE.
I JUST DON'T LIKE BULLIES.
EAT UP, TAWNY.
I CAN OUTRUN THEM, FREDDY, YOU CAN'T.
YES...
...YES, YOU DO HAVE POTENTIAL, I SUPPOSE.
NNGGG.
ARE YOU OKAY?
WE NEED...TO HURRY. HE'LL COME FOR ME. AND I'M FAR TOO WEAK TO SURVIVE THIS TIME.
THE MAGIC WORD. SAY IT. SAY "SHAZAM!"
SHAZAM?

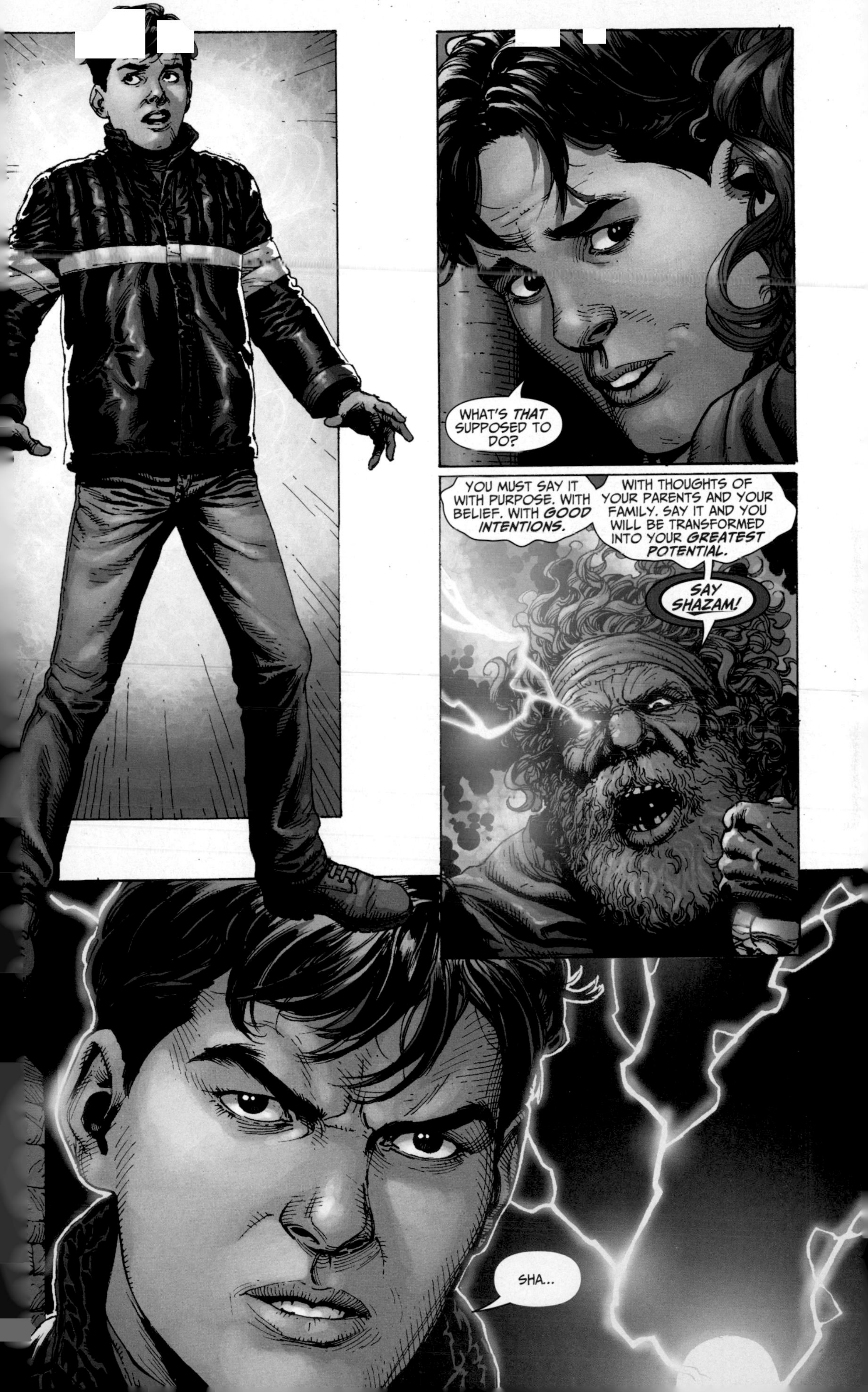
WHAT'S *THAT* SUPPOSED TO DO?
YOU MUST SAY IT WITH PURPOSE. WITH BELIEF. WITH *GOOD INTENTIONS.*
WITH THOUGHTS OF YOUR PARENTS AND YOUR FAMILY. SAY IT AND YOU WILL BE TRANSFORMED INTO YOUR *GREATEST POTENTIAL.*
SAY SHAZAM!
SHA...

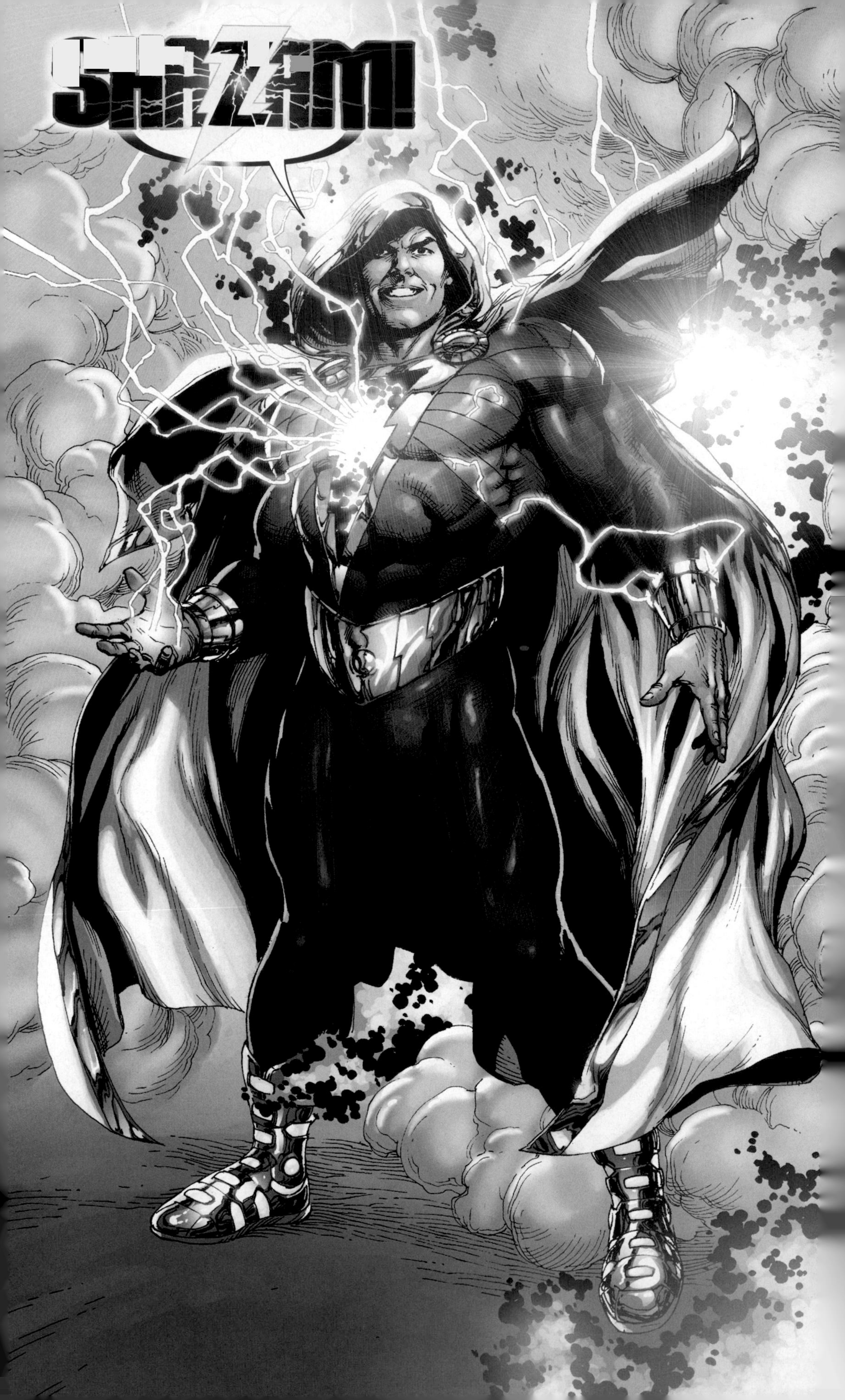
SHAZAM!

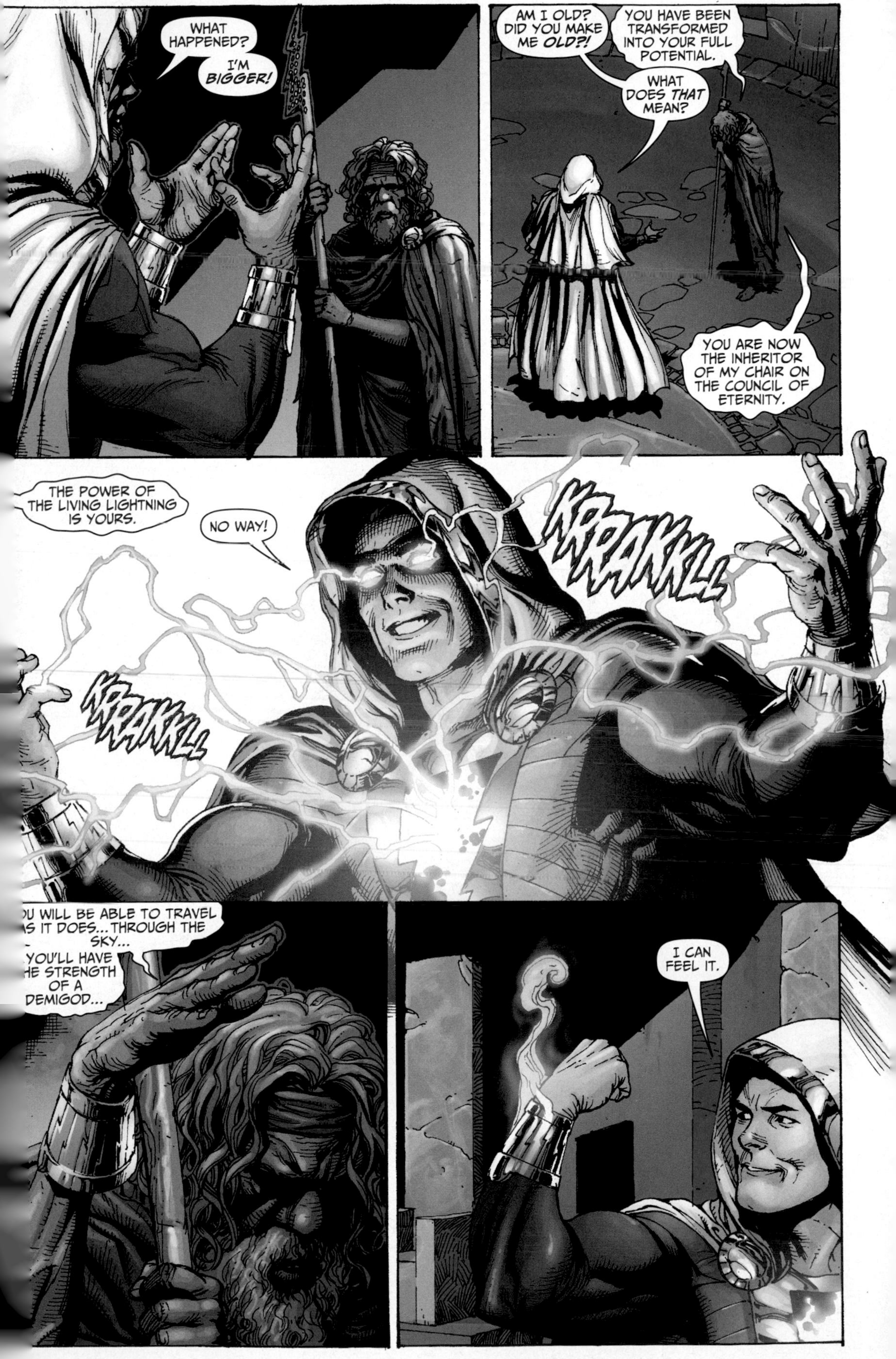
WHAT HAPPENED? I'M BIGGER!
AM I OLD? DID YOU MAKE ME OLD?!
YOU HAVE BEEN TRANSFORMED INTO YOUR FULL POTENTIAL.
WHAT DOES THAT MEAN?
YOU ARE NOW THE INHERITOR OF MY CHAIR ON THE COUNCIL OF ETERNITY.
THE POWER OF THE LIVING LIGHTNING IS YOURS.
NO WAY!
KRRAKKLL
KRRAKKLL
OU WILL BE ABLE TO TRAVEL AS IT DOES... THROUGH THE SKY...
YOU'LL HAVE HE STRENGTH OF A DEMIGOD...
I CAN FEEL IT.

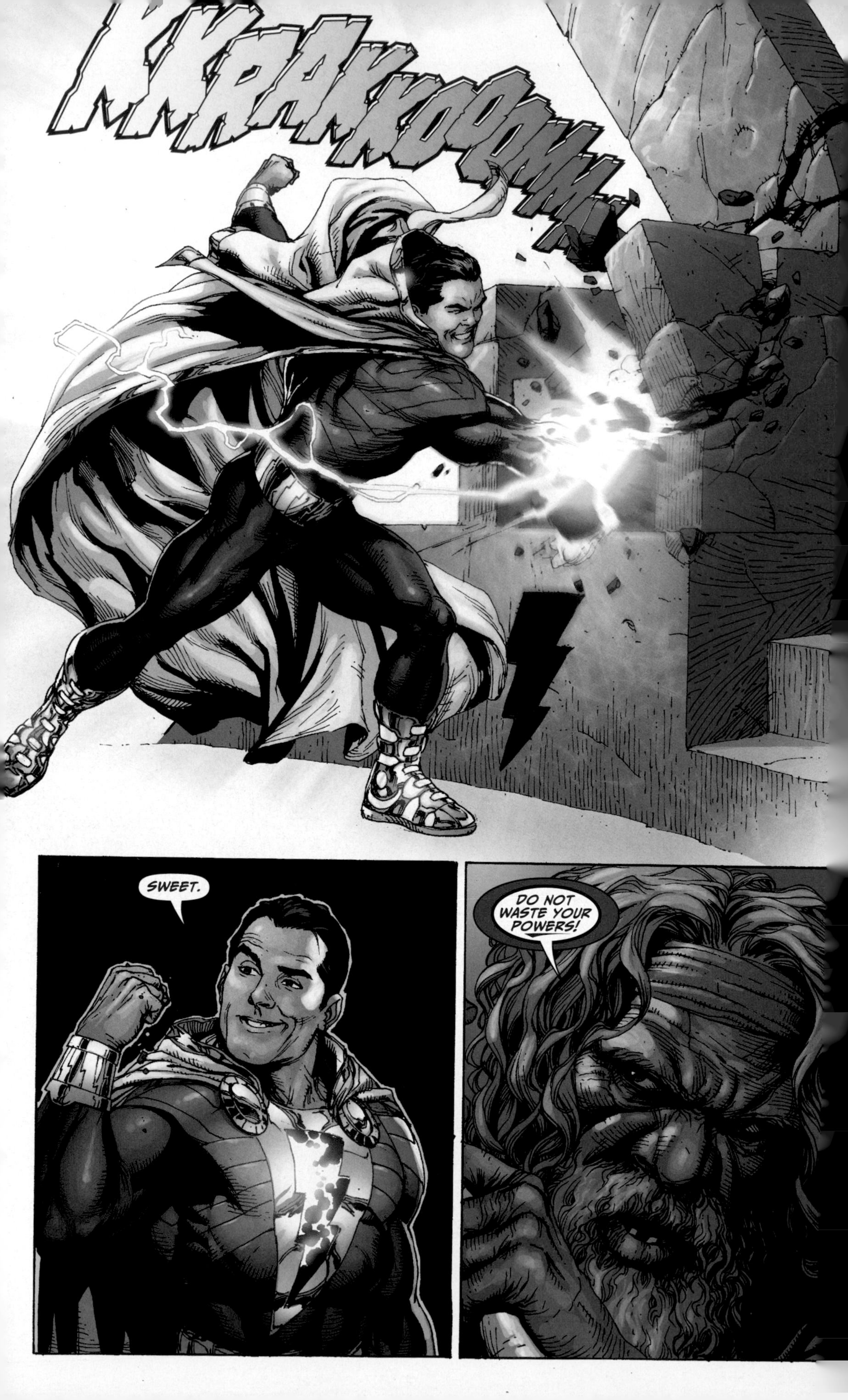
KKRAKKOOOMM...
SWEET.
DO NOT WASTE YOUR POWERS!

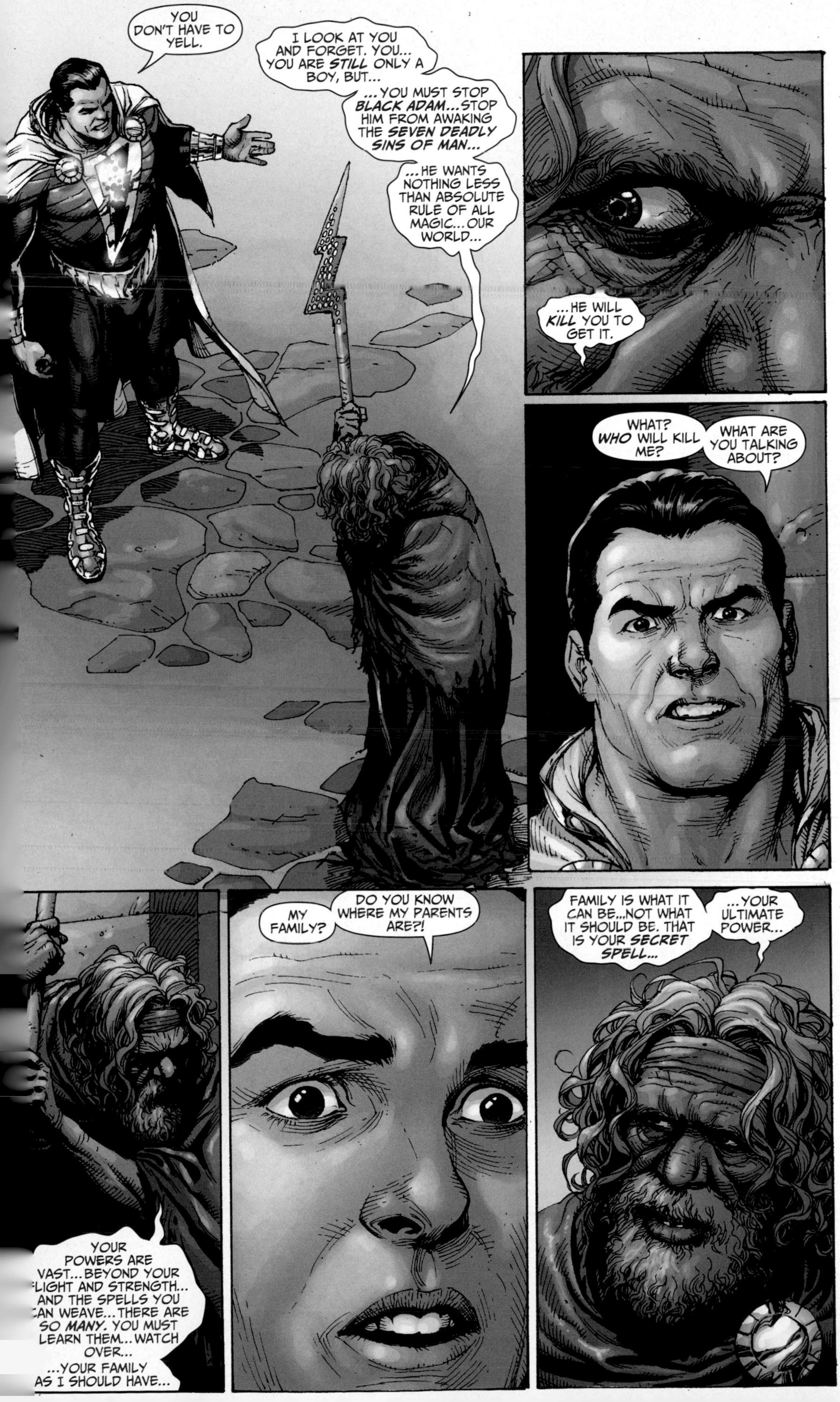
YOU DON'T HAVE TO YELL.
I LOOK AT YOU AND FORGET. YOU... YOU ARE STILL ONLY A BOY, BUT...
...YOU MUST STOP BLACK ADAM...STOP HIM FROM AWAKING THE SEVEN DEADLY SINS OF MAN...
...HE WANTS NOTHING LESS THAN ABSOLUTE RULE OF ALL MAGIC...OUR WORLD...
...HE WILL KILL YOU TO GET IT.
WHAT? WHO WILL KILL ME?
WHAT ARE YOU TALKING ABOUT?
YOUR POWERS ARE VAST...BEYOND YOUR FLIGHT AND STRENGTH... AND THE SPELLS YOU CAN WEAVE...THERE ARE SO MANY. YOU MUST LEARN THEM...WATCH OVER...
...YOUR FAMILY AS I SHOULD HAVE...
MY FAMILY?
DO YOU KNOW WHERE MY PARENTS ARE?!
FAMILY IS WHAT IT CAN BE...NOT WHAT IT SHOULD BE. THAT IS YOUR SECRET SPELL...
...YOUR ULTIMATE POWER...

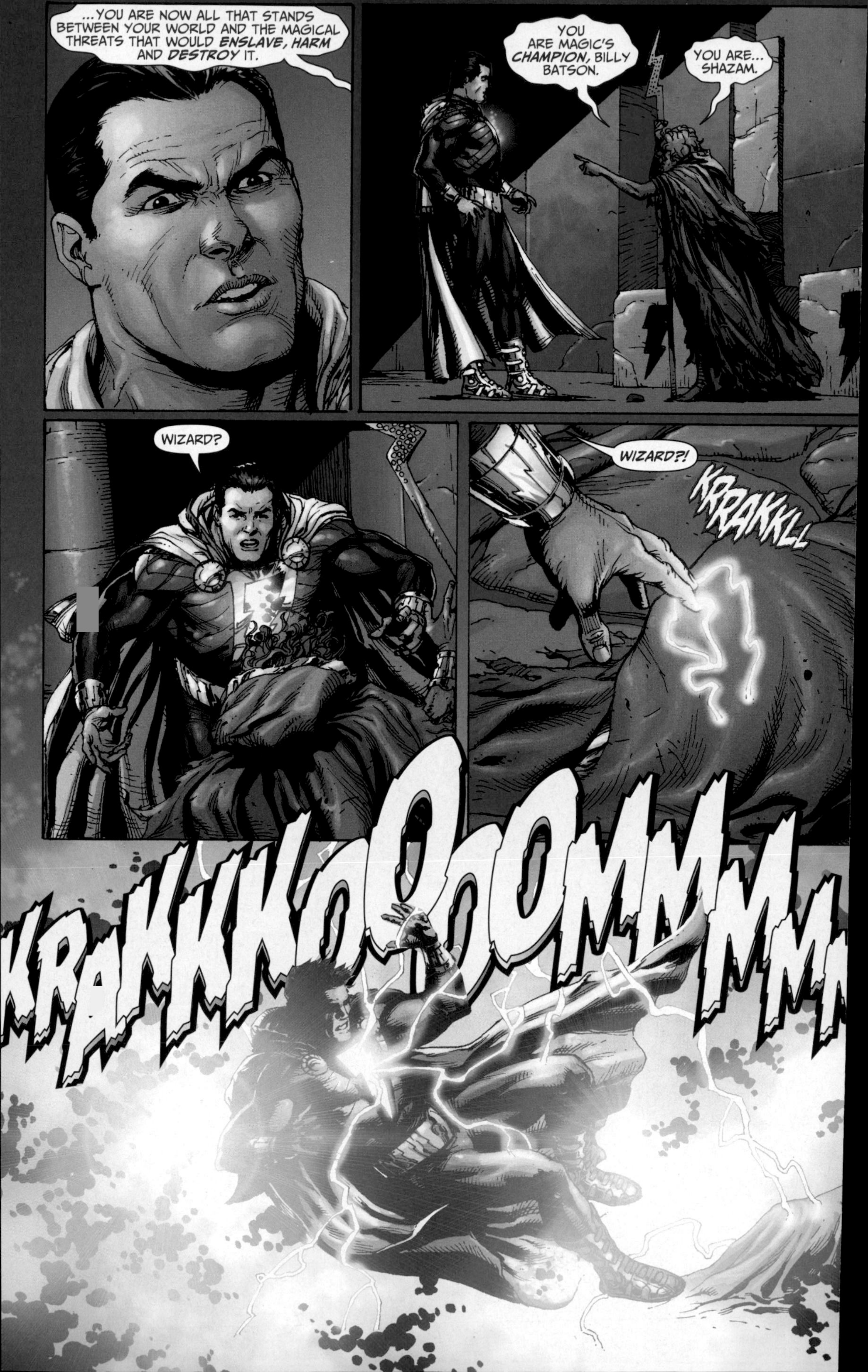
...YOU ARE NOW ALL THAT STANDS BETWEEN YOUR WORLD AND THE MAGICAL THREATS THAT WOULD *ENSLAVE, HARM* AND *DESTROY* IT.
YOU ARE MAGIC'S *CHAMPION*, BILLY BATSON.
YOU ARE... SHAZAM.
WIZARD?
WIZARD?!
KRRAKKLL
KRAKKKOOOOMMMMM

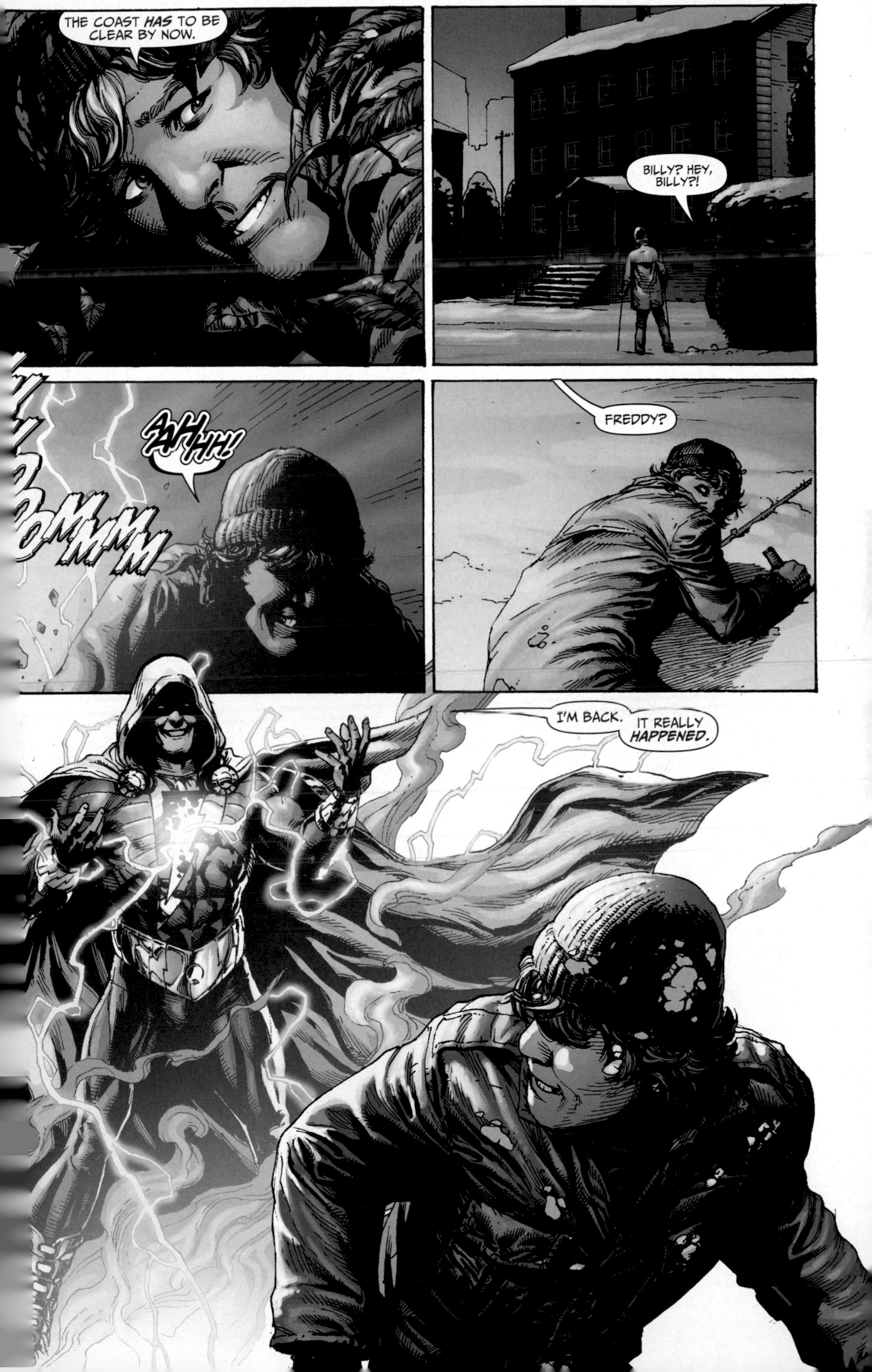
THE COAST HAS TO BE CLEAR BY NOW.
BILLY? HEY, BILLY?!
AAHHH!
VOOOMMMM
FREDDY?
I'M BACK.
IT REALLY HAPPENED.

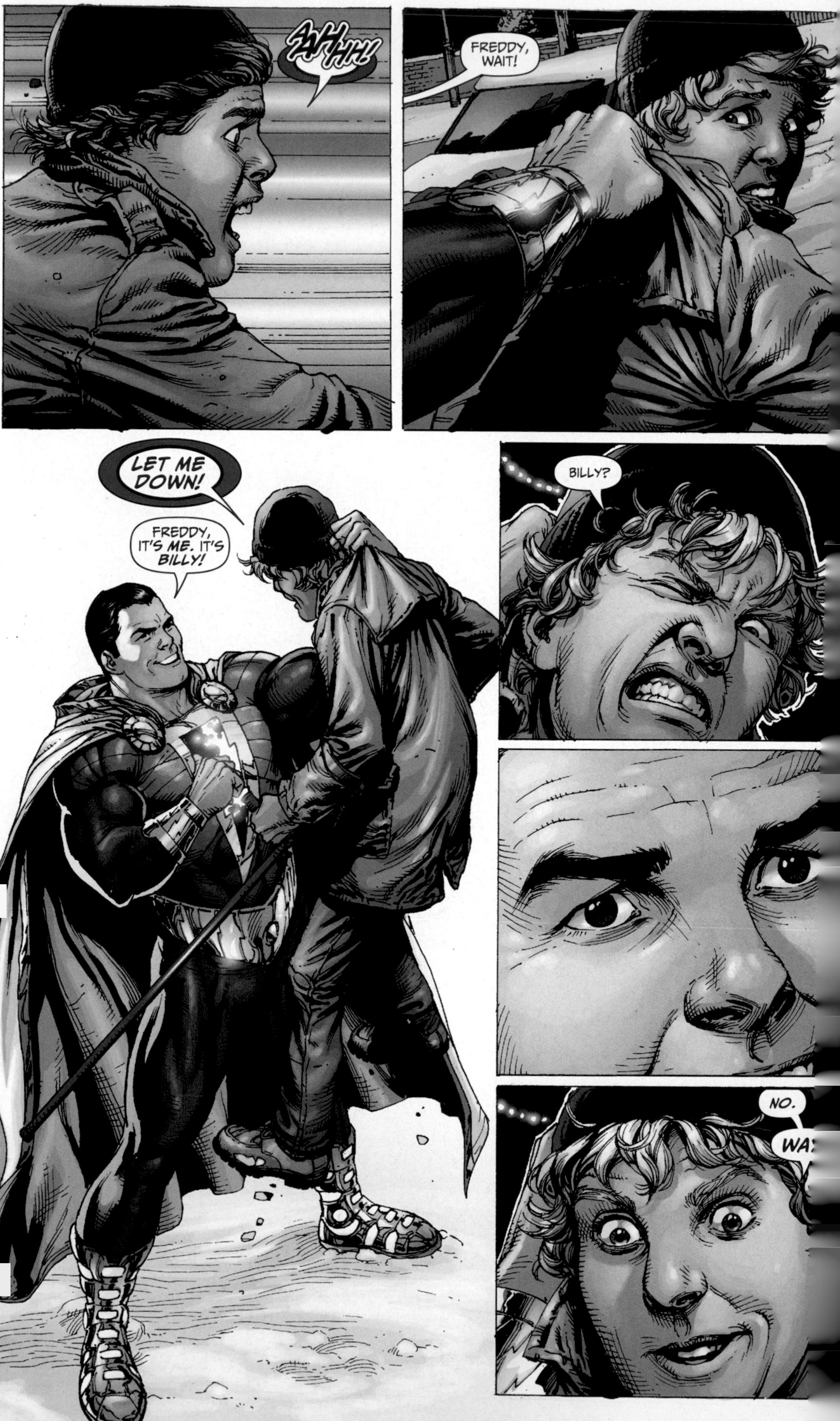
AAHHH!
FREDDY, WAIT!
LET ME DOWN!
FREDDY, IT'S ME. IT'S BILLY!
BILLY?
NO.
WA

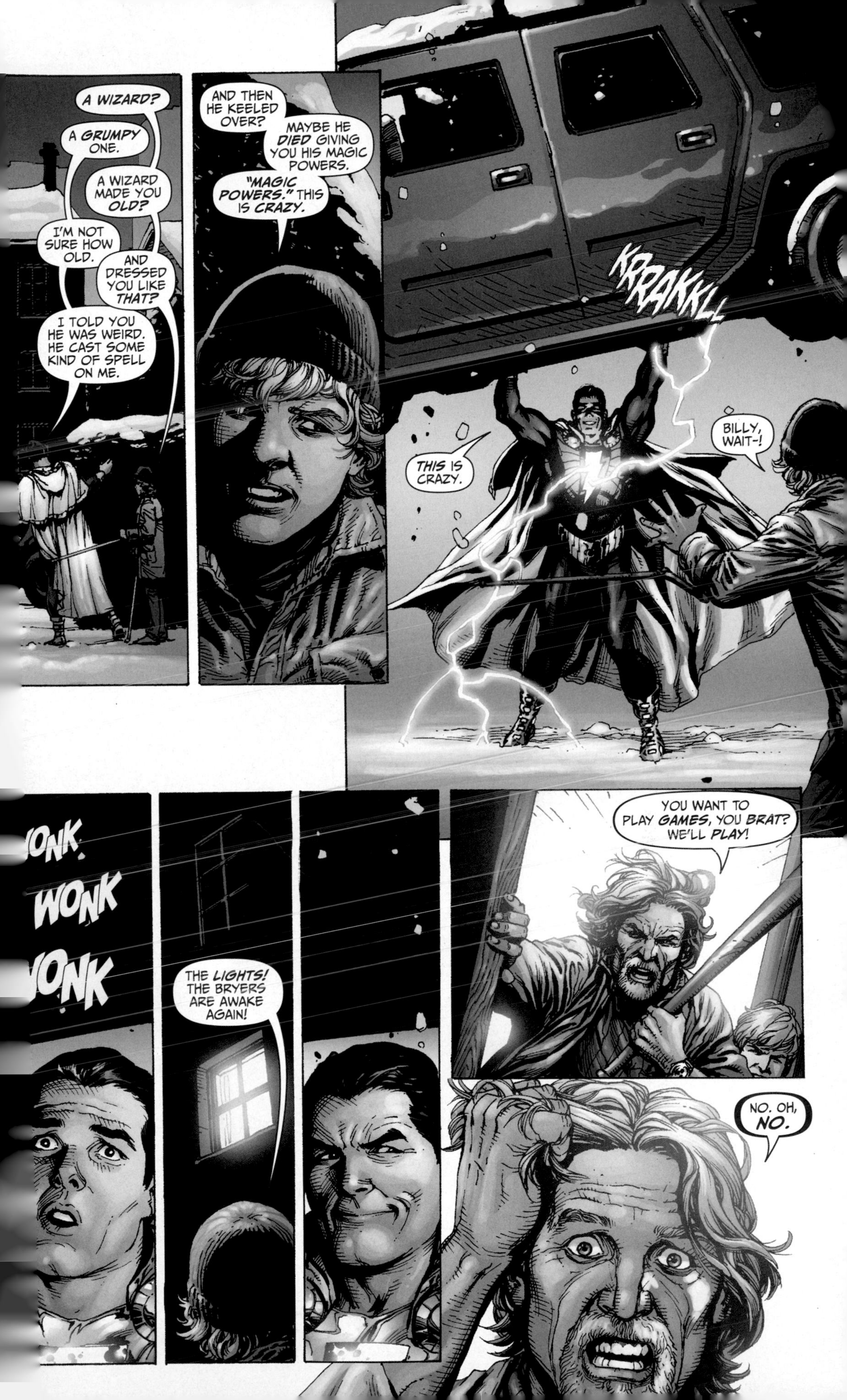
A WIZARD?
A GRUMPY ONE.
A WIZARD MADE YOU OLD?
I'M NOT SURE HOW OLD.
AND DRESSED YOU LIKE THAT?
I TOLD YOU HE WAS WEIRD. HE CAST SOME KIND OF SPELL ON ME.
AND THEN HE KEELED OVER?
MAYBE HE DIED GIVING YOU HIS MAGIC POWERS.
"MAGIC POWERS." THIS IS CRAZY.
KRRAKKL!
THIS IS CRAZY.
BILLY, WAIT-!
WONK
WONK
WONK
THE LIGHTS! THE BRYERS ARE AWAKE AGAIN!
YOU WANT TO PLAY GAMES, YOU BRAT? WE'LL PLAY!
NO. OH, NO.

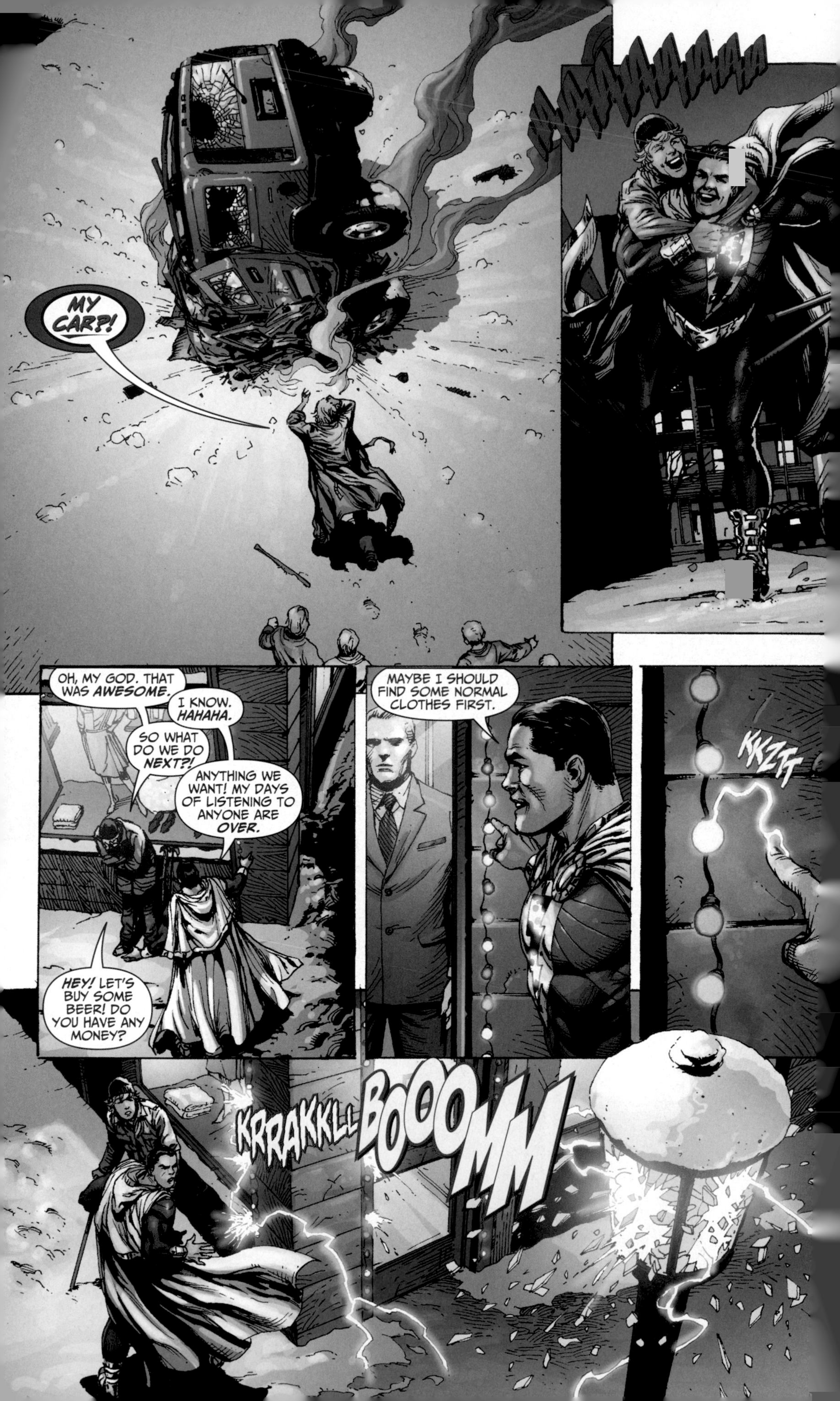
MY CAR?!
AAAAAAAAAAAA
OH, MY GOD. THAT WAS AWESOME.
I KNOW. HAHAHA.
SO WHAT DO WE DO NEXT?!
ANYTHING WE WANT! MY DAYS OF LISTENING TO ANYONE ARE OVER.
HEY! LET'S BUY SOME BEER! DO YOU HAVE ANY MONEY?
MAYBE I SHOULD FIND SOME NORMAL CLOTHES FIRST.
KKZTT
KRRAKKLL BOOOMM

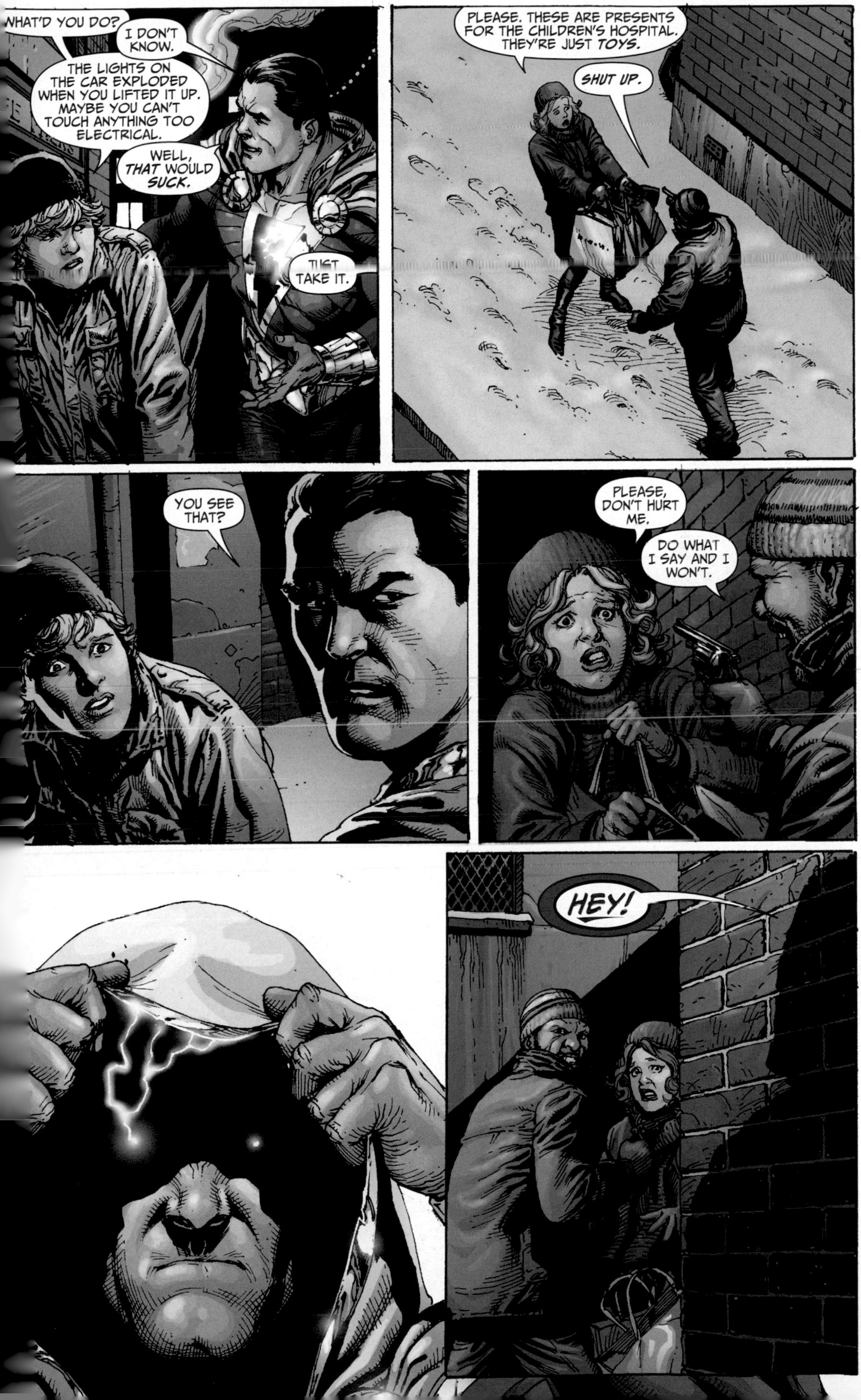
WHAT'D YOU DO?
I DON'T KNOW.
THE LIGHTS ON THE CAR EXPLODED WHEN YOU LIFTED IT UP. MAYBE YOU CAN'T TOUCH ANYTHING TOO ELECTRICAL.
WELL, THAT WOULD SUCK.
JUST TAKE IT.
PLEASE. THESE ARE PRESENTS FOR THE CHILDREN'S HOSPITAL. THEY'RE JUST TOYS.
SHUT UP.
YOU SEE THAT?
PLEASE, DON'T HURT ME.
DO WHAT I SAY AND I WON'T.
HEY!

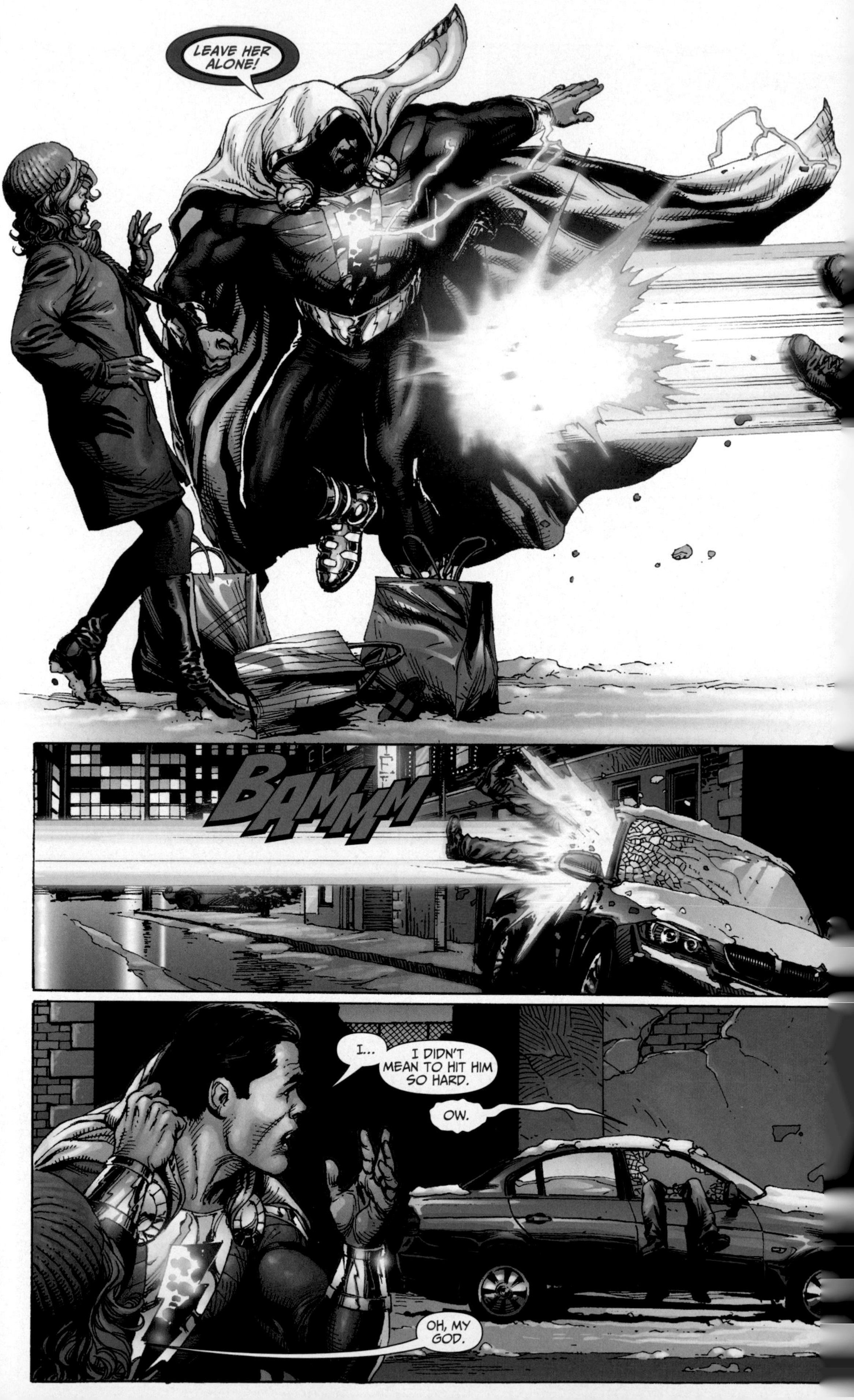
LEAVE HER ALONE!
BAMMM
I... I DIDN'T MEAN TO HIT HIM SO HARD.
OW.
OH, MY GOD.

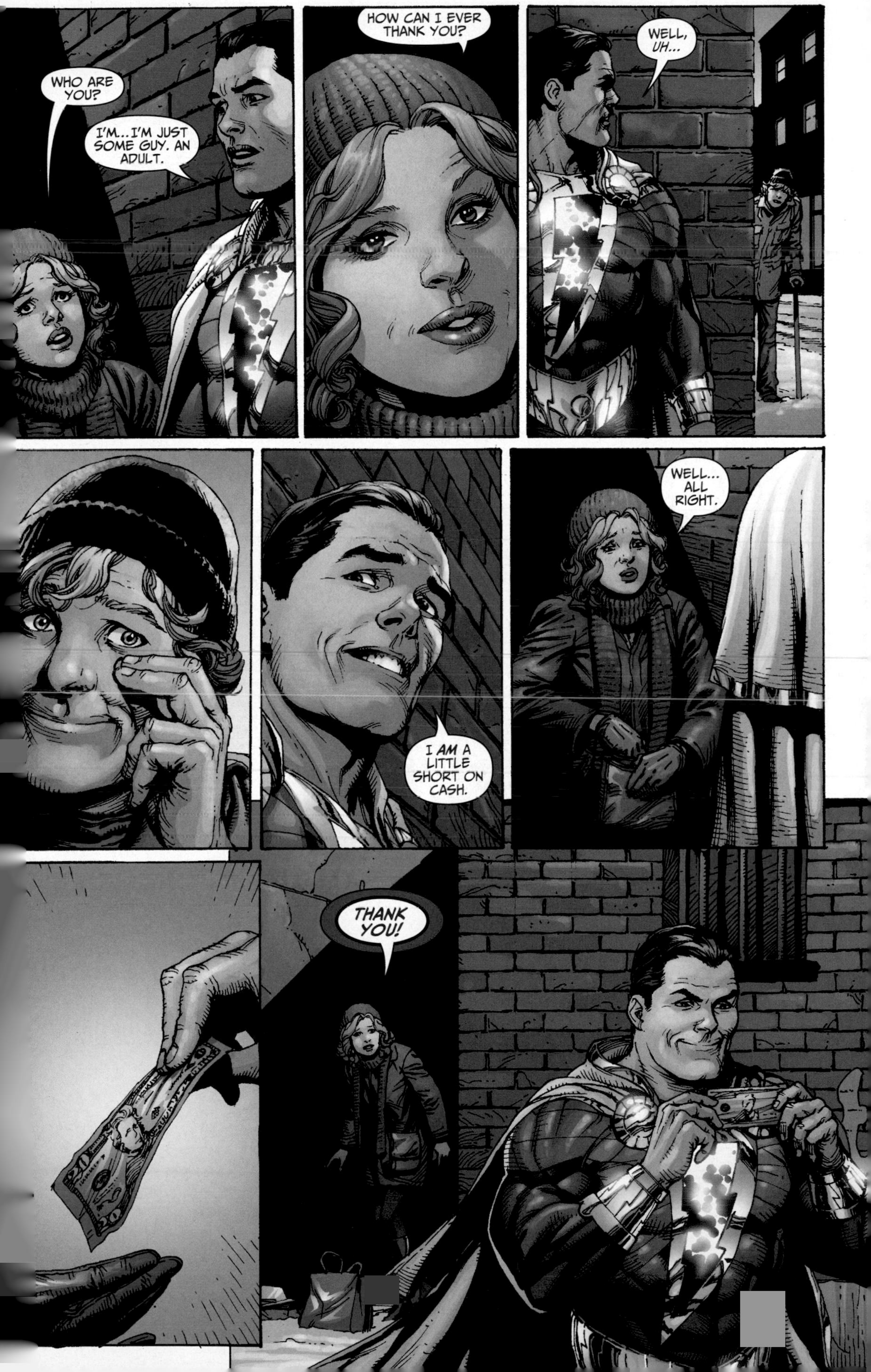
WHO ARE YOU?
I'M...I'M JUST SOME GUY. AN ADULT.
HOW CAN I EVER THANK YOU?
WELL, UH...
I *AM* A LITTLE SHORT ON CASH.
WELL... ALL RIGHT.
THANK YOU!

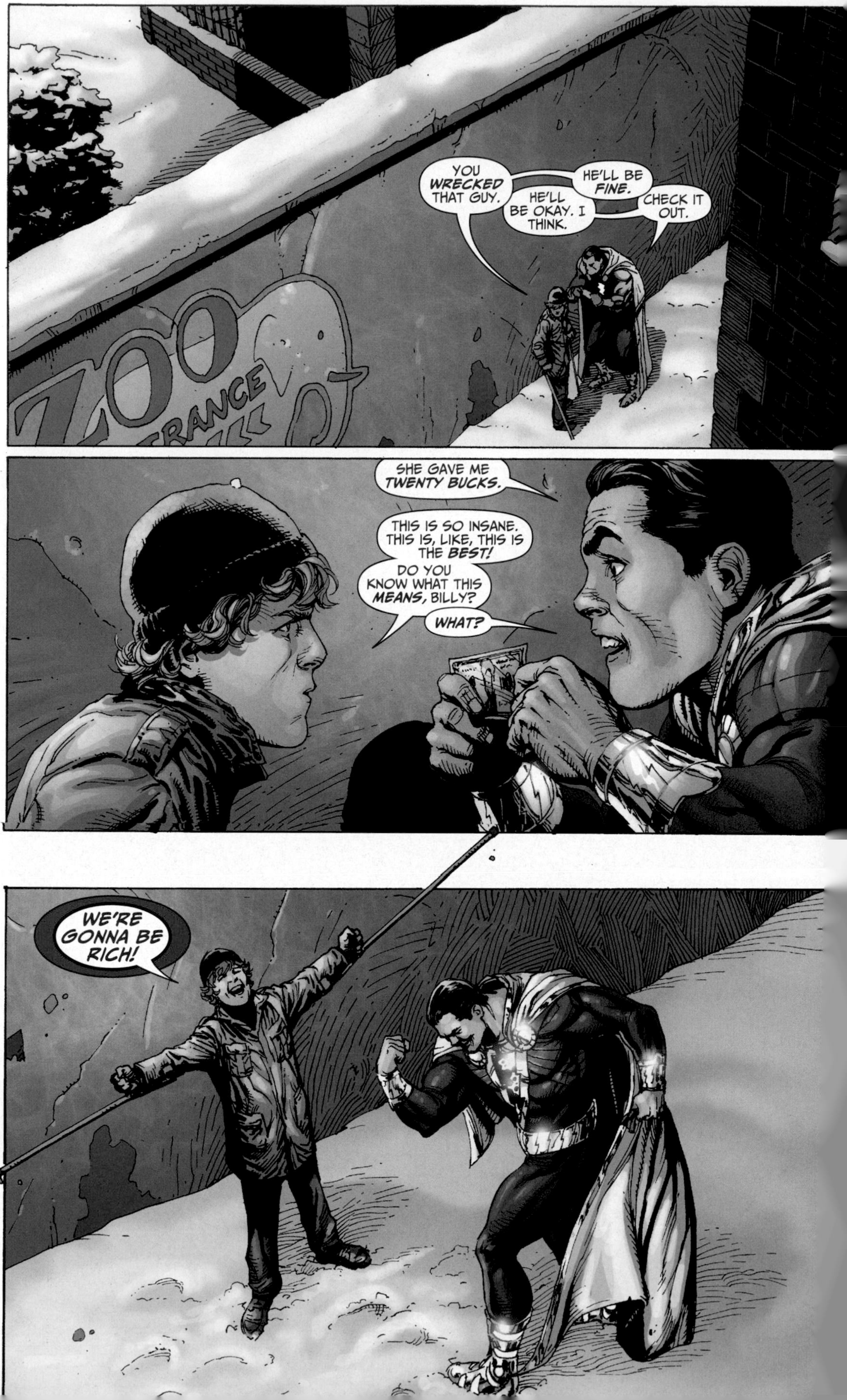

YOU *WRECKED* THAT GUY.
HE'LL BE *FINE.*
HE'LL BE OKAY. I THINK.
CHECK IT OUT.
ZOO
SHE GAVE ME *TWENTY BUCKS.*
THIS IS SO INSANE. THIS IS, LIKE, THIS IS THE *BEST!*
DO YOU KNOW WHAT THIS *MEANS,* BILLY?
WHAT?
WE'RE GONNA BE RICH!

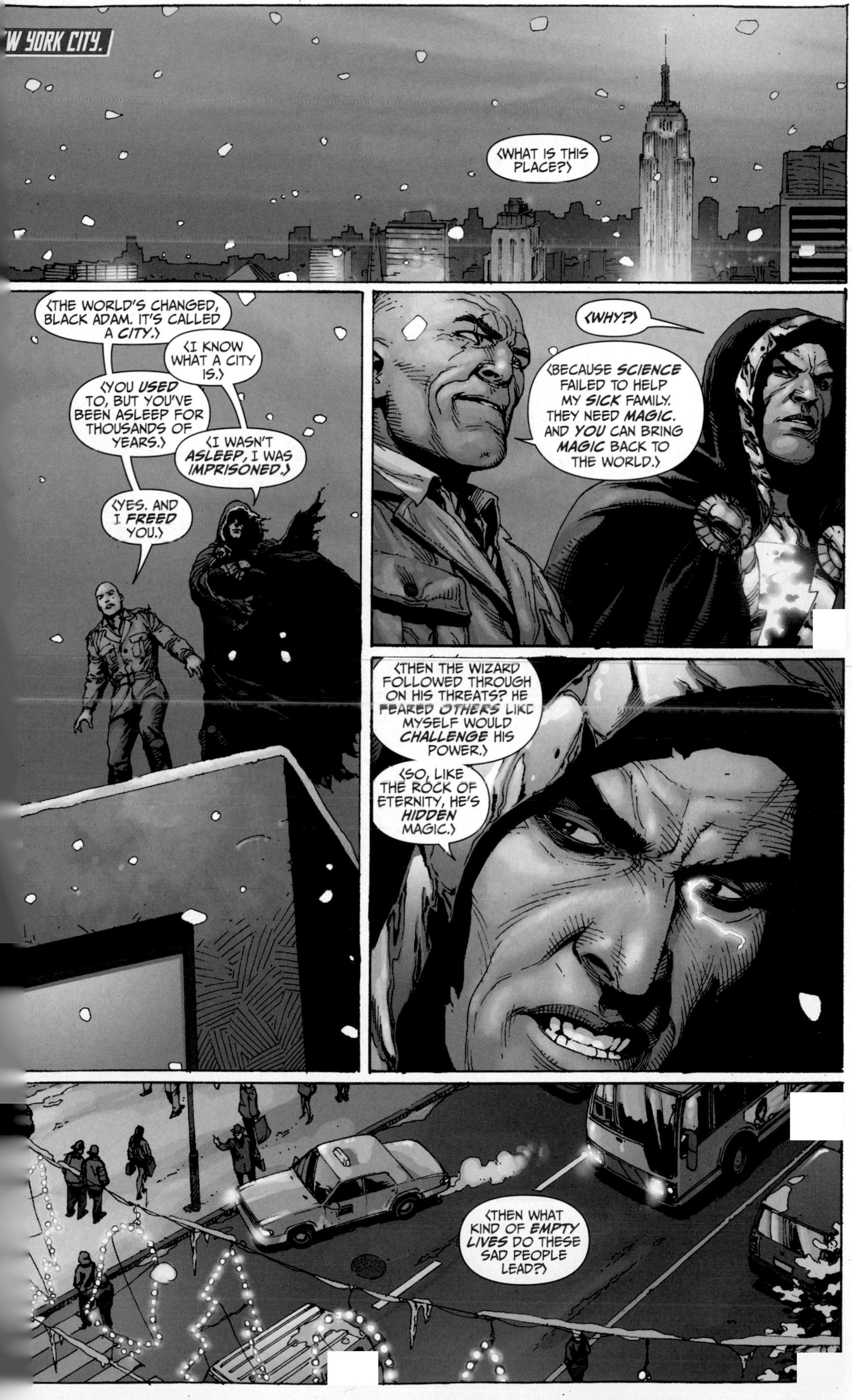
W YORK CITY.
⟨WHAT IS THIS PLACE?⟩
⟨THE WORLD'S CHANGED, BLACK ADAM. IT'S CALLED A CITY.⟩
⟨I KNOW WHAT A CITY IS.⟩
⟨YOU USED TO, BUT YOU'VE BEEN ASLEEP FOR THOUSANDS OF YEARS.⟩
⟨I WASN'T ASLEEP, I WAS IMPRISONED.⟩
⟨YES. AND I FREED YOU.⟩
⟨WHY?⟩
⟨BECAUSE SCIENCE FAILED TO HELP MY SICK FAMILY. THEY NEED MAGIC. AND YOU CAN BRING MAGIC BACK TO THE WORLD.⟩
⟨THEN THE WIZARD FOLLOWED THROUGH ON HIS THREATS? HE FEARED OTHERS LIKE MYSELF WOULD CHALLENGE HIS POWER.⟩
⟨SO, LIKE THE ROCK OF ETERNITY, HE'S HIDDEN MAGIC.⟩
⟨THEN WHAT KIND OF EMPTY LIVES DO THESE SAD PEOPLE LEAD?⟩

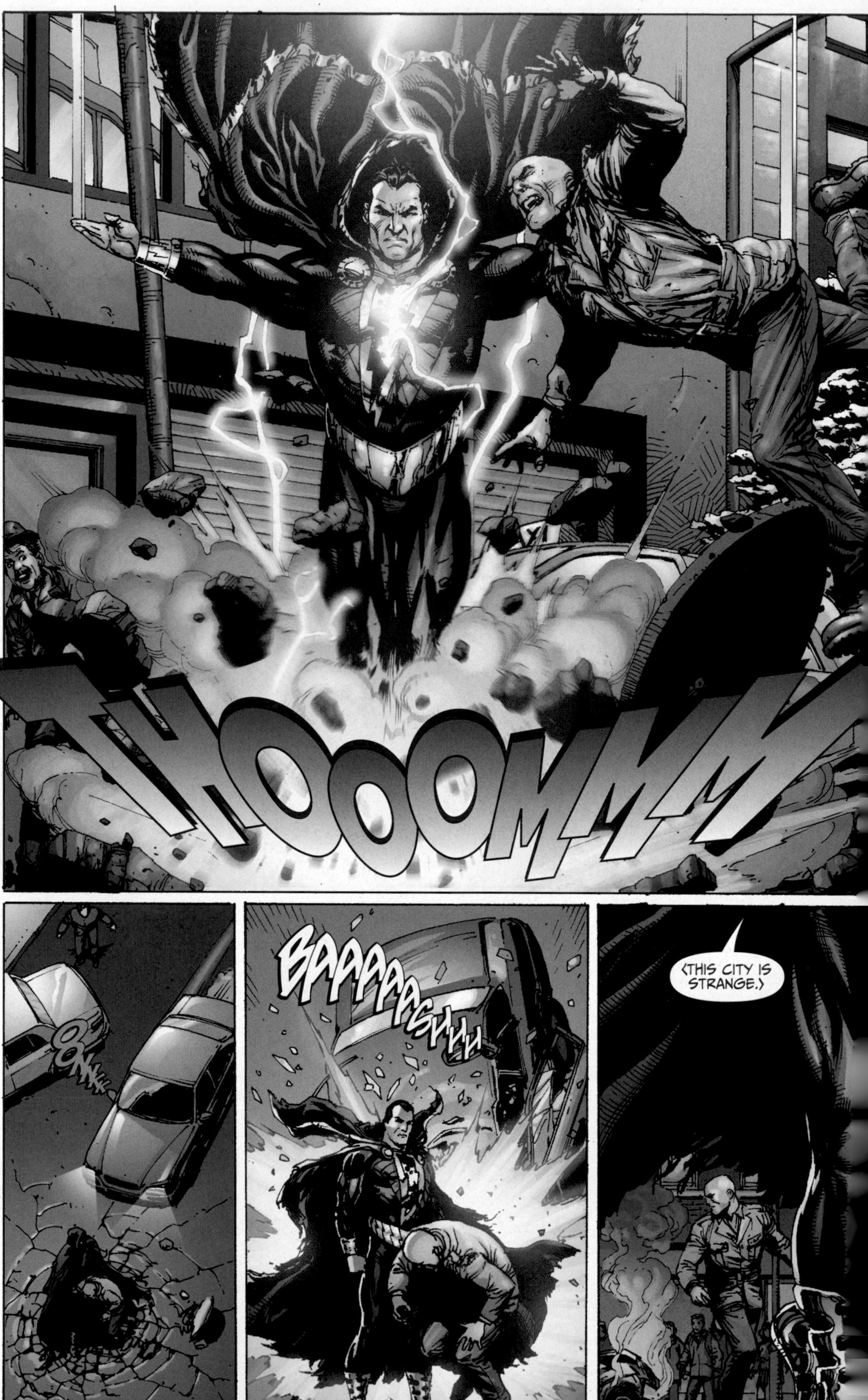

THOOOMMM
OONK
BAAAAASHHH
‹THIS CITY IS STRANGE.›

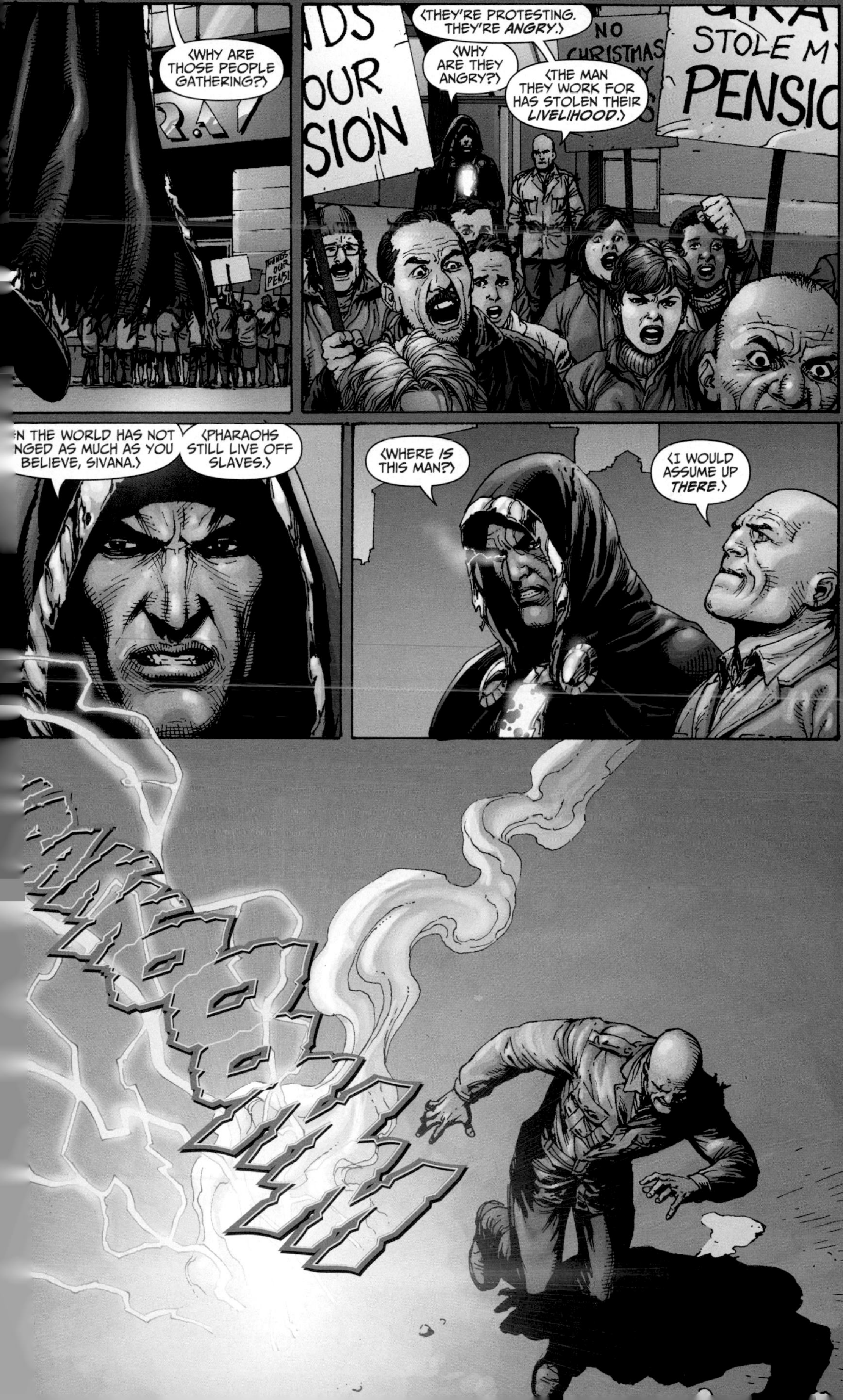
‹WHY ARE THOSE PEOPLE GATHERING?›
‹THEY'RE PROTESTING. THEY'RE *ANGRY*.›
‹WHY ARE THEY ANGRY?›
‹THE MAN THEY WORK FOR HAS STOLEN THEIR *LIVELIHOOD*.›
N THE WORLD HAS NOT NGED AS MUCH AS YOU BELIEVE, SIVANA.›
‹PHARAOHS STILL LIVE OFF SLAVES.›
‹WHERE *IS* THIS MAN?›
‹I WOULD ASSUME UP *THERE*.›

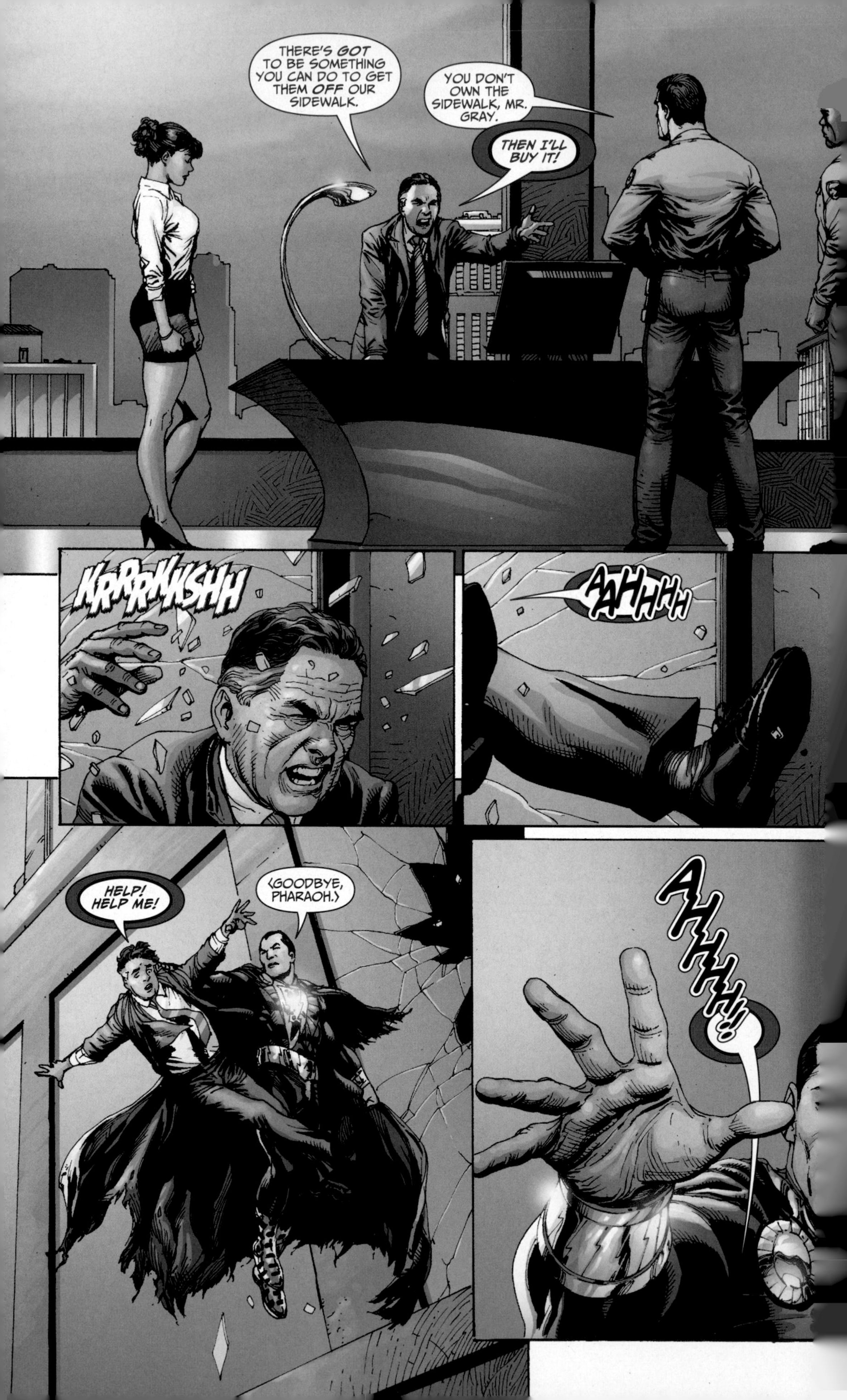
THERE'S GOT TO BE SOMETHING YOU CAN DO TO GET THEM OFF OUR SIDEWALK.
YOU DON'T OWN THE SIDEWALK, MR. GRAY.
THEN I'LL BUY IT!
KRRRKKSHH
AAHHHH
HELP! HELP ME!
<GOODBYE, PHARAOH.>
AHHHH!!

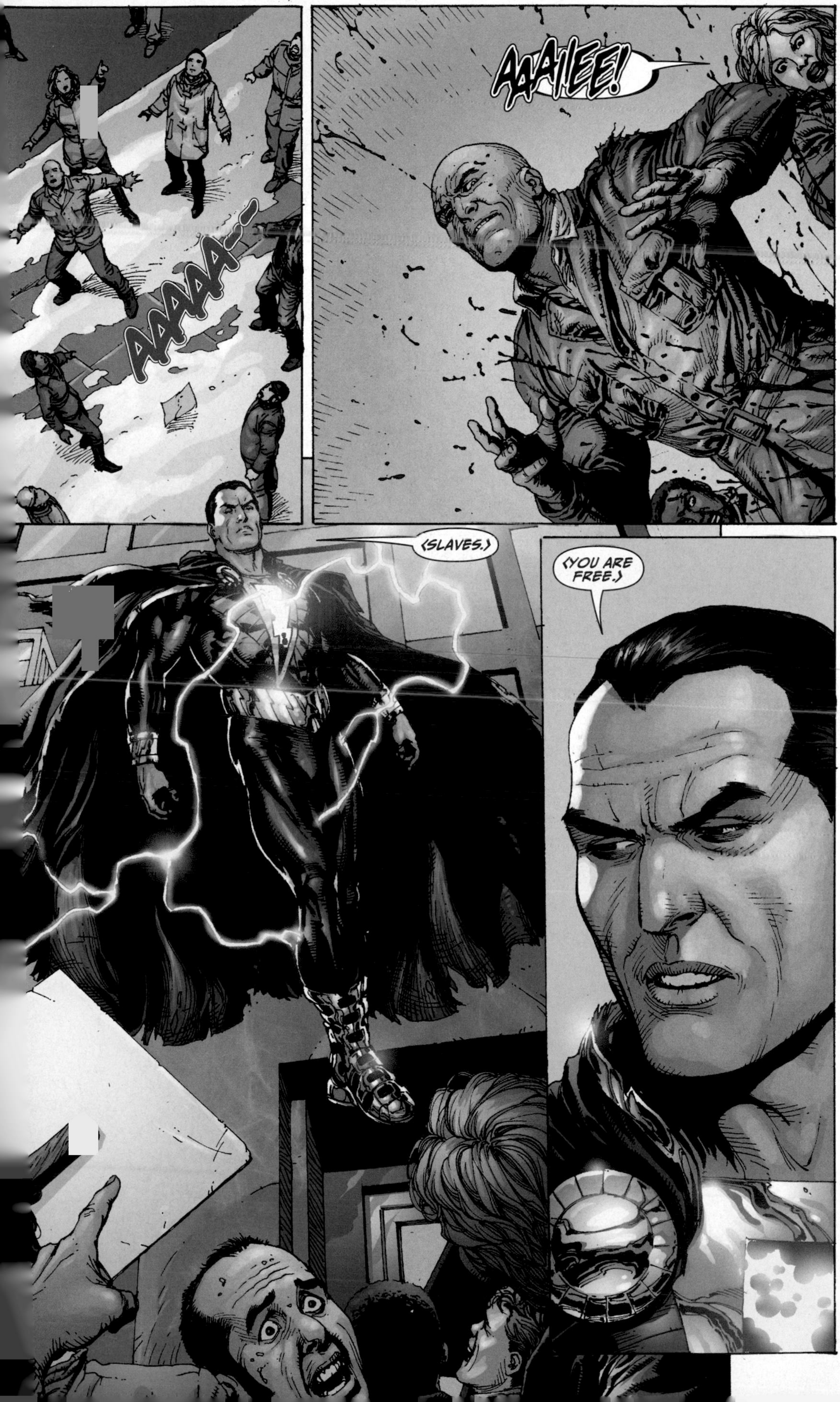
AAAAA--
AAAIIEE!
⟨SLAVES.⟩
⟨YOU ARE FREE.⟩

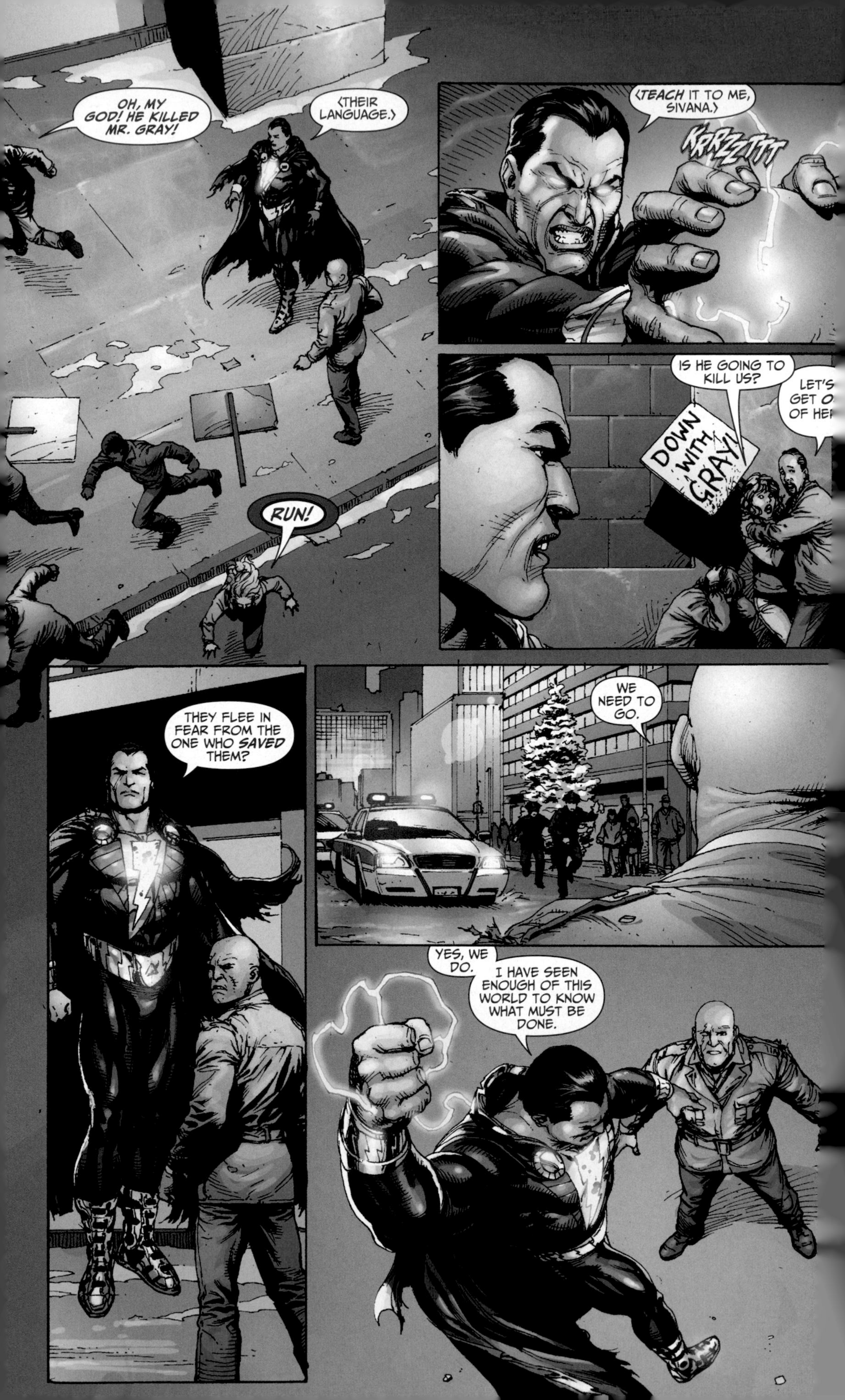

OH, MY GOD! HE KILLED MR. GRAY!
‹THEIR LANGUAGE.›
RUN!
‹TEACH IT TO ME, SIVANA.›
KRRZZTTT
IS HE GOING TO KILL US?
DOWN WITH GRAY!
THEY FLEE IN FEAR FROM THE ONE WHO SAVED THEM?
WE NEED TO GO.
YES, WE DO.
I HAVE SEEN ENOUGH OF THIS WORLD TO KNOW WHAT MUST BE DONE.

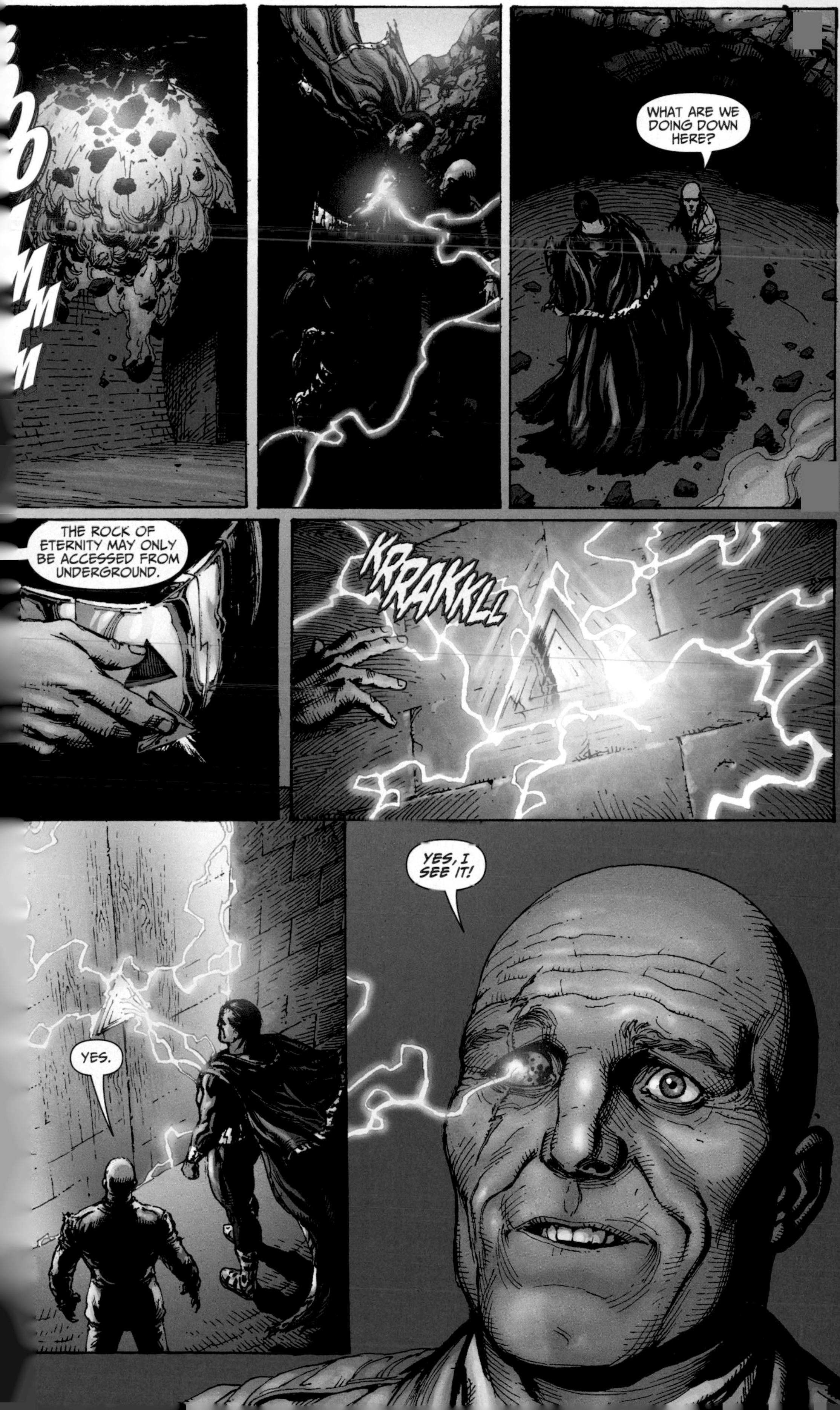
BOOM
WHAT ARE WE DOING DOWN HERE?
THE ROCK OF ETERNITY MAY ONLY BE ACCESSED FROM UNDERGROUND.
KRRAKKLL
YES, I SEE IT!
YES.

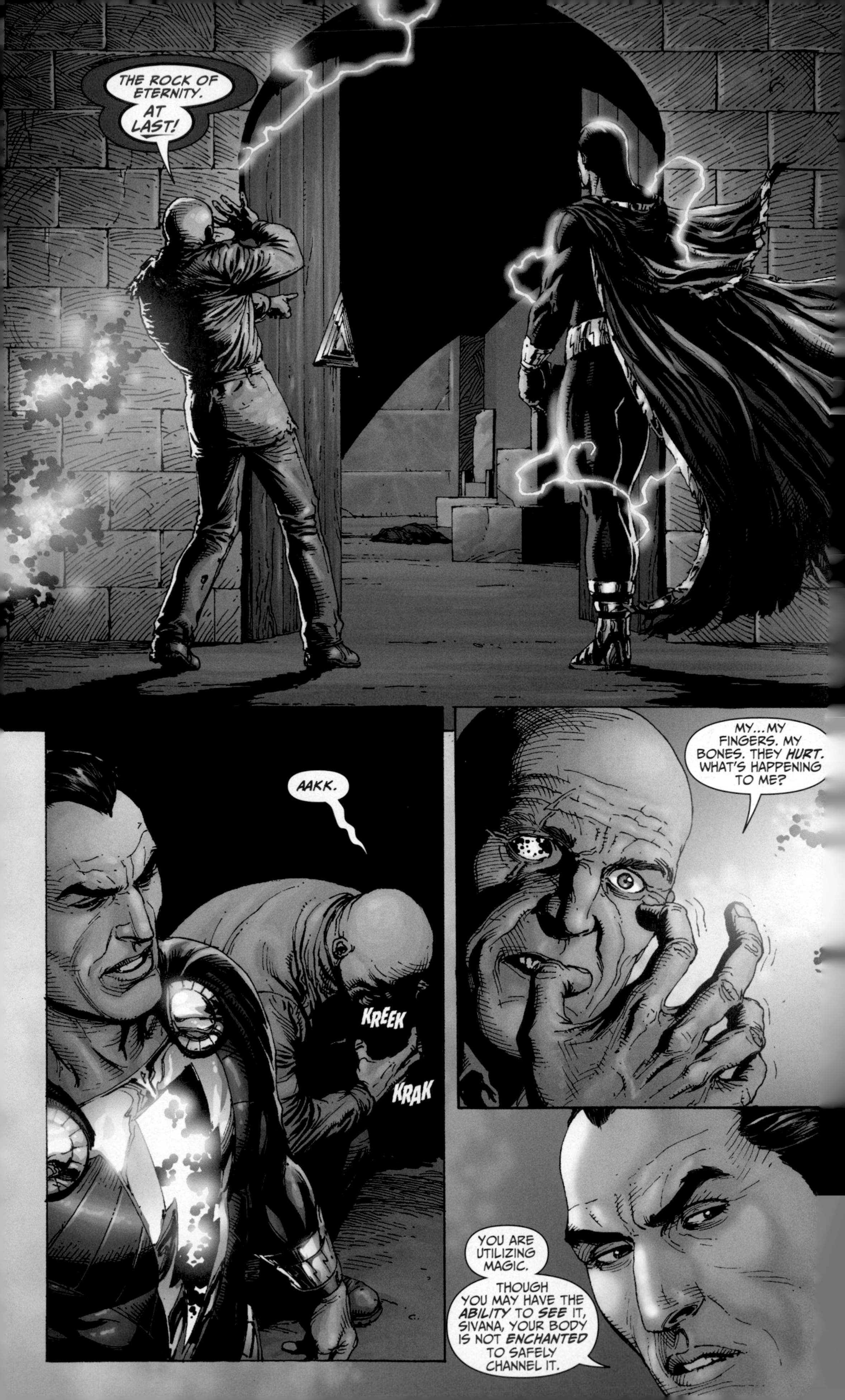
THE ROCK OF ETERNITY. AT LAST!
AAKK.
KREEK
KRAK
MY...MY FINGERS. MY BONES. THEY HURT. WHAT'S HAPPENING TO ME?
YOU ARE UTILIZING MAGIC.
THOUGH YOU MAY HAVE THE ABILITY TO SEE IT, SIVANA, YOUR BODY IS NOT ENCHANTED TO SAFELY CHANNEL IT.

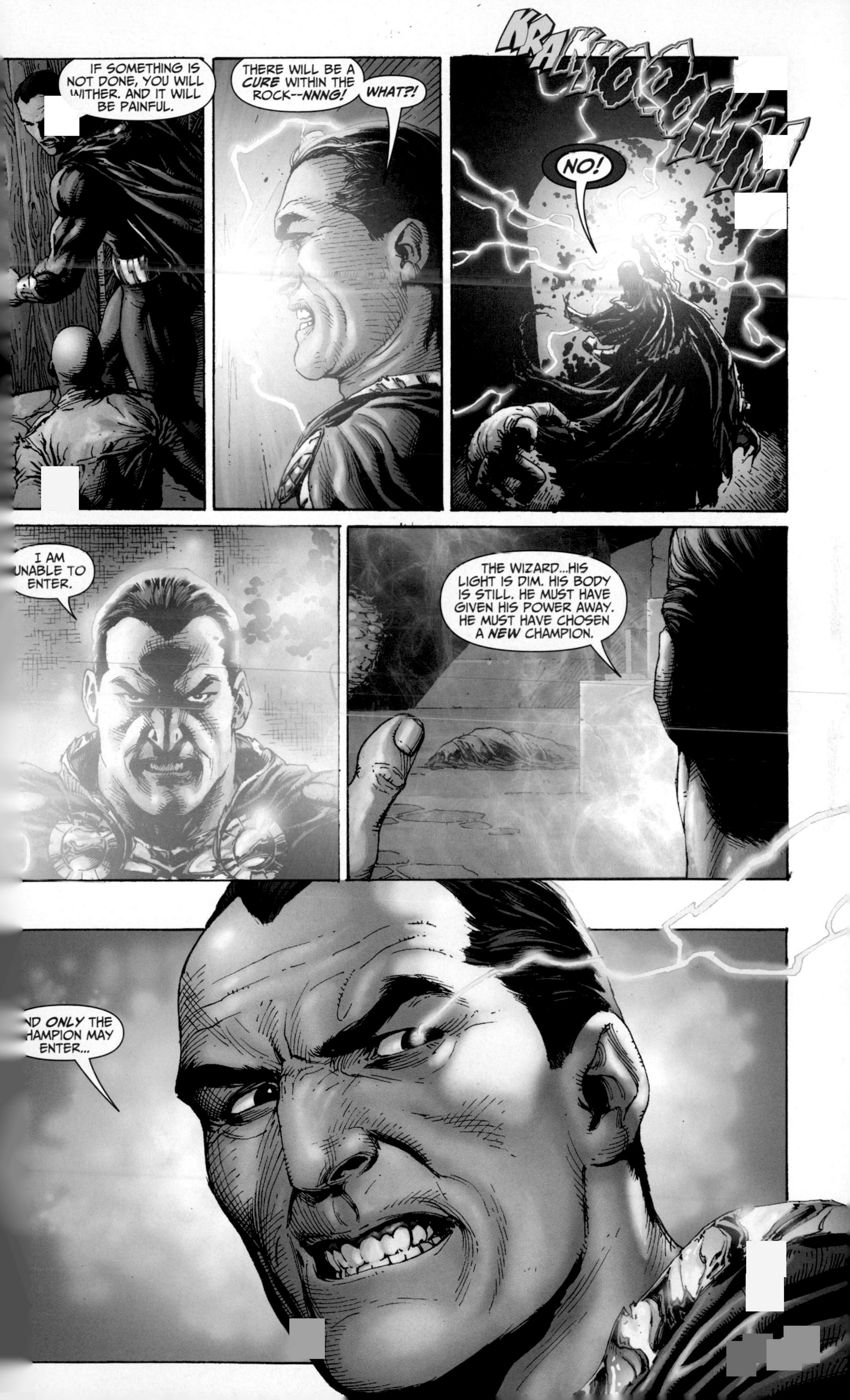
IF SOMETHING IS NOT DONE, YOU WILL WITHER. AND IT WILL BE PAINFUL.
THERE WILL BE A *CURE* WITHIN THE ROCK--*NNNG!*
WHAT?!
NO!
I AM UNABLE TO ENTER.
THE WIZARD...HIS LIGHT IS DIM. HIS BODY IS STILL. HE MUST HAVE GIVEN HIS POWER AWAY. HE MUST HAVE CHOSEN A *NEW* CHAMPION.
ND *ONLY* THE HAMPION MAY ENTER...

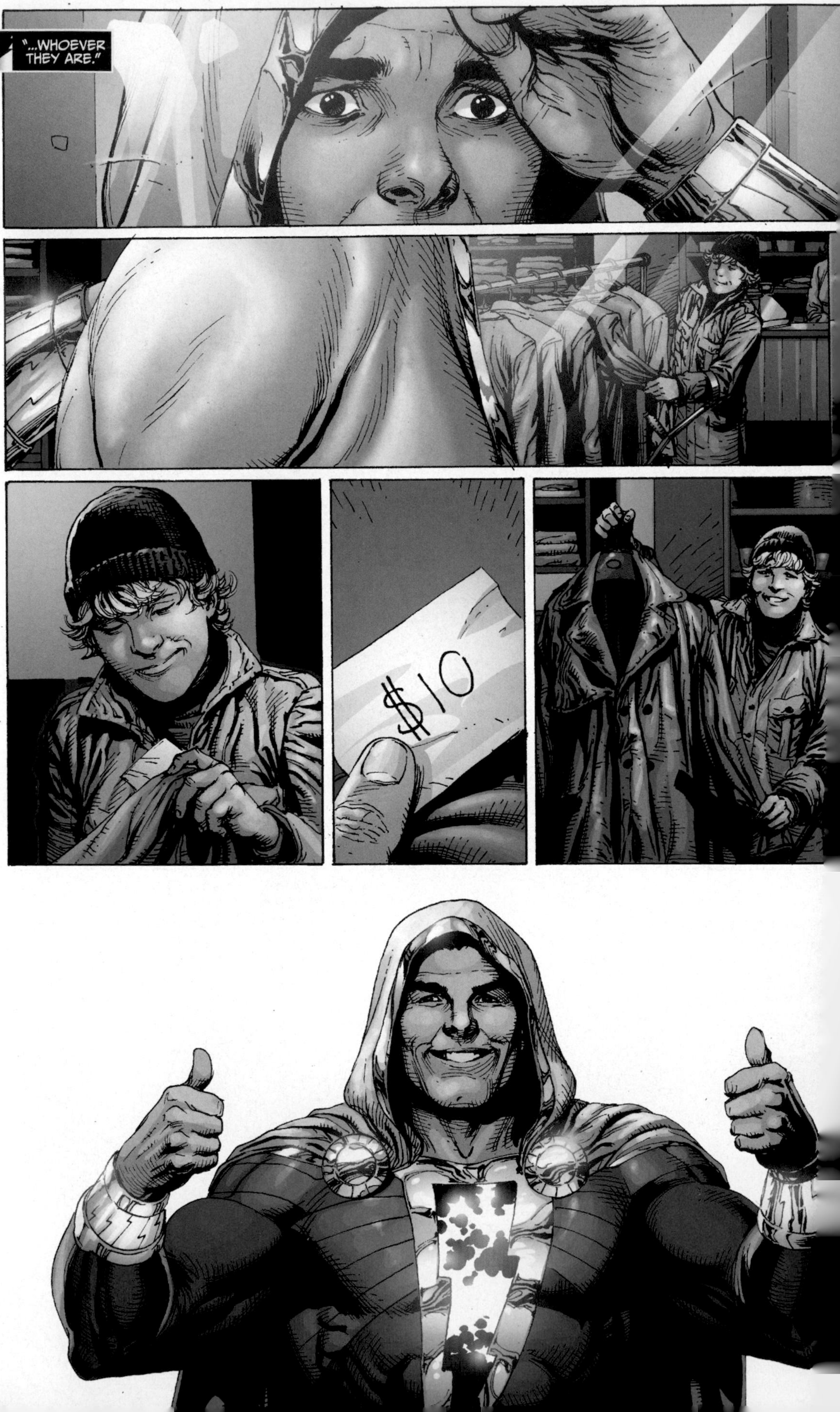
"...WHOEVER THEY ARE."
$10

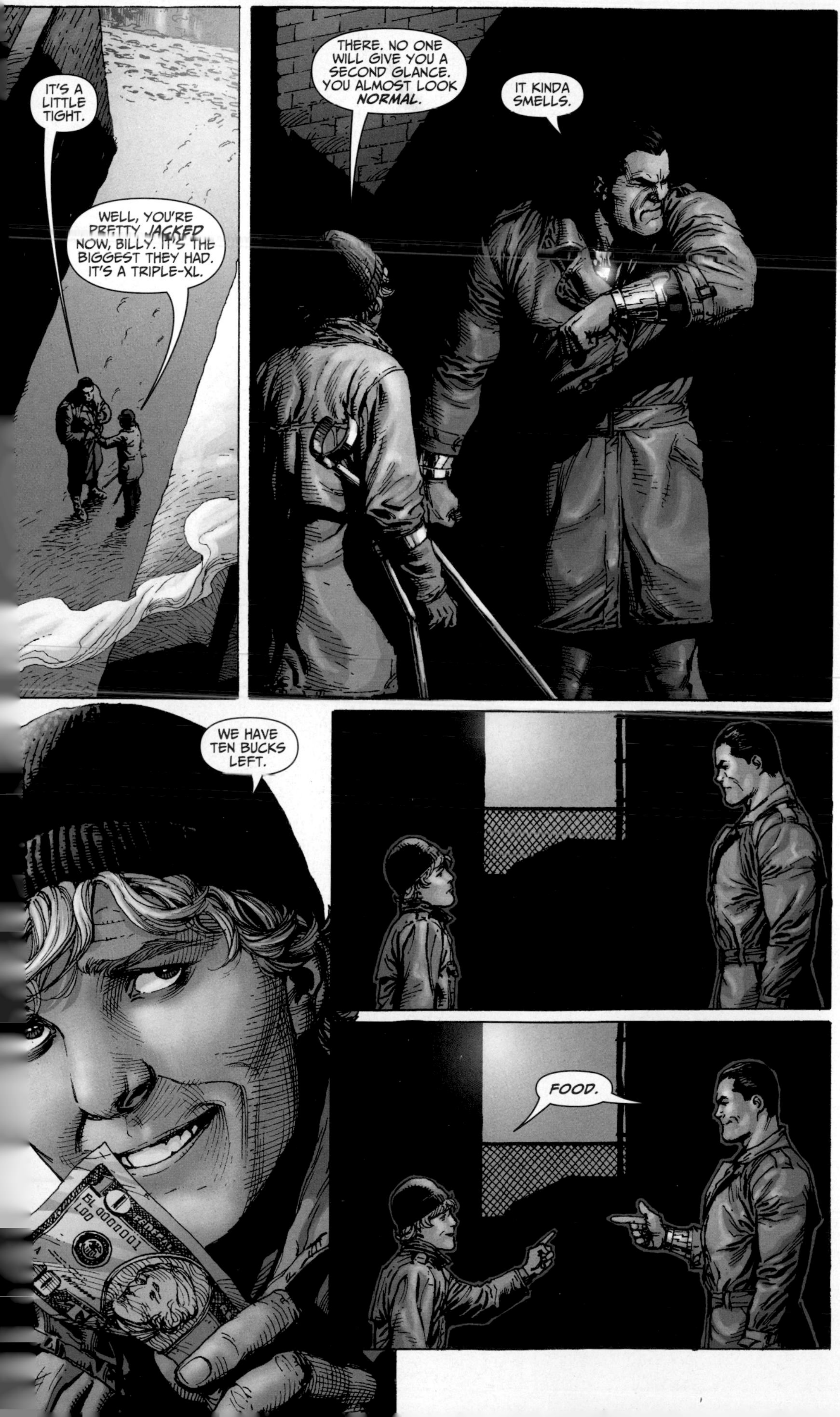

IT'S A LITTLE TIGHT.
WELL, YOU'RE PRETTY JACKED NOW, BILLY. IT'S THE BIGGEST THEY HAD. IT'S A TRIPLE-XL.
THERE. NO ONE WILL GIVE YOU A SECOND GLANCE. YOU ALMOST LOOK NORMAL.
IT KINDA SMELLS.
WE HAVE TEN BUCKS LEFT.
FOOD.

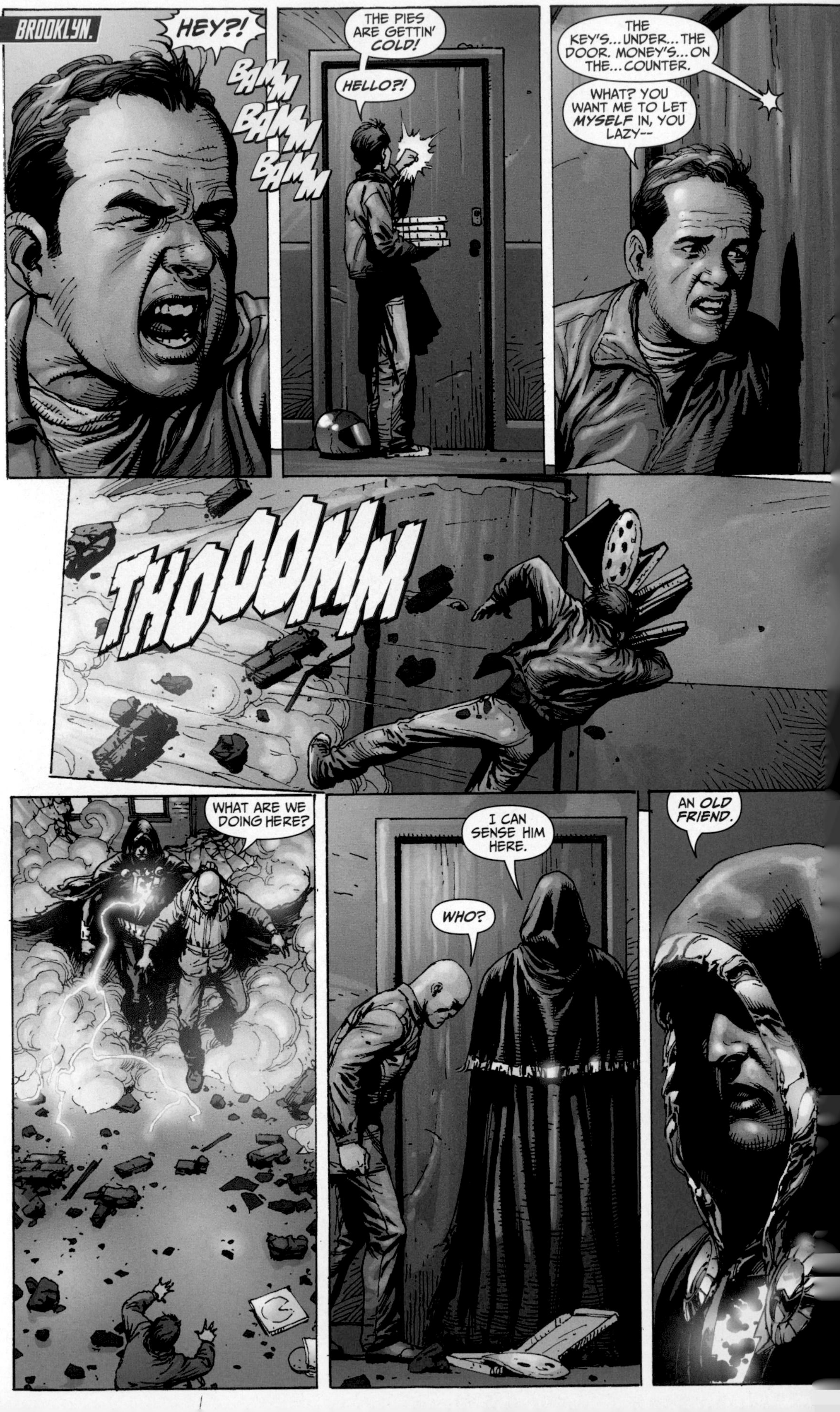
BROOKLYN.
HEY?!
BAMM
BAMM
BAMM
THE PIES ARE GETTIN' COLD!
HELLO?!
THE KEY'S... UNDER... THE DOOR. MONEY'S... ON THE... COUNTER.
WHAT? YOU WANT ME TO LET MYSELF IN, YOU LAZY--
THOOOMM
WHAT ARE WE DOING HERE?
I CAN SENSE HIM HERE.
WHO?
AN OLD FRIEND.

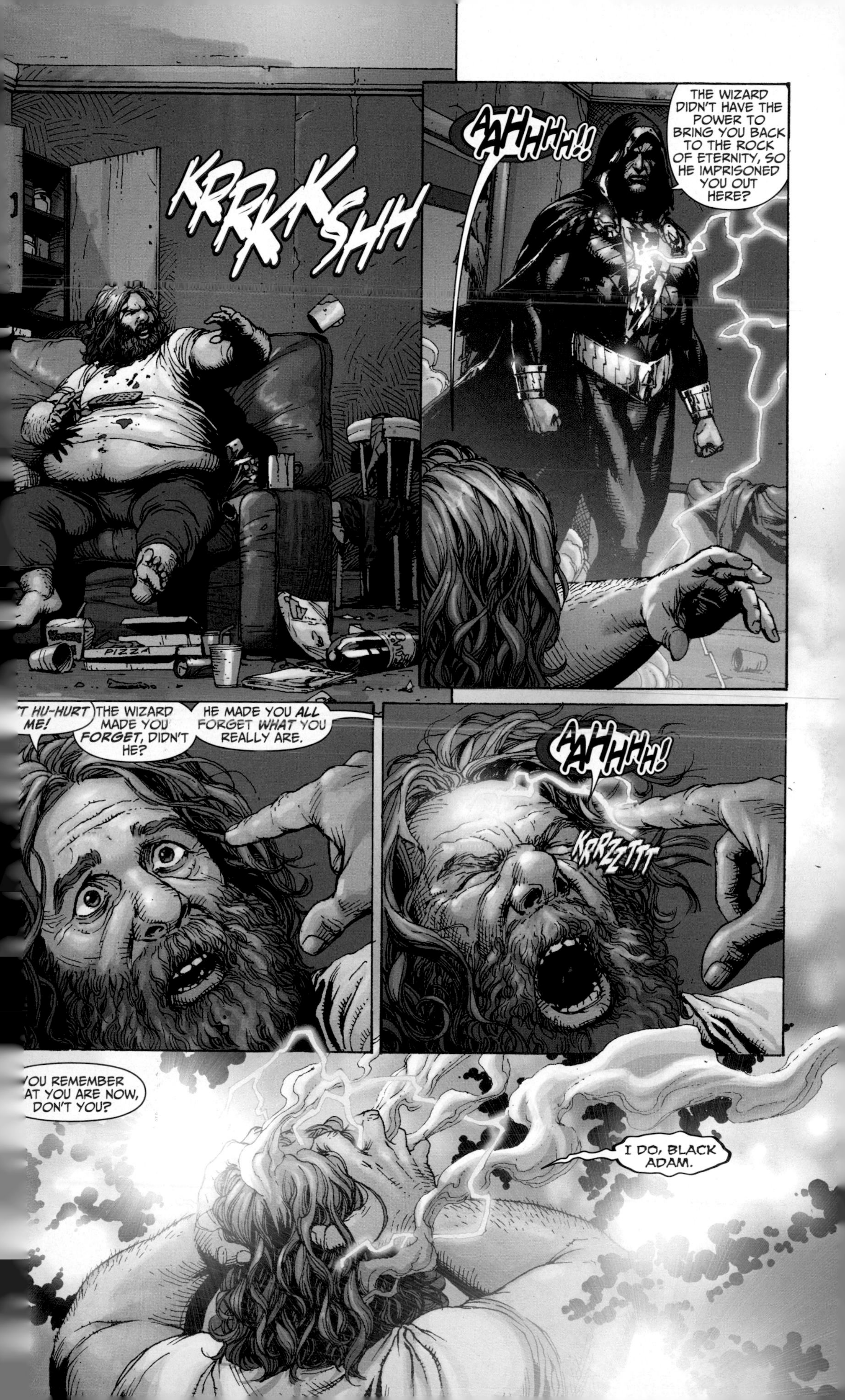
KRRKKSHH
AAHHHH!!
THE WIZARD DIDN'T HAVE THE POWER TO BRING YOU BACK TO THE ROCK OF ETERNITY, SO HE IMPRISONED YOU OUT HERE?
T HU-HURT ME!
THE WIZARD MADE YOU FORGET, DIDN'T HE?
HE MADE YOU ALL FORGET WHAT YOU REALLY ARE.
AAHHHH!
KRRZZTTT
YOU REMEMBER AT YOU ARE NOW, DON'T YOU?
I DO, BLACK ADAM.

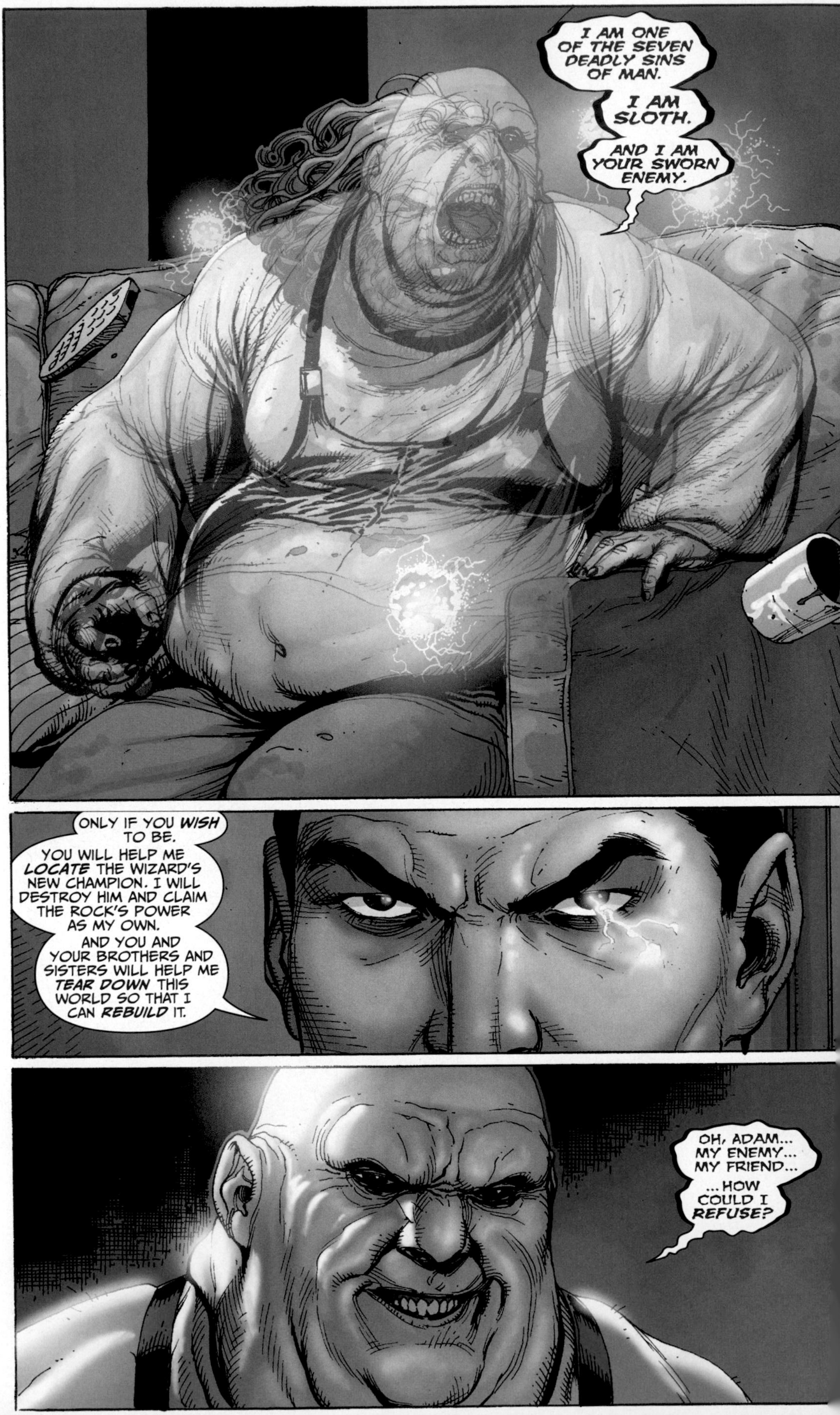
I AM ONE OF THE SEVEN DEADLY SINS OF MAN.
I AM SLOTH.
AND I AM YOUR SWORN ENEMY.
ONLY IF YOU WISH TO BE.
YOU WILL HELP ME LOCATE THE WIZARD'S NEW CHAMPION. I WILL DESTROY HIM AND CLAIM THE ROCK'S POWER AS MY OWN.
AND YOU AND YOUR BROTHERS AND SISTERS WILL HELP ME TEAR DOWN THIS WORLD SO THAT I CAN REBUILD IT.
OH, ADAM... MY ENEMY... MY FRIEND...
...HOW COULD I REFUSE?

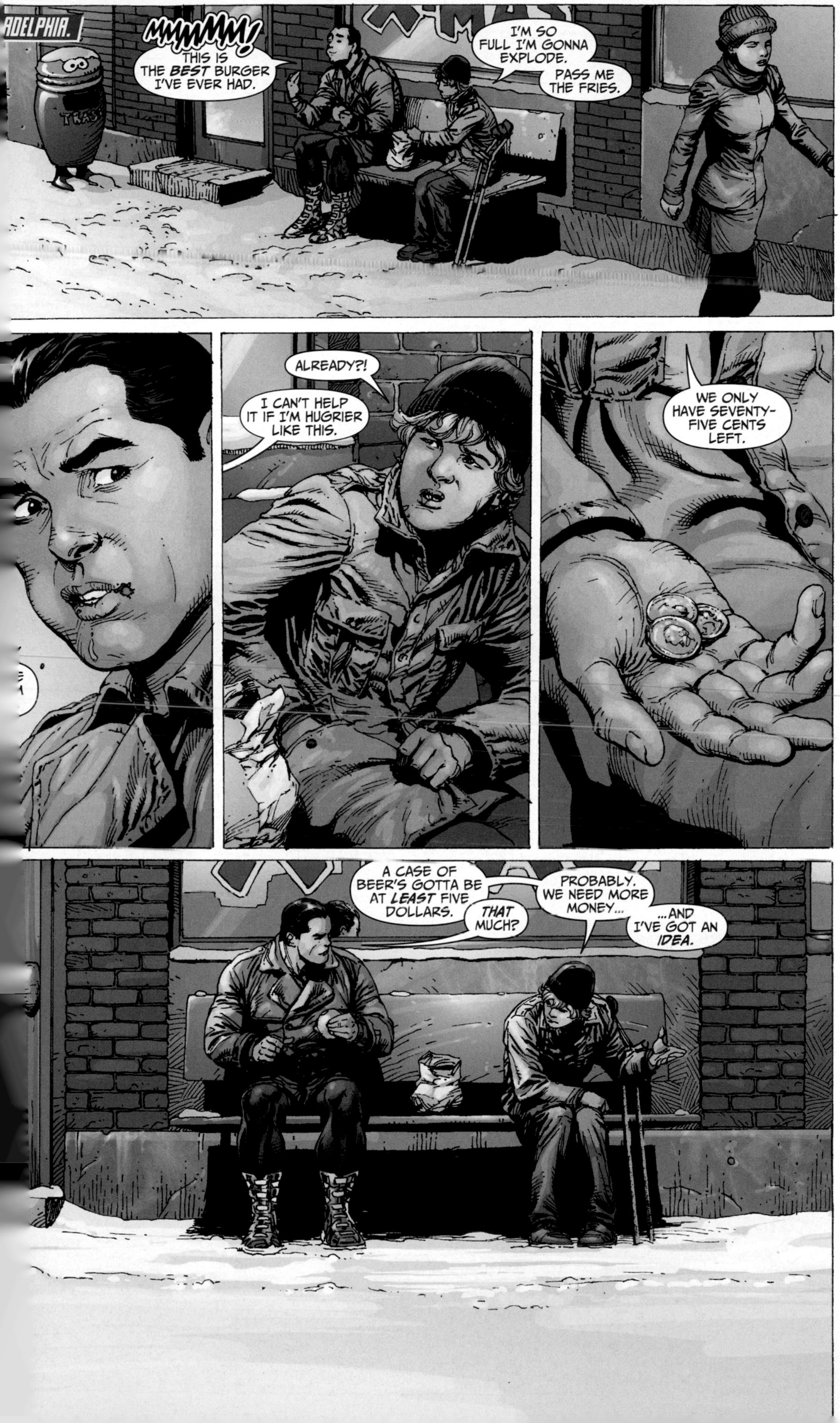
ADELPHIA.
MMMMM! THIS IS THE BEST BURGER I'VE EVER HAD.
I'M SO FULL I'M GONNA EXPLODE.
PASS ME THE FRIES.
ALREADY?!
I CAN'T HELP IT IF I'M HUGRIER LIKE THIS.
WE ONLY HAVE SEVENTY-FIVE CENTS LEFT.
A CASE OF BEER'S GOTTA BE AT LEAST FIVE DOLLARS.
THAT MUCH?
PROBABLY. WE NEED MORE MONEY...
...AND I'VE GOT AN IDEA.

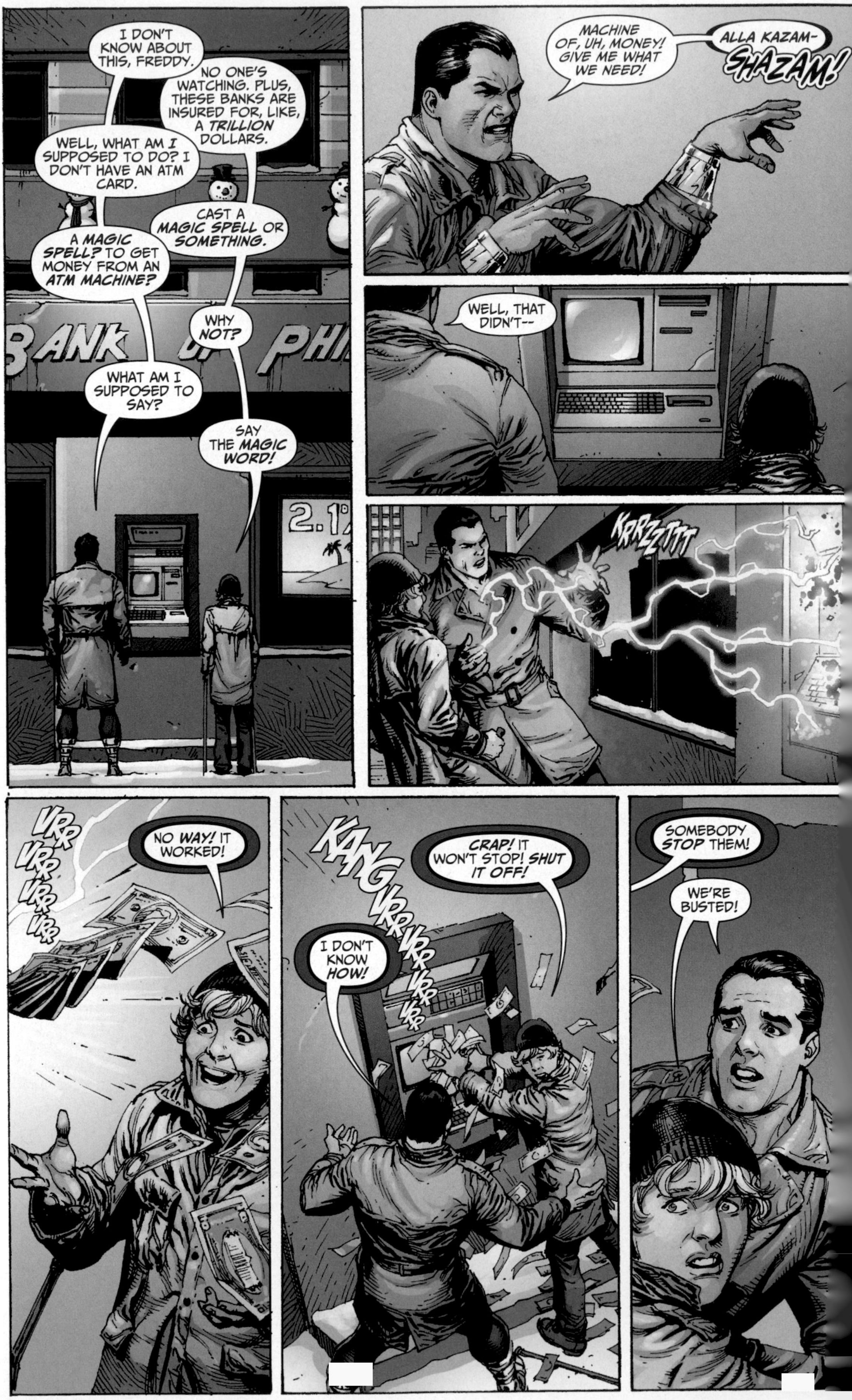
I DON'T KNOW ABOUT THIS, FREDDY.
NO ONE'S WATCHING. PLUS, THESE BANKS ARE INSURED FOR, LIKE, A TRILLION DOLLARS.
WELL, WHAT AM I SUPPOSED TO DO? I DON'T HAVE AN ATM CARD.
CAST A MAGIC SPELL OR SOMETHING.
A MAGIC SPELL? TO GET MONEY FROM AN ATM MACHINE?
WHY NOT?
BANK OF PHI
WHAT AM I SUPPOSED TO SAY?
SAY THE MAGIC WORD!
MACHINE OF, UH, MONEY! GIVE ME WHAT WE NEED!
ALLA KAZAM-
SHAZAM!
WELL, THAT DIDN'T--
KRRZZTTT
VRR VRR VRR VRR
NO WAY! IT WORKED!
KANG
VRR VRR VRR VRR
CRAP! IT WON'T STOP! SHUT IT OFF!
I DON'T KNOW HOW!
SOMEBODY STOP THEM!
WE'RE BUSTED!

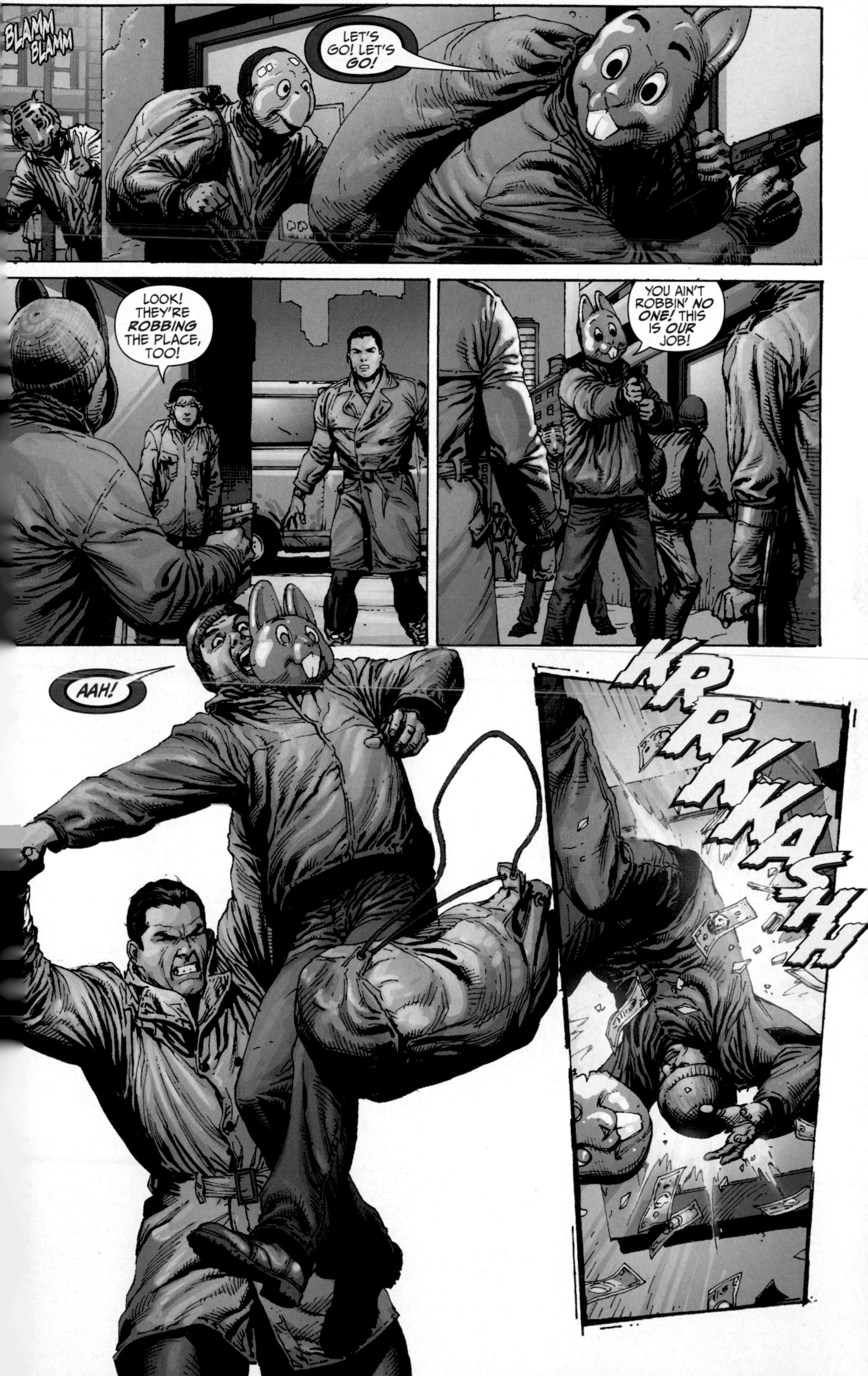
BLAMM BLAMM
LET'S GO! LET'S GO!
LOOK! THEY'RE ROBBING THE PLACE, TOO!
YOU AIN'T ROBBIN' NO ONE! THIS IS OUR JOB!
AAH!
KRRKKASH

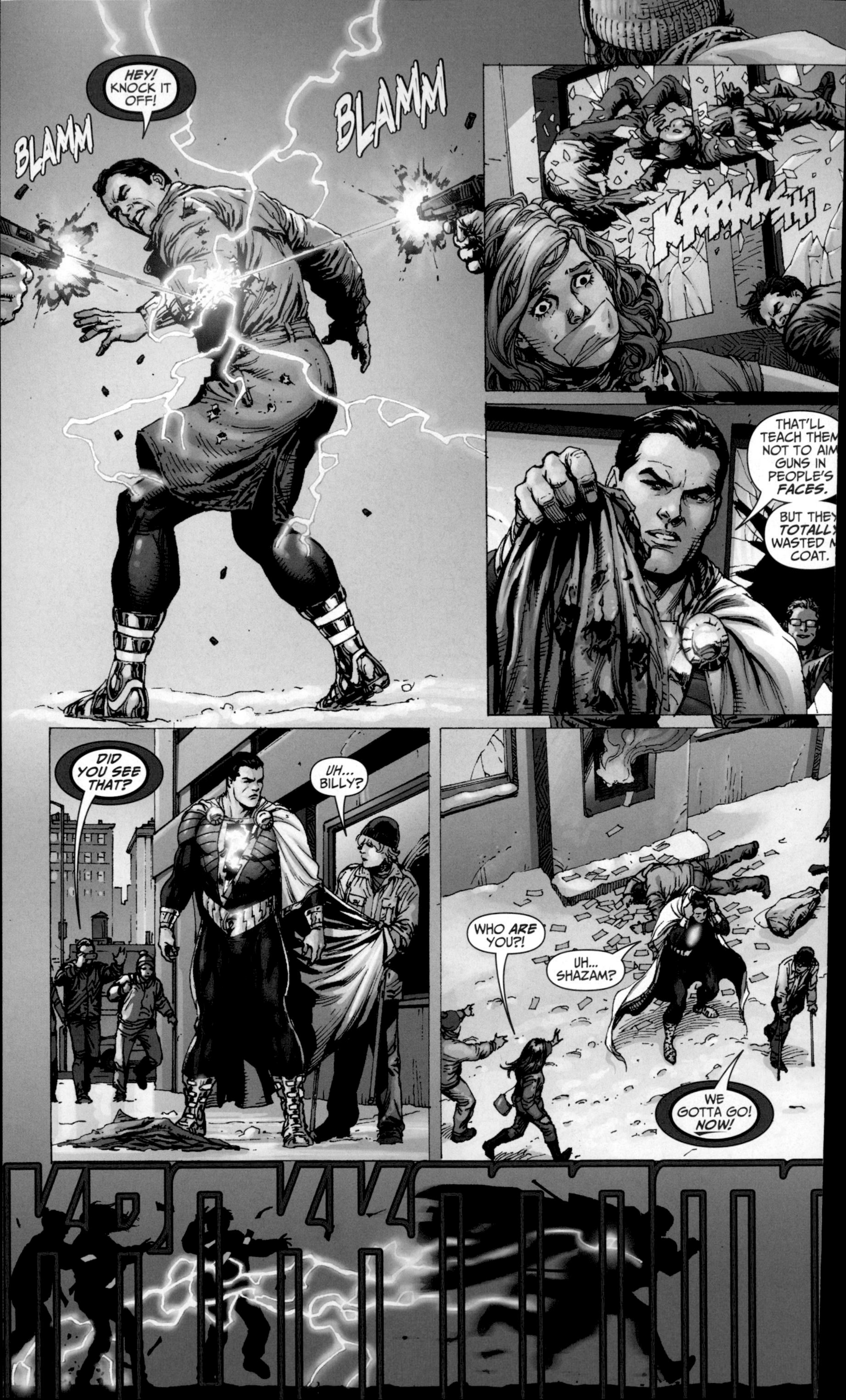
BLAMM
HEY! KNOCK IT OFF!
BLAMM
THAT'LL TEACH THEM NOT TO AIM GUNS IN PEOPLE'S FACES.
BUT THEY TOTALLY WASTED M COAT.
DID YOU SEE THAT?
UH... BILLY?
WHO ARE YOU?!
UH... SHAZAM?
WE GOTTA GO! NOW!

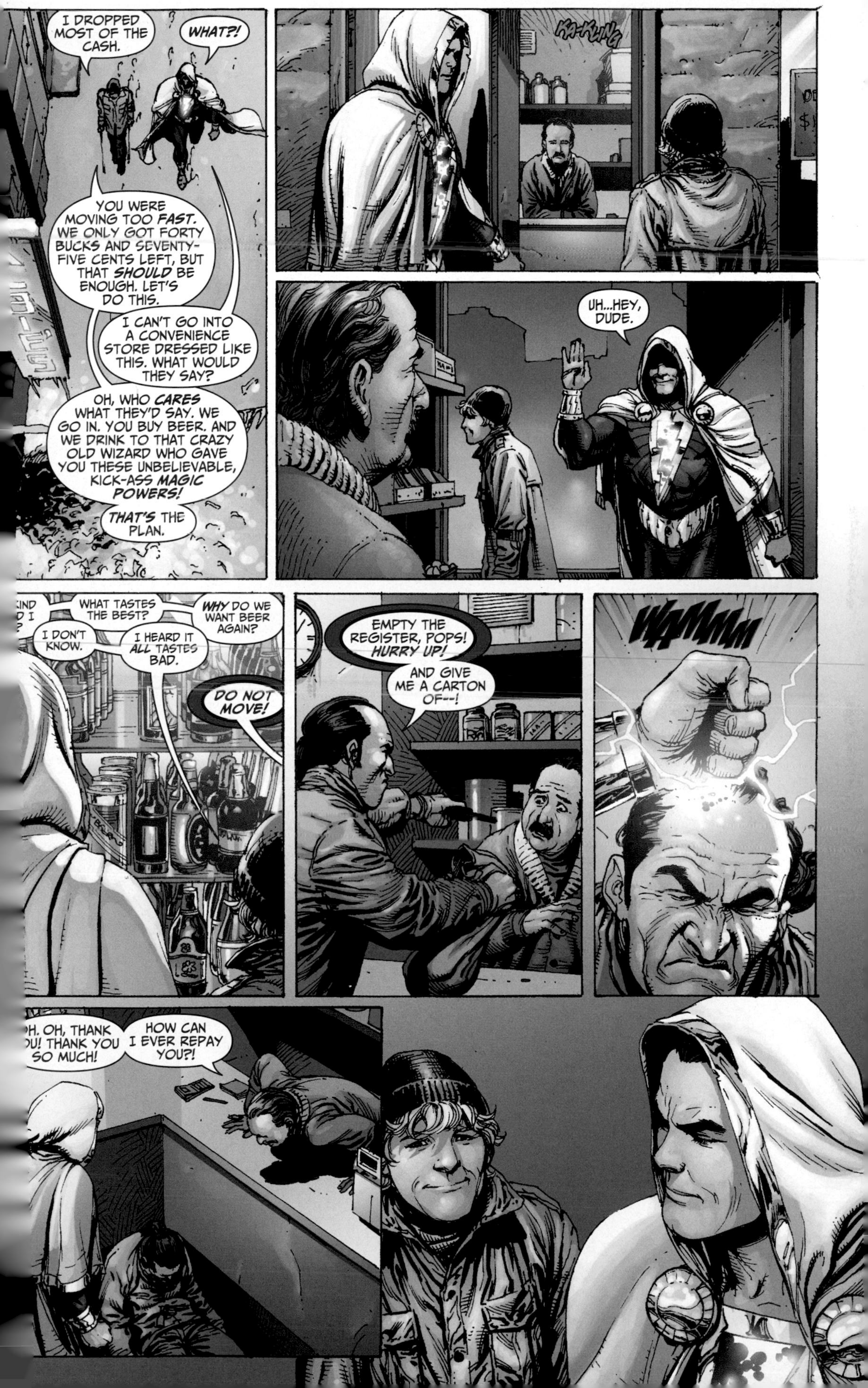

I DROPPED MOST OF THE CASH.
WHAT?!
YOU WERE MOVING TOO FAST. WE ONLY GOT FORTY BUCKS AND SEVENTY-FIVE CENTS LEFT, BUT THAT SHOULD BE ENOUGH. LET'S DO THIS.
I CAN'T GO INTO A CONVENIENCE STORE DRESSED LIKE THIS. WHAT WOULD THEY SAY?
OH, WHO CARES WHAT THEY'D SAY. WE GO IN. YOU BUY BEER. AND WE DRINK TO THAT CRAZY OLD WIZARD WHO GAVE YOU THESE UNBELIEVABLE, KICK-ASS MAGIC POWERS!
THAT'S THE PLAN.
KA-KLING
UH...HEY, DUDE.
WHAT TASTES THE BEST?
WHY DO WE WANT BEER AGAIN?
I DON'T KNOW.
I HEARD IT ALL TASTES BAD.
DO NOT MOVE!
EMPTY THE REGISTER, POPS! HURRY UP!
AND GIVE ME A CARTON OF--!
WHAMMM
H. OH, THANK OU! THANK YOU SO MUCH!
HOW CAN I EVER REPAY YOU?!

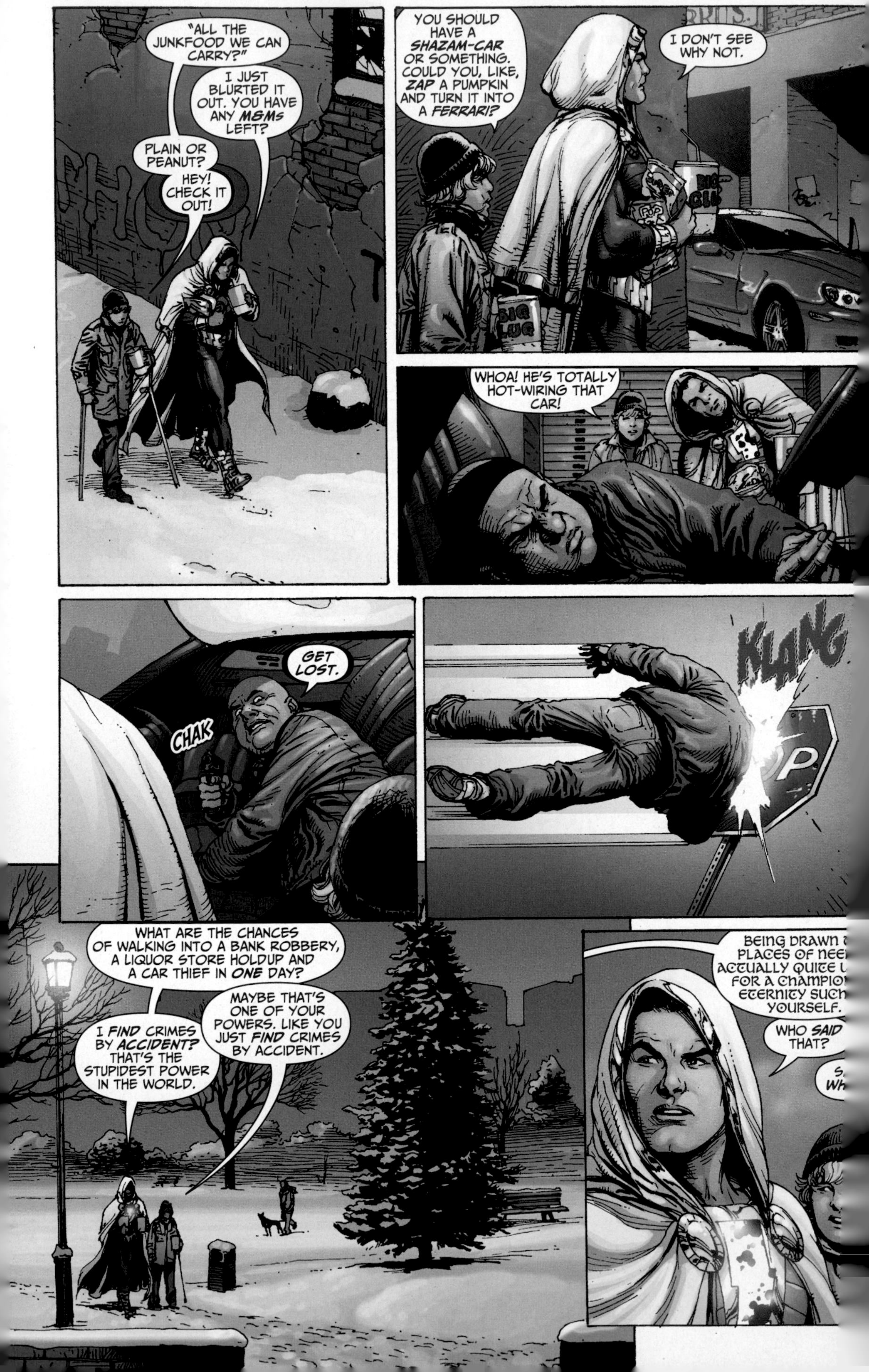
"ALL THE JUNKFOOD WE CAN CARRY?"
I JUST BLURTED IT OUT. YOU HAVE ANY M&Ms LEFT?
PLAIN OR PEANUT?
HEY! CHECK IT OUT!
YOU SHOULD HAVE A SHAZAM-CAR OR SOMETHING. COULD YOU, LIKE, ZAP A PUMPKIN AND TURN IT INTO A FERRARI?
I DON'T SEE WHY NOT.
BIG GLUG
WHOA! HE'S TOTALLY HOT-WIRING THAT CAR!
GET LOST.
CHAK
KLANG
WHAT ARE THE CHANCES OF WALKING INTO A BANK ROBBERY, A LIQUOR STORE HOLDUP AND A CAR THIEF IN ONE DAY?
MAYBE THAT'S ONE OF YOUR POWERS. LIKE YOU JUST FIND CRIMES BY ACCIDENT.
I FIND CRIMES BY ACCIDENT? THAT'S THE STUPIDEST POWER IN THE WORLD.
BEING DRAWN T
PLACES OF NEE
ACTUALLY QUITE U
FOR A CHAMPION
ETERNITY SUCH
YOURSELF.
WHO SAID THAT?

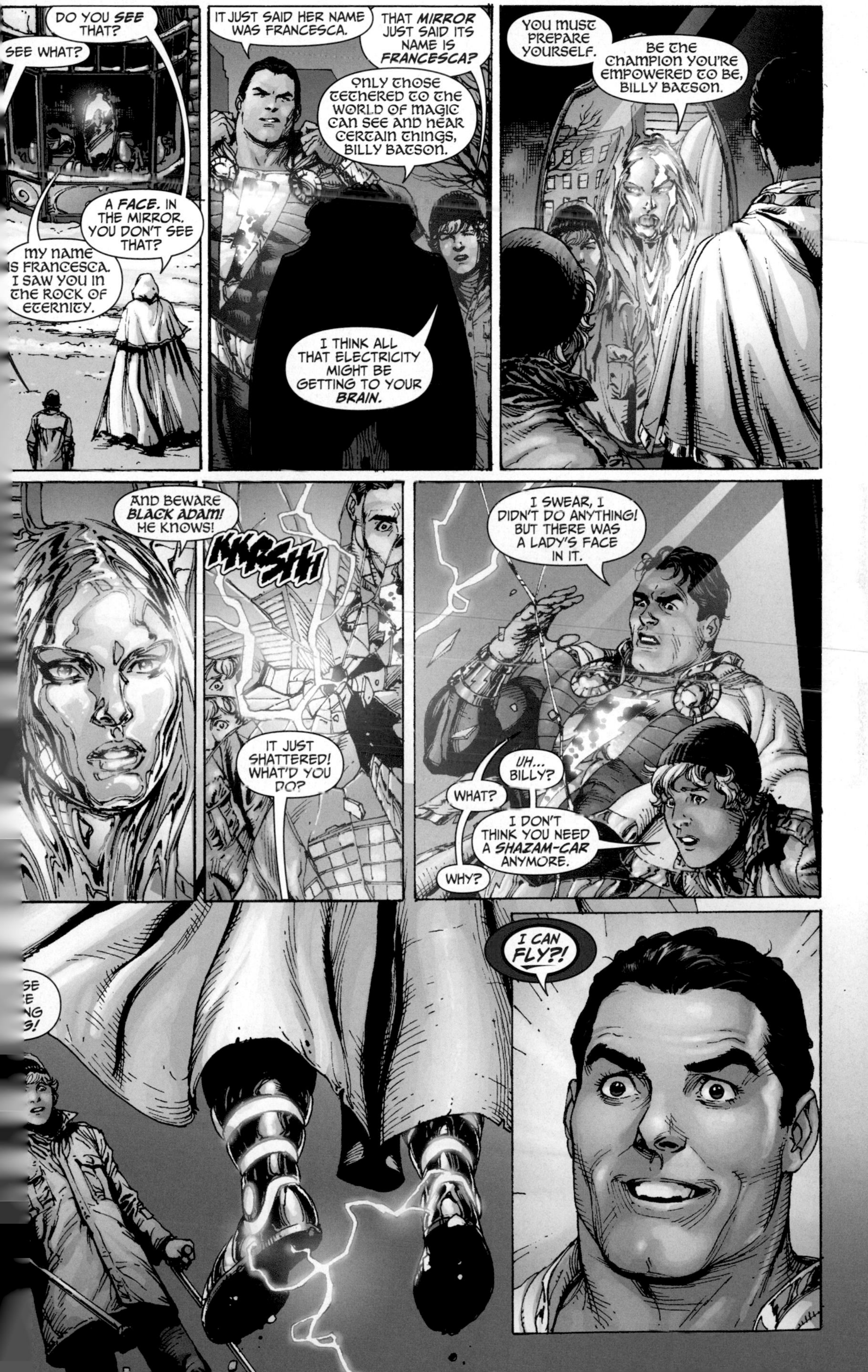

DO YOU SEE THAT?
SEE WHAT?
A FACE. IN THE MIRROR. YOU DON'T SEE THAT?
MY NAME IS FRANCESCA. I SAW YOU IN THE ROCK OF ETERNITY.
IT JUST SAID HER NAME WAS FRANCESCA.
THAT MIRROR JUST SAID ITS NAME IS FRANCESCA?
ONLY THOSE TETHERED TO THE WORLD OF MAGIC CAN SEE AND HEAR CERTAIN THINGS, BILLY BATSON.
I THINK ALL THAT ELECTRICITY MIGHT BE GETTING TO YOUR BRAIN.
YOU MUST PREPARE YOURSELF.
BE THE CHAMPION YOU'RE EMPOWERED TO BE, BILLY BATSON.
AND BEWARE BLACK ADAM! HE KNOWS!
KKRSHH
IT JUST SHATTERED! WHAT'D YOU DO?
I SWEAR, I DIDN'T DO ANYTHING! BUT THERE WAS A LADY'S FACE IN IT.
UH... BILLY?
WHAT?
I DON'T THINK YOU NEED A SHAZAM-CAR ANYMORE.
WHY?
I CAN FLY?!

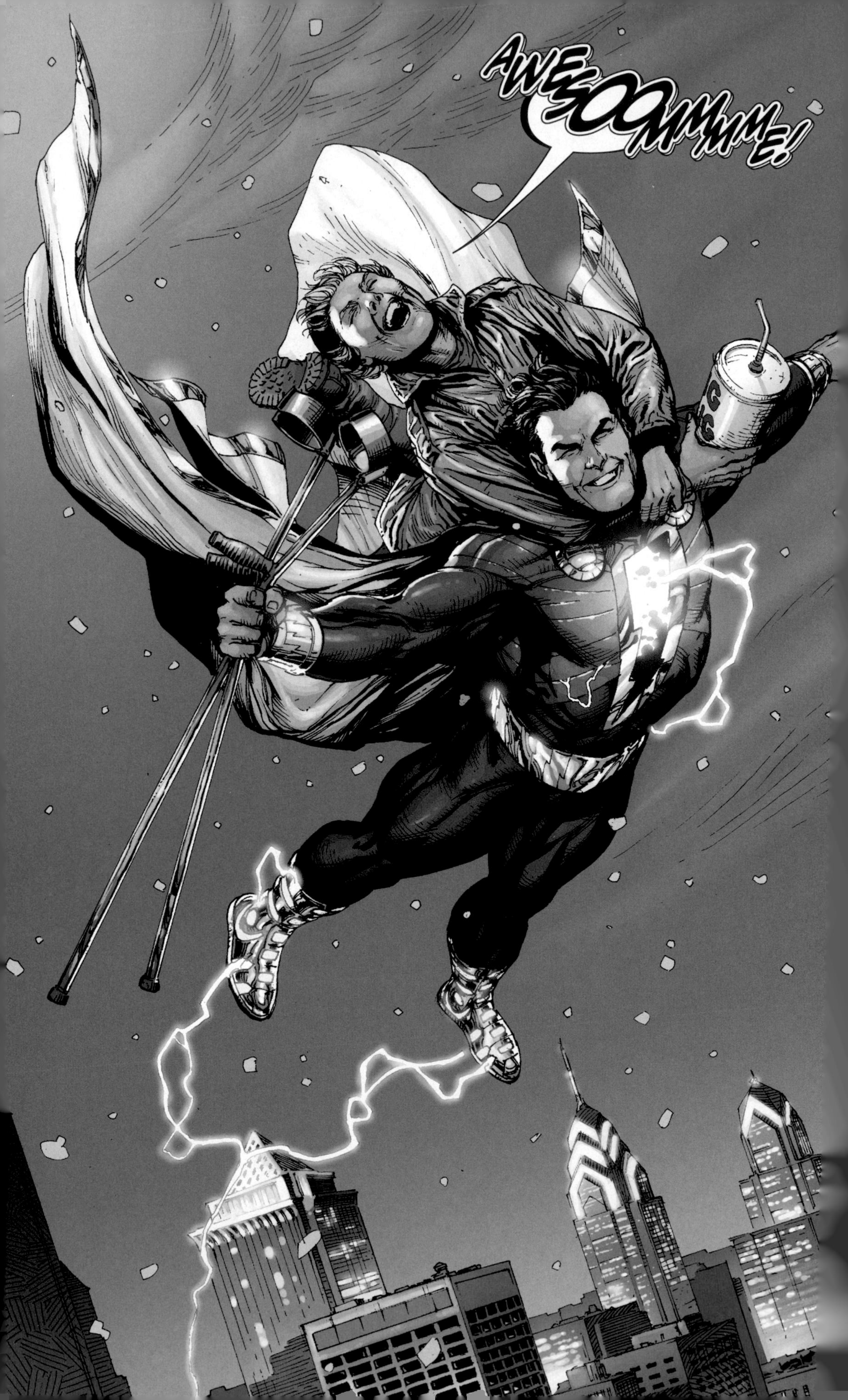
AWESOOMMMMME!

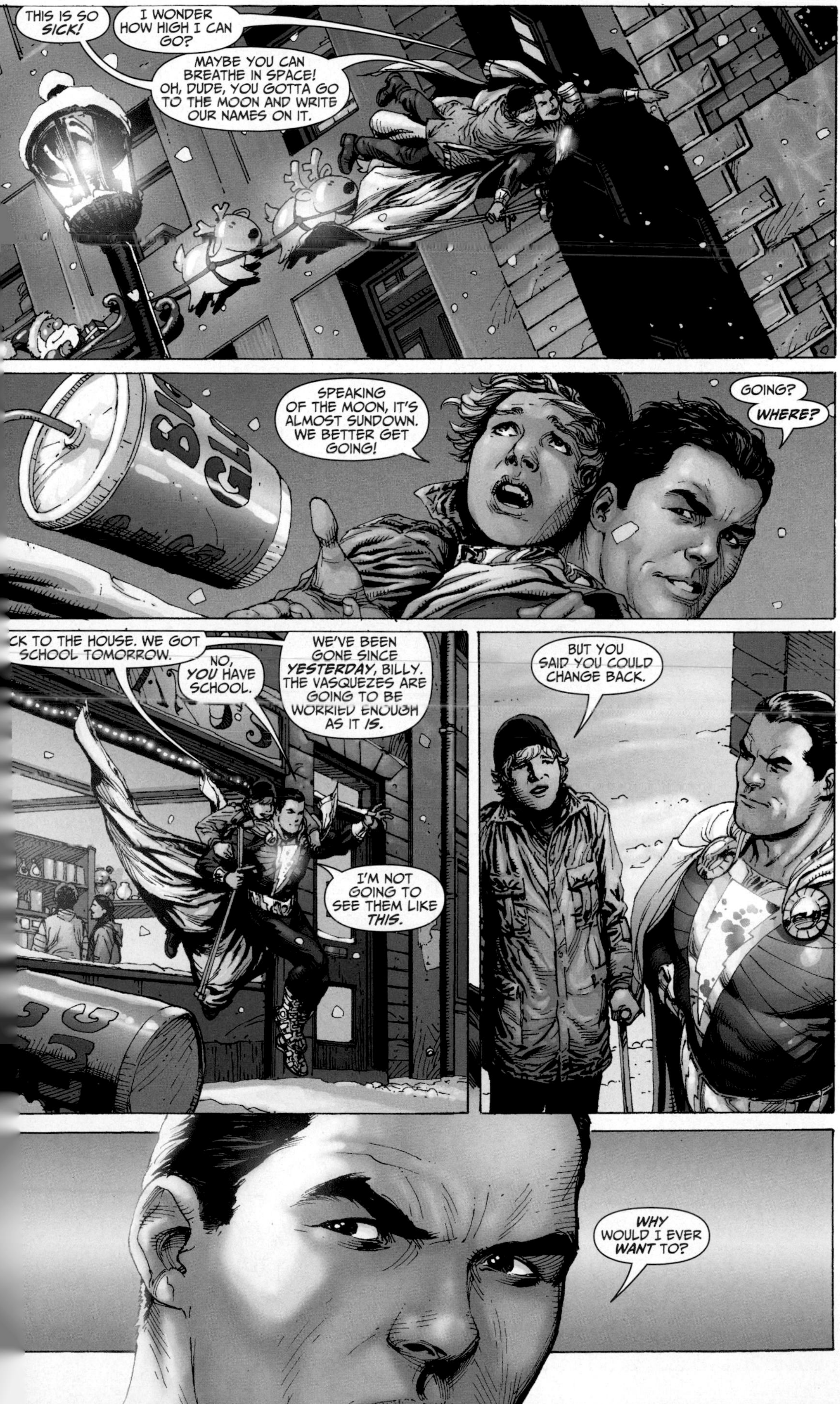

THIS IS SO SICK!
I WONDER HOW HIGH I CAN GO?
MAYBE YOU CAN BREATHE IN SPACE! OH, DUDE, YOU GOTTA GO TO THE MOON AND WRITE OUR NAMES ON IT.
SPEAKING OF THE MOON, IT'S ALMOST SUNDOWN. WE BETTER GET GOING!
GOING? WHERE?
CK TO THE HOUSE. WE GOT SCHOOL TOMORROW.
NO, YOU HAVE SCHOOL.
WE'VE BEEN GONE SINCE YESTERDAY, BILLY. THE VASQUEZES ARE GOING TO BE WORRIED ENOUGH AS IT IS.
I'M NOT GOING TO SEE THEM LIKE THIS.
BUT YOU SAID YOU COULD CHANGE BACK.
WHY WOULD I EVER WANT TO?

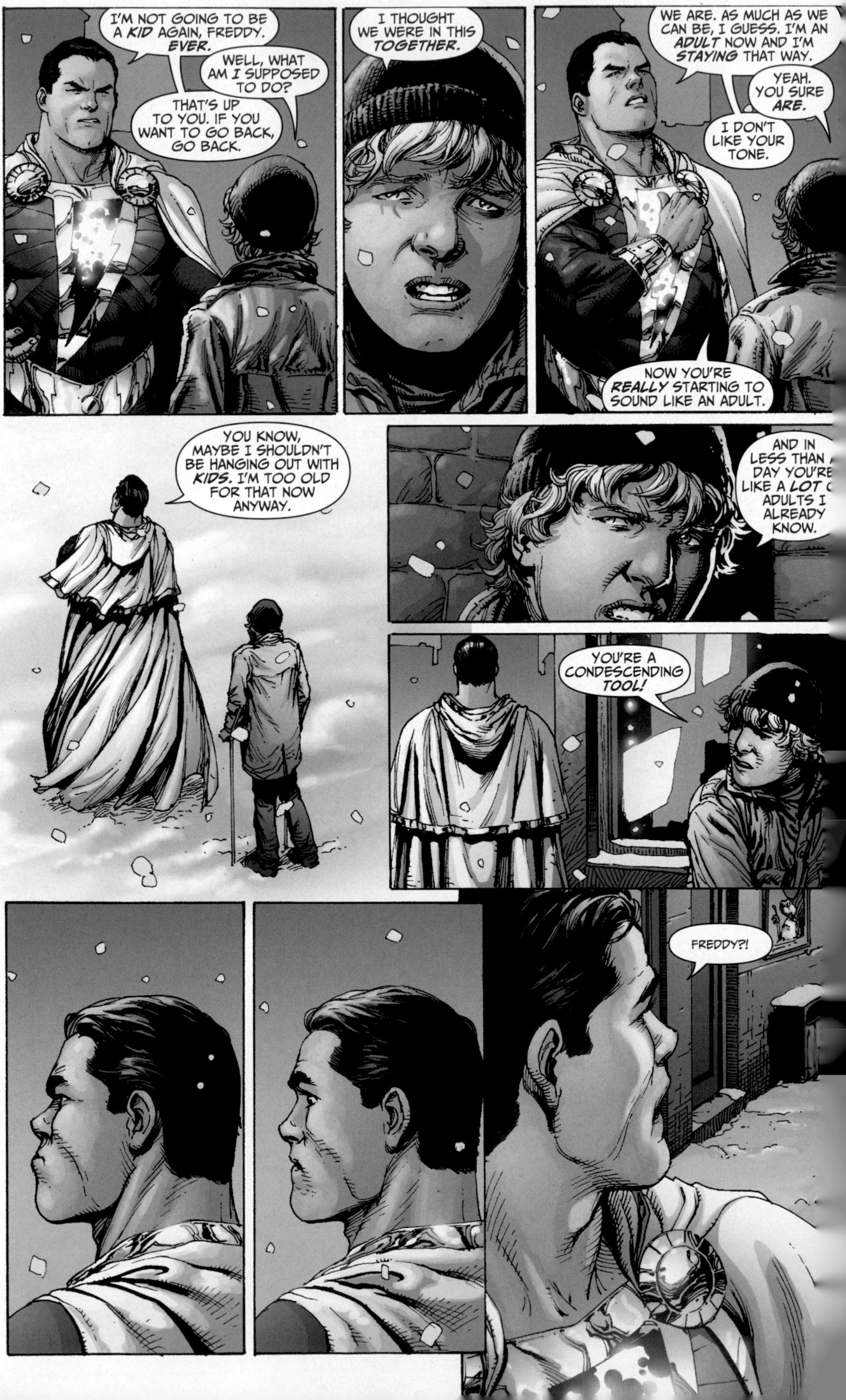

I'M NOT GOING TO BE A KID AGAIN, FREDDY. EVER.
WELL, WHAT AM I SUPPOSED TO DO?
THAT'S UP TO YOU. IF YOU WANT TO GO BACK, GO BACK.
I THOUGHT WE WERE IN THIS TOGETHER.
WE ARE. AS MUCH AS WE CAN BE, I GUESS. I'M AN ADULT NOW AND I'M STAYING THAT WAY.
YEAH. YOU SURE ARE.
I DON'T LIKE YOUR TONE.
NOW YOU'RE REALLY STARTING TO SOUND LIKE AN ADULT.
YOU KNOW, MAYBE I SHOULDN'T BE HANGING OUT WITH KIDS. I'M TOO OLD FOR THAT NOW ANYWAY.
AND IN LESS THAN DAY YOU'RE LIKE A LOT ADULTS I ALREADY KNOW.
YOU'RE A CONDESCENDING TOOL!
FREDDY?!

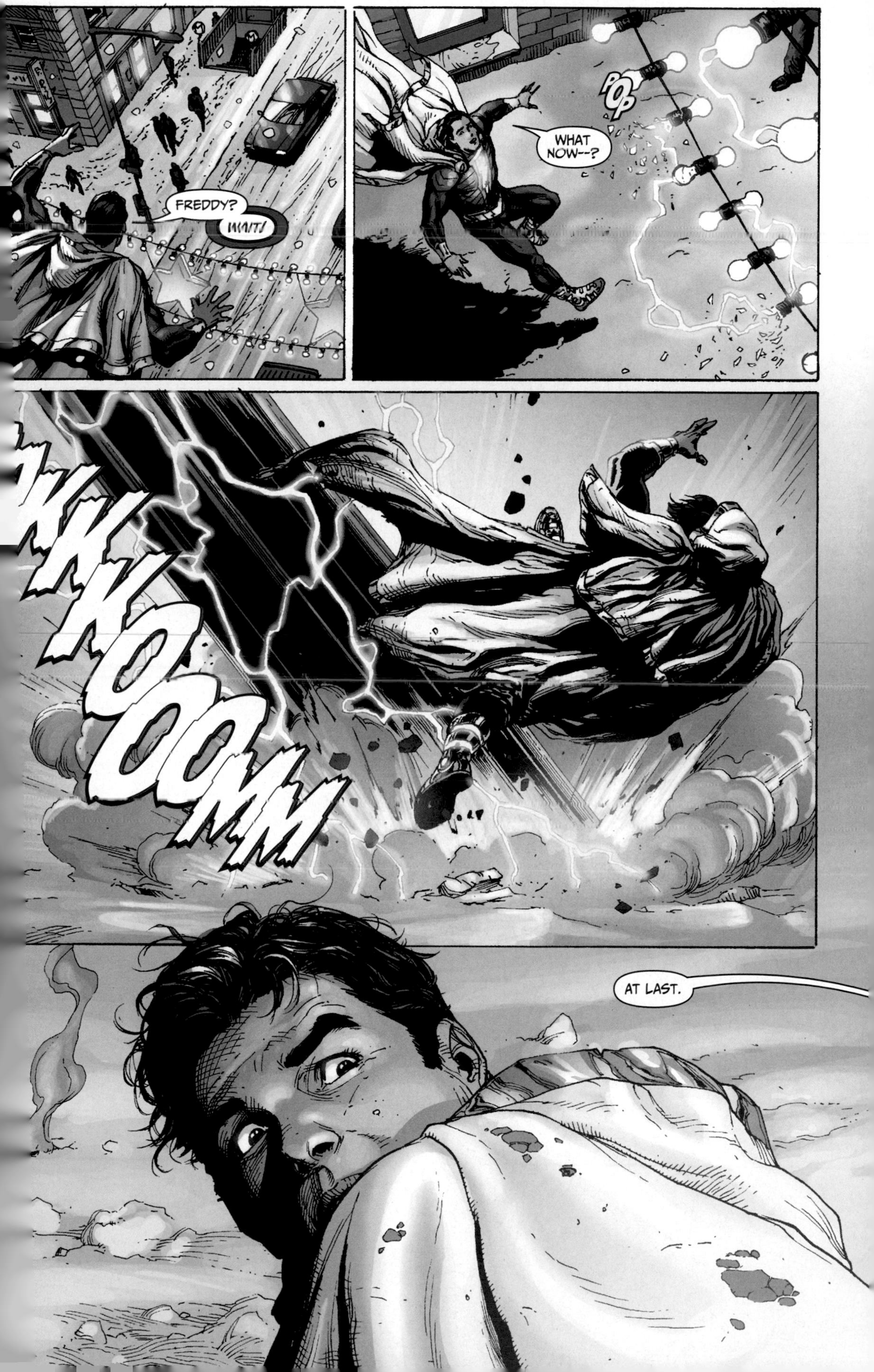
FREDDY?
WAIT!
POP
WHAT NOW--?
KKKOOOMM
AT LAST.

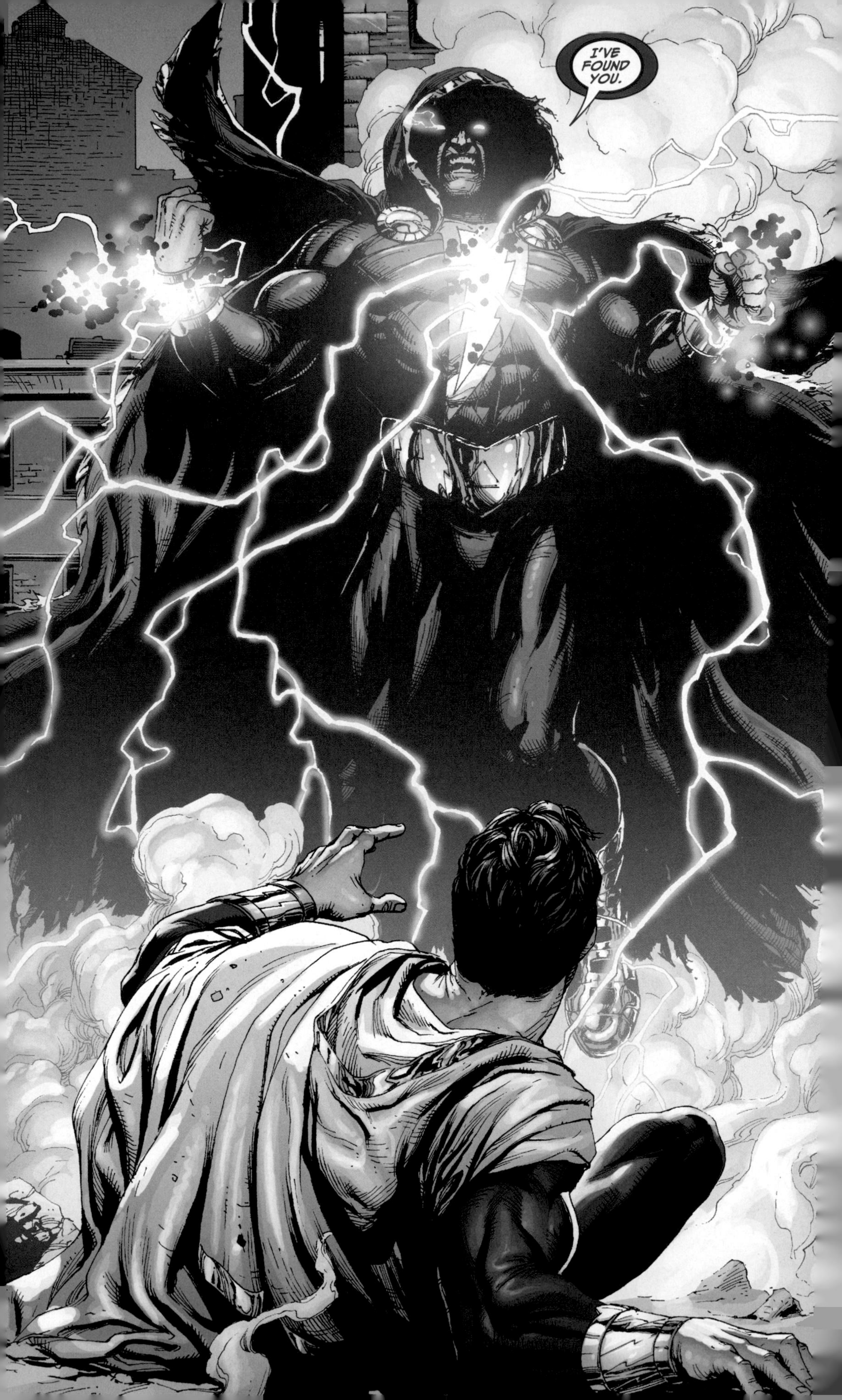
I'VE FOUND YOU.

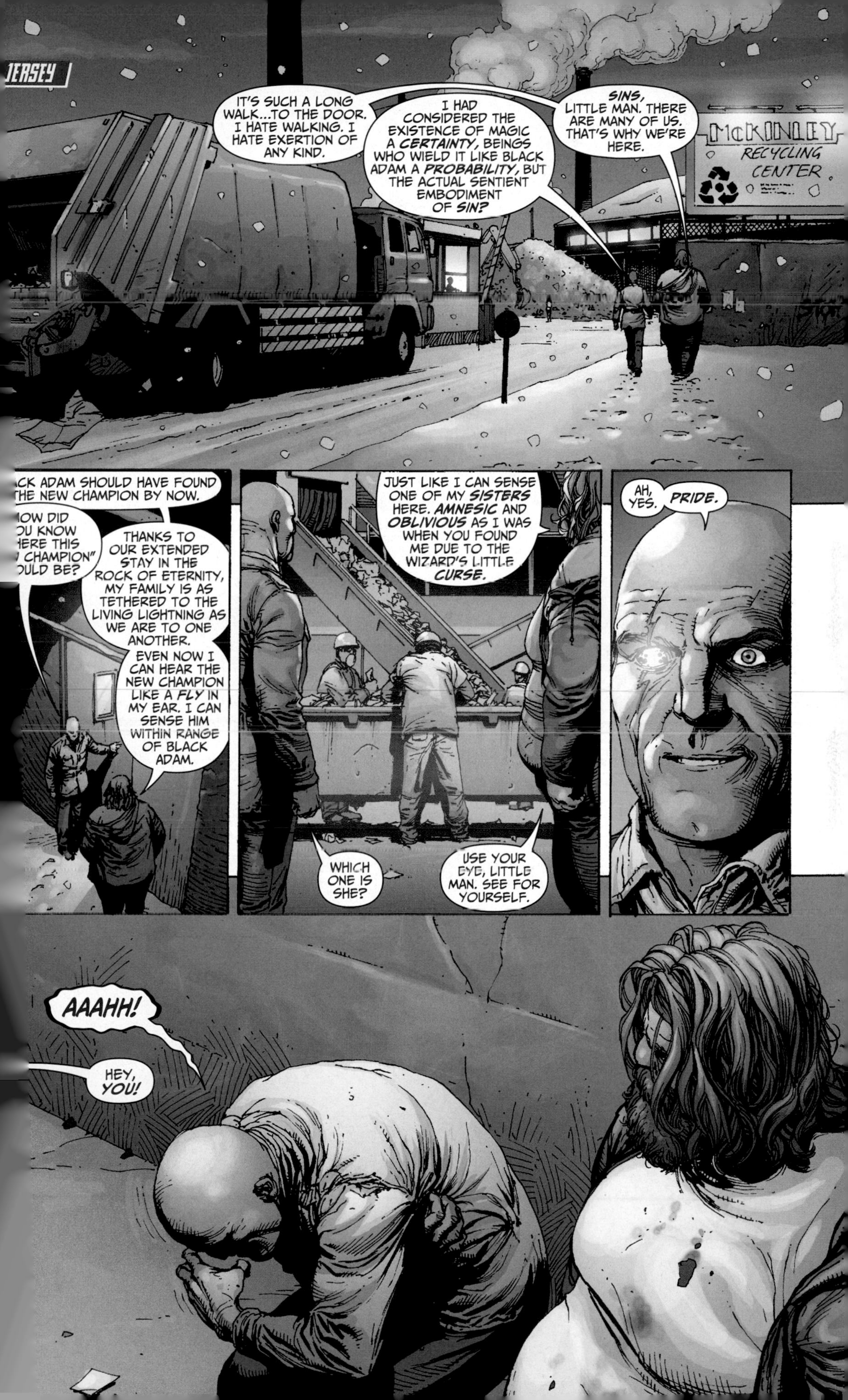
JERSEY
IT'S SUCH A LONG WALK...TO THE DOOR. I HATE WALKING. I HATE EXERTION OF ANY KIND.
I HAD CONSIDERED THE EXISTENCE OF MAGIC A *CERTAINTY,* BEINGS WHO WIELD IT LIKE BLACK ADAM A *PROBABILITY,* BUT THE ACTUAL SENTIENT EMBODIMENT OF *SIN?*
SINS, LITTLE MAN. THERE ARE MANY OF US. THAT'S WHY WE'RE HERE.
McKINLEY RECYCLING CENTER
CK ADAM SHOULD HAVE FOUND THE NEW CHAMPION BY NOW.
HOW DID OU KNOW HERE THIS CHAMPION" OULD BE?
THANKS TO OUR EXTENDED STAY IN THE ROCK OF ETERNITY, MY FAMILY IS AS TETHERED TO THE LIVING LIGHTNING AS WE ARE TO ONE ANOTHER.
EVEN NOW I CAN HEAR THE NEW CHAMPION LIKE A *FLY* IN MY EAR. I CAN SENSE HIM WITHIN RANGE OF BLACK ADAM.
JUST LIKE I CAN SENSE ONE OF MY *SISTERS* HERE. *AMNESIC* AND *OBLIVIOUS* AS I WAS WHEN YOU FOUND ME DUE TO THE WIZARD'S LITTLE *CURSE.*
WHICH ONE IS SHE?
USE YOUR EYE, LITTLE MAN. SEE FOR YOURSELF.
AH, YES. *PRIDE.*
AAAHH!
HEY, *YOU!*

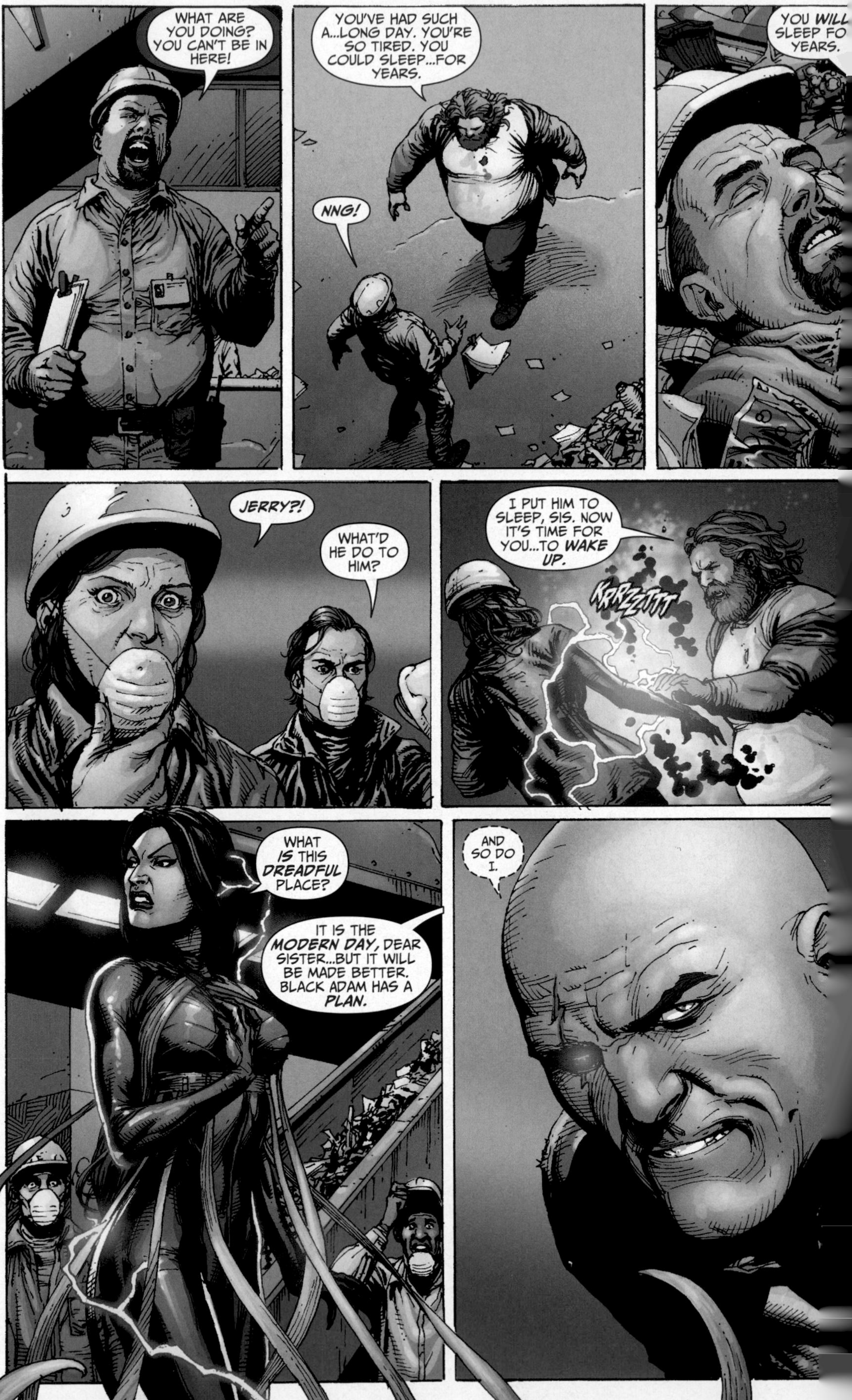
WHAT ARE YOU DOING? YOU CAN'T BE IN HERE!
YOU'VE HAD SUCH A...LONG DAY. YOU'RE SO TIRED. YOU COULD SLEEP...FOR YEARS.
NNG!
YOU WILL SLEEP FO YEARS.
JERRY?!
WHAT'D HE DO TO HIM?
I PUT HIM TO SLEEP, SIS. NOW IT'S TIME FOR YOU...TO WAKE UP.
KRRZZTTT
WHAT IS THIS DREADFUL PLACE?
IT IS THE MODERN DAY, DEAR SISTER...BUT IT WILL BE MADE BETTER. BLACK ADAM HAS A PLAN.
AND SO DO I.

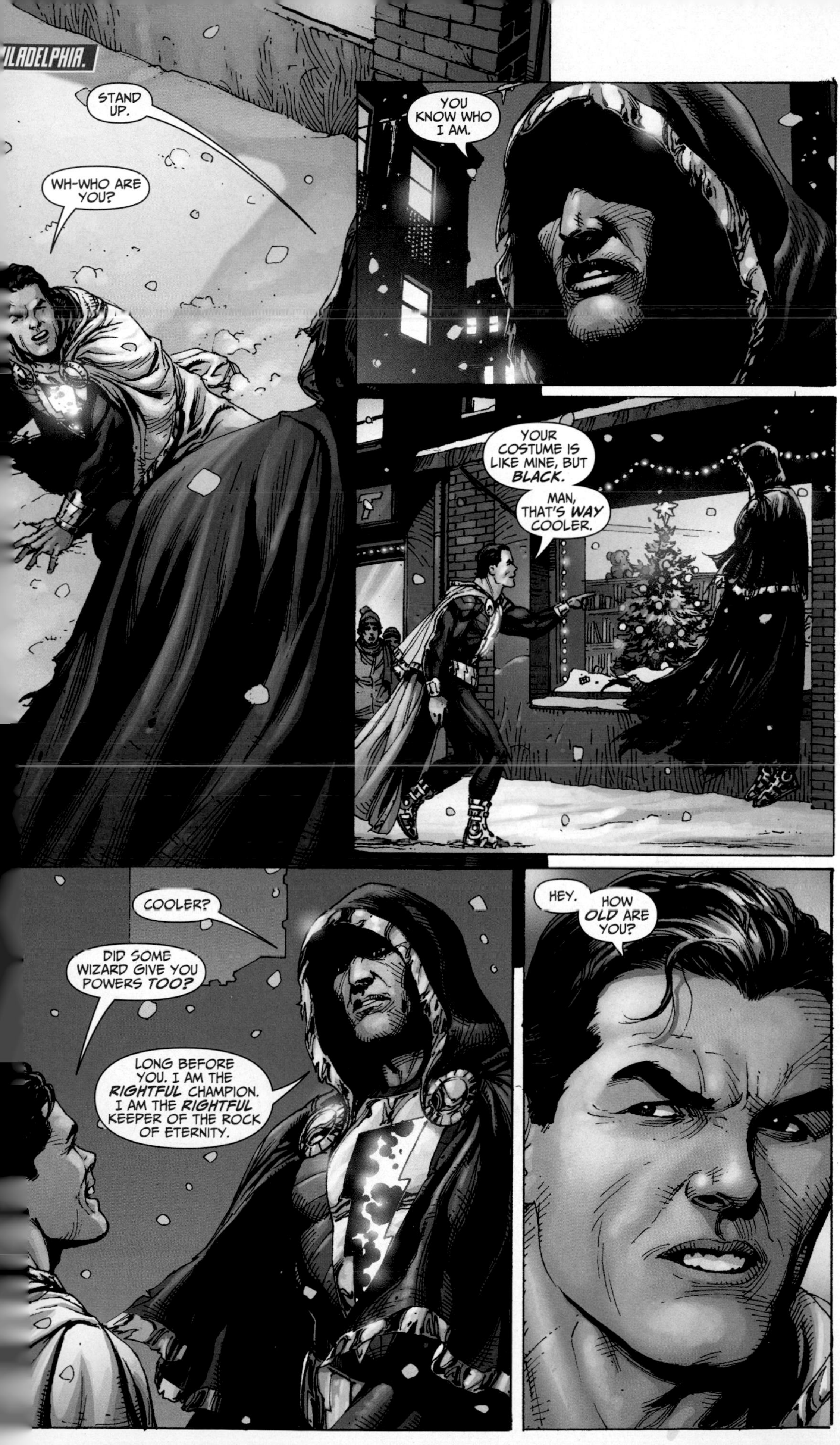

...ILADELPHIA.
STAND UP.
WH-WHO ARE YOU?
YOU KNOW WHO I AM.
YOUR COSTUME IS LIKE MINE, BUT BLACK.
MAN, THAT'S WAY COOLER.
COOLER?
DID SOME WIZARD GIVE YOU POWERS TOO?
LONG BEFORE YOU. I AM THE RIGHTFUL CHAMPION. I AM THE RIGHTFUL KEEPER OF THE ROCK OF ETERNITY.
HEY.
HOW OLD ARE YOU?

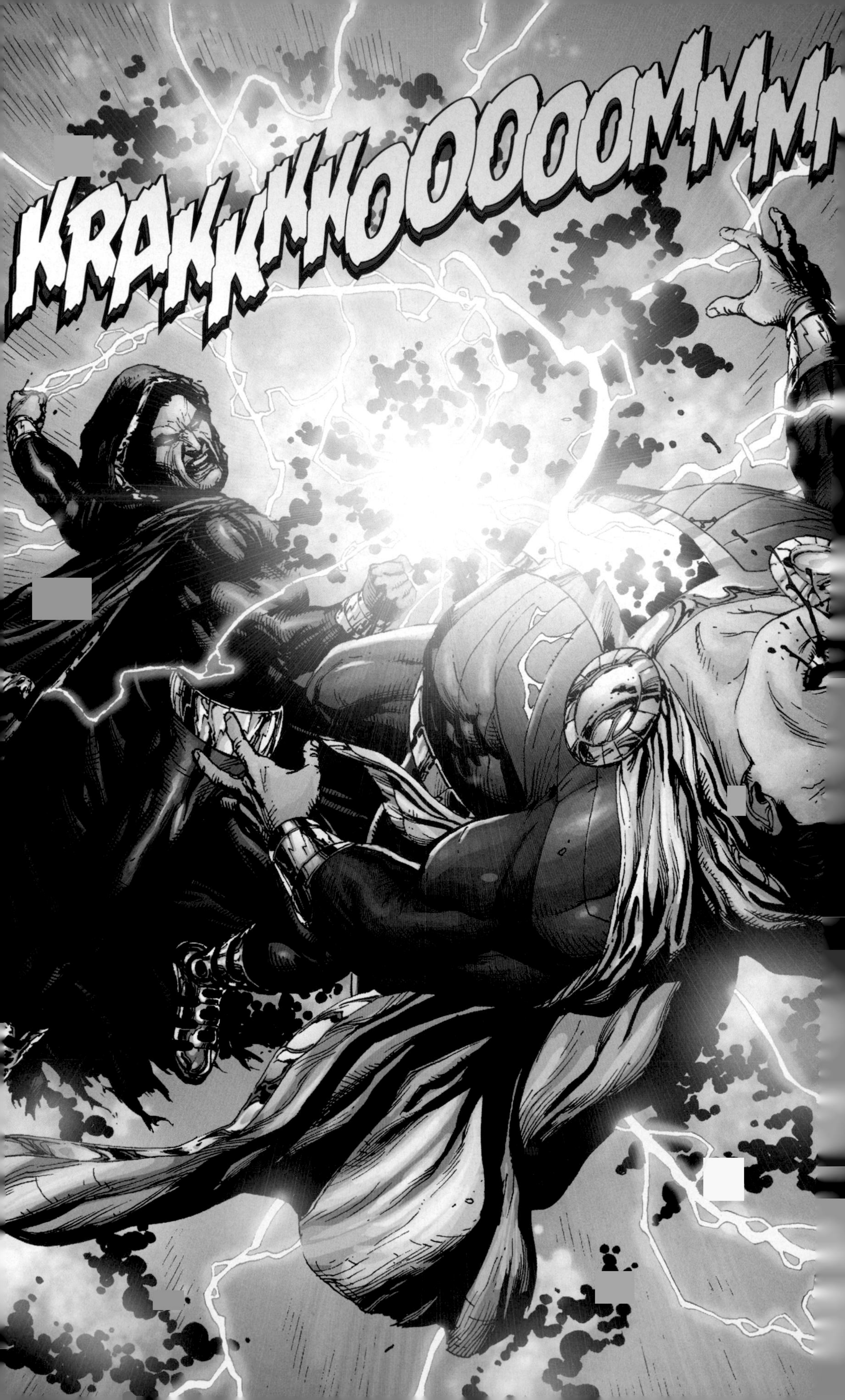
KRAKKKOOOOOOMMM

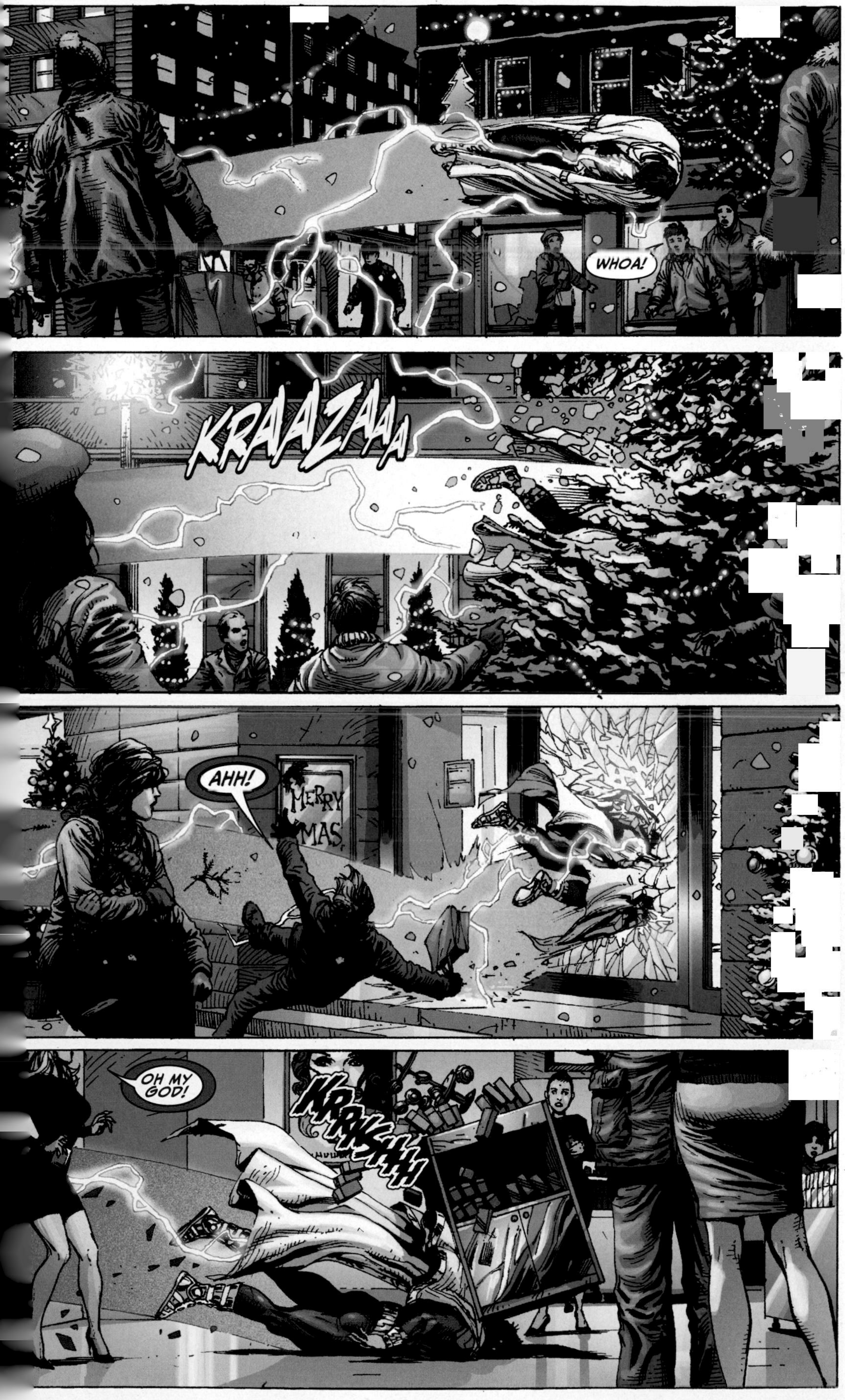
WHOA!
KRAAZAAA
AHH!
MERRY
MAS
OH MY GOD!
KRRASHH

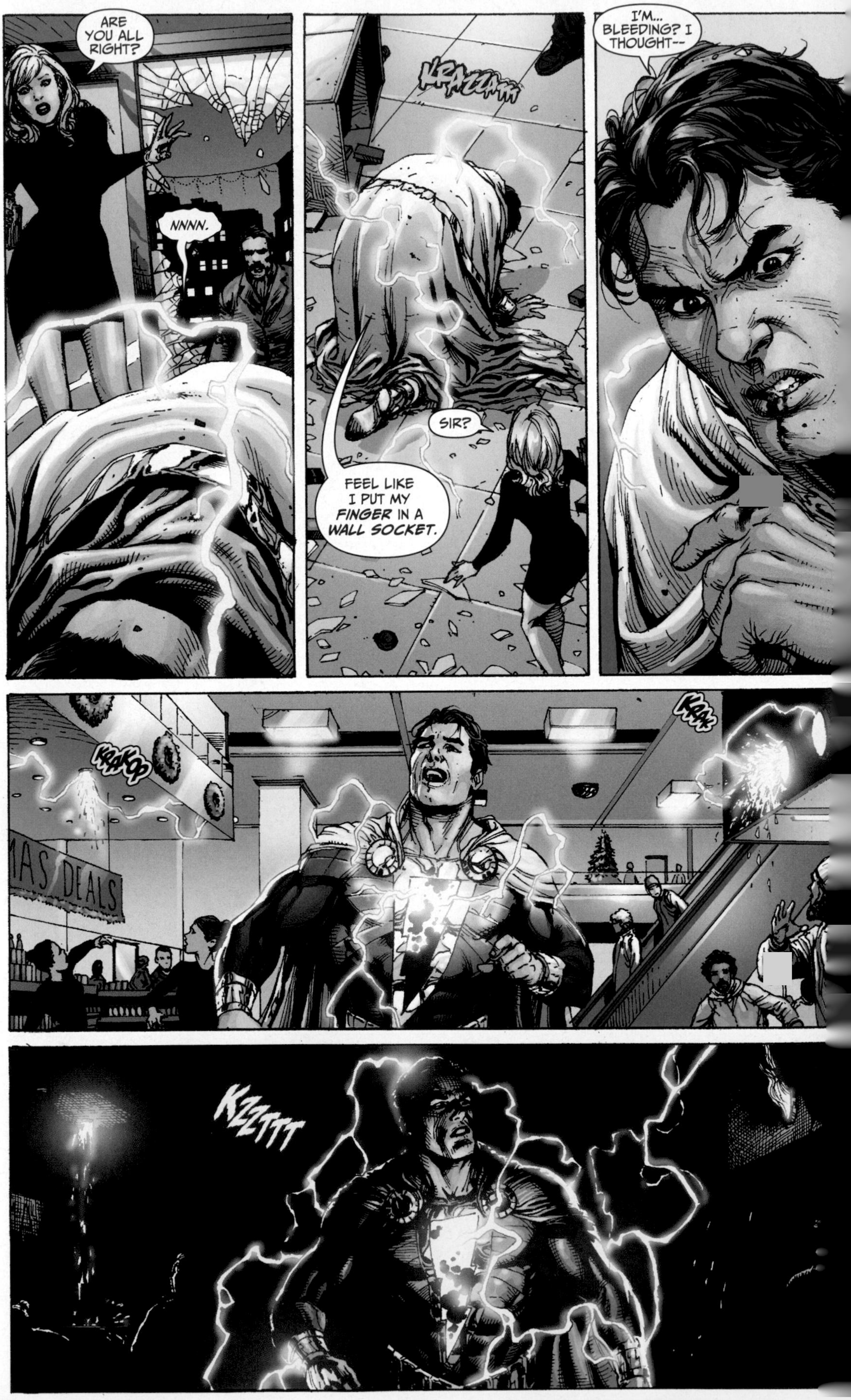
ARE YOU ALL RIGHT?
NNNN.
KRAZZAM
SIR?
FEEL LIKE I PUT MY FINGER IN A WALL SOCKET.
I'M... BLEEDING? I THOUGHT--
KRAKOP
KRAK
MAS DEALS
KZZTTT

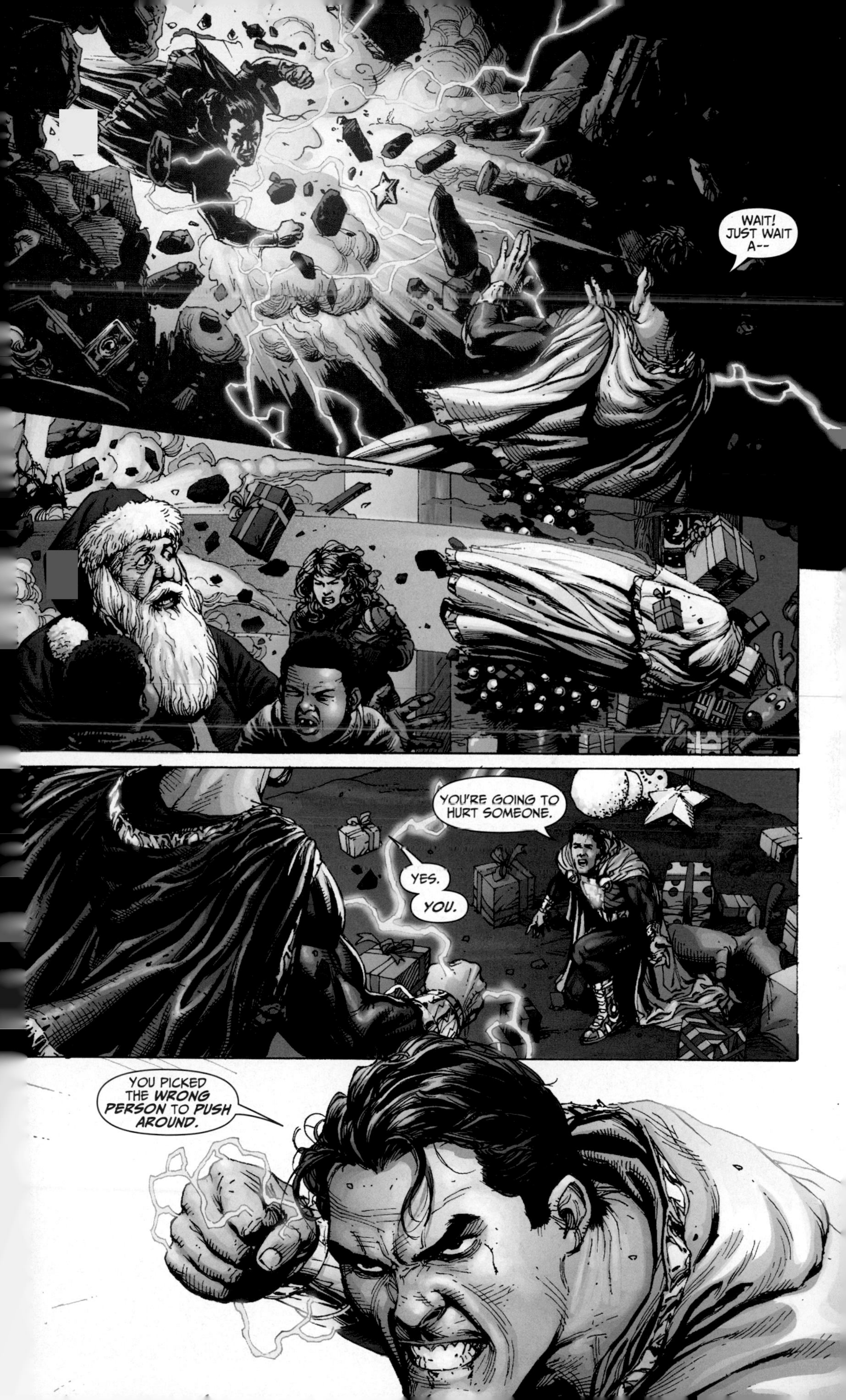
WAIT! JUST WAIT A--
YOU'RE GOING TO HURT SOMEONE.
YES.
YOU.
YOU PICKED THE WRONG PERSON TO PUSH AROUND.

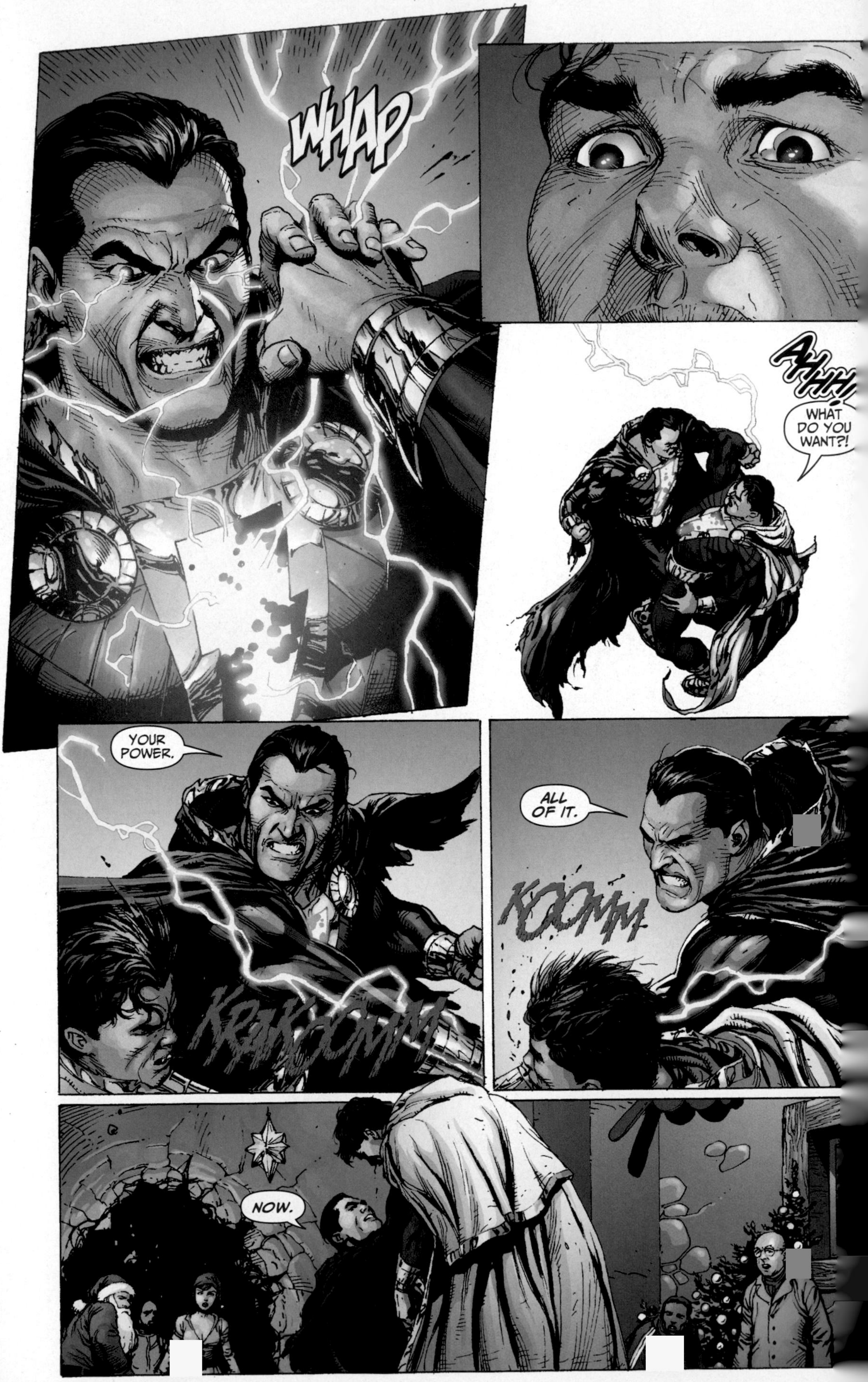
WHAP
AHHH!
WHAT DO YOU WANT?!
YOUR POWER.
KRAKOOMM
ALL OF IT.
KOOMM
NOW.

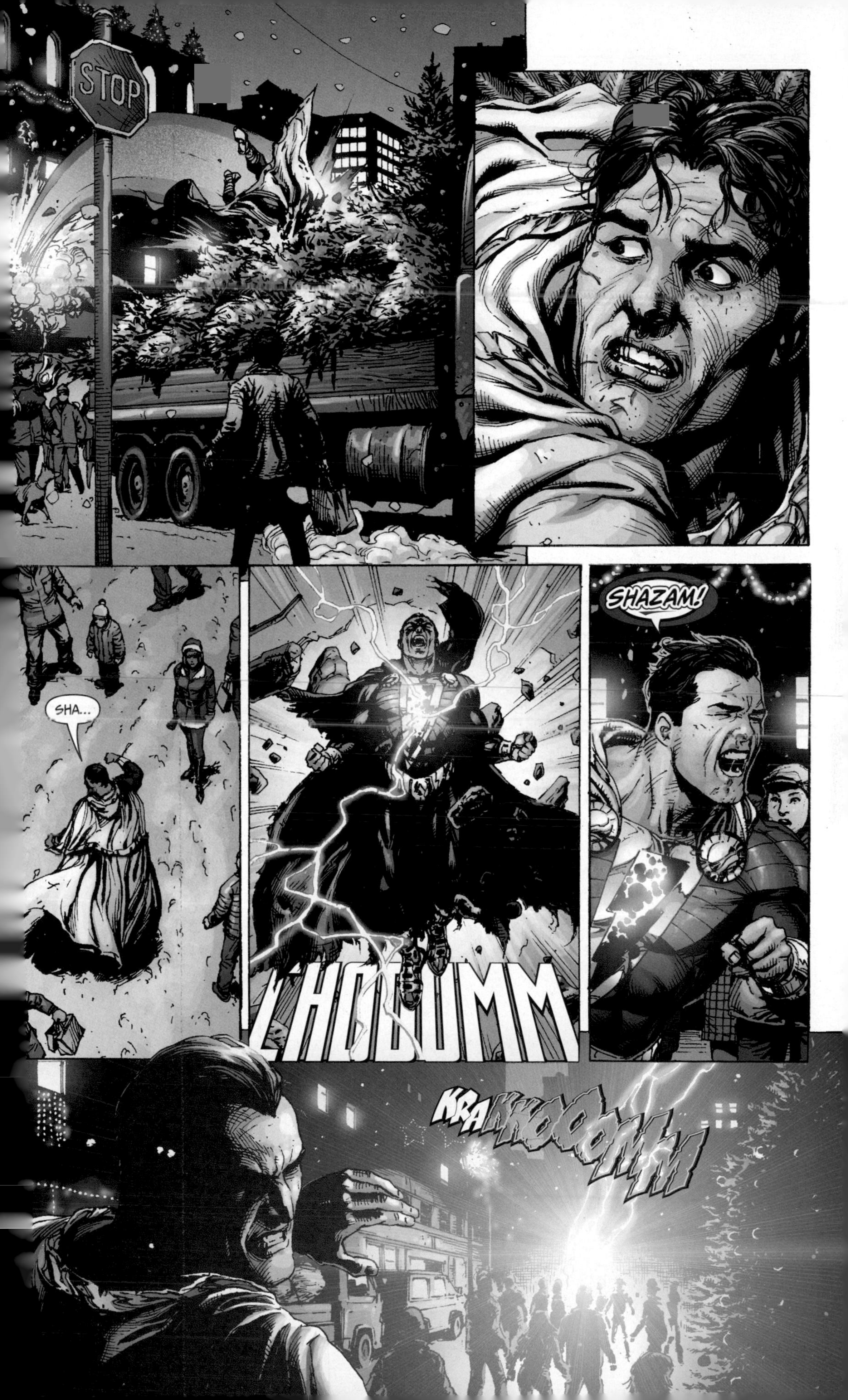
STOP
SHA...
CHOOOMM
SHAZAM!
KRAKKOOOMM

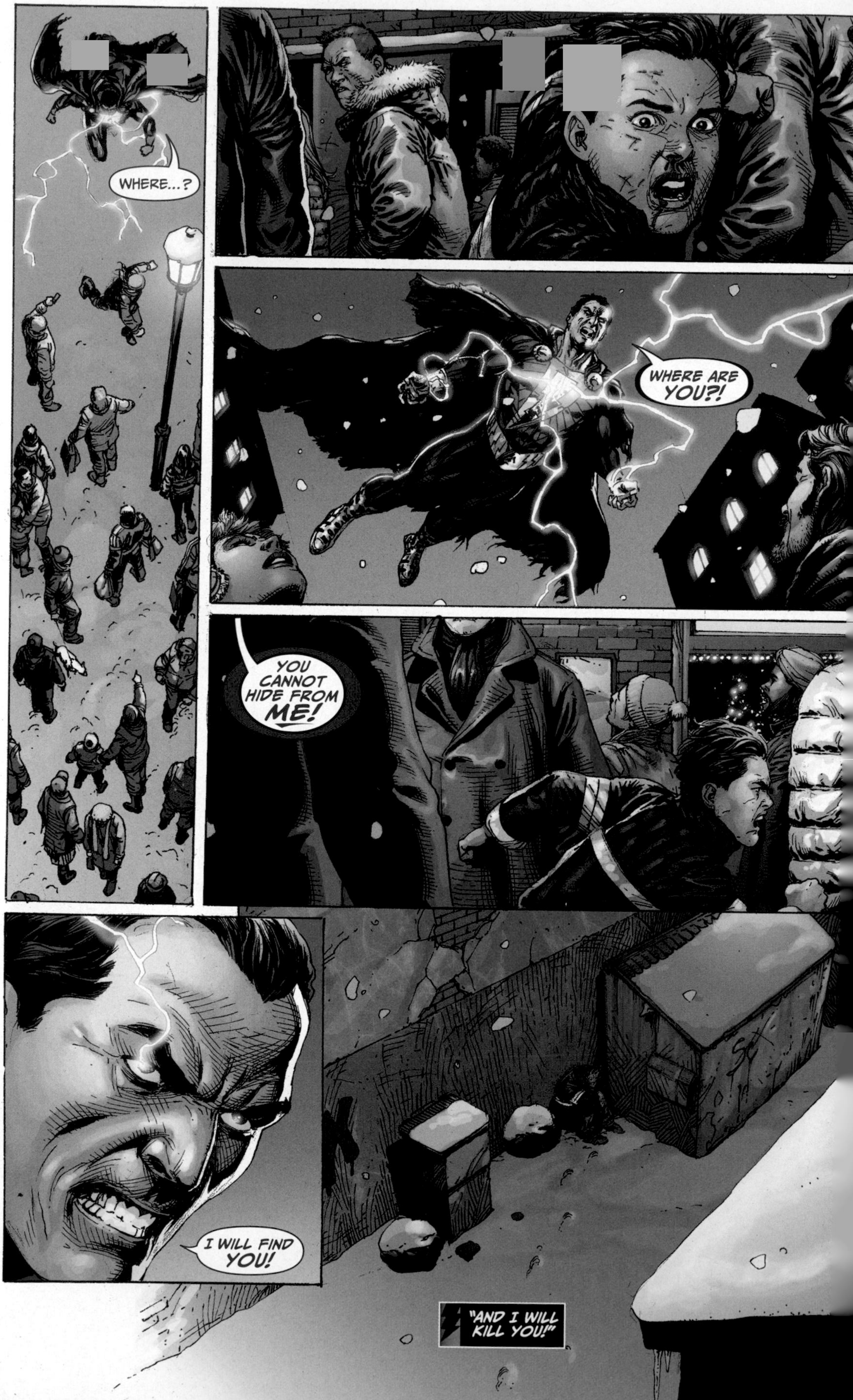
WHERE...?
WHERE ARE YOU?!
YOU CANNOT HIDE FROM ME!
I WILL FIND YOU!
"AND I WILL KILL YOU!"

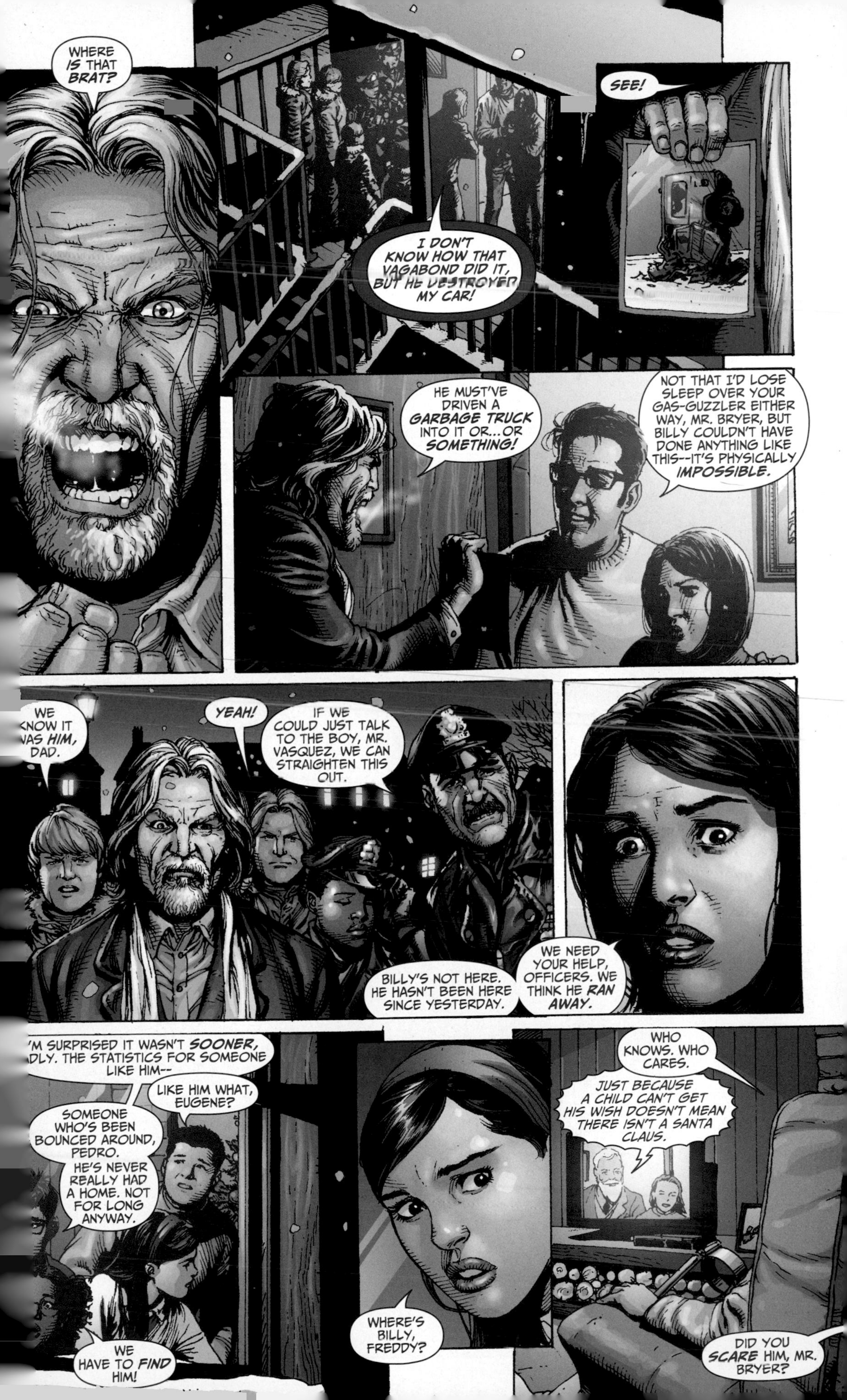

WHERE IS THAT BRAT?
SEE!
I DON'T KNOW HOW THAT VAGABOND DID IT, BUT HE DESTROYED MY CAR!
HE MUST'VE DRIVEN A GARBAGE TRUCK INTO IT OR...OR SOMETHING!
NOT THAT I'D LOSE SLEEP OVER YOUR GAS-GUZZLER EITHER WAY, MR. BRYER, BUT BILLY COULDN'T HAVE DONE ANYTHING LIKE THIS--IT'S PHYSICALLY IMPOSSIBLE.
WE KNOW IT VAS HIM, DAD.
YEAH!
IF WE COULD JUST TALK TO THE BOY, MR. VASQUEZ, WE CAN STRAIGHTEN THIS OUT.
BILLY'S NOT HERE. HE HASN'T BEEN HERE SINCE YESTERDAY.
WE NEED YOUR HELP, OFFICERS. WE THINK HE RAN AWAY.
'M SURPRISED IT WASN'T SOONER, ADLY. THE STATISTICS FOR SOMEONE LIKE HIM--
LIKE HIM WHAT, EUGENE?
SOMEONE WHO'S BEEN BOUNCED AROUND, PEDRO.
HE'S NEVER REALLY HAD A HOME. NOT FOR LONG ANYWAY.
WE HAVE TO FIND HIM!
WHERE'S BILLY, FREDDY?
WHO KNOWS. WHO CARES.
JUST BECAUSE A CHILD CAN'T GET HIS WISH DOESN'T MEAN THERE ISN'T A SANTA CLAUS.
DID YOU SCARE HIM, MR. BRYER?

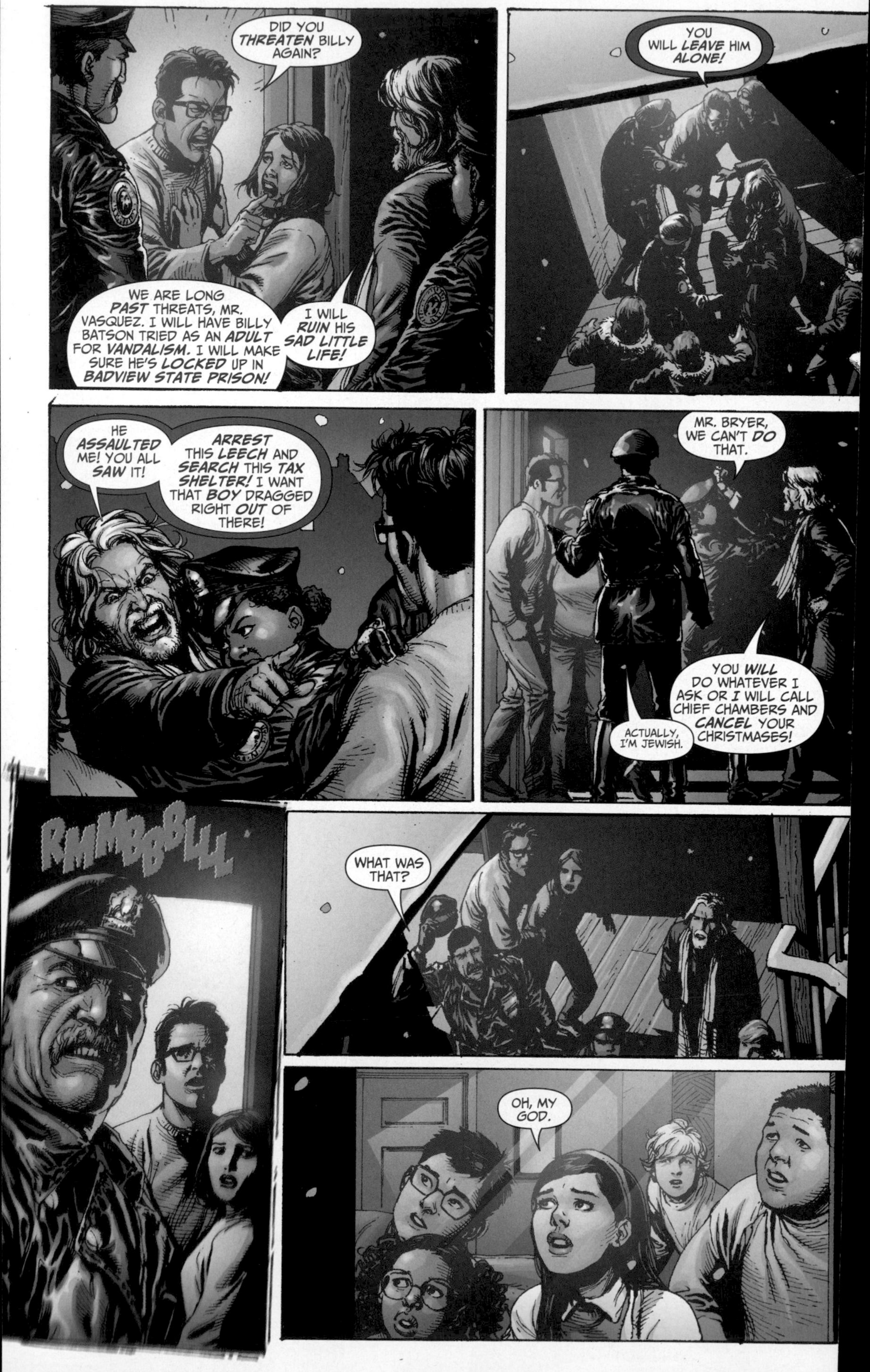
DID YOU THREATEN BILLY AGAIN?
WE ARE LONG PAST THREATS, MR. VASQUEZ. I WILL HAVE BILLY BATSON TRIED AS AN ADULT FOR VANDALISM. I WILL MAKE SURE HE'S LOCKED UP IN BADVIEW STATE PRISON!
I WILL RUIN HIS SAD LITTLE LIFE!
YOU WILL LEAVE HIM ALONE!
HE ASSAULTED ME! YOU ALL SAW IT!
ARREST THIS LEECH AND SEARCH THIS TAX SHELTER! I WANT THAT BOY DRAGGED RIGHT OUT OF THERE!
MR. BRYER, WE CAN'T DO THAT.
YOU WILL DO WHATEVER I ASK OR I WILL CALL CHIEF CHAMBERS AND CANCEL YOUR CHRISTMASES!
ACTUALLY, I'M JEWISH.
RMMBBBLLL
WHAT WAS THAT?
OH, MY GOD.

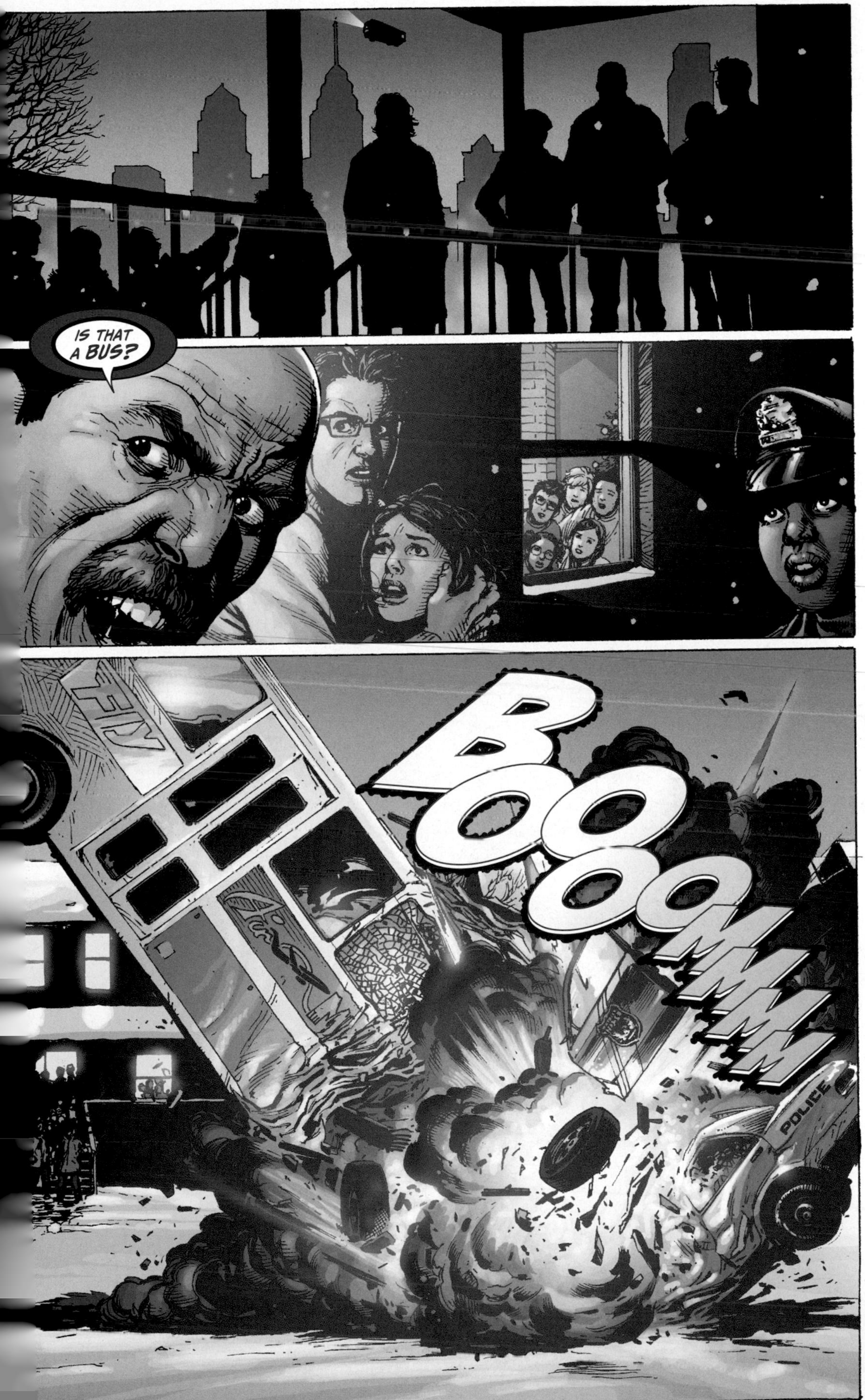
IS THAT A BUS?
BOOOMMM
POLICE

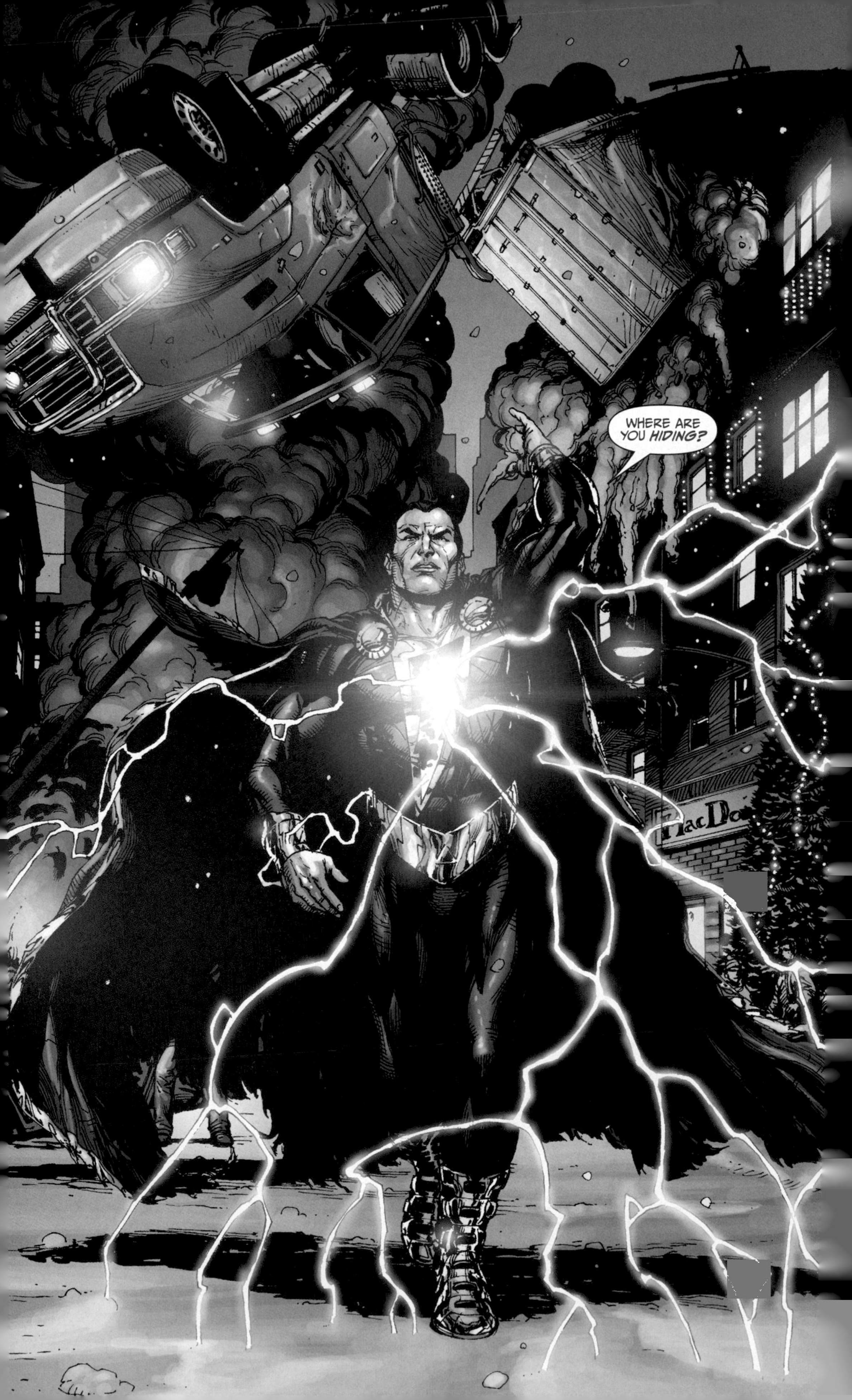
WHERE ARE YOU HIDING?

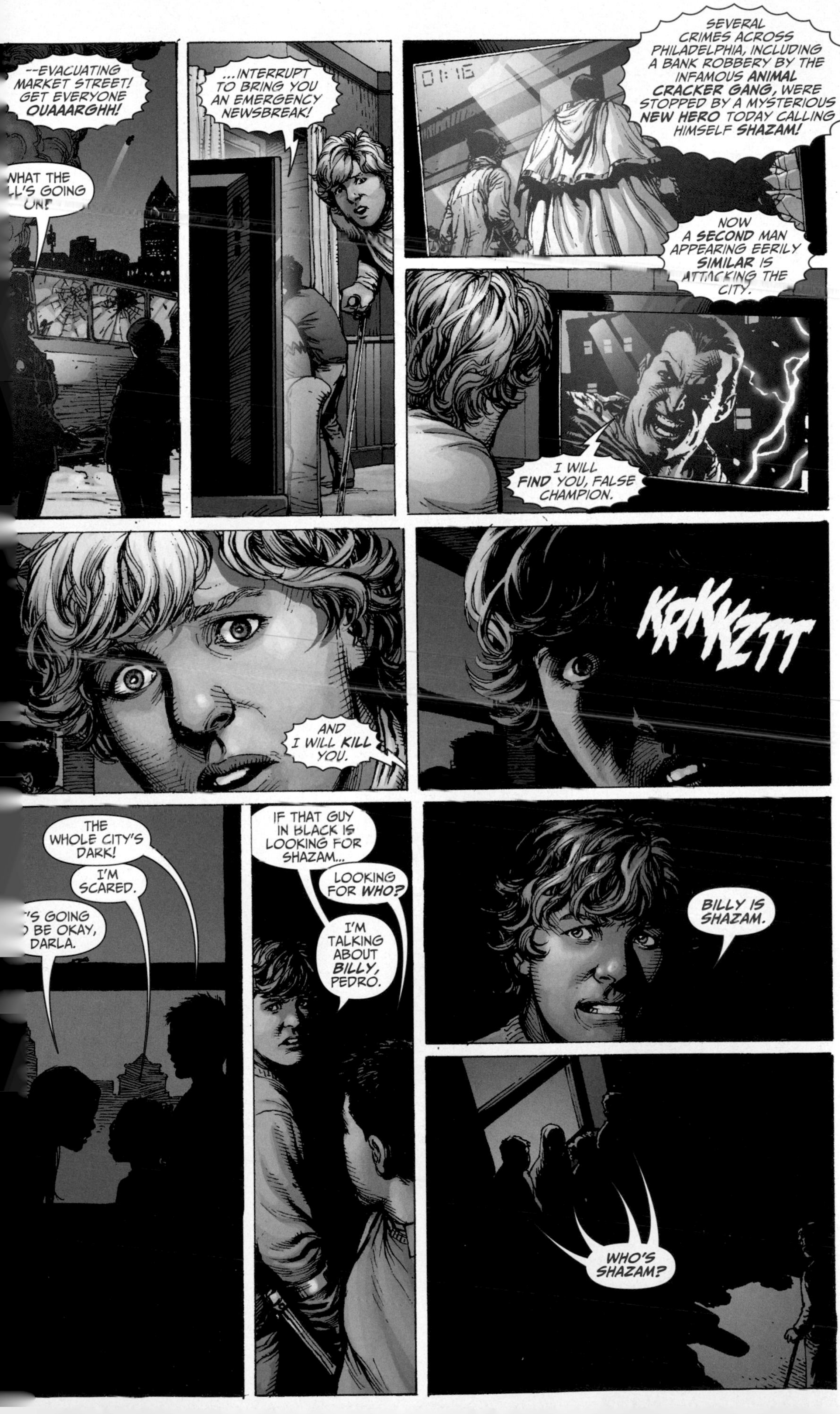
--EVACUATING MARKET STREET! GET EVERYONE OUAAARGHH!
WHAT THE ...LL'S GOING ON?
...INTERRUPT TO BRING YOU AN EMERGENCY NEWSBREAK!
SEVERAL CRIMES ACROSS PHILADELPHIA, INCLUDING A BANK ROBBERY BY THE INFAMOUS ANIMAL CRACKER GANG, WERE STOPPED BY A MYSTERIOUS NEW HERO TODAY CALLING HIMSELF SHAZAM!
01:16
NOW A SECOND MAN APPEARING EERILY SIMILAR IS ATTACKING THE CITY.
I WILL FIND YOU, FALSE CHAMPION.
AND I WILL KILL YOU.
KRKKZTT
THE WHOLE CITY'S DARK!
I'M SCARED.
...'S GOING ...O BE OKAY, DARLA.
IF THAT GUY IN BLACK IS LOOKING FOR SHAZAM...
LOOKING FOR WHO?
I'M TALKING ABOUT BILLY, PEDRO.
BILLY IS SHAZAM.
WHO'S SHAZAM?

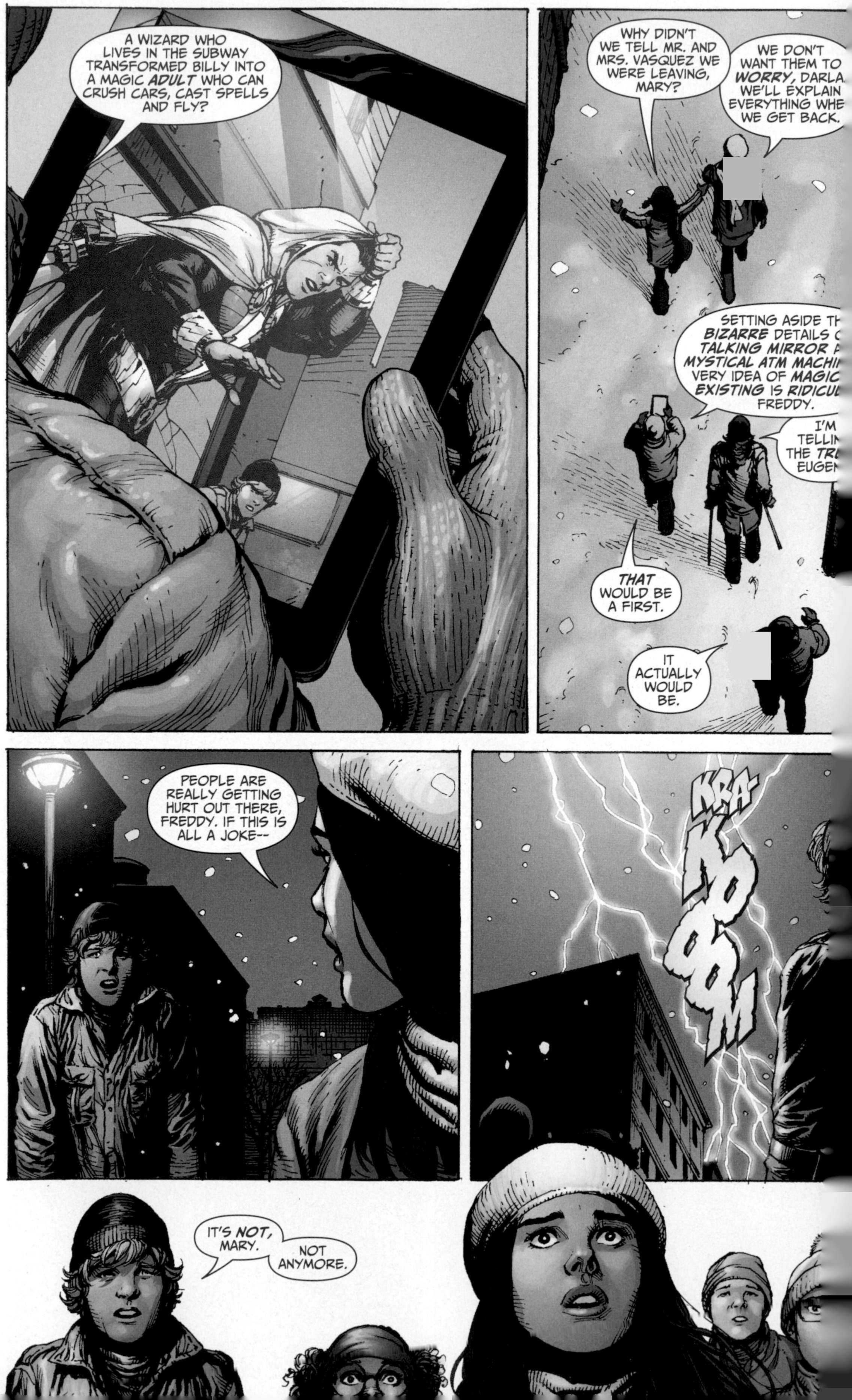

A WIZARD WHO LIVES IN THE SUBWAY TRANSFORMED BILLY INTO A MAGIC ADULT WHO CAN CRUSH CARS, CAST SPELLS AND FLY?
WHY DIDN'T WE TELL MR. AND MRS. VASQUEZ WE WERE LEAVING, MARY?
WE DON'T WANT THEM TO WORRY, DARLA. WE'LL EXPLAIN EVERYTHING WHE WE GET BACK.
SETTING ASIDE TH BIZARRE DETAILS C TALKING MIRROR A MYSTICAL ATM MACHI VERY IDEA OF MAGIC EXISTING IS RIDICUL FREDDY.
I'M TELLIN THE TR EUGEN
THAT WOULD BE A FIRST.
IT ACTUALLY WOULD BE.
PEOPLE ARE REALLY GETTING HURT OUT THERE, FREDDY. IF THIS IS ALL A JOKE--
KRA-KOOOOM
IT'S NOT, MARY.
NOT ANYMORE.

"THINK I KNOW WHERE WE CAN FIND BILLY."

YOU'D GO BACK AND FIGHT, WOULDN'T YOU, TAWNY?

BECAUSE YOU'RE A TIGER.

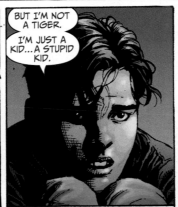

BUT I'M NOT A TIGER.

I'M JUST A KID...A STUPID KID.

BILLY?

FREDDY?

WHAT ARE YOU DOING HERE? AND WHY DID YOU BRING THE GOONIES?

WHAT ARE THE GOONIES?

YOU TURNED BACK TO YOU? YOU SAID YOU NEVER WOULD AGAIN, BUT--

WHY DID YOU BRING THEM?

BECAUSE WE WANT TO SEE YOU CHANGE INTO SHAZAM!

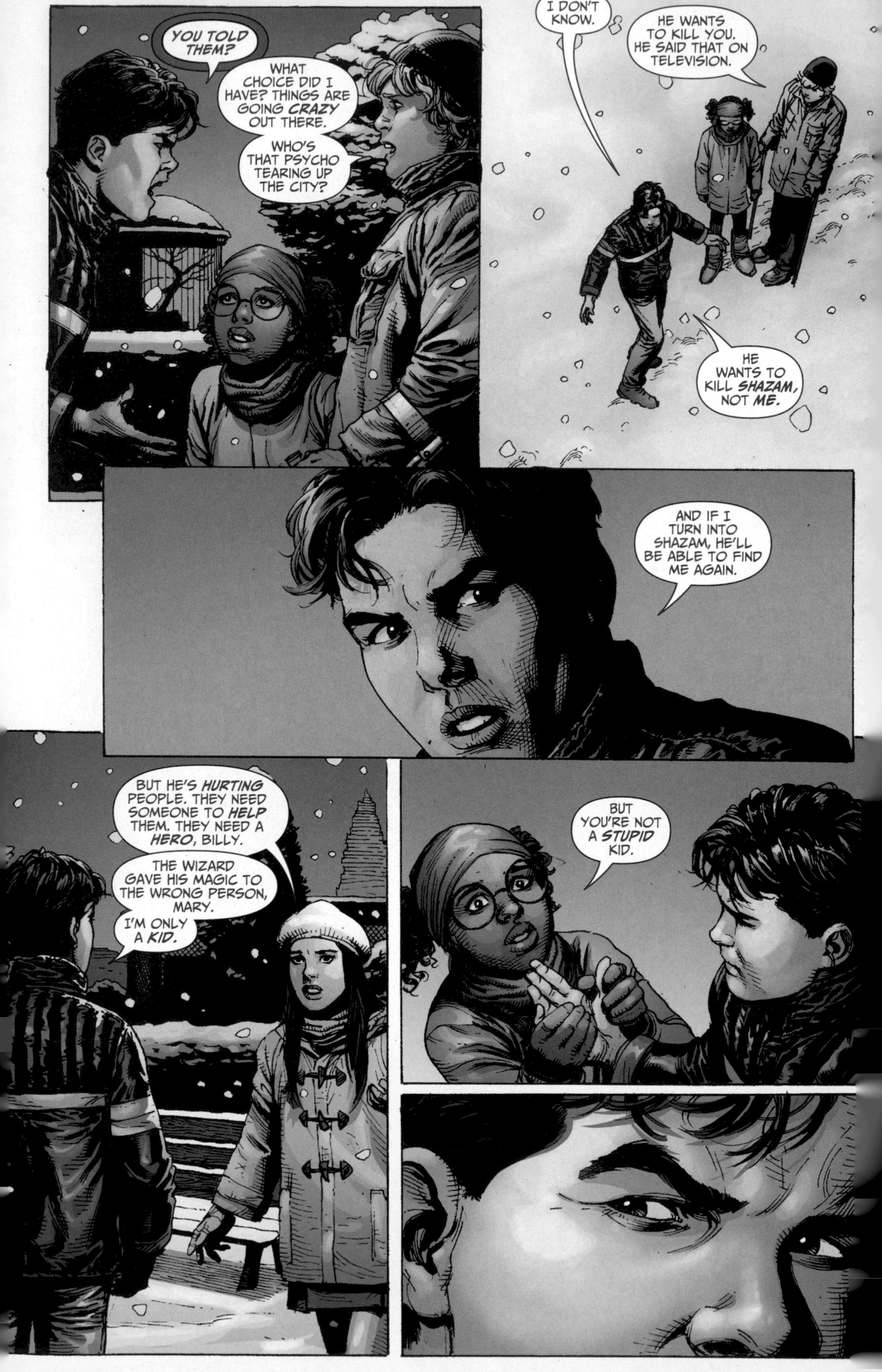
YOU TOLD THEM?
WHAT CHOICE DID I HAVE? THINGS ARE GOING CRAZY OUT THERE.
WHO'S THAT PSYCHO TEARING UP THE CITY?
I DON'T KNOW.
HE WANTS TO KILL YOU. HE SAID THAT ON TELEVISION.
HE WANTS TO KILL SHAZAM, NOT ME.
AND IF I TURN INTO SHAZAM, HE'LL BE ABLE TO FIND ME AGAIN.
BUT HE'S HURTING PEOPLE. THEY NEED SOMEONE TO HELP THEM. THEY NEED A HERO, BILLY.
THE WIZARD GAVE HIS MAGIC TO THE WRONG PERSON, MARY.
I'M ONLY A KID.
BUT YOU'RE NOT A STUPID KID.

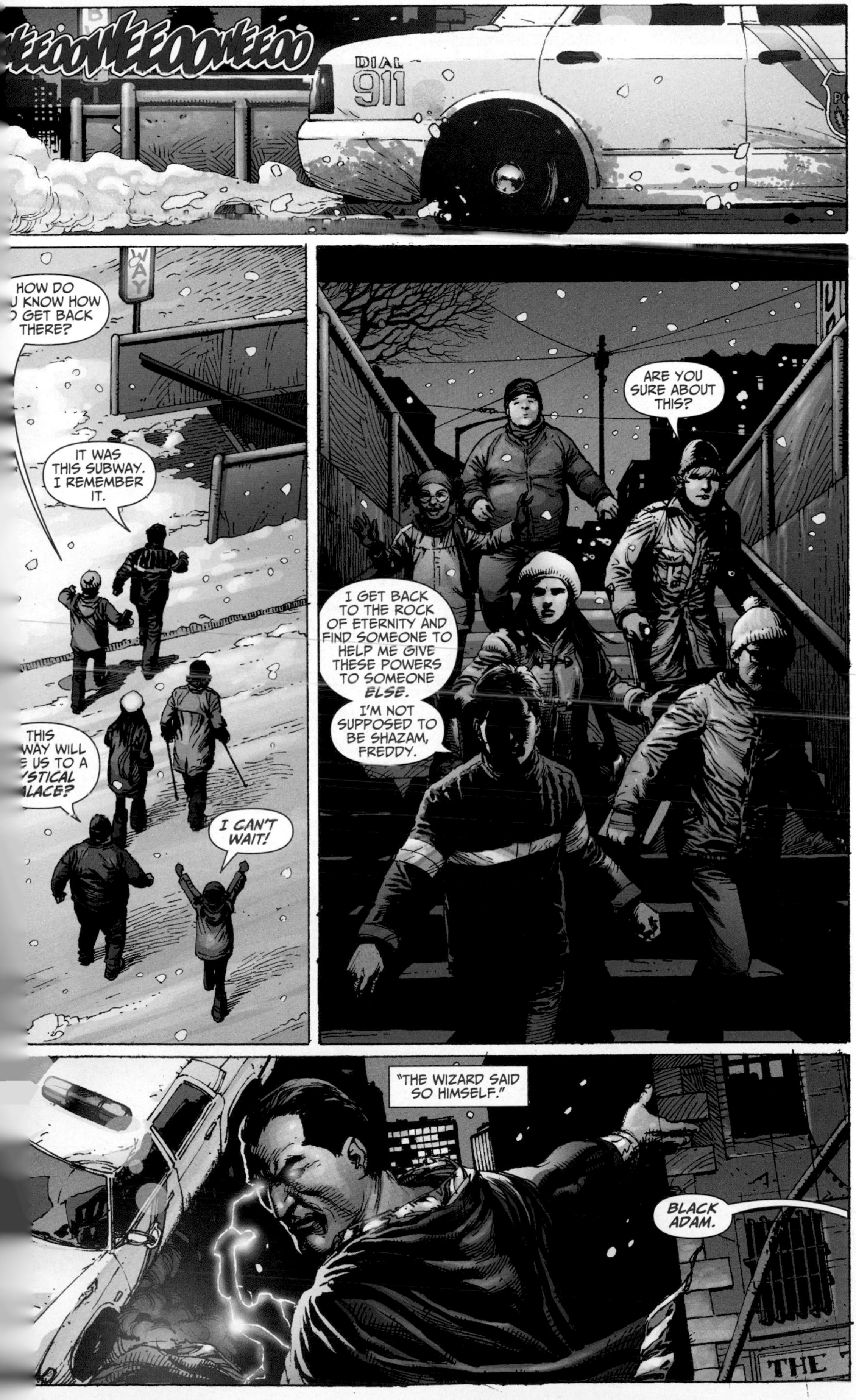
EEOOWEEOOWEEOO
DIAL 911
HOW DO U KNOW HOW D GET BACK THERE?
IT WAS THIS SUBWAY. I REMEMBER IT.
THIS WAY WILL E US TO A YSTICAL ALACE?
I CAN'T WAIT!
ARE YOU SURE ABOUT THIS?
I GET BACK TO THE ROCK OF ETERNITY AND FIND SOMEONE TO HELP ME GIVE THESE POWERS TO SOMEONE ELSE.
I'M NOT SUPPOSED TO BE SHAZAM, FREDDY.
"THE WIZARD SAID SO HIMSELF."
BLACK ADAM.
THE

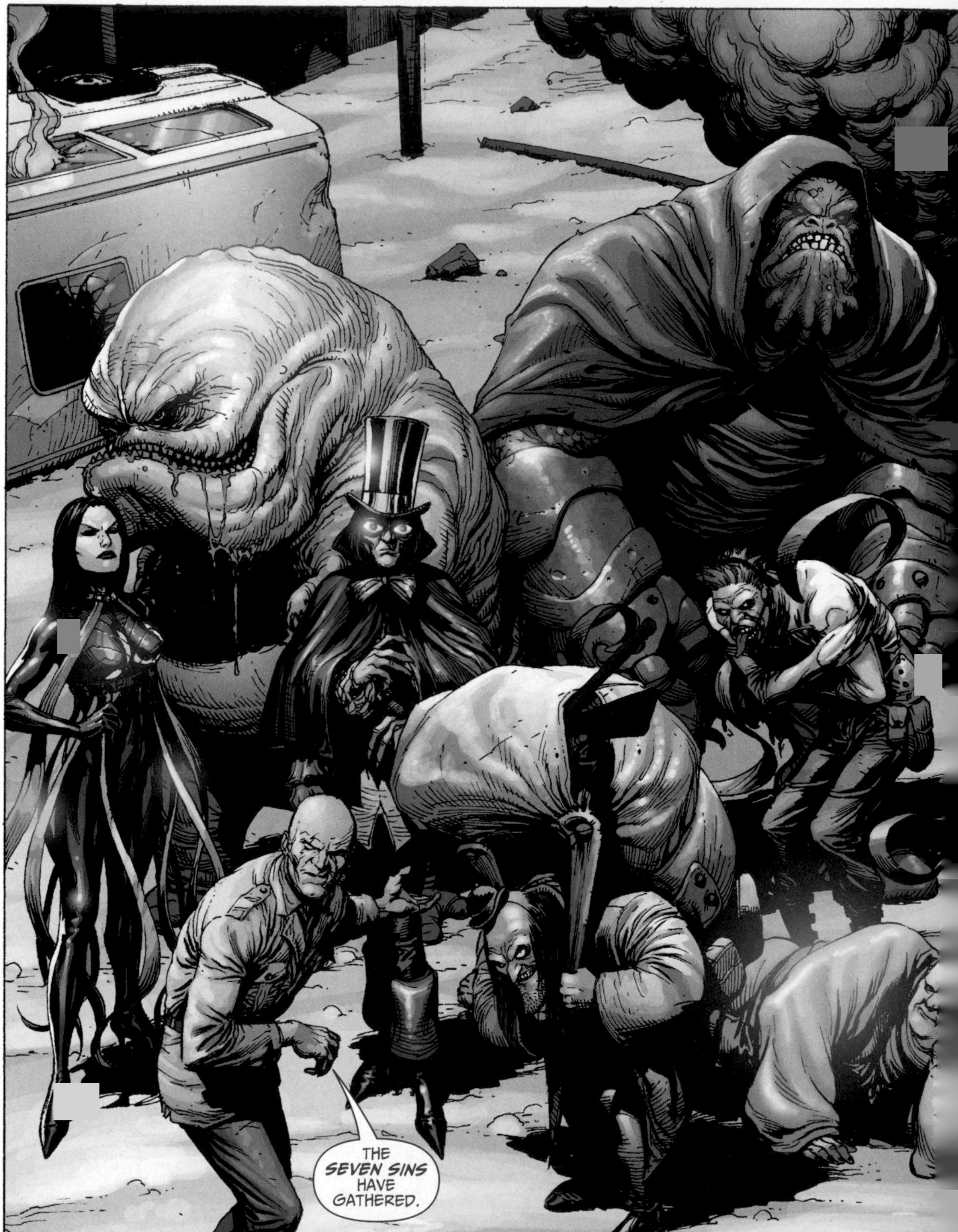
THE SEVEN SINS HAVE GATHERED.

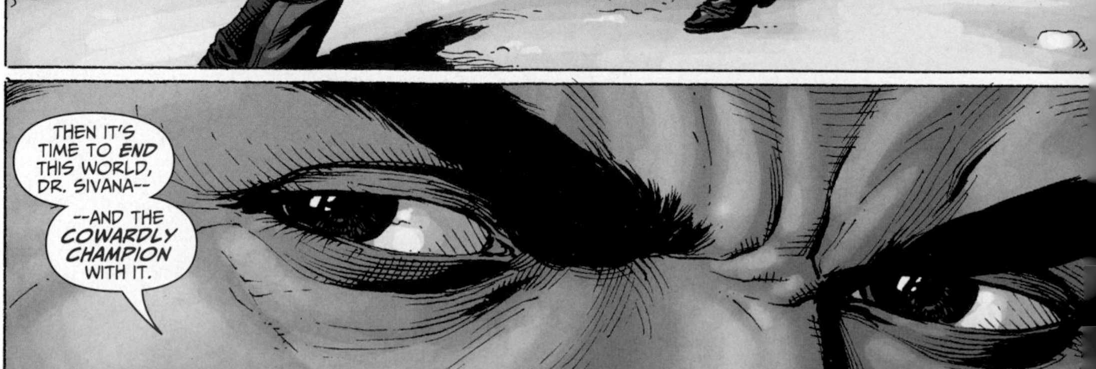
THEN IT'S TIME TO END THIS WORLD, DR. SIVANA--
--AND THE COWARDLY CHAMPION WITH IT.

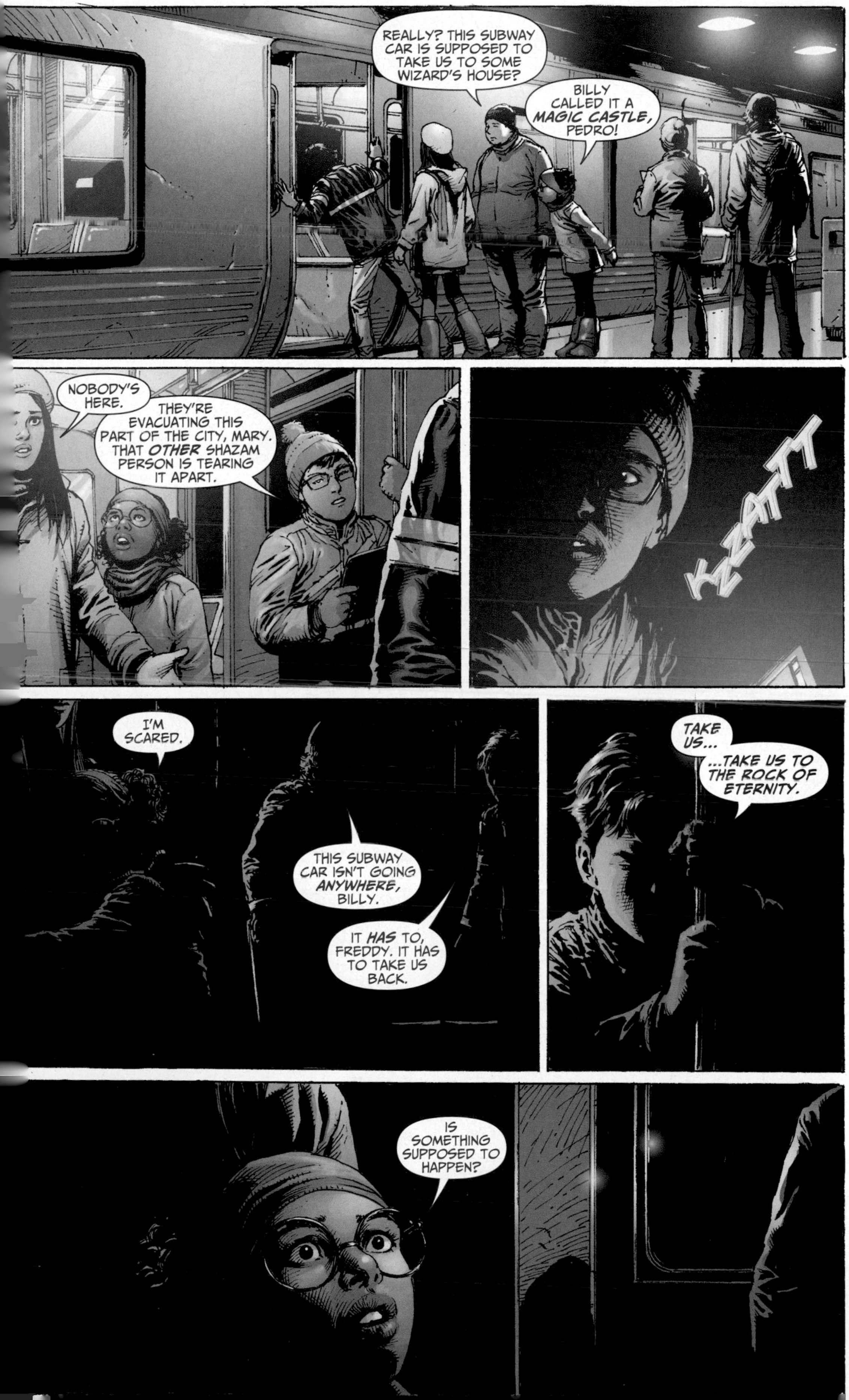
REALLY? THIS SUBWAY CAR IS SUPPOSED TO TAKE US TO SOME WIZARD'S HOUSE?
BILLY CALLED IT A MAGIC CASTLE, PEDRO!
NOBODY'S HERE.
THEY'RE EVACUATING THIS PART OF THE CITY, MARY. THAT OTHER SHAZAM PERSON IS TEARING IT APART.
KZZATTT
I'M SCARED.
THIS SUBWAY CAR ISN'T GOING ANYWHERE, BILLY.
IT HAS TO, FREDDY. IT HAS TO TAKE US BACK.
TAKE US...
...TAKE US TO THE ROCK OF ETERNITY.
IS SOMETHING SUPPOSED TO HAPPEN?

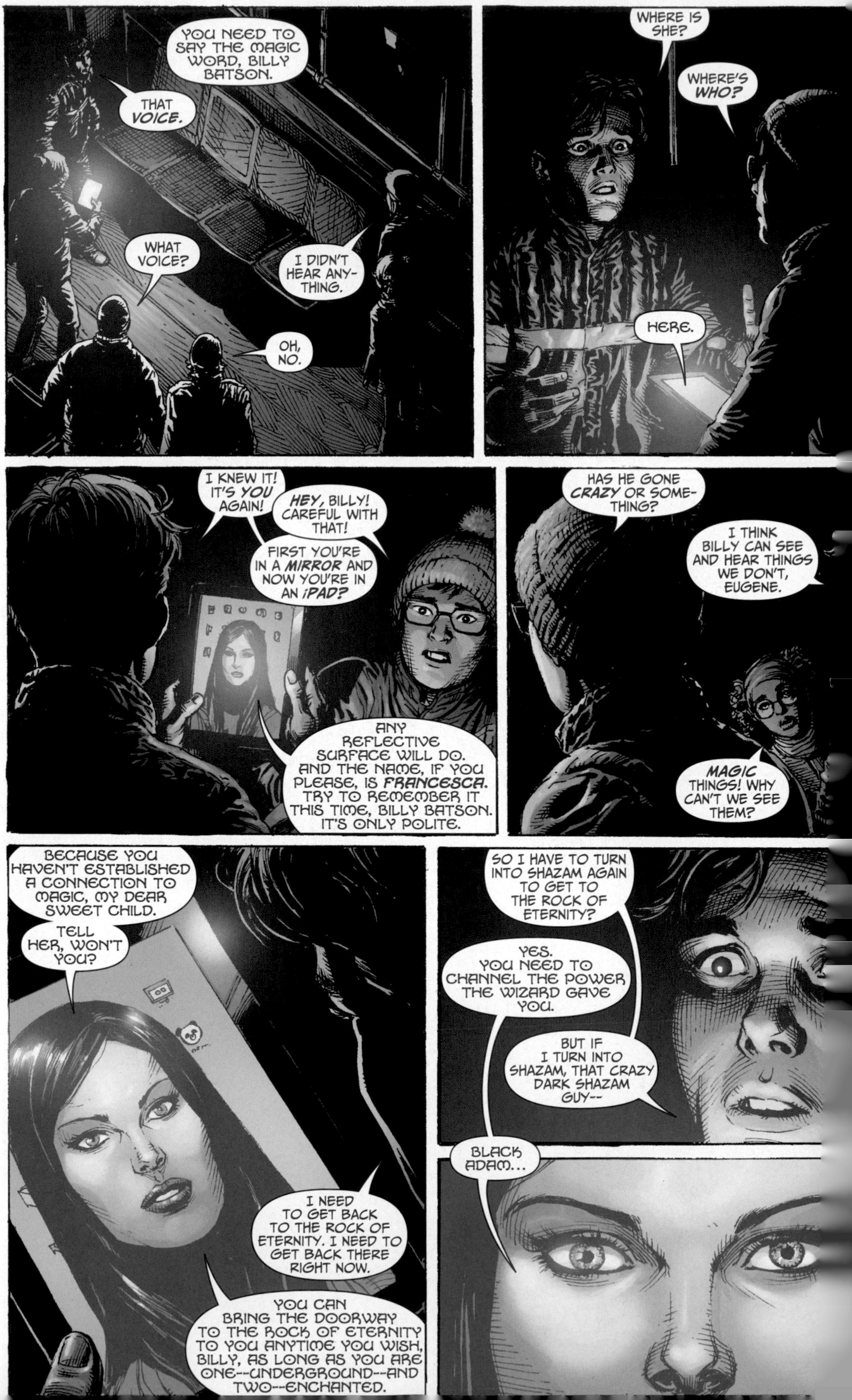

YOU NEED TO SAY THE MAGIC WORD, BILLY BATSON.
THAT VOICE.
WHAT VOICE?
I DIDN'T HEAR ANY-THING.
OH, NO.
WHERE IS SHE?
WHERE'S WHO?
HERE.
I KNEW IT! IT'S YOU AGAIN!
HEY, BILLY! CAREFUL WITH THAT!
FIRST YOU'RE IN A MIRROR AND NOW YOU'RE IN AN iPAD?
ANY REFLECTIVE SURFACE WILL DO. AND THE NAME, IF YOU PLEASE, IS FRANCESCA. TRY TO REMEMBER IT THIS TIME, BILLY BATSON. IT'S ONLY POLITE.
HAS HE GONE CRAZY OR SOME-THING?
I THINK BILLY CAN SEE AND HEAR THINGS WE DON'T, EUGENE.
MAGIC THINGS! WHY CAN'T WE SEE THEM?
BECAUSE YOU HAVEN'T ESTABLISHED A CONNECTION TO MAGIC, MY DEAR SWEET CHILD.
TELL HER, WON'T YOU?
I NEED TO GET BACK TO THE ROCK OF ETERNITY. I NEED TO GET BACK THERE RIGHT NOW.
YOU CAN BRING THE DOORWAY TO THE ROCK OF ETERNITY TO YOU ANYTIME YOU WISH, BILLY, AS LONG AS YOU ARE ONE--UNDERGROUND--AND TWO--ENCHANTED.
SO I HAVE TO TURN INTO SHAZAM AGAIN TO GET TO THE ROCK OF ETERNITY?
YES. YOU NEED TO CHANNEL THE POWER THE WIZARD GAVE YOU.
BUT IF I TURN INTO SHAZAM, THAT CRAZY DARK SHAZAM GUY--
BLACK ADAM...

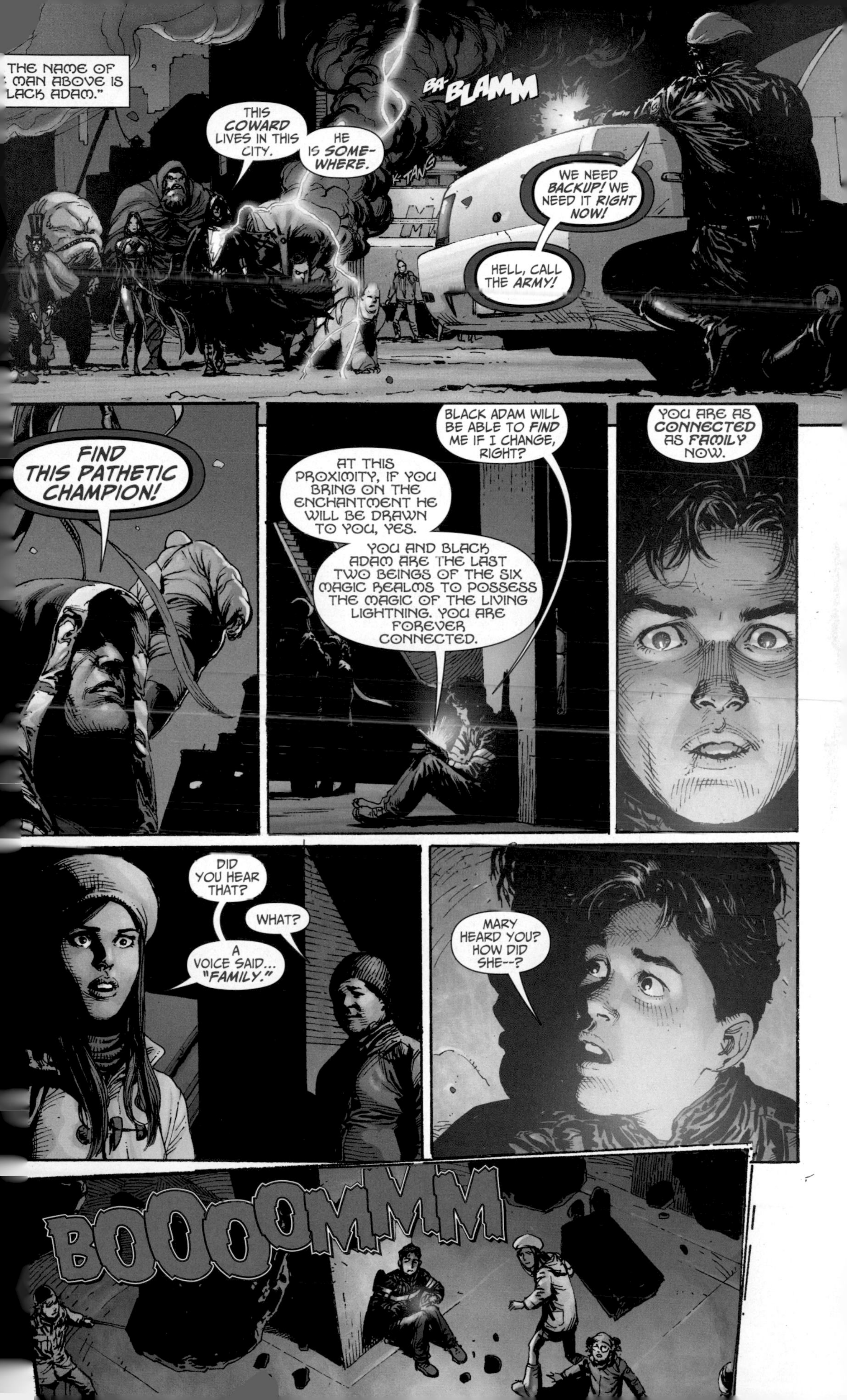

THE NAME OF
MAN ABOVE IS
LACK ADAM."
THIS COWARD LIVES IN THIS CITY.
HE IS SOMEWHERE.
BA-BLAMM
K-TANG
WE NEED BACKUP! WE NEED IT RIGHT NOW!
HELL, CALL THE ARMY!
FIND THIS PATHETIC CHAMPION!
BLACK ADAM WILL BE ABLE TO FIND ME IF I CHANGE, RIGHT?
AT THIS PROXIMITY, IF YOU BRING ON THE ENCHANTMENT HE WILL BE DRAWN TO YOU, YES.
YOU AND BLACK ADAM ARE THE LAST TWO BEINGS OF THE SIX MAGIC REALMS TO POSSESS THE MAGIC OF THE LIVING LIGHTNING. YOU ARE FOREVER CONNECTED.
YOU ARE AS CONNECTED AS FAMILY NOW.
DID YOU HEAR THAT?
WHAT?
A VOICE SAID... "FAMILY."
MARY HEARD YOU? HOW DID SHE--?
BOOOOMMM

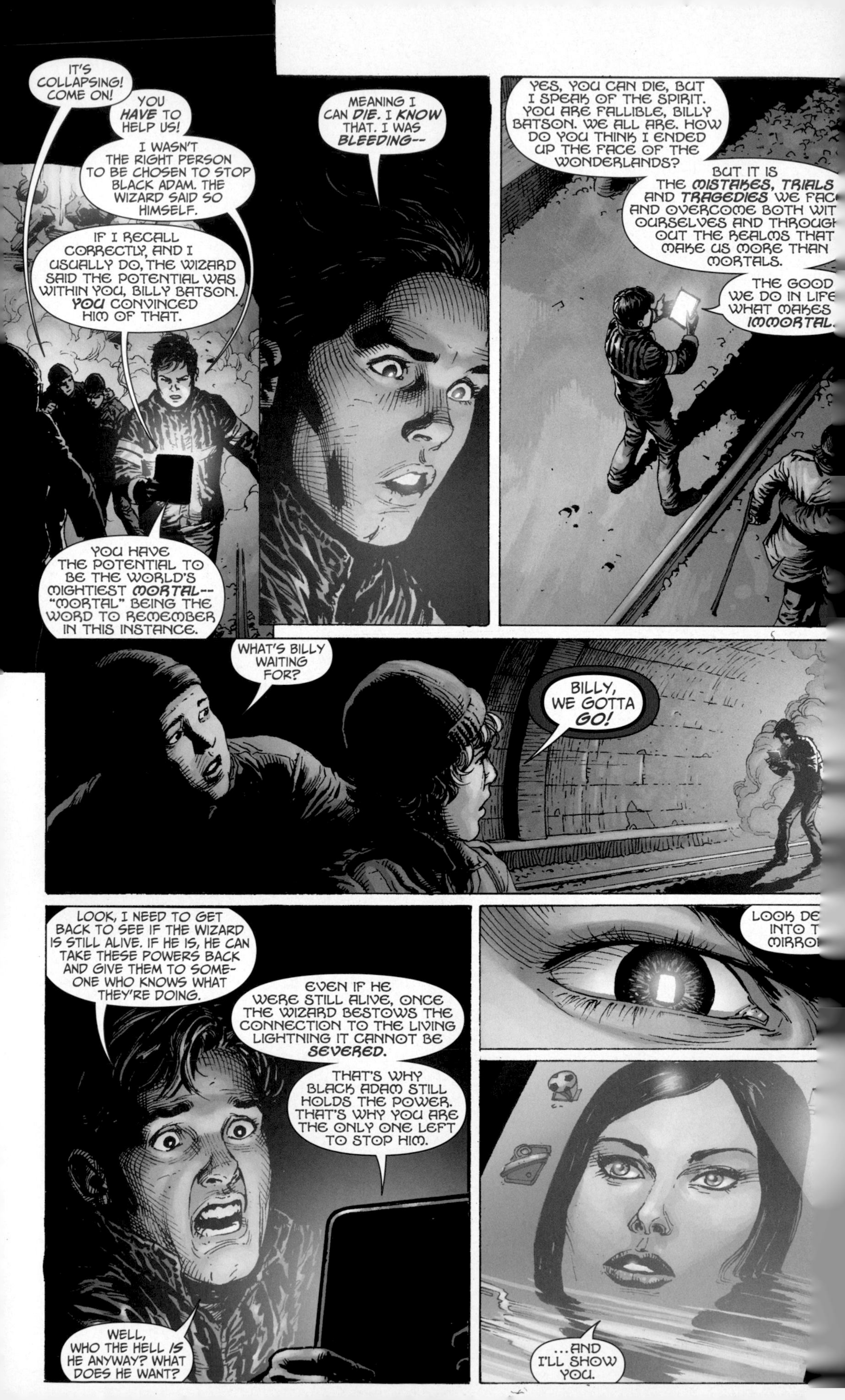
IT'S COLLAPSING! COME ON!
YOU HAVE TO HELP US!
I WASN'T THE RIGHT PERSON TO BE CHOSEN TO STOP BLACK ADAM. THE WIZARD SAID SO HIMSELF.
IF I RECALL CORRECTLY, AND I USUALLY DO, THE WIZARD SAID THE POTENTIAL WAS WITHIN YOU, BILLY BATSON. YOU CONVINCED HIM OF THAT.
YOU HAVE THE POTENTIAL TO BE THE WORLD'S MIGHTIEST MORTAL-- "MORTAL" BEING THE WORD TO REMEMBER IN THIS INSTANCE.
MEANING I CAN DIE. I KNOW THAT. I WAS BLEEDING--
YES, YOU CAN DIE, BUT I SPEAK OF THE SPIRIT. YOU ARE FALLIBLE, BILLY BATSON. WE ALL ARE. HOW DO YOU THINK I ENDED UP THE FACE OF THE WONDERLANDS?
BUT IT IS THE MISTAKES, TRIALS AND TRAGEDIES WE FAC AND OVERCOME BOTH WIT OURSELVES AND THROUGH OUT THE REALMS THAT MAKE US MORE THAN MORTALS.
THE GOOD WE DO IN LIFE WHAT MAKES IMMORTAL.
WHAT'S BILLY WAITING FOR?
BILLY, WE GOTTA GO!
LOOK, I NEED TO GET BACK TO SEE IF THE WIZARD IS STILL ALIVE. IF HE IS, HE CAN TAKE THESE POWERS BACK AND GIVE THEM TO SOME-ONE WHO KNOWS WHAT THEY'RE DOING.
EVEN IF HE WERE STILL ALIVE, ONCE THE WIZARD BESTOWS THE CONNECTION TO THE LIVING LIGHTNING IT CANNOT BE SEVERED.
THAT'S WHY BLACK ADAM STILL HOLDS THE POWER. THAT'S WHY YOU ARE THE ONLY ONE LEFT TO STOP HIM.
WELL, WHO THE HELL IS HE ANYWAY? WHAT DOES HE WANT?
LOOK DE INTO T MIRRO
...AND I'LL SHOW YOU.

"RE
NE?"

"IT'S NOT WHERE
WE ARE, BILLY
BATSON, IT'S
WHAT YOU SEE.

WHAT YOU SEE IS
ANCIENT WORLD.
E COUNTRY OF
DAQ--BIRTHPLACE
LIVING LIGHTNING
HE WIZARD WHO
STOWED YOUR
ERS UPON YOU.

AS YEARS AFTER THE
ARD HAD ESCAPED
NDAQ'S BRUTALITY.

IF HE HAD STAYED
HE WOULD HAVE
BEEN ENSLAVED..."

AS *THIS*
Y WAS."

A
BOY?

"A BOY AMONG THOUSANDS OF OTHER
MEN, WOMEN AND CHILDREN WHO HAD
BEEN CAPTURED BY THE INVADING
FORCES OF THE BARBARIC IBAC AND HIS
ARMY--*THE MEN WHO INVENTED EVIL.*

"THE BOY WAS TORN AWAY FROM
THE REST OF HIS FAMILY--"

<MOTHER!
PATHER!>

"FOR MONTHS, THIS
OY WAS AMONG MANY
ENT DOWN INTO THE
CAVES TO WORK.

"WHEN HE COLLAPSED
BECAUSE OF THE HEAT OR
XHAUSTION...HE SUFFERED AT
THE HANDS OF IBAC'S MEN."

ET
?!>

AHH!

"MANY TIMES
HE WISHED
HIMSELF DEAD.

"HE CLOSED HIS
EYES AND *WISHED*
FOR HELP."

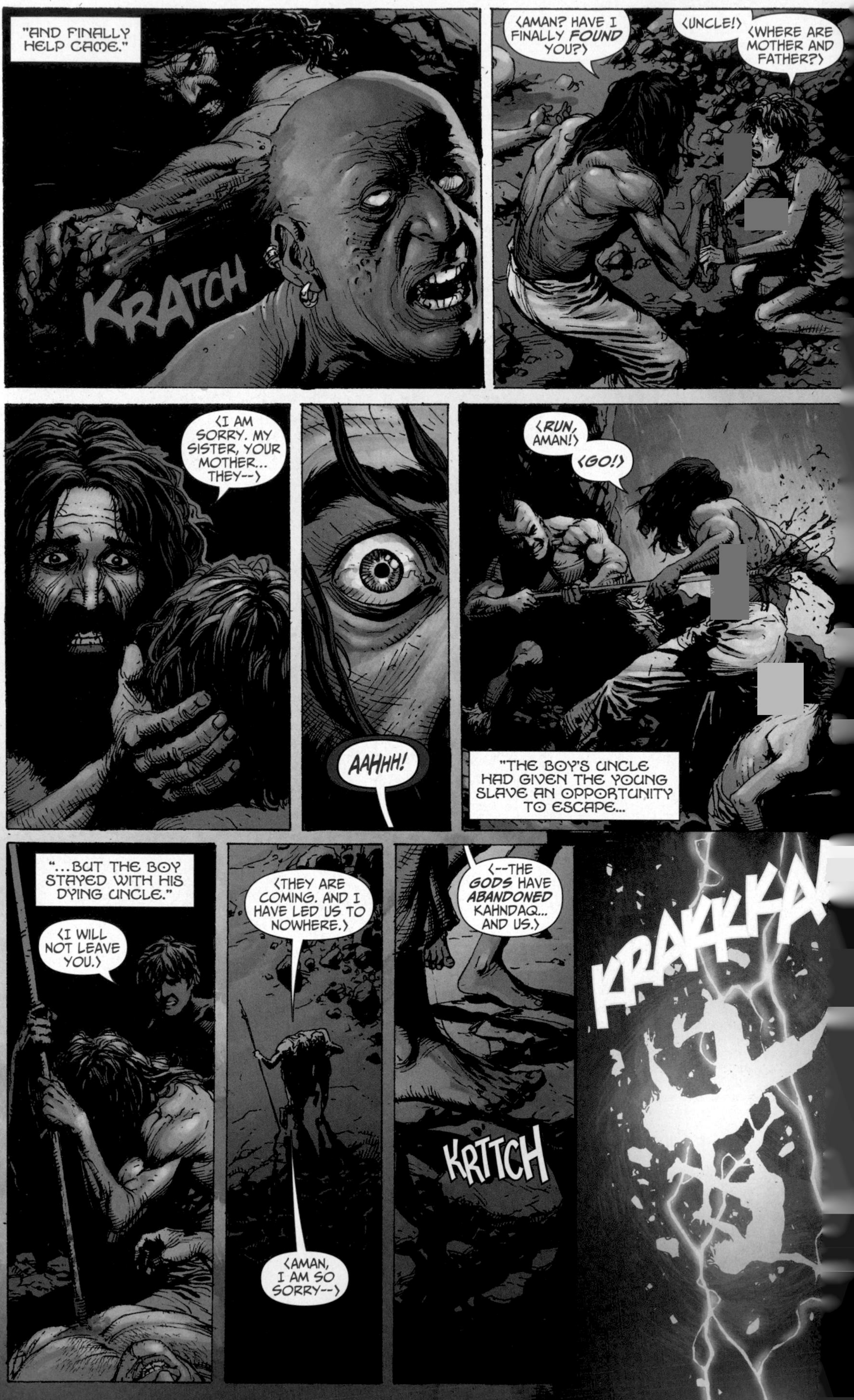
"AND FINALLY HELP CAME."
KRATCH
<AMAN? HAVE I FINALLY *FOUND* YOU?>
<UNCLE!>
<WHERE ARE MOTHER AND FATHER?>
<I AM SORRY. MY SISTER, YOUR MOTHER... THEY-->
AAHHH!
<*RUN*, AMAN!>
<*GO!*>
"THE BOY'S UNCLE HAD GIVEN THE YOUNG SLAVE AN OPPORTUNITY TO ESCAPE...
"...BUT THE BOY STAYED WITH HIS DYING UNCLE."
<I WILL NOT LEAVE YOU.>
<THEY ARE COMING. AND I HAVE LED US TO NOWHERE.>
<AMAN, I AM SO SORRY-->
<--THE *GODS* HAVE *ABANDONED* KAHNDAQ... AND US.>
KRTTCH
KRAKKA

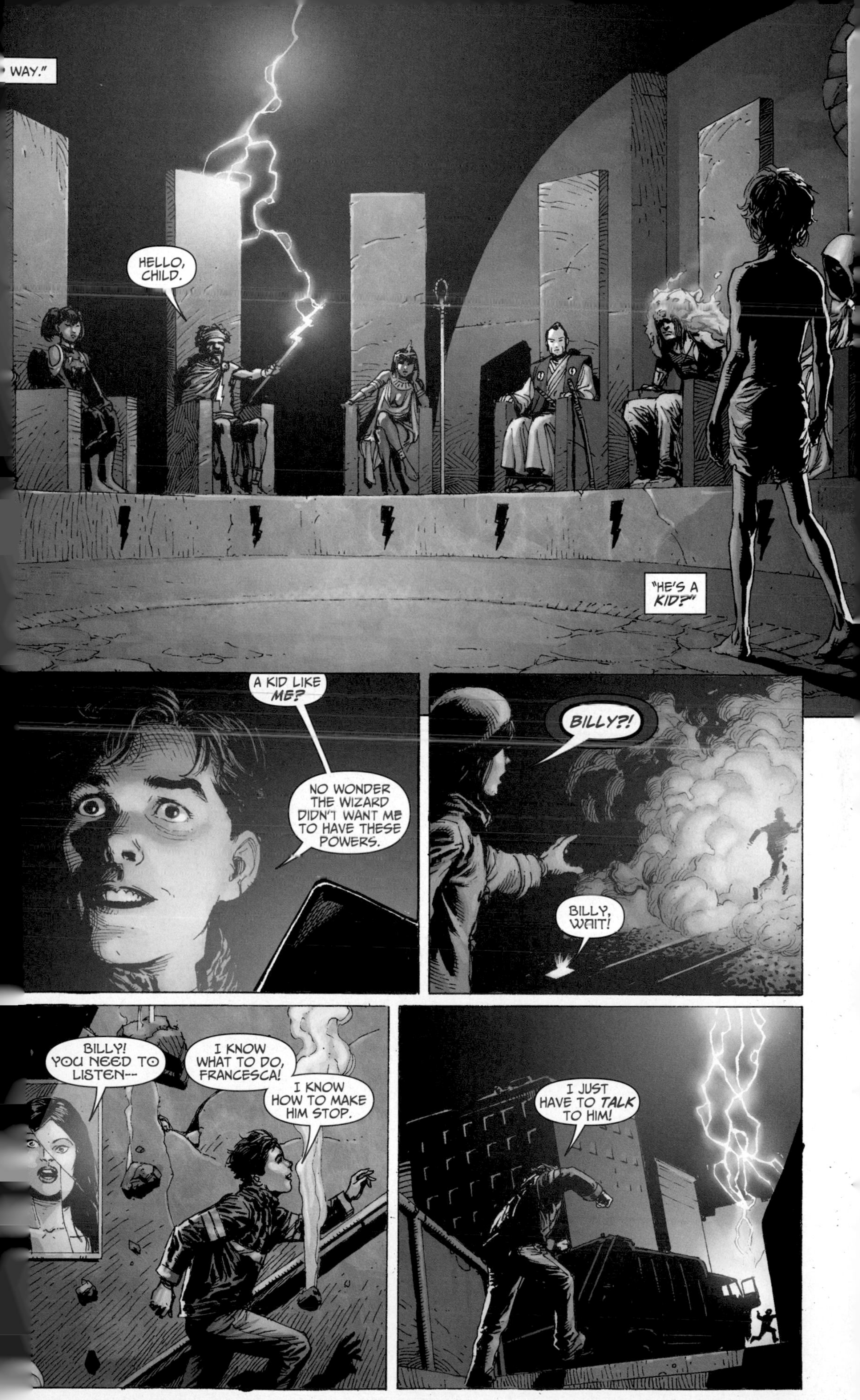
WAY."
HELLO, CHILD.
"HE'S A KID?"
A KID LIKE ME?
NO WONDER THE WIZARD DIDN'T WANT ME TO HAVE THESE POWERS.
BILLY?!
BILLY, WAIT!
BILLY! YOU NEED TO LISTEN--
I KNOW WHAT TO DO, FRANCESCA!
I KNOW HOW TO MAKE HIM STOP.
I JUST HAVE TO TALK TO HIM!

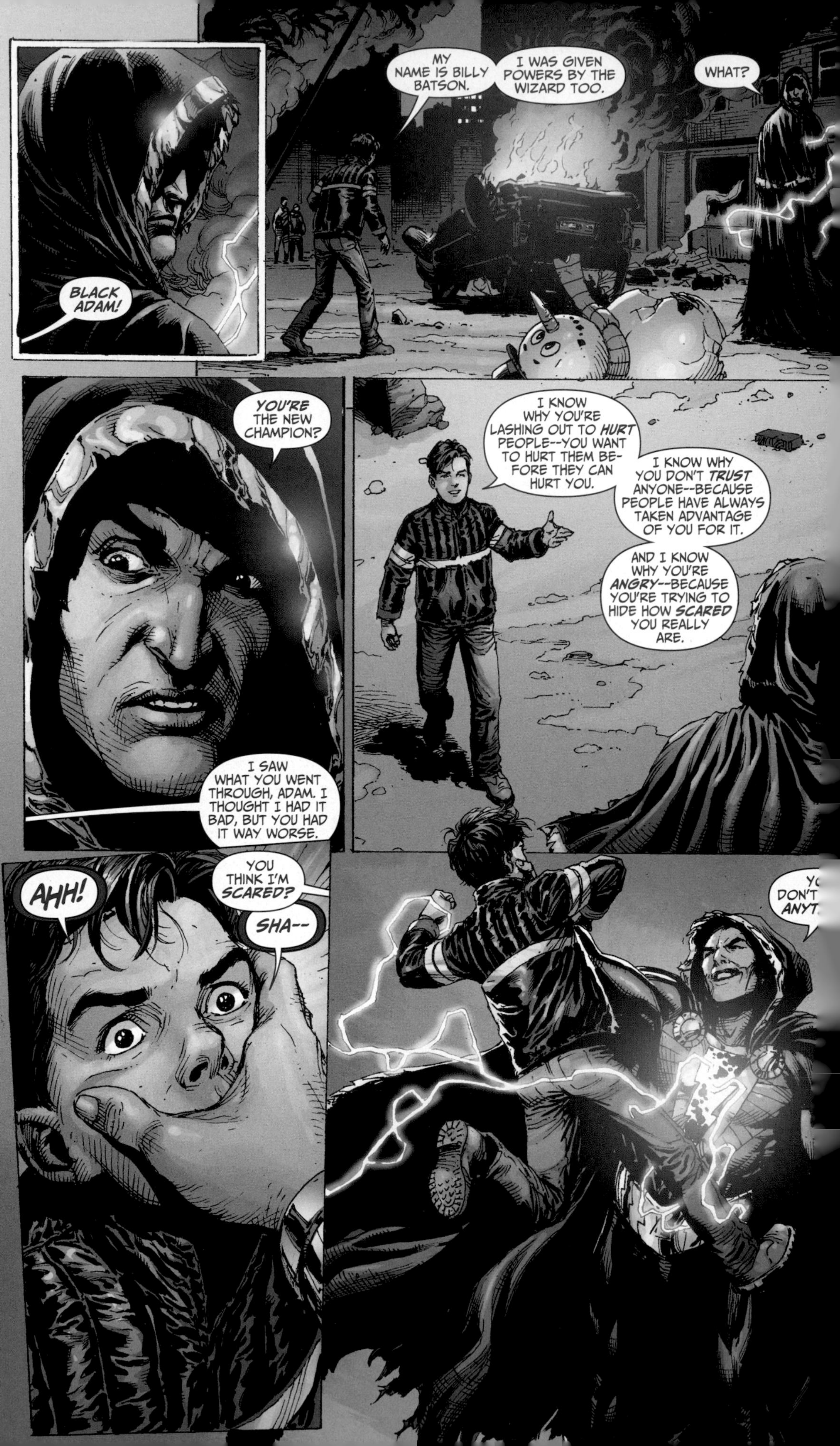
BLACK ADAM!
MY NAME IS BILLY BATSON.
I WAS GIVEN POWERS BY THE WIZARD TOO.
WHAT?
YOU'RE THE NEW CHAMPION?
I SAW WHAT YOU WENT THROUGH, ADAM. I THOUGHT I HAD IT BAD, BUT YOU HAD IT WAY WORSE.
I KNOW WHY YOU'RE LASHING OUT TO HURT PEOPLE--YOU WANT TO HURT THEM BEFORE THEY CAN HURT YOU.
I KNOW WHY YOU DON'T TRUST ANYONE--BECAUSE PEOPLE HAVE ALWAYS TAKEN ADVANTAGE OF YOU FOR IT.
AND I KNOW WHY YOU'RE ANGRY--BECAUSE YOU'RE TRYING TO HIDE HOW SCARED YOU REALLY ARE.
AHH!
YOU THINK I'M SCARED?
SHA--

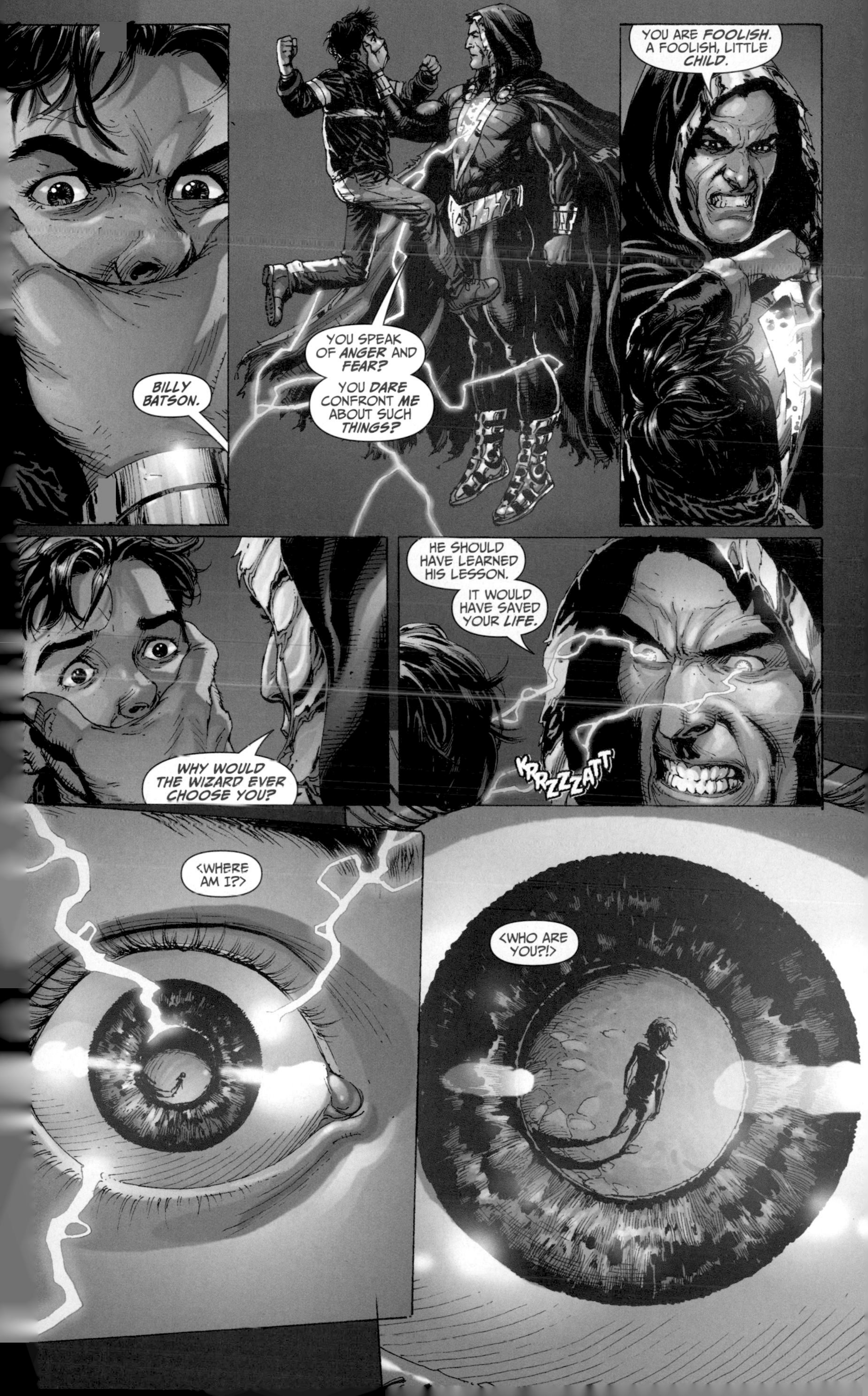
BILLY BATSON.
YOU SPEAK OF ANGER AND FEAR?
YOU DARE CONFRONT ME ABOUT SUCH THINGS?
YOU ARE FOOLISH. A FOOLISH, LITTLE CHILD.
WHY WOULD THE WIZARD EVER CHOOSE YOU?
HE SHOULD HAVE LEARNED HIS LESSON.
IT WOULD HAVE SAVED YOUR LIFE.
KRRZZZZATT
<WHERE AM I?>
<WHO ARE YOU?!>

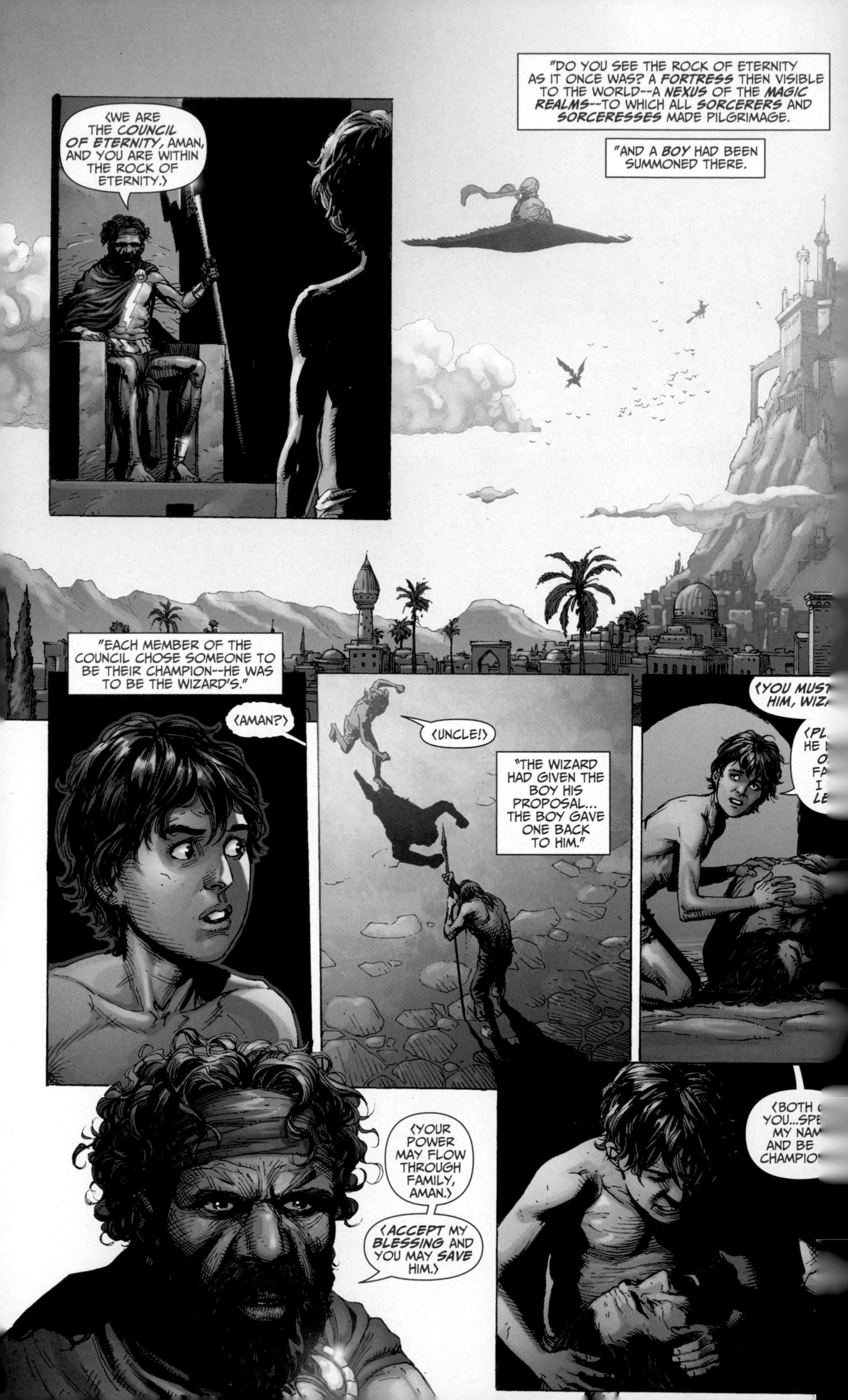

"DO YOU SEE THE ROCK OF ETERNITY AS IT ONCE WAS? A FORTRESS THEN VISIBLE TO THE WORLD--A NEXUS OF THE MAGIC REALMS--TO WHICH ALL SORCERERS AND SORCERESSES MADE PILGRIMAGE.
"AND A BOY HAD BEEN SUMMONED THERE.
‹WE ARE THE COUNCIL OF ETERNITY, AMAN, AND YOU ARE WITHIN THE ROCK OF ETERNITY.›
"EACH MEMBER OF THE COUNCIL CHOSE SOMEONE TO BE THEIR CHAMPION--HE WAS TO BE THE WIZARD'S."
‹AMAN?›
‹UNCLE!›
"THE WIZARD HAD GIVEN THE BOY HIS PROPOSAL... THE BOY GAVE ONE BACK TO HIM."
‹YOU MUST
HIM, WIZ
‹YOUR POWER MAY FLOW THROUGH FAMILY, AMAN.›
‹ACCEPT MY BLESSING AND YOU MAY SAVE HIM.›
‹BOTH
YOU...SPE
MY NAM
AND BE
CHAMPIO

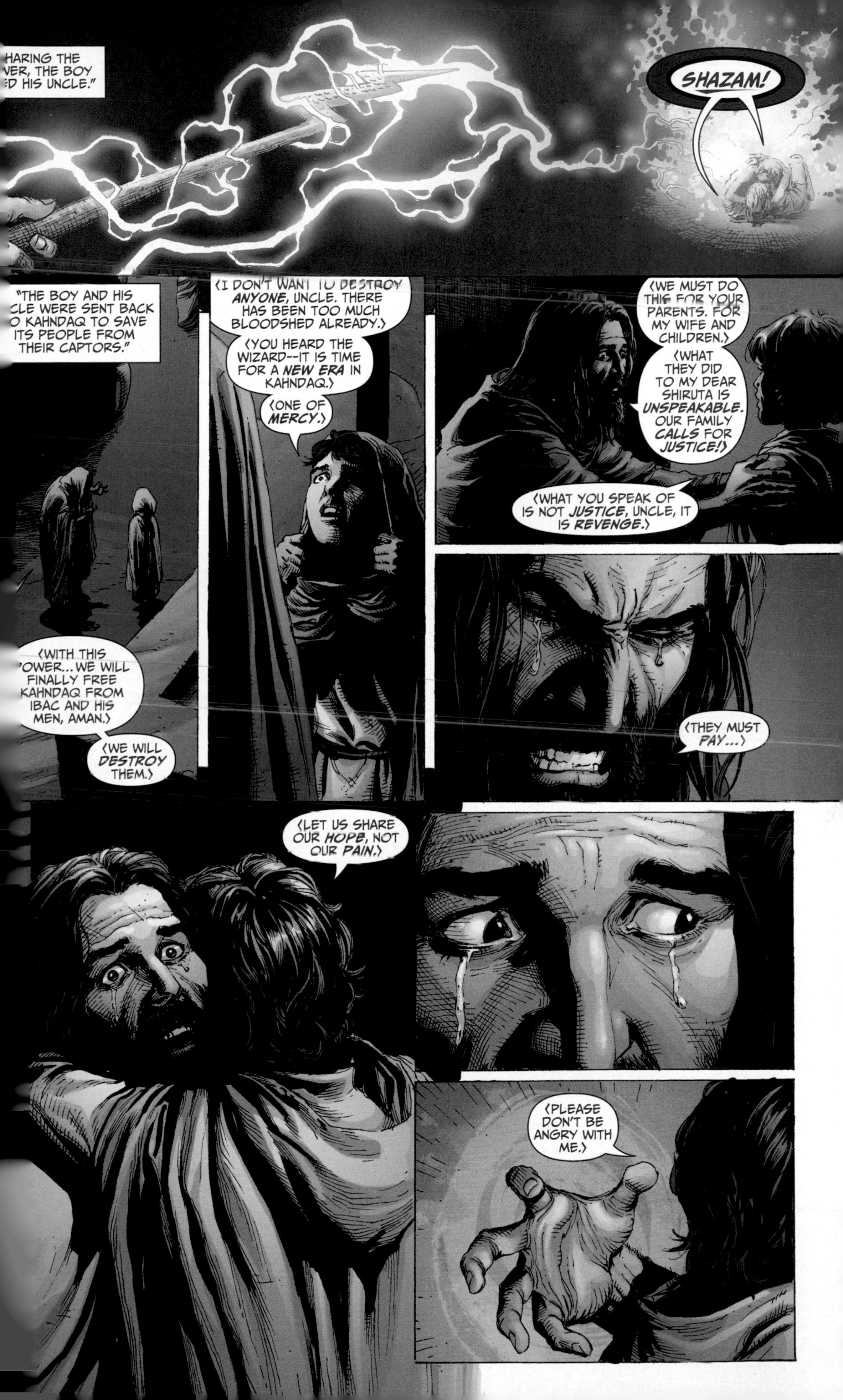

HARING THE VER, THE BOY ED HIS UNCLE."
SHAZAM!
"THE BOY AND HIS CLE WERE SENT BACK O KAHNDAQ TO SAVE ITS PEOPLE FROM THEIR CAPTORS."
‹WITH THIS POWER... WE WILL FINALLY FREE KAHNDAQ FROM IBAC AND HIS MEN, AMAN.›
‹WE WILL DESTROY THEM.›
‹I DON'T WANT TO DESTROY ANYONE, UNCLE. THERE HAS BEEN TOO MUCH BLOODSHED ALREADY.›
‹YOU HEARD THE WIZARD--IT IS TIME FOR A NEW ERA IN KAHNDAQ.›
‹ONE OF MERCY.›
‹WE MUST DO THIS FOR YOUR PARENTS. FOR MY WIFE AND CHILDREN.›
‹WHAT THEY DID TO MY DEAR SHIRUTA IS UNSPEAKABLE. OUR FAMILY CALLS FOR JUSTICE!›
‹WHAT YOU SPEAK OF IS NOT JUSTICE, UNCLE, IT IS REVENGE.›
‹THEY MUST PAY...›
‹LET US SHARE OUR HOPE, NOT OUR PAIN.›
‹PLEASE DON'T BE ANGRY WITH ME.›

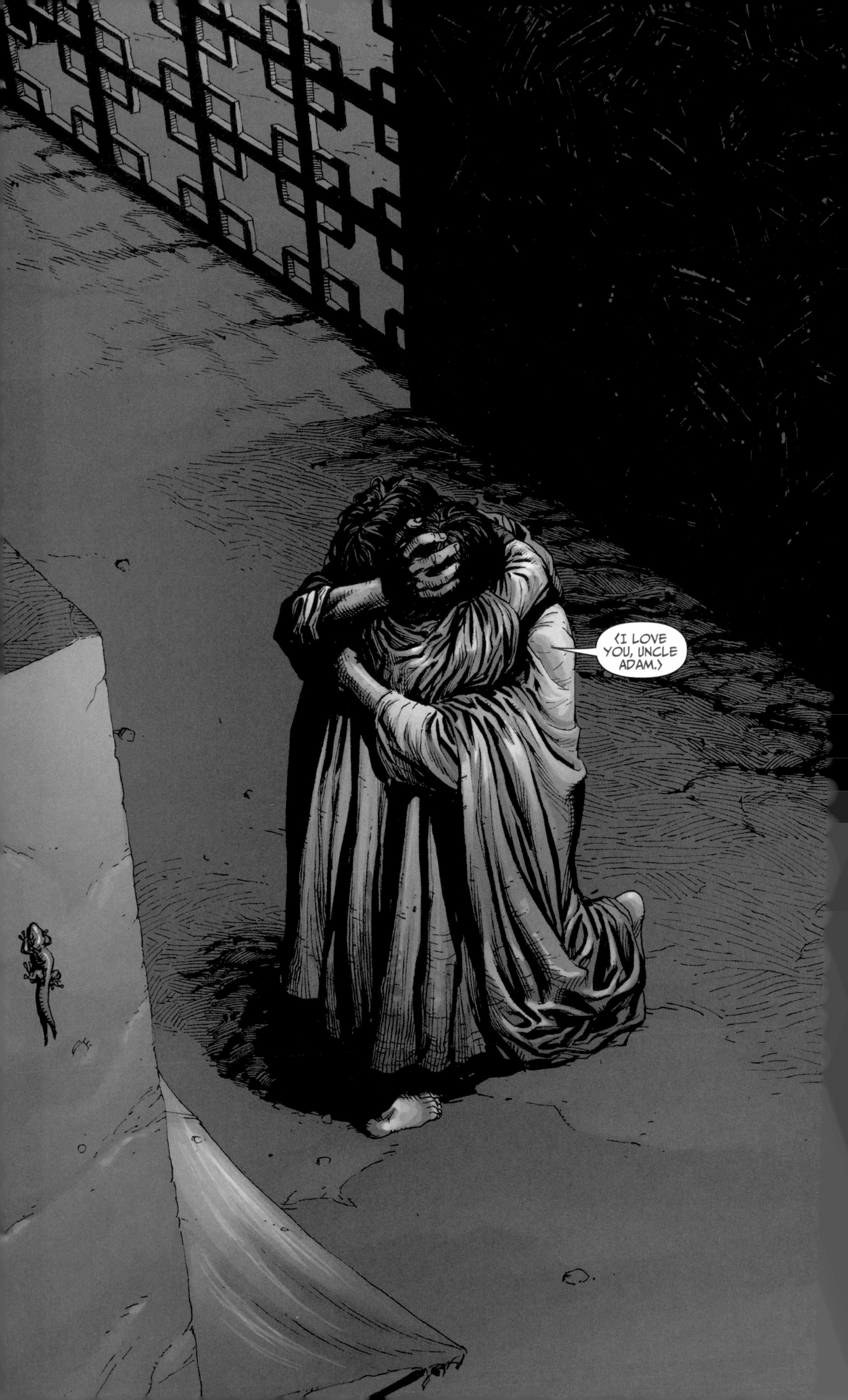
<I LOVE YOU, UNCLE ADAM.>

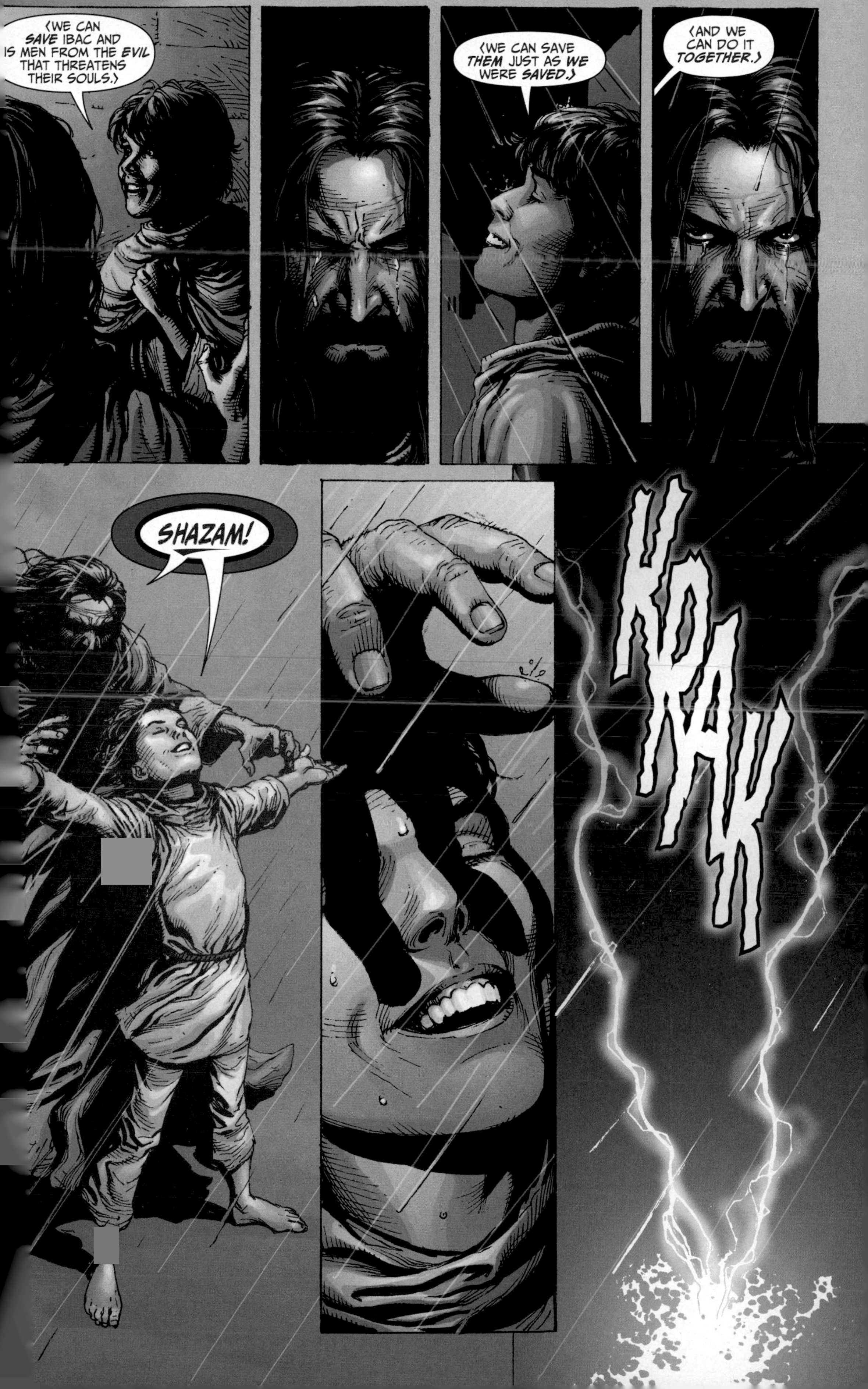
⟨WE CAN SAVE IBAC AND IS MEN FROM THE EVIL THAT THREATENS THEIR SOULS.⟩
⟨WE CAN SAVE THEM JUST AS WE WERE SAVED.⟩
⟨AND WE CAN DO IT TOGETHER.⟩
SHAZAM!
KRAAK

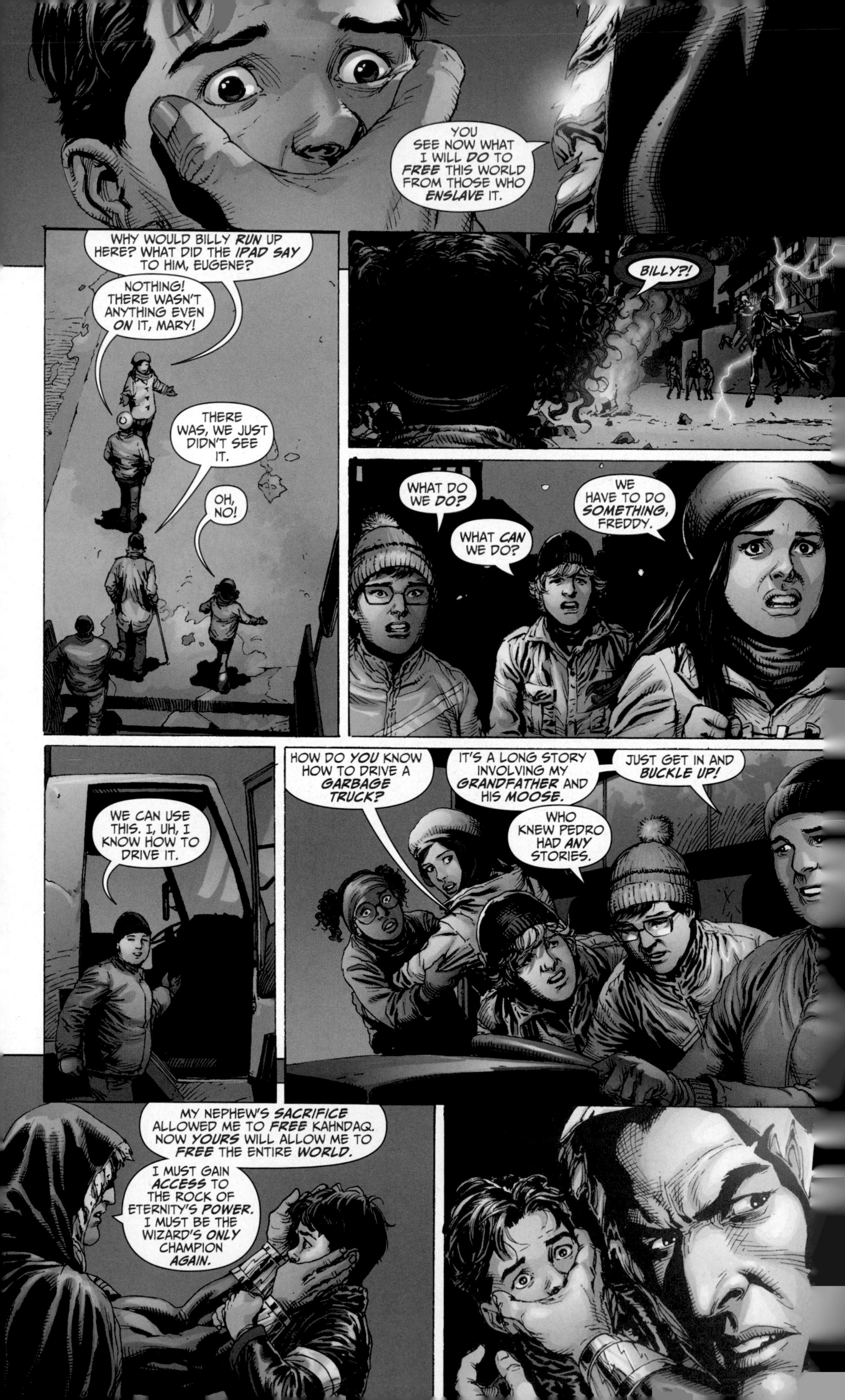
YOU SEE NOW WHAT I WILL DO TO FREE THIS WORLD FROM THOSE WHO ENSLAVE IT.
WHY WOULD BILLY RUN UP HERE? WHAT DID THE IPAD SAY TO HIM, EUGENE?
NOTHING! THERE WASN'T ANYTHING EVEN ON IT, MARY!
THERE WAS, WE JUST DIDN'T SEE IT.
OH, NO!
BILLY?!
WHAT DO WE DO?
WHAT CAN WE DO?
WE HAVE TO DO SOMETHING, FREDDY.
WE CAN USE THIS. I, UH, I KNOW HOW TO DRIVE IT.
HOW DO YOU KNOW HOW TO DRIVE A GARBAGE TRUCK?
IT'S A LONG STORY INVOLVING MY GRANDFATHER AND HIS MOOSE.
JUST GET IN AND BUCKLE UP!
WHO KNEW PEDRO HAD ANY STORIES.
MY NEPHEW'S SACRIFICE ALLOWED ME TO FREE KAHNDAQ. NOW YOURS WILL ALLOW ME TO FREE THE ENTIRE WORLD.
I MUST GAIN ACCESS TO THE ROCK OF ETERNITY'S POWER. I MUST BE THE WIZARD'S ONLY CHAMPION AGAIN.

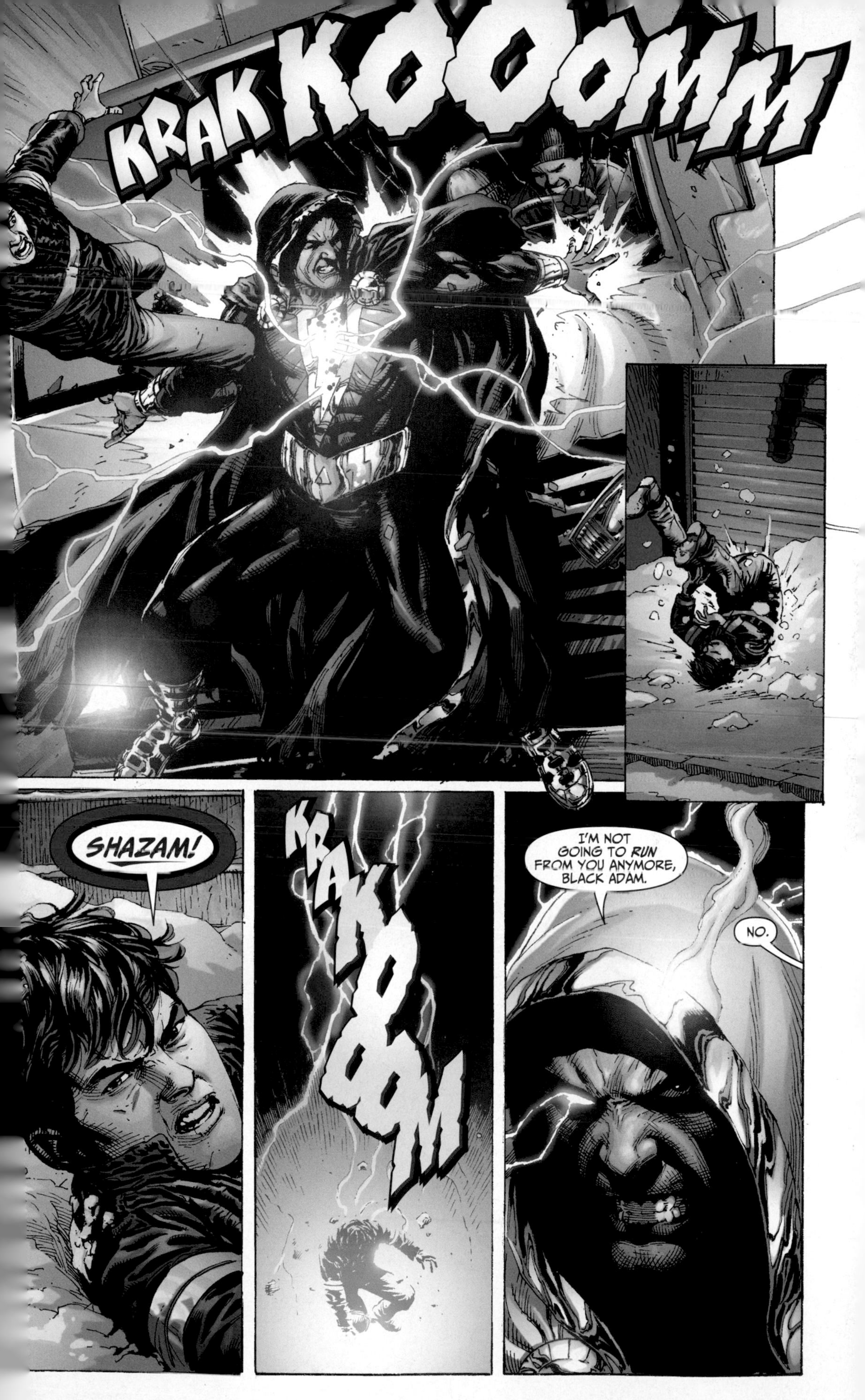
KRAK KOOOMM
SHAZAM!
KRAKOOOM
I'M NOT GOING TO RUN FROM YOU ANYMORE, BLACK ADAM.
NO.

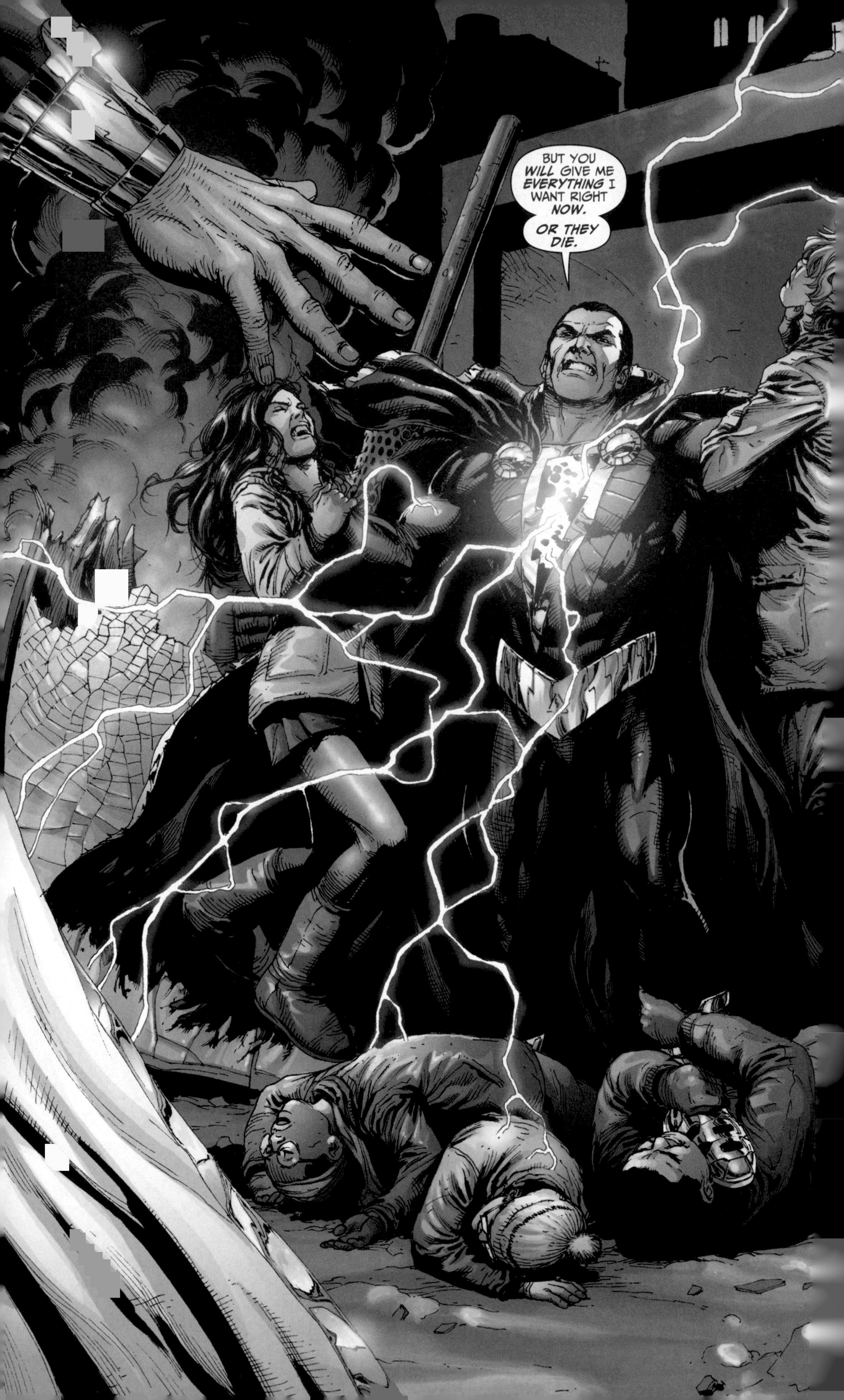
BUT YOU *WILL* GIVE ME *EVERYTHING* I WANT RIGHT *NOW*. *OR THEY DIE*.

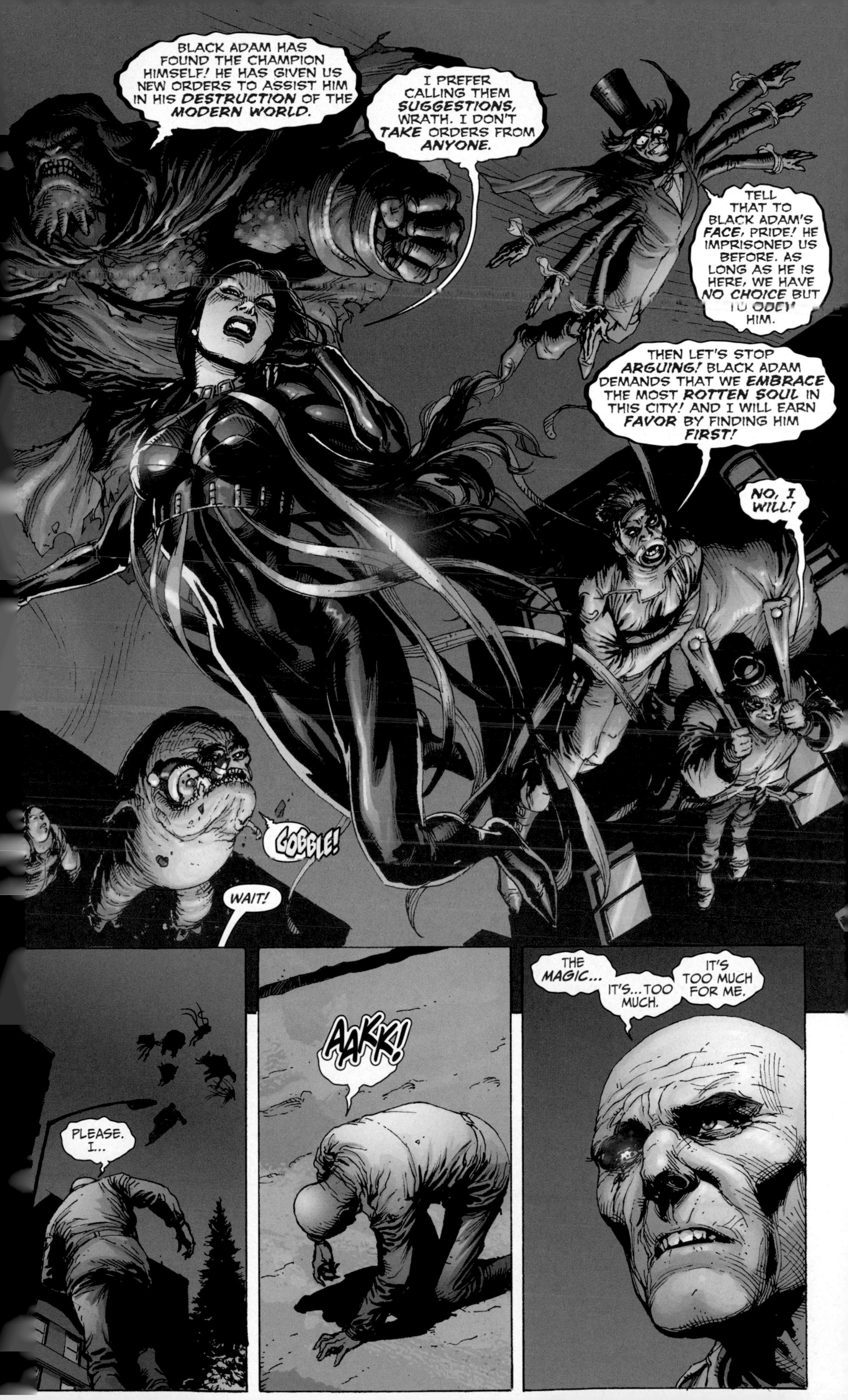
BLACK ADAM HAS FOUND THE CHAMPION HIMSELF! HE HAS GIVEN US NEW ORDERS TO ASSIST HIM IN HIS DESTRUCTION OF THE MODERN WORLD.
I PREFER CALLING THEM SUGGESTIONS, WRATH. I DON'T TAKE ORDERS FROM ANYONE.
TELL THAT TO BLACK ADAM'S FACE, PRIDE! HE IMPRISONED US BEFORE. AS LONG AS HE IS HERE, WE HAVE NO CHOICE BUT TO OBEY HIM.
THEN LET'S STOP ARGUING! BLACK ADAM DEMANDS THAT WE EMBRACE THE MOST ROTTEN SOUL IN THIS CITY! AND I WILL EARN FAVOR BY FINDING HIM FIRST!
NO, I WILL!
GOBBLE!
WAIT!
PLEASE. I...
AAKK!
THE MAGIC...
IT'S...TOO MUCH.
IT'S TOO MUCH FOR ME.

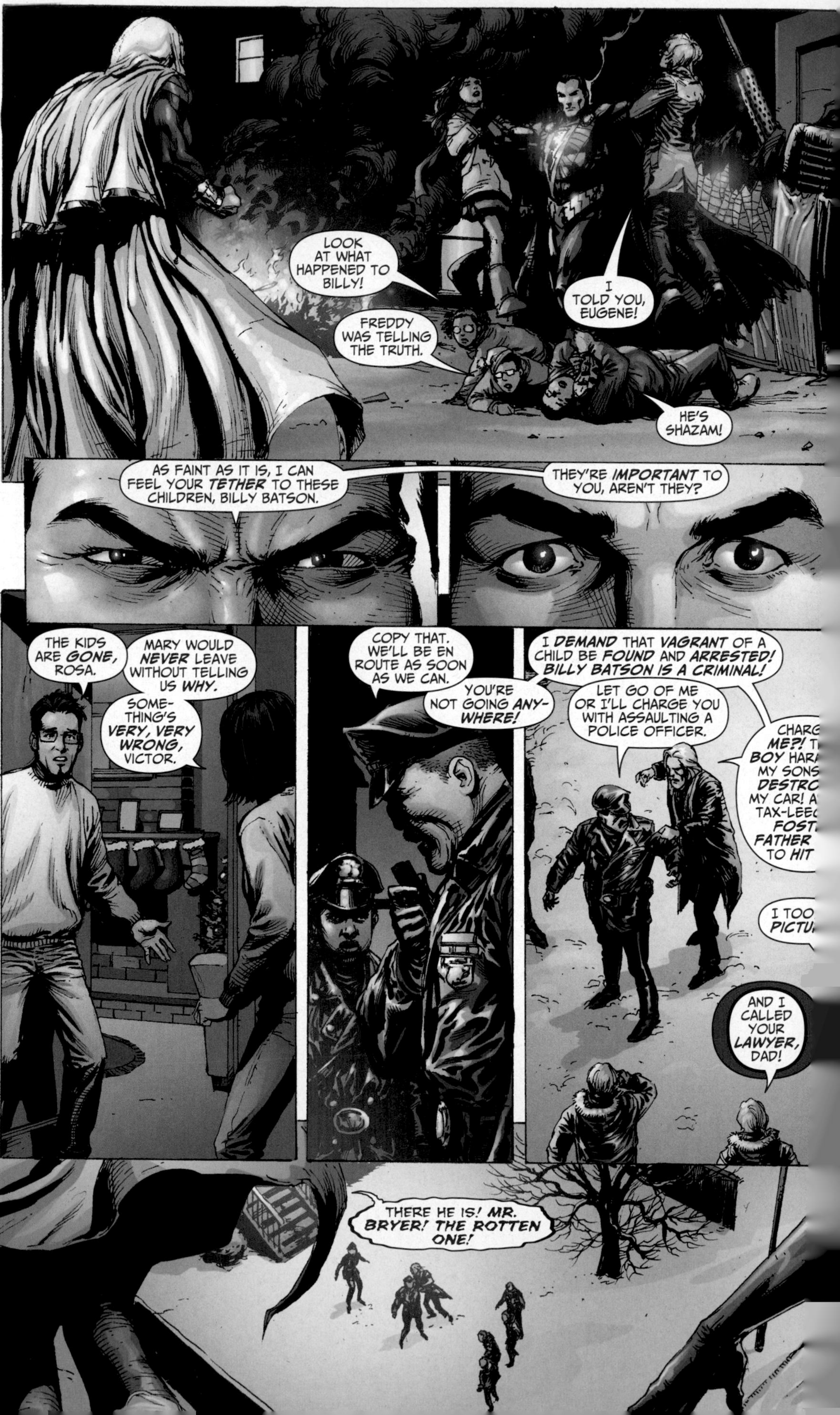
LOOK AT WHAT HAPPENED TO BILLY!
FREDDY WAS TELLING THE TRUTH.
I TOLD YOU, EUGENE!
HE'S SHAZAM!
AS FAINT AS IT IS, I CAN FEEL YOUR TETHER TO THESE CHILDREN, BILLY BATSON.
THEY'RE IMPORTANT TO YOU, AREN'T THEY?
THE KIDS ARE GONE, ROSA.
MARY WOULD NEVER LEAVE WITHOUT TELLING US WHY.
SOME-THING'S VERY, VERY WRONG, VICTOR.
COPY THAT. WE'LL BE EN ROUTE AS SOON AS WE CAN.
YOU'RE NOT GOING ANY-WHERE!
I DEMAND THAT VAGRANT OF A CHILD BE FOUND AND ARRESTED! BILLY BATSON IS A CRIMINAL!
LET GO OF ME OR I'LL CHARGE YOU WITH ASSAULTING A POLICE OFFICER.
CHARG ME?! T BOY HARA MY SONS DESTRO MY CAR! A TAX-LEEC FOST FATHER TO HIT
I TOO PICTU
AND I CALLED YOUR LAWYER, DAD!
THERE HE IS! MR. BRYER! THE ROTTEN ONE!

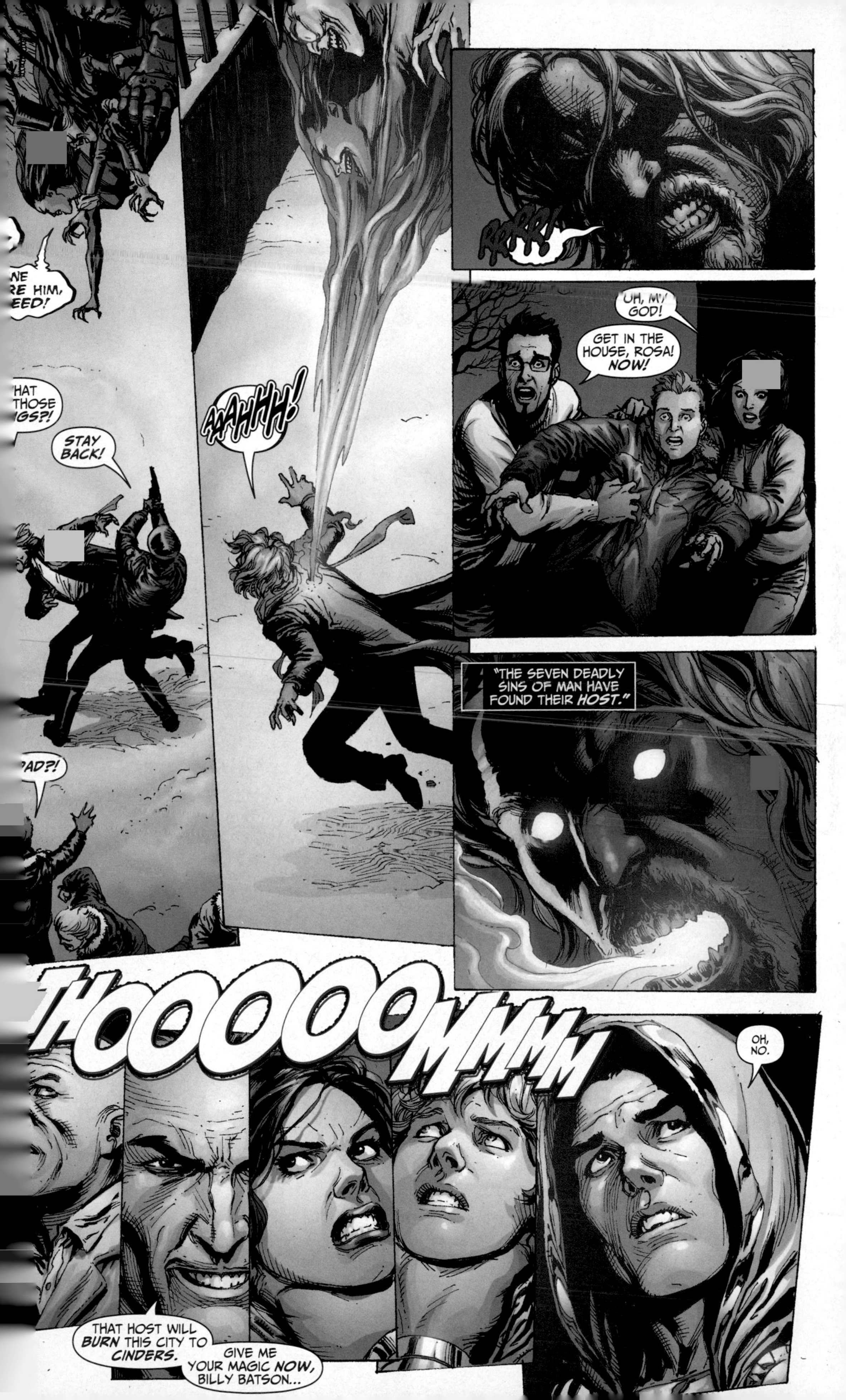
NE
RE HIM,
EED!
HAT
THOSE
GS?!
STAY BACK!
AD?!
AAAHHH!
RRRR!
OH, MY GOD!
GET IN THE HOUSE, ROSA! NOW!
"THE SEVEN DEADLY SINS OF MAN HAVE FOUND THEIR HOST."
THOOOOOMMMM
OH, NO.
THAT HOST WILL BURN THIS CITY TO CINDERS.
GIVE ME YOUR MAGIC NOW, BILLY BATSON...

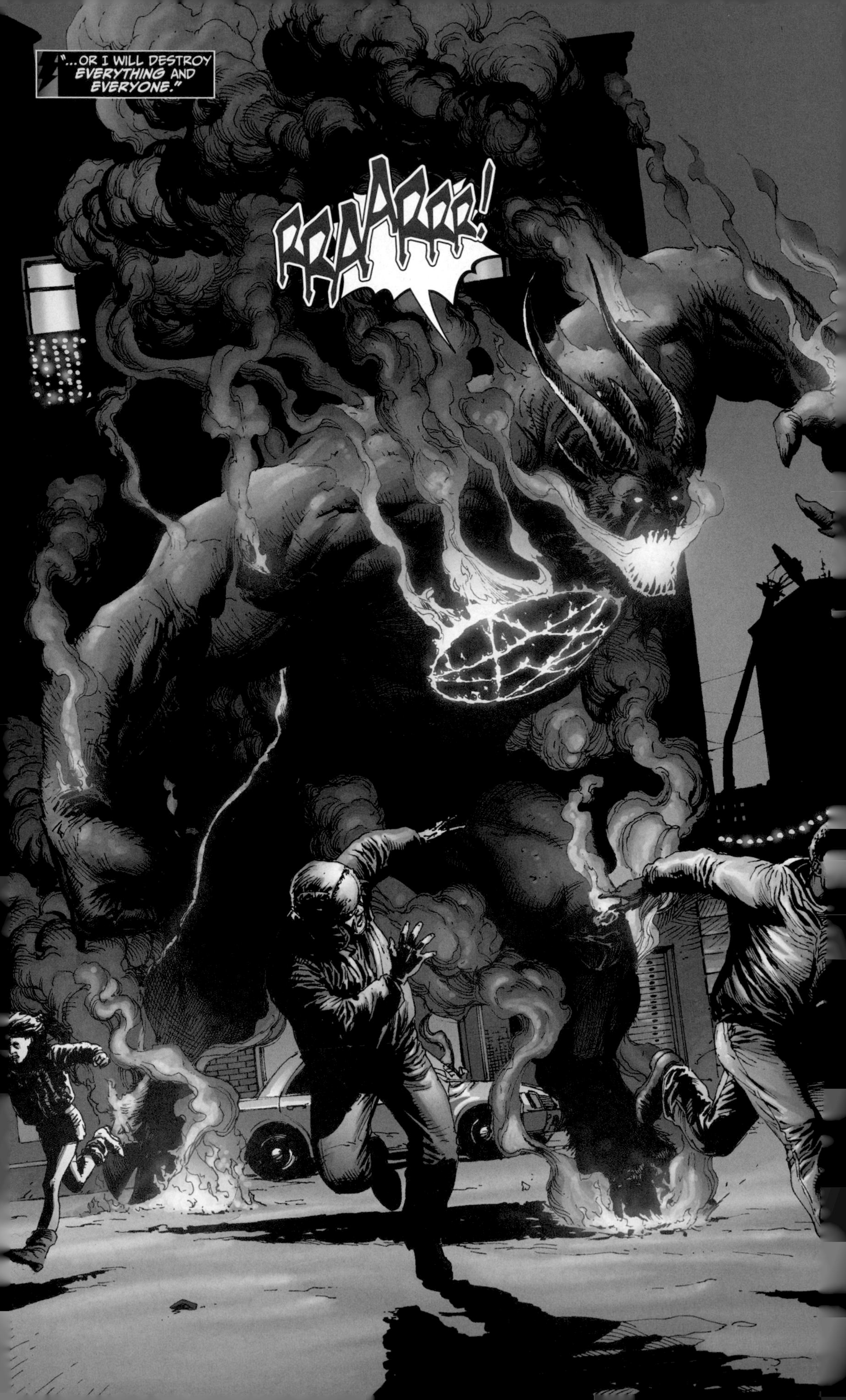
"...OR I WILL DESTROY EVERYTHING AND EVERYONE."
RRRAAARR!

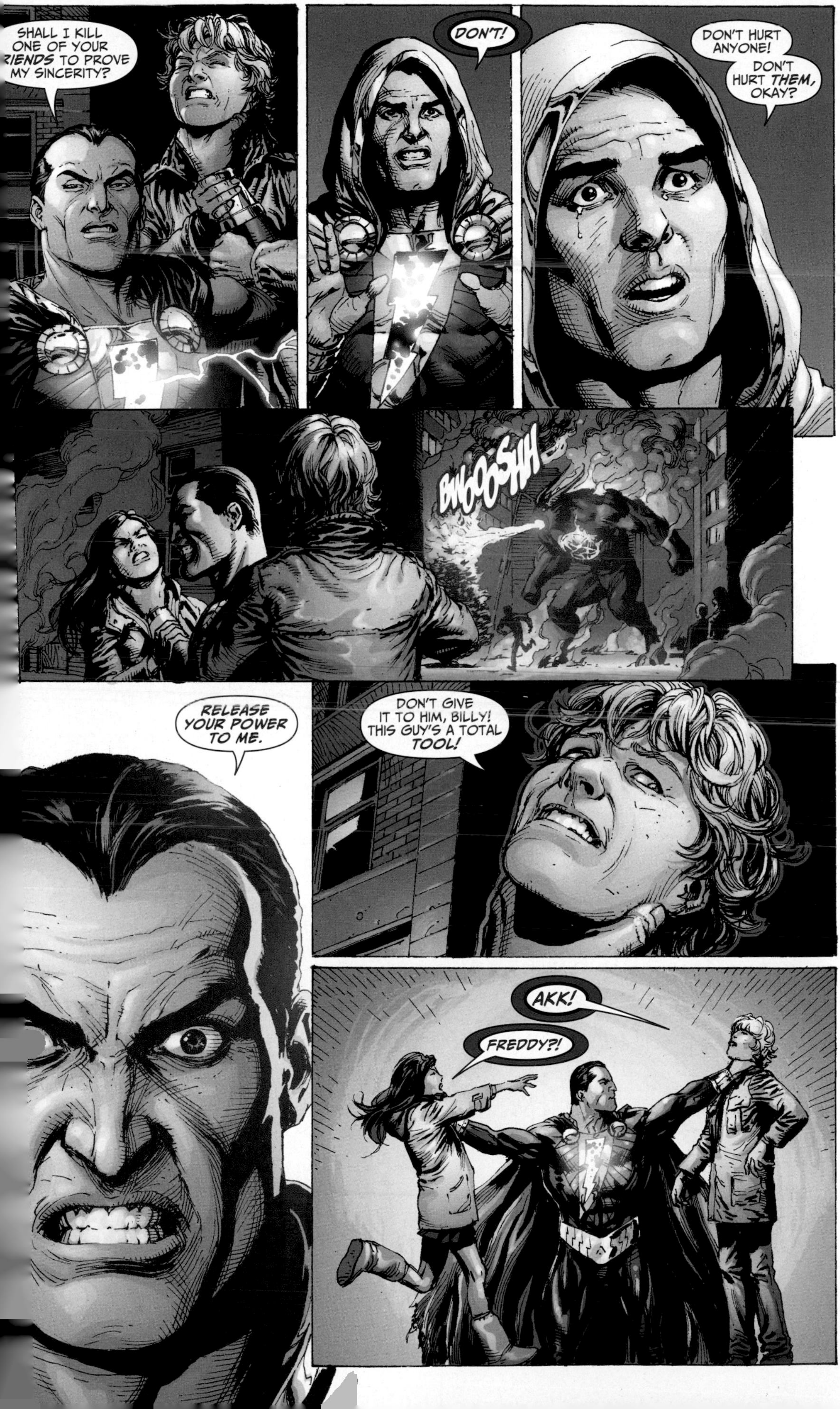
SHALL I KILL ONE OF YOUR FRIENDS TO PROVE MY SINCERITY?
DON'T!
DON'T HURT ANYONE!
DON'T HURT THEM, OKAY?
BWOOOSHH
RELEASE YOUR POWER TO ME.
DON'T GIVE IT TO HIM, BILLY! THIS GUY'S A TOTAL TOOL!
AKK!
FREDDY?!

OKAY! OKAY, THE POWER IS *YOURS!*

I DON'T EVEN KNOW HOW...HOW DO I DO IT?

WE ARE AS *CONNECTED* AS *FAMILY* THANKS TO THE WIZARD'S BLESSING.

AND THIS LIGHTNING FLOWS THROUGH FAMILY.

BILLY?

DO NOT FORGET WHAT THE WIZARD TOLD YOU.

FRANCESCA?

FAMILY IS WHAT IT CAN BE, NOT WHAT IT SHOULD BE.

SAY THE *WORD* AND *RELEASE* THE *LIVING LIGHTNING* TO ME.

"FAMILY IS WHAT IT CAN BE, NOT WHAT IT SHOULD BE"? *THE SECRET SPELL!*

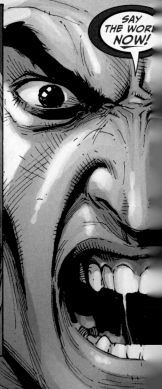

SAY THE WORD *NOW!*

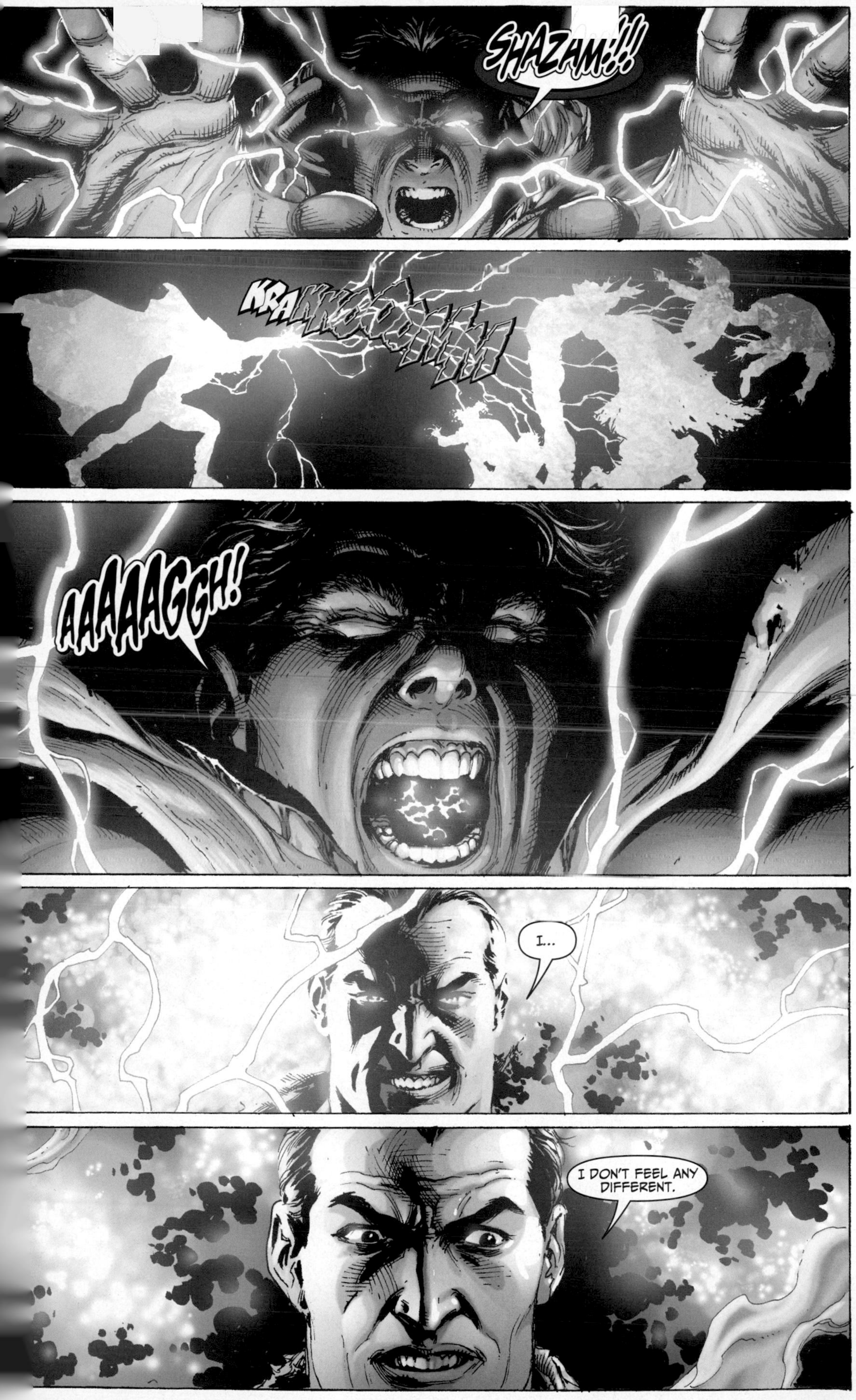
SHAZAM!!!
KRAKKOOOMM
AAAAAGGH!
I...
I DON'T FEEL ANY DIFFERENT.

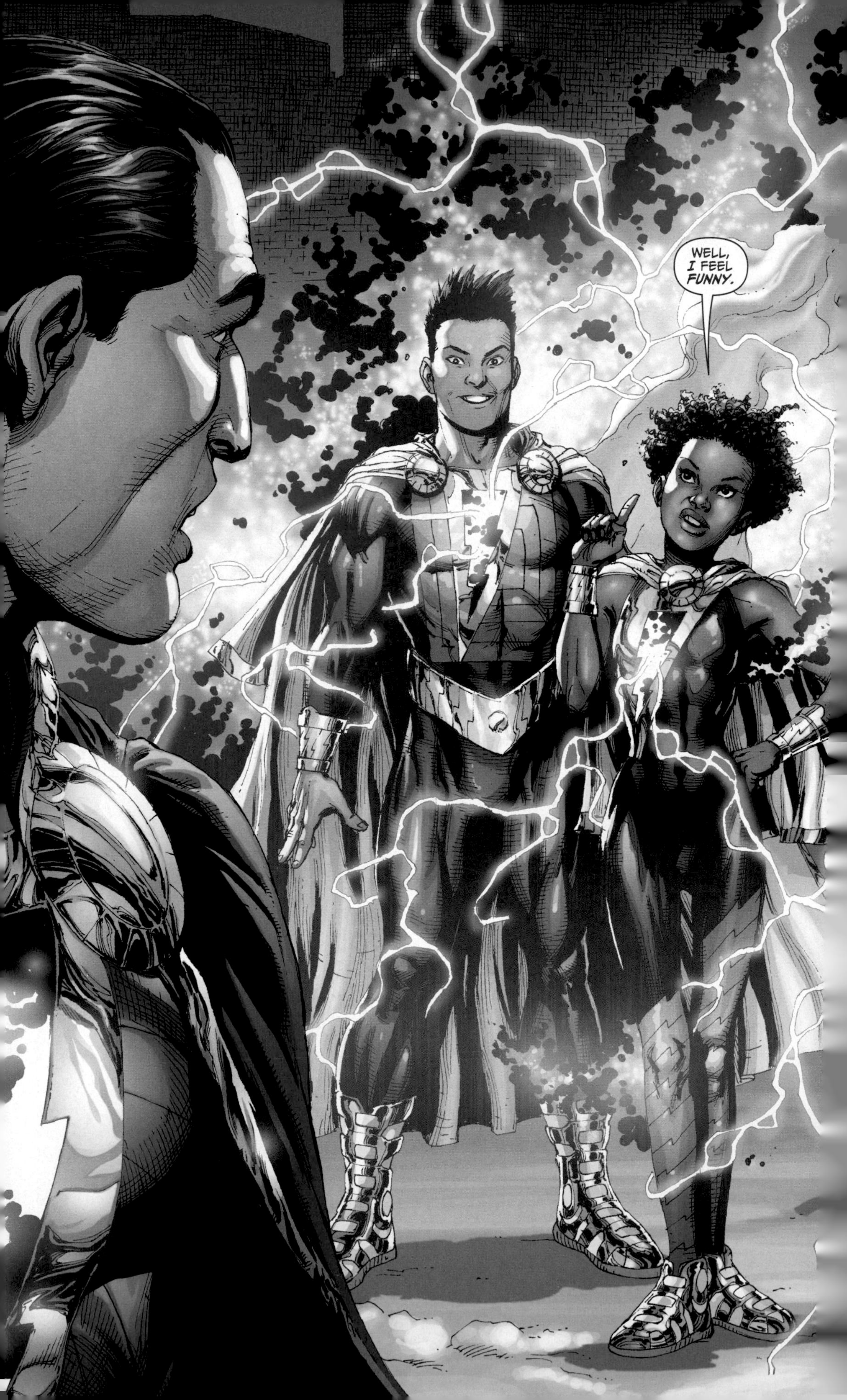
WELL, I FEEL FUNNY.

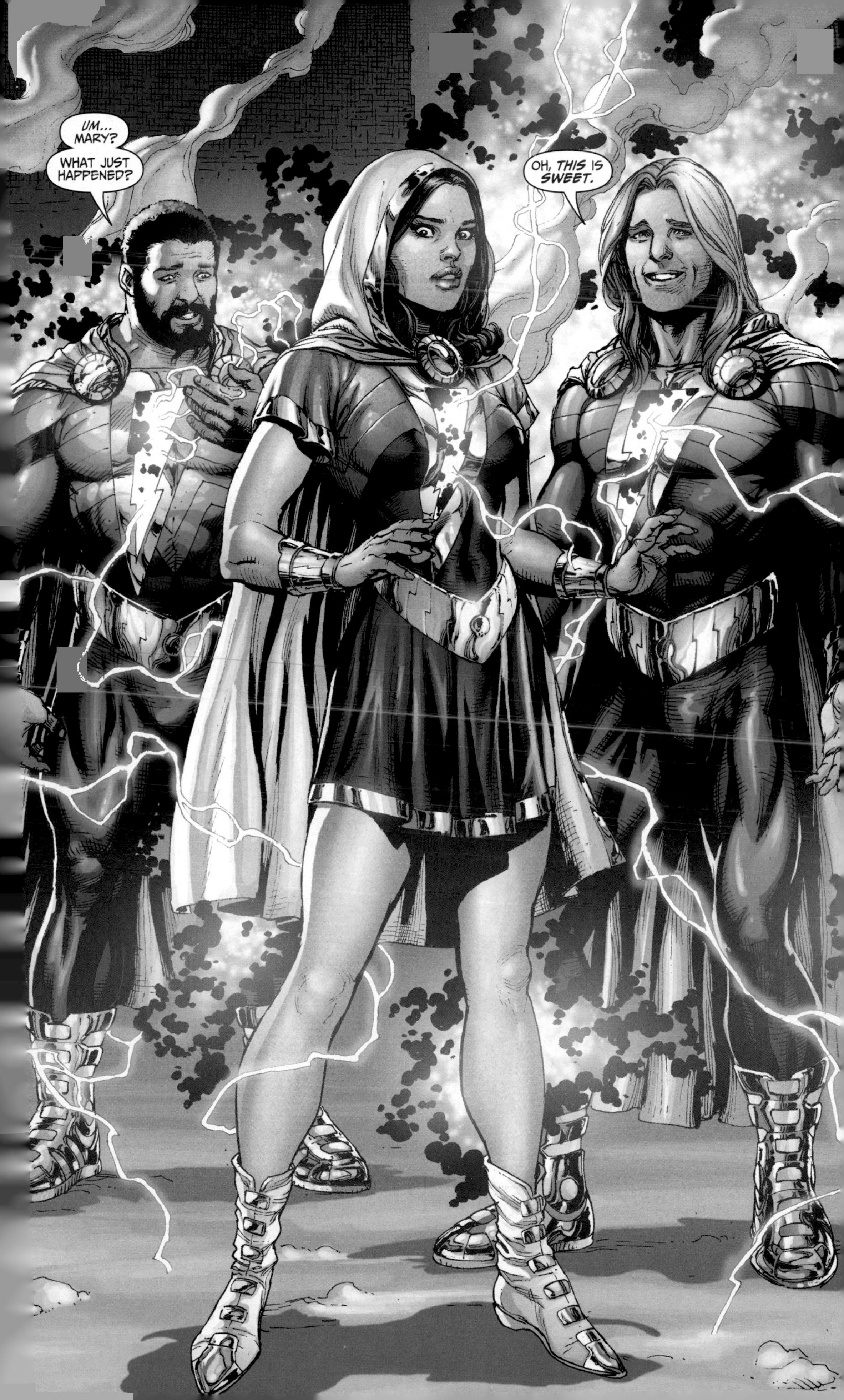
UM... MARY?
WHAT JUST HAPPENED?
OH, THIS IS SWEET.

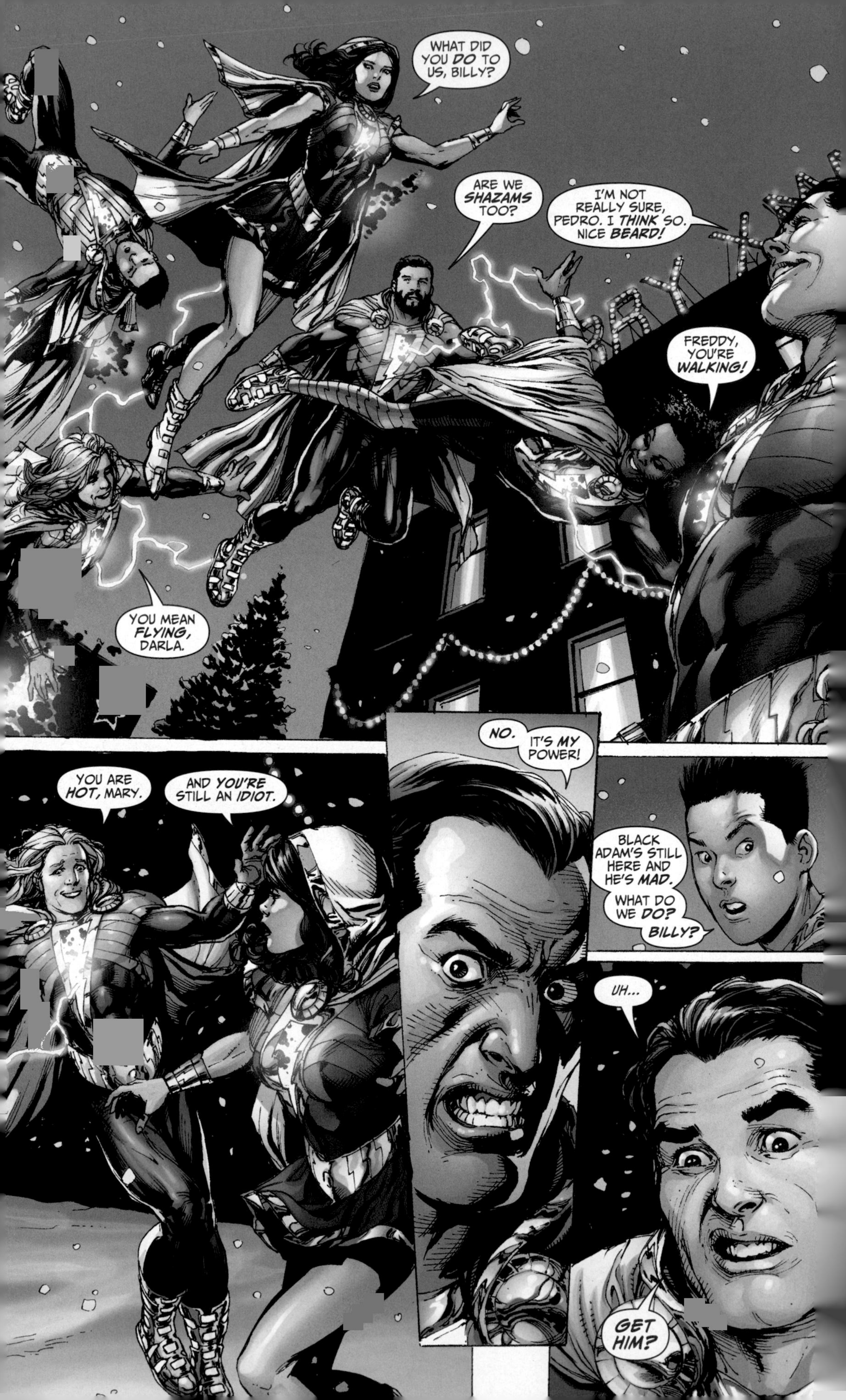
WHAT DID YOU DO TO US, BILLY?
ARE WE SHAZAMS TOO?
I'M NOT REALLY SURE, PEDRO. I THINK SO. NICE BEARD!
FREDDY, YOU'RE WALKING!
YOU MEAN FLYING, DARLA.
YOU ARE HOT, MARY.
AND YOU'RE STILL AN IDIOT.
NO.
IT'S MY POWER!
BLACK ADAM'S STILL HERE AND HE'S MAD.
WHAT DO WE DO?
BILLY?
UH...
GET HIM?

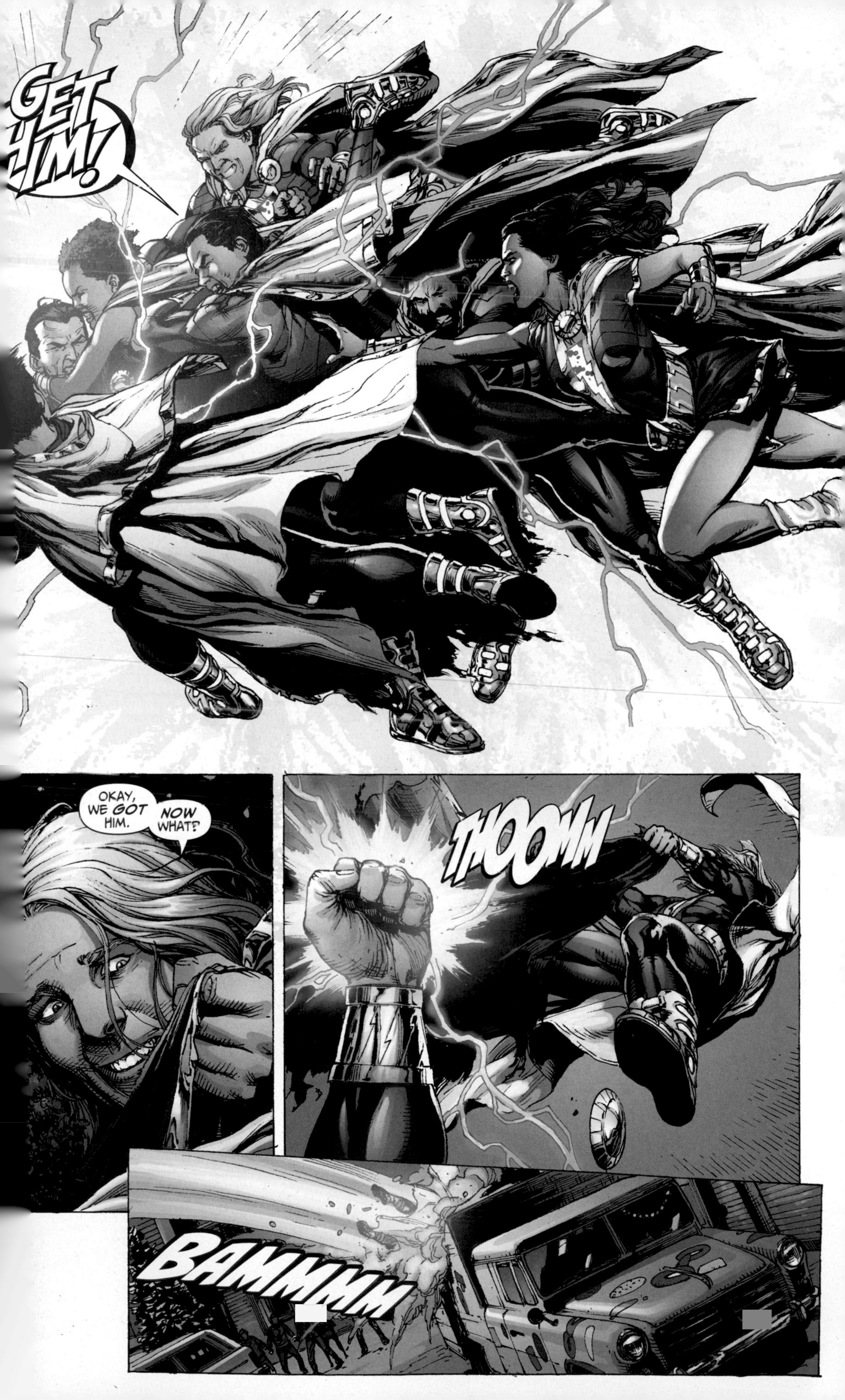
GET HIM!
OKAY, WE GOT HIM.
NOW WHAT?
THOOMM
BAMMMMM

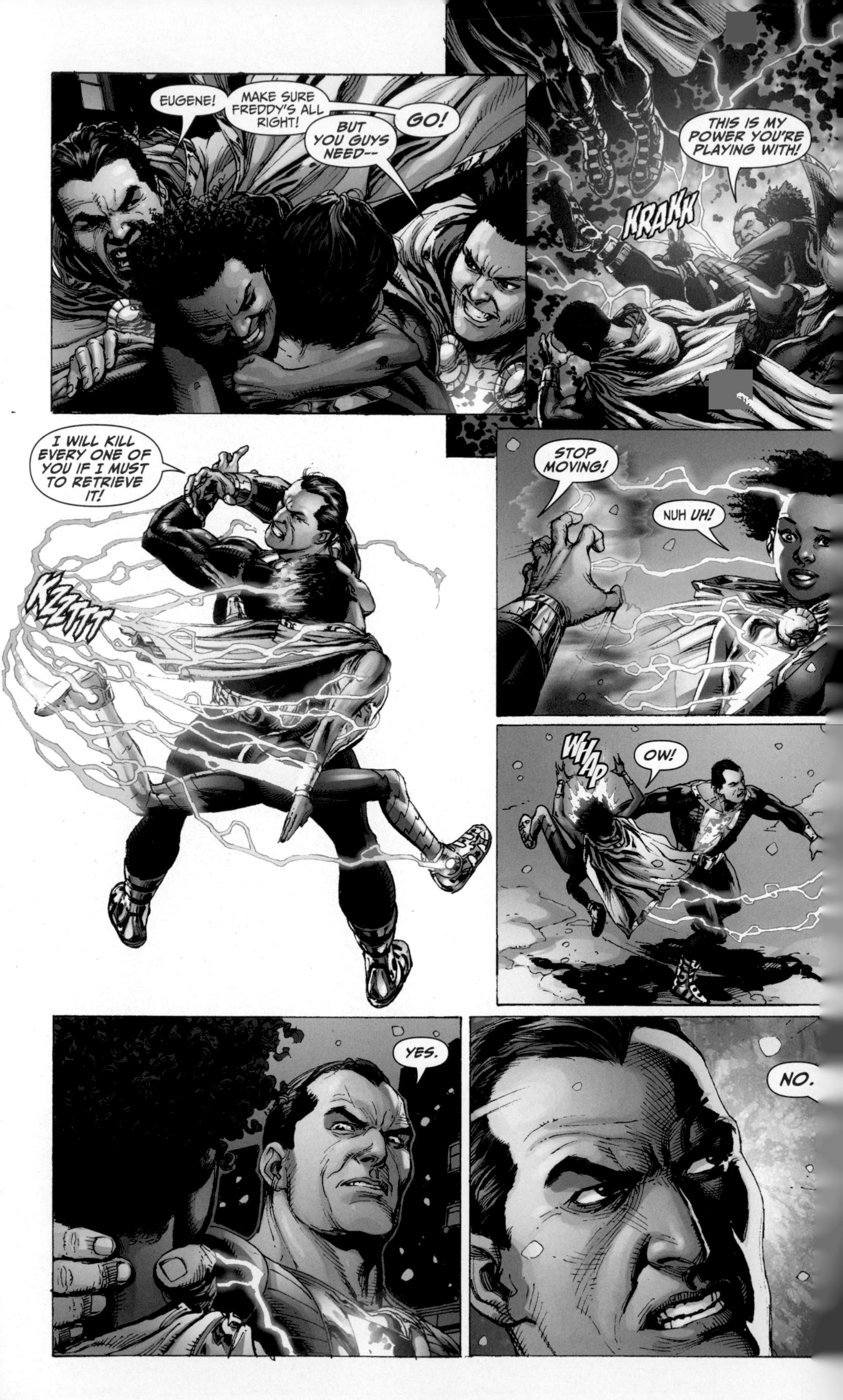
EUGENE!
MAKE SURE FREDDY'S ALL RIGHT!
GO!
BUT YOU GUYS NEED--
THIS IS MY POWER YOU'RE PLAYING WITH!
KRAKK
I WILL KILL EVERY ONE OF YOU IF I MUST TO RETRIEVE IT!
KZZTTT
STOP MOVING!
NUH UH!
WHAP
OW!
YES.
NO.

LET HER GO!

KRRAKOOOOMMM

FREDDY?

OH, GEEZ. I NEED TO MOVE THIS VAN--

HONK HONK

VROOMM

DID THAT VAN JUST DO WHAT YOU *ASKED* IT TO?

I CAN HEAR THEM TALKING TO ME, FREDDY.

I CAN HEAR EVERY CAR, COMPUTER, EVEN THE CELL PHONES.

THEY'RE ASKING ME HOW THEY CAN HELP.

HOW ARE YOU DOING *THAT*, EUGENE?

MY DIGITAL DEVICES. WHEN BILLY CHANGED US, THEY ALL *VANISHED*.

MAYBE THEY [ME]RGED INTO YOU! [LI]KE *"THE FLY"*!

HEY, TELL THAT VAN *THANKS A LOT* FOR BREAKING MY FALL!

UH, GOOD JOB, VAN?

HONK HO-

88 · 15

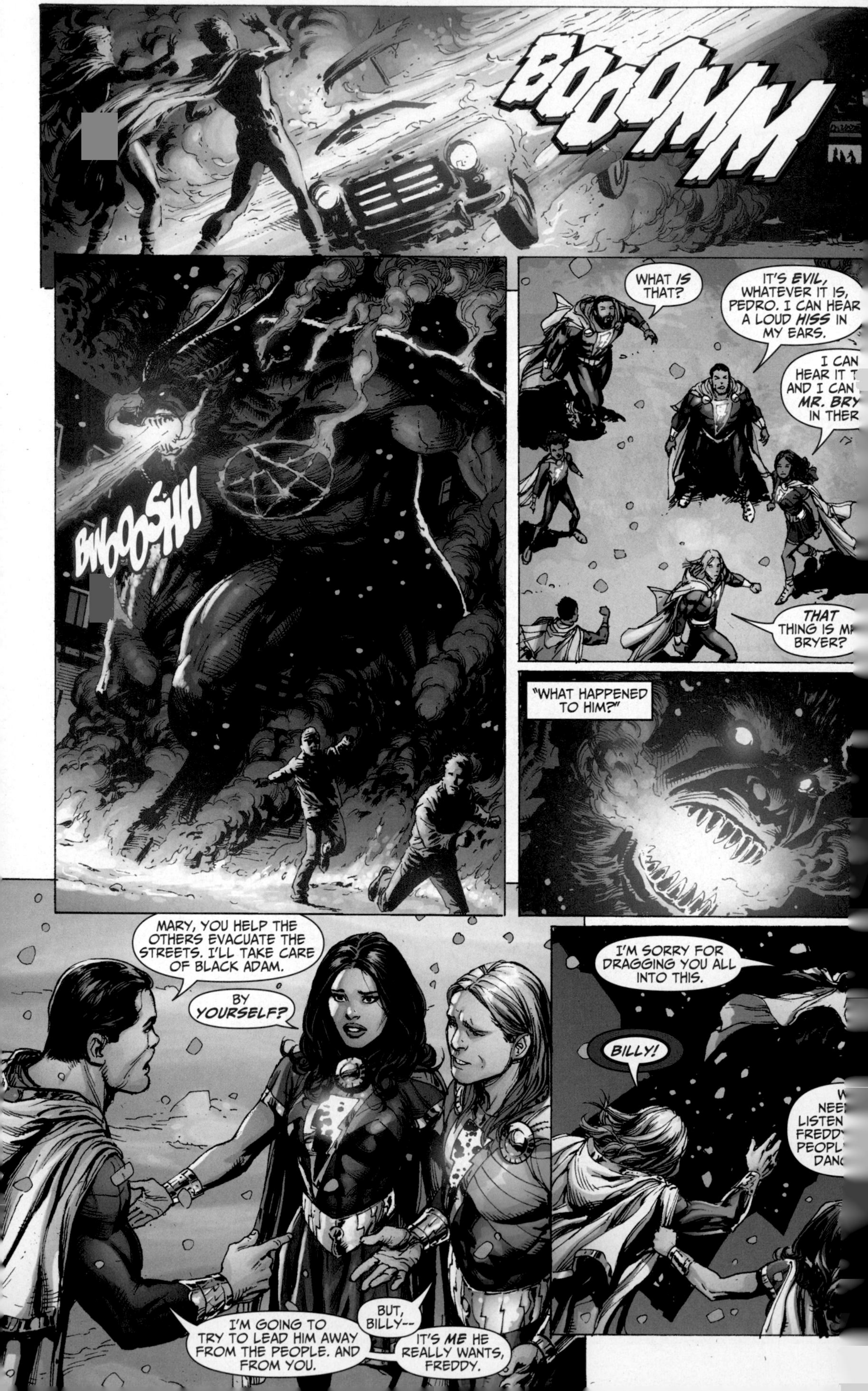
BOOOMM
BWOOOSHH
WHAT IS THAT?
IT'S EVIL, WHATEVER IT IS, PEDRO. I CAN HEAR A LOUD HISS IN MY EARS.
I CAN HEAR IT T AND I CAN MR. BRY IN THER
THAT THING IS MR BRYER?
"WHAT HAPPENED TO HIM?"
MARY, YOU HELP THE OTHERS EVACUATE THE STREETS. I'LL TAKE CARE OF BLACK ADAM.
BY YOURSELF?
I'M GOING TO TRY TO LEAD HIM AWAY FROM THE PEOPLE. AND FROM YOU.
BUT, BILLY--
IT'S ME HE REALLY WANTS, FREDDY.
I'M SORRY FOR DRAGGING YOU ALL INTO THIS.
BILLY!
W NEE LISTEN FREDDY PEOPL DANG

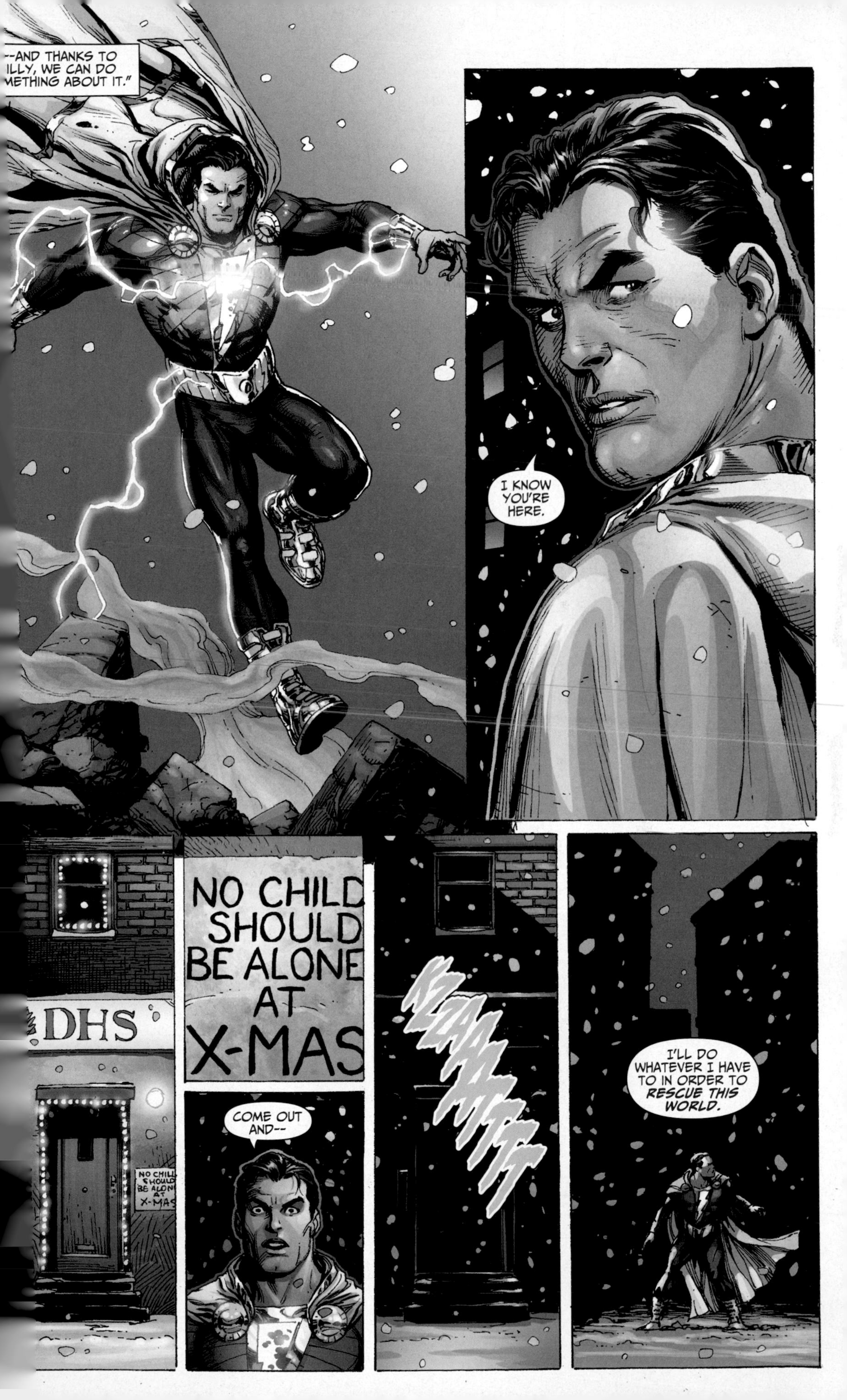
--AND THANKS TO
ILLY, WE CAN DO
METHING ABOUT IT."
I KNOW YOU'RE HERE.
DHS
NO CHILD SHOULD BE ALONE AT X-MAS
COME OUT AND--
KKZAAAKTTTT
I'LL DO WHATEVER I HAVE TO IN ORDER TO RESCUE THIS WORLD.

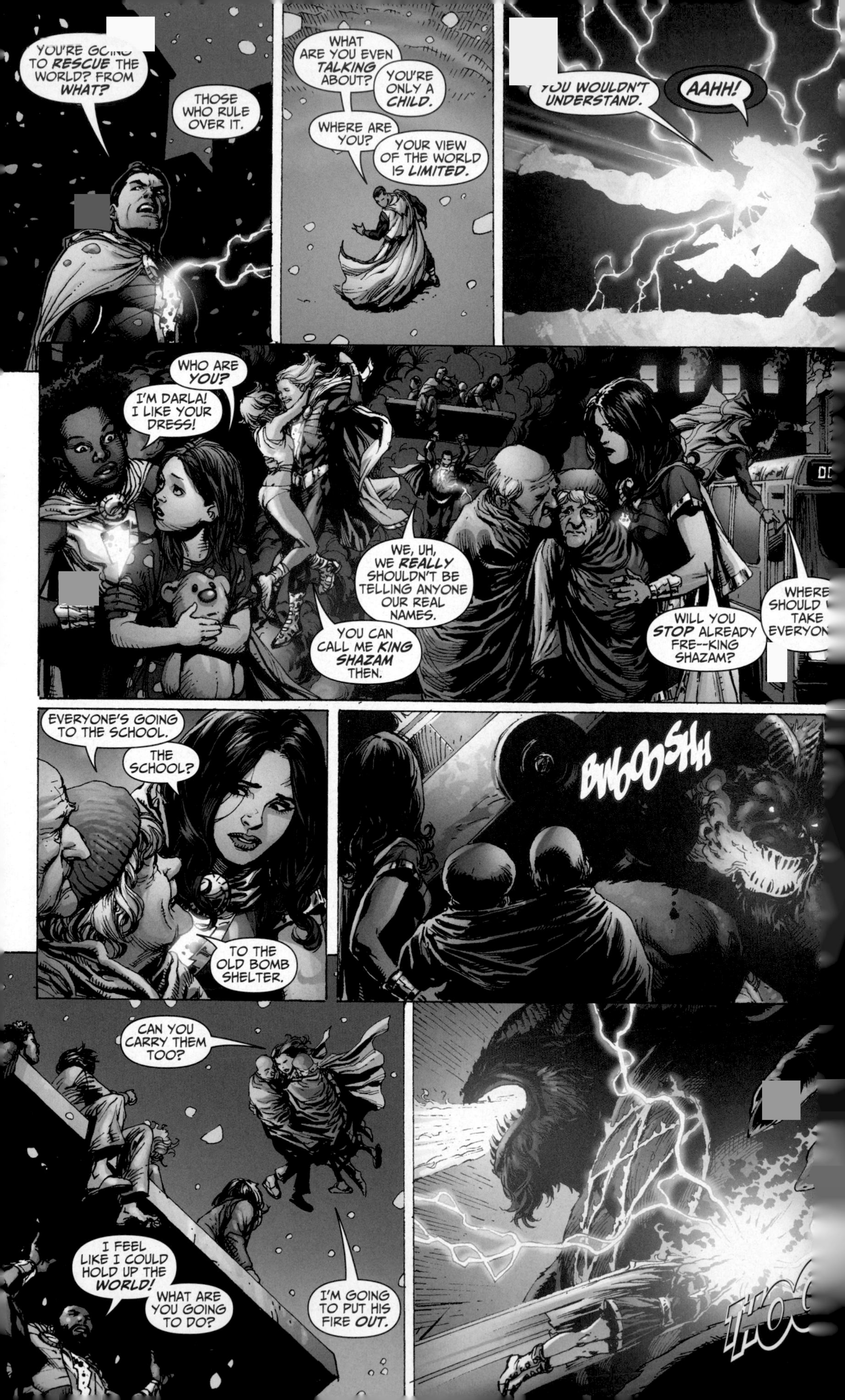

TO RESCUE THE WORLD? FROM WHAT?
THOSE WHO RULE OVER IT.
WHAT ARE YOU EVEN TALKING ABOUT?
YOU'RE ONLY A CHILD.
WHERE ARE YOU?
YOUR VIEW OF THE WORLD IS LIMITED.
UNDERSTAND.
AAHH!
WHO ARE YOU?
I'M DARLA! I LIKE YOUR DRESS!
WE, UH, WE REALLY SHOULDN'T BE TELLING ANYONE OUR REAL NAMES.
YOU CAN CALL ME KING SHAZAM THEN.
WILL YOU STOP ALREADY FRE--KING SHAZAM?
TAKE
EVERYONE'S GOING TO THE SCHOOL.
THE SCHOOL?
TO THE OLD BOMB SHELTER.
BWOOOSHH
CAN YOU CARRY THEM TOO?
I FEEL LIKE I COULD HOLD UP THE WORLD!
WHAT ARE YOU GOING TO DO?
I'M GOING TO PUT HIS FIRE OUT.

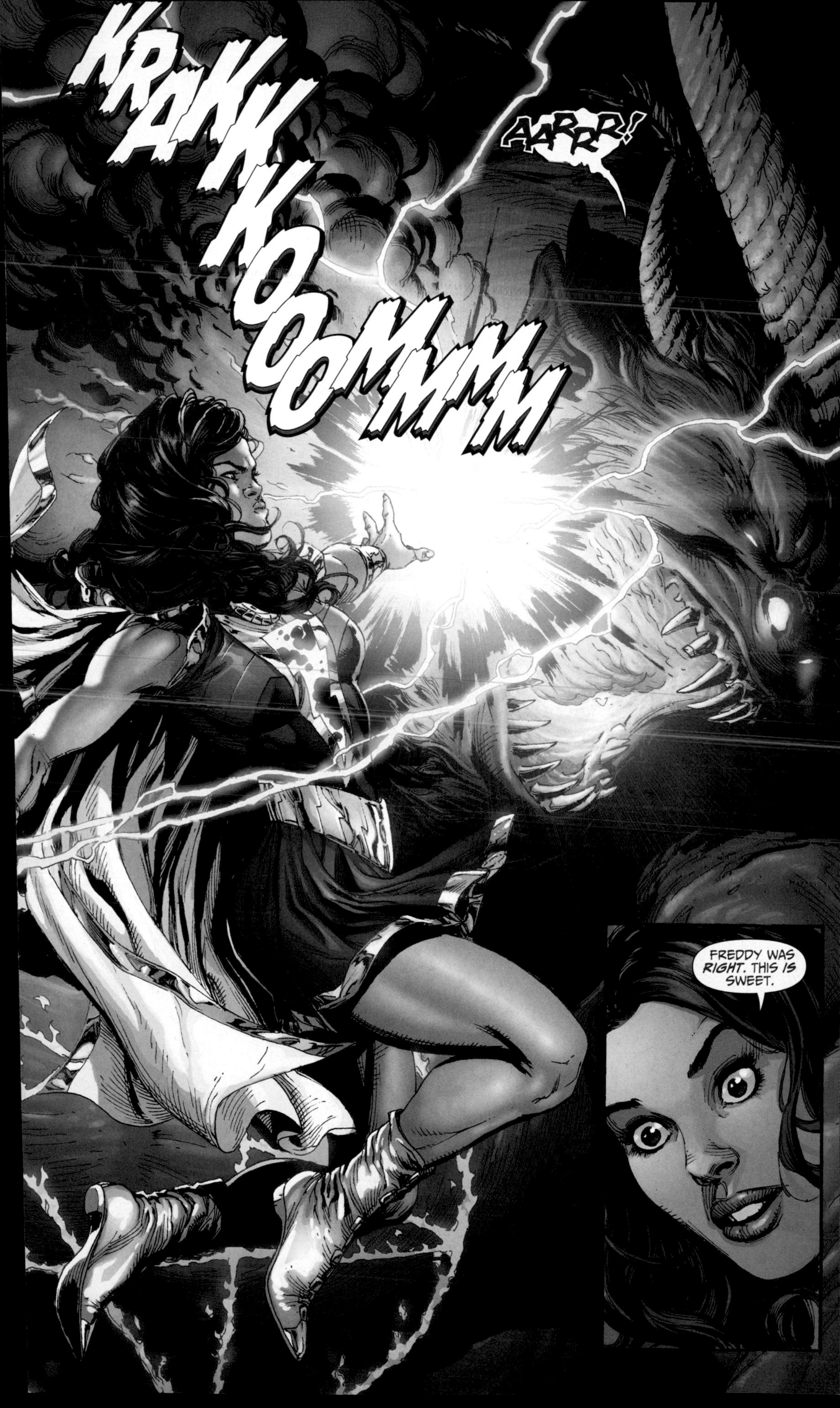
KRAKKKOOOMMM
AARRR!
FREDDY WAS RIGHT. THIS IS SWEET.

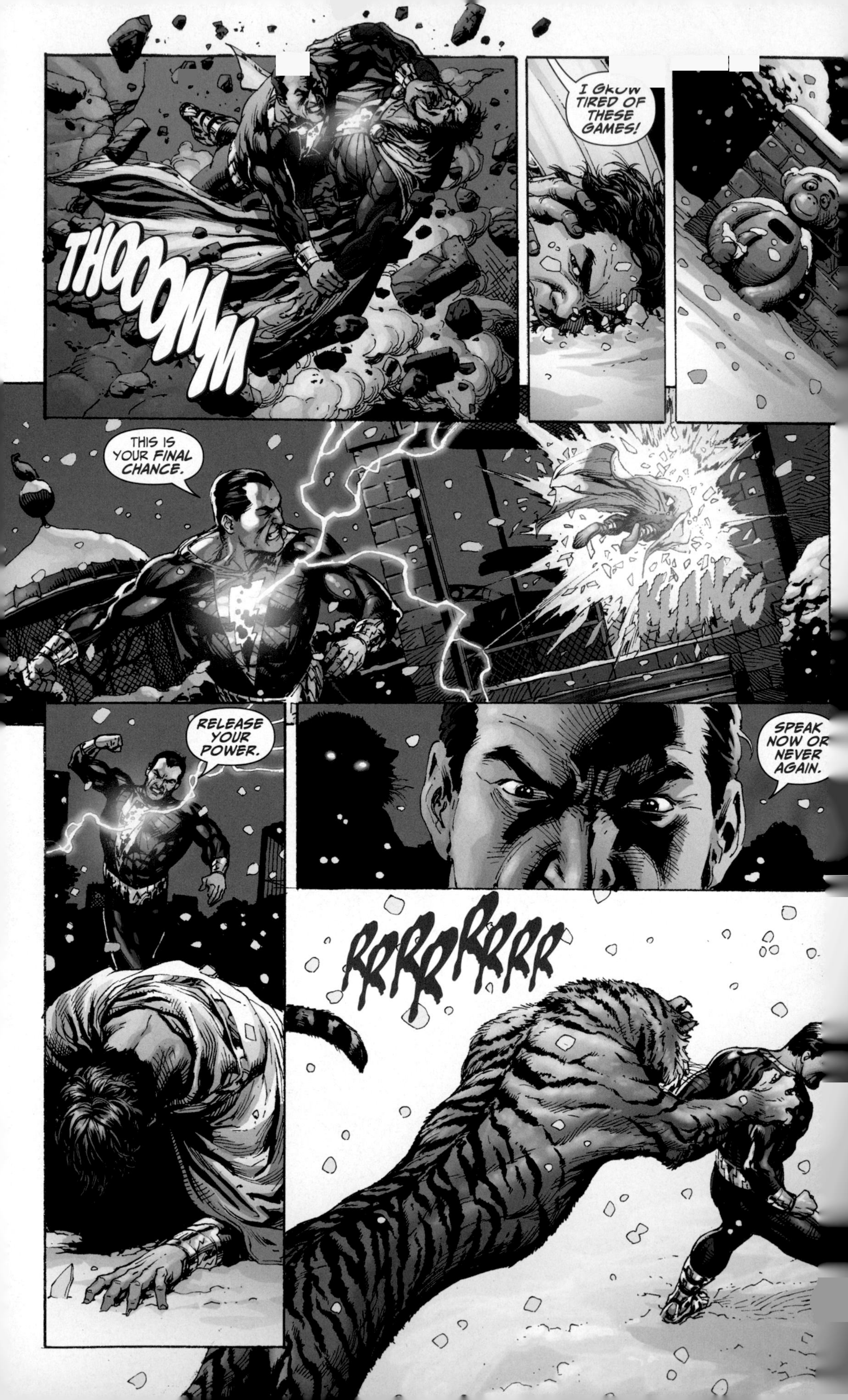
THOOOMM
I GROW TIRED OF THESE GAMES!
THIS IS YOUR FINAL CHANCE.
KLANGG
RELEASE YOUR POWER.
SPEAK NOW OR NEVER AGAIN.
RRRRRRRRR

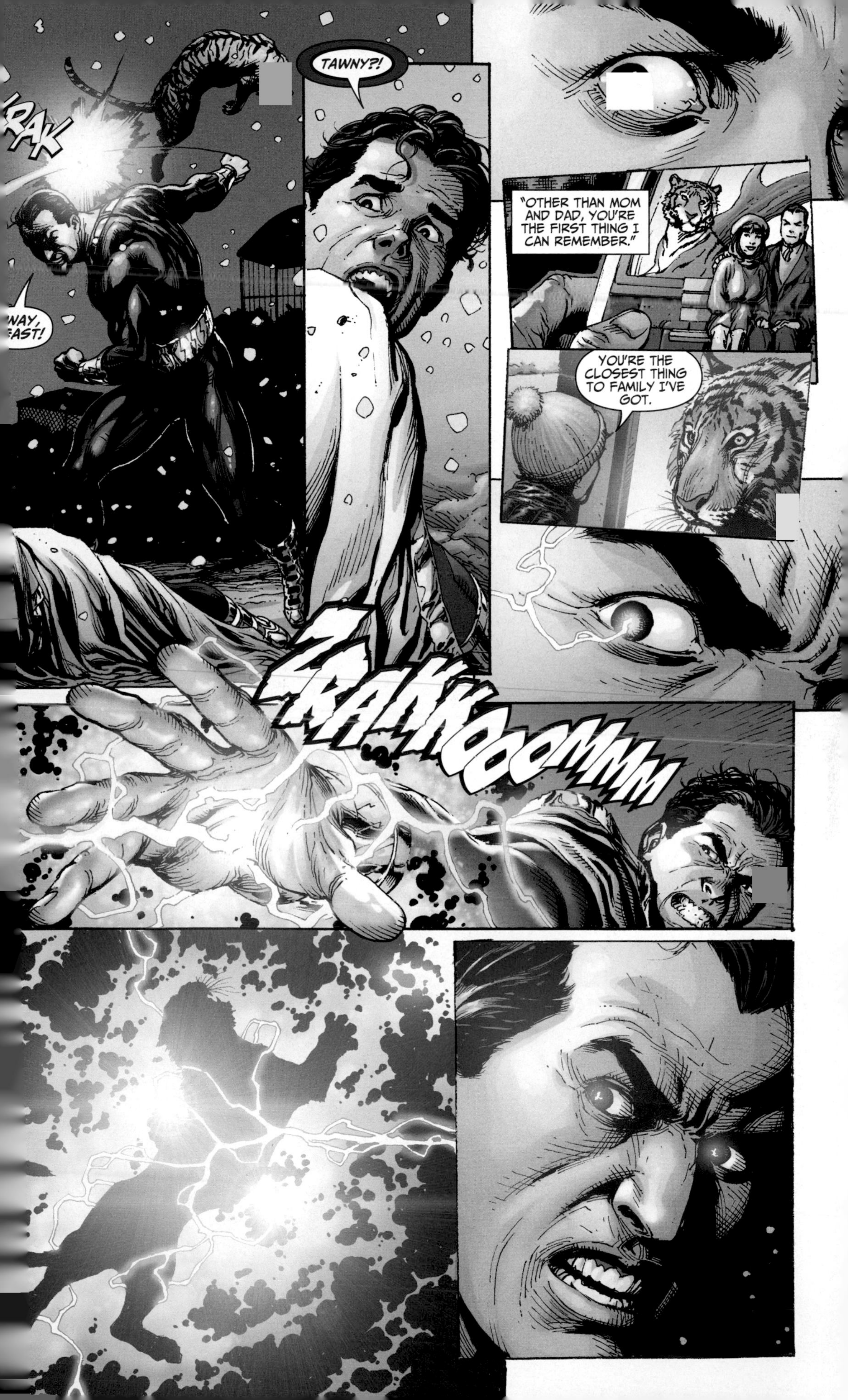
TAWNY?!
"OTHER THAN MOM AND DAD, YOU'RE THE FIRST THING I CAN REMEMBER."
YOU'RE THE CLOSEST THING TO FAMILY I'VE GOT.
ZRAKKOOOMMM

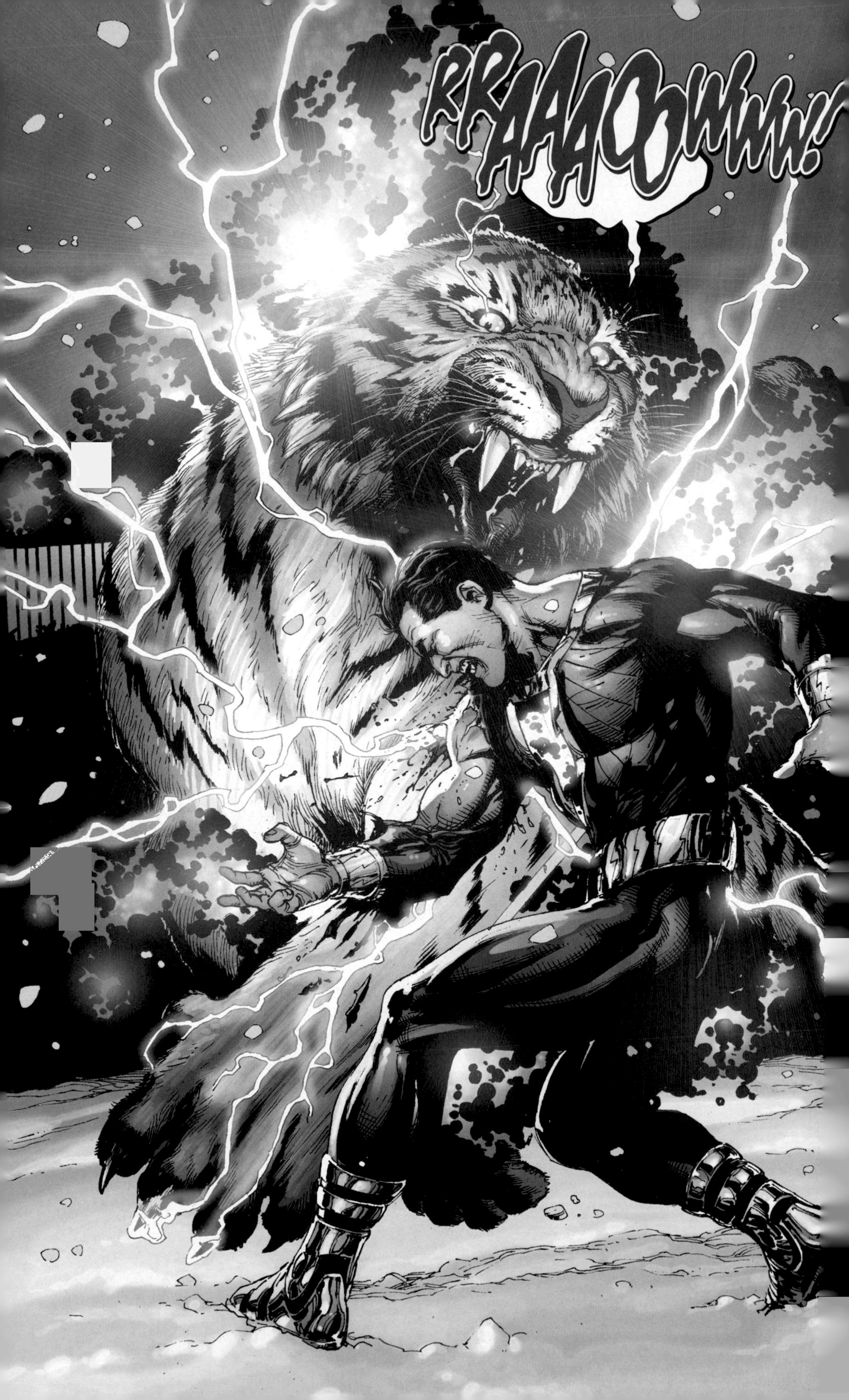
RRAAAOOWWW!

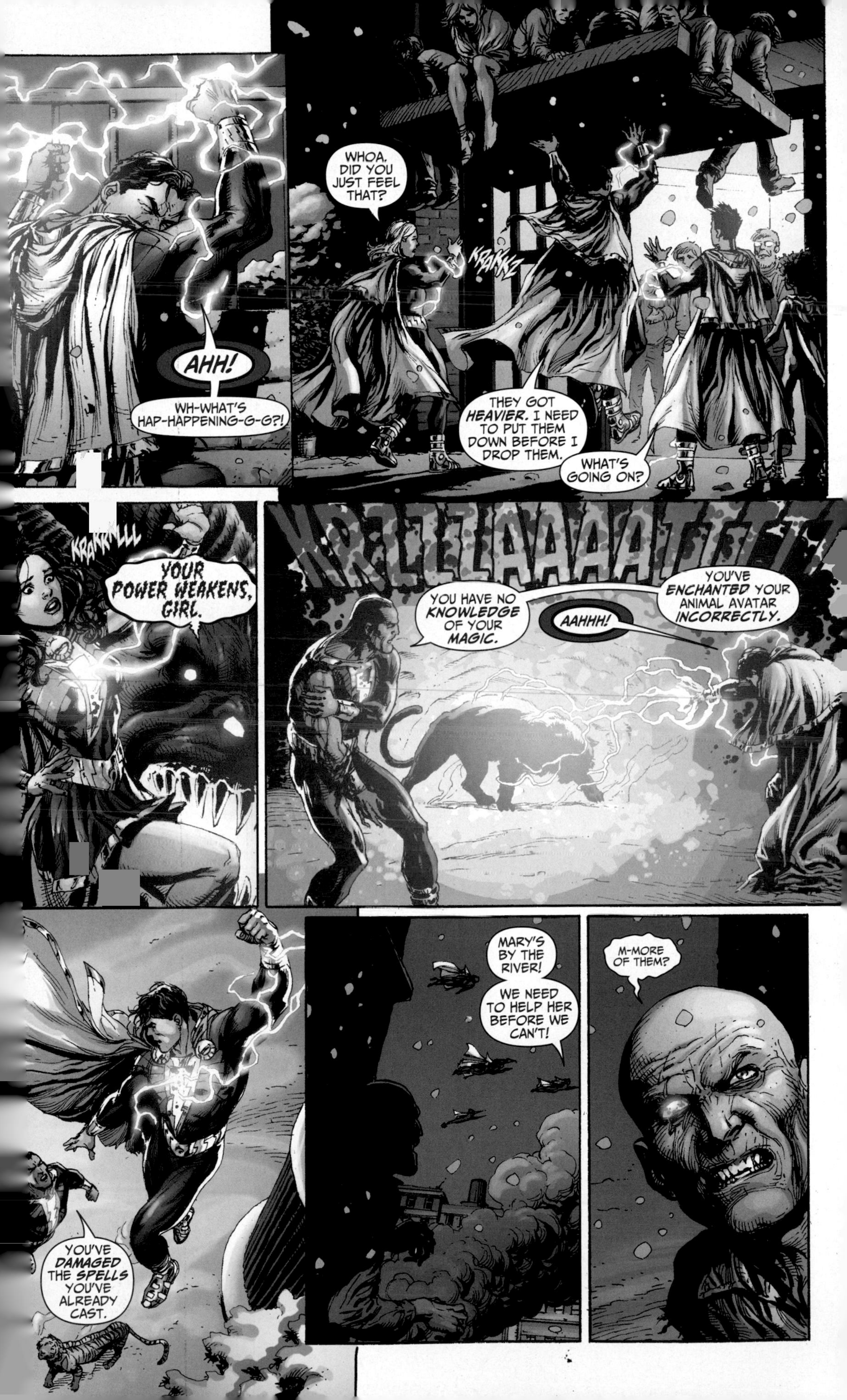
AHH!
WH-WHAT'S HAP-HAPPENING-G-G?!
WHOA. DID YOU JUST FEEL THAT?
KRAKKZ
THEY GOT HEAVIER. I NEED TO PUT THEM DOWN BEFORE I DROP THEM.
WHAT'S GOING ON?
KRAKRLLL
YOUR POWER WEAKENS, GIRL.
YOU HAVE NO KNOWLEDGE OF YOUR MAGIC.
AAHHH!
YOU'VE ENCHANTED YOUR ANIMAL AVATAR INCORRECTLY.
YOU'VE DAMAGED THE SPELLS YOU'VE ALREADY CAST.
MARY'S BY THE RIVER!
WE NEED TO HELP HER BEFORE WE CAN'T!
M-MORE OF THEM?

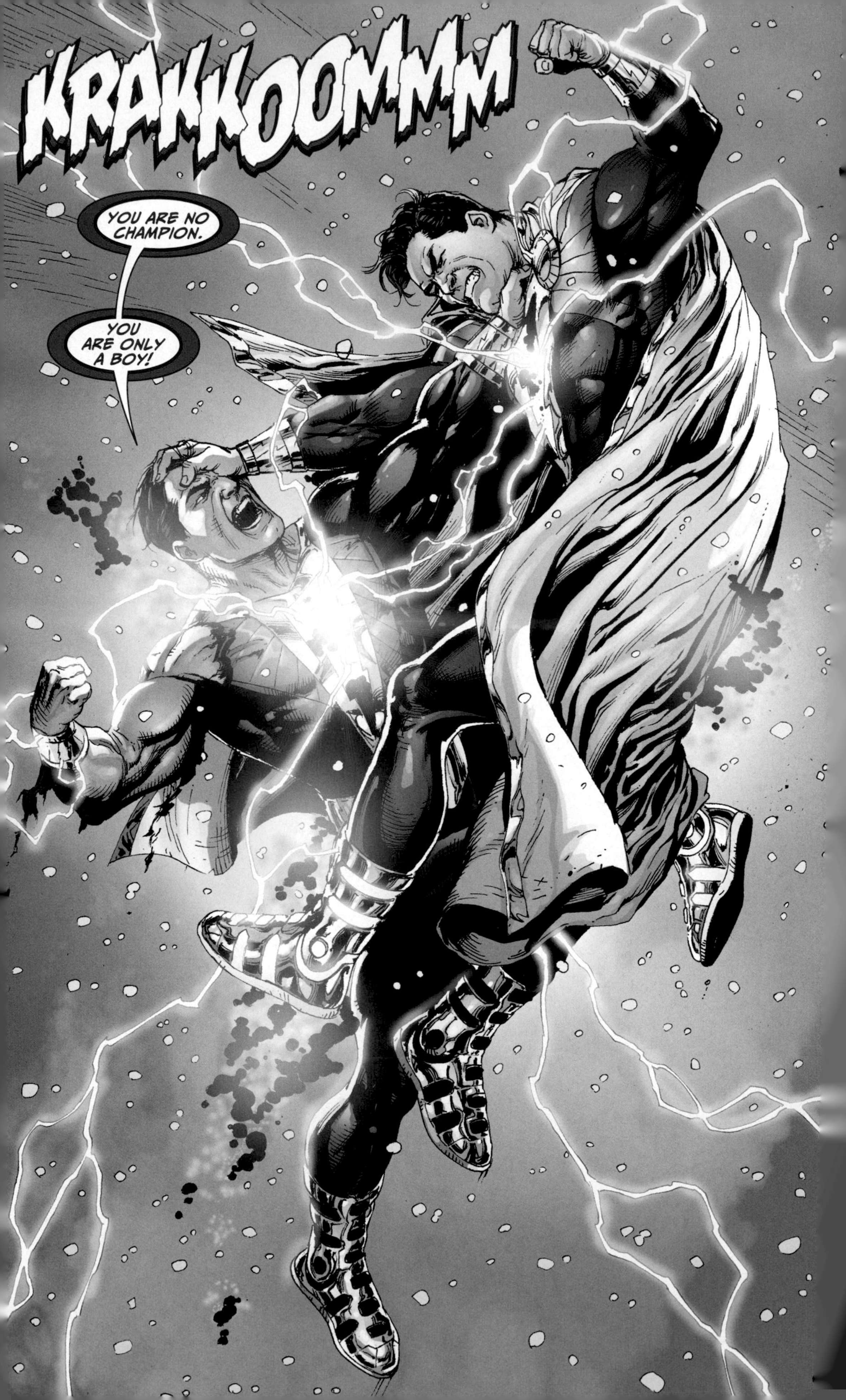
KRAKKOOMMM
YOU ARE NO CHAMPION.
YOU ARE ONLY A BOY!

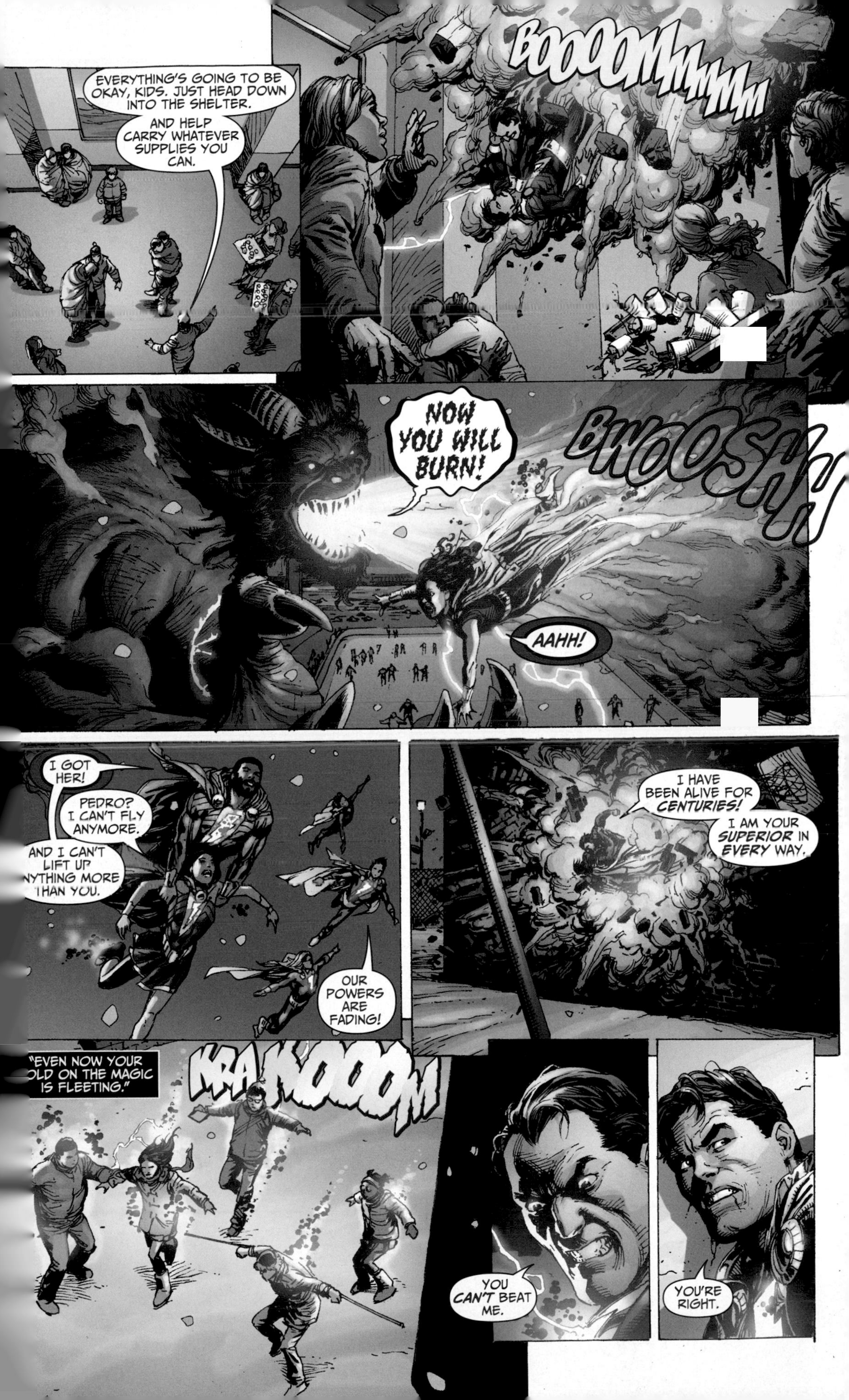
EVERYTHING'S GOING TO BE OKAY, KIDS. JUST HEAD DOWN INTO THE SHELTER.
AND HELP CARRY WHATEVER SUPPLIES YOU CAN.
BOOOOMMMMMM
NOW YOU WILL BURN!
BWOOSH
AAHH!
I GOT HER!
PEDRO? I CAN'T FLY ANYMORE.
AND I CAN'T LIFT UP ANYTHING MORE THAN YOU.
OUR POWERS ARE FADING!
I HAVE BEEN ALIVE FOR CENTURIES!
I AM YOUR SUPERIOR IN EVERY WAY.
"EVEN NOW YOUR HOLD ON THE MAGIC IS FLEETING."
KRA KOOOM
YOU CAN'T BEAT ME.
YOU'RE RIGHT.

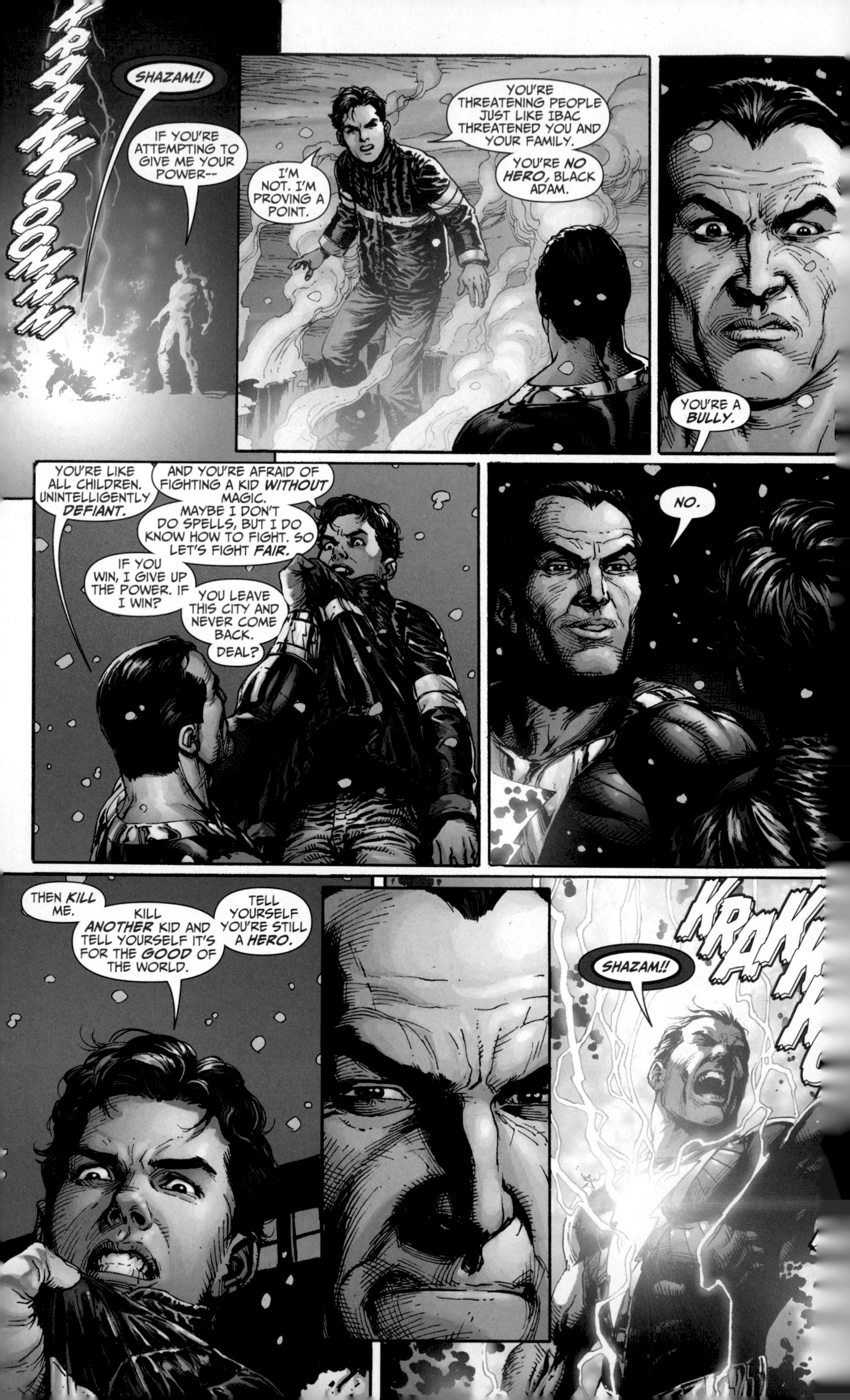
KRAAKHOOOOMMM
SHAZAM!!
IF YOU'RE ATTEMPTING TO GIVE ME YOUR POWER--
I'M NOT. I'M PROVING A POINT.
YOU'RE THREATENING PEOPLE JUST LIKE IBAC THREATENED YOU AND YOUR FAMILY.
YOU'RE NO HERO, BLACK ADAM.
YOU'RE A BULLY.
YOU'RE LIKE ALL CHILDREN. UNINTELLIGENTLY DEFIANT.
AND YOU'RE AFRAID OF FIGHTING A KID WITHOUT MAGIC.
MAYBE I DON'T DO SPELLS, BUT I DO KNOW HOW TO FIGHT. SO LET'S FIGHT FAIR.
IF YOU WIN, I GIVE UP THE POWER. IF I WIN?
YOU LEAVE THIS CITY AND NEVER COME BACK.
DEAL?
NO.
THEN KILL ME.
KILL ANOTHER KID AND TELL YOURSELF IT'S FOR THE GOOD OF THE WORLD.
TELL YOURSELF YOU'RE STILL A HERO.
SHAZAM!!
KRAKK

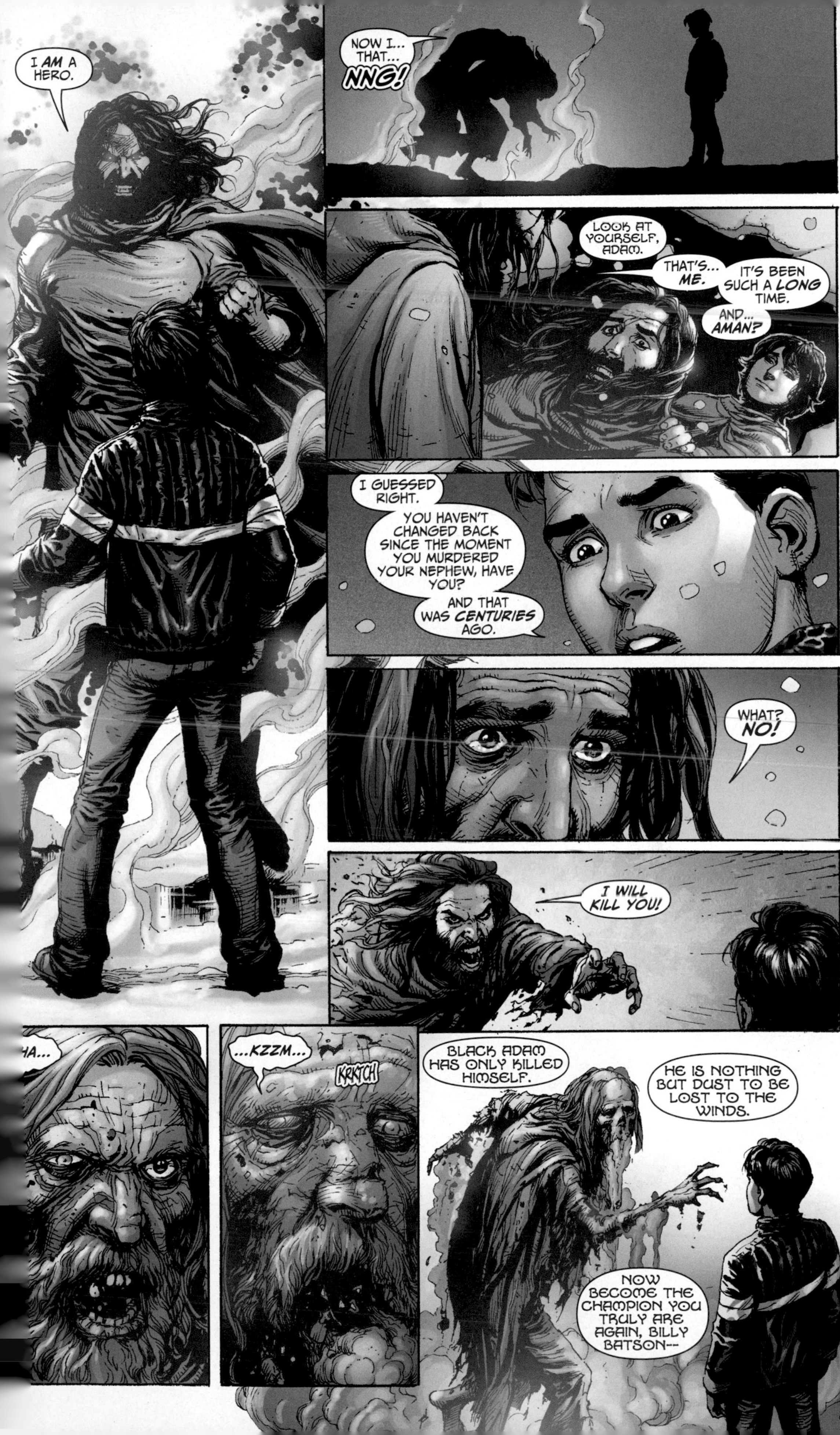
I AM A HERO.
NOW I... THAT... NNG!
LOOK AT YOURSELF, ADAM.
THAT'S... ME.
IT'S BEEN SUCH A LONG TIME.
AND... AMAN?
I GUESSED RIGHT.
YOU HAVEN'T CHANGED BACK SINCE THE MOMENT YOU MURDERED YOUR NEPHEW, HAVE YOU?
AND THAT WAS CENTURIES AGO.
WHAT? NO!
I WILL KILL YOU!
HA...
...KZZM...
KRKTCH
BLACK ADAM HAS ONLY KILLED HIMSELF.
HE IS NOTHING BUT DUST TO BE LOST TO THE WINDS.
NOW BECOME THE CHAMPION YOU TRULY ARE AGAIN, BILLY BATSON--

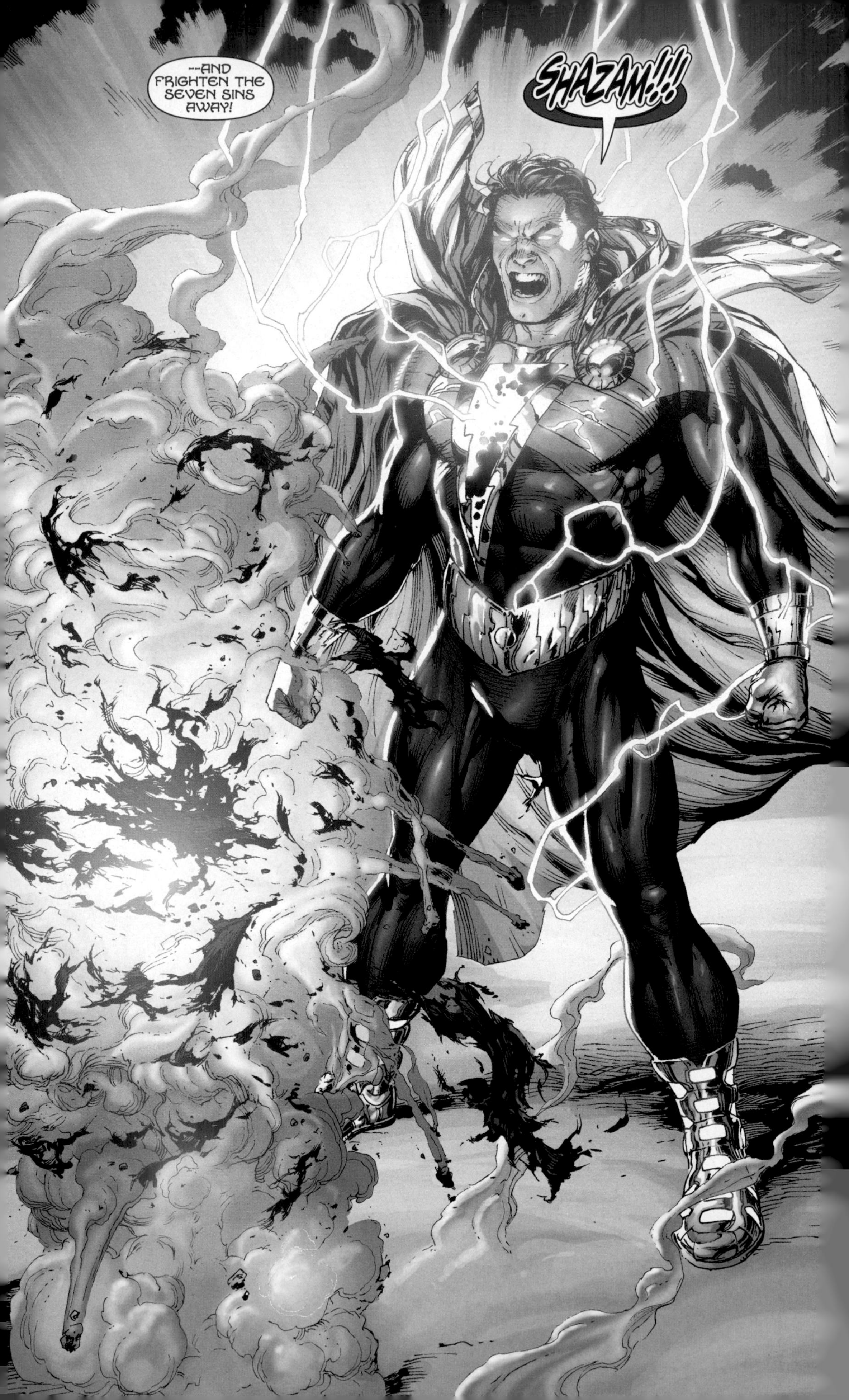
--AND FRIGHTEN THE SEVEN SINS AWAY!
SHAZAM!!!

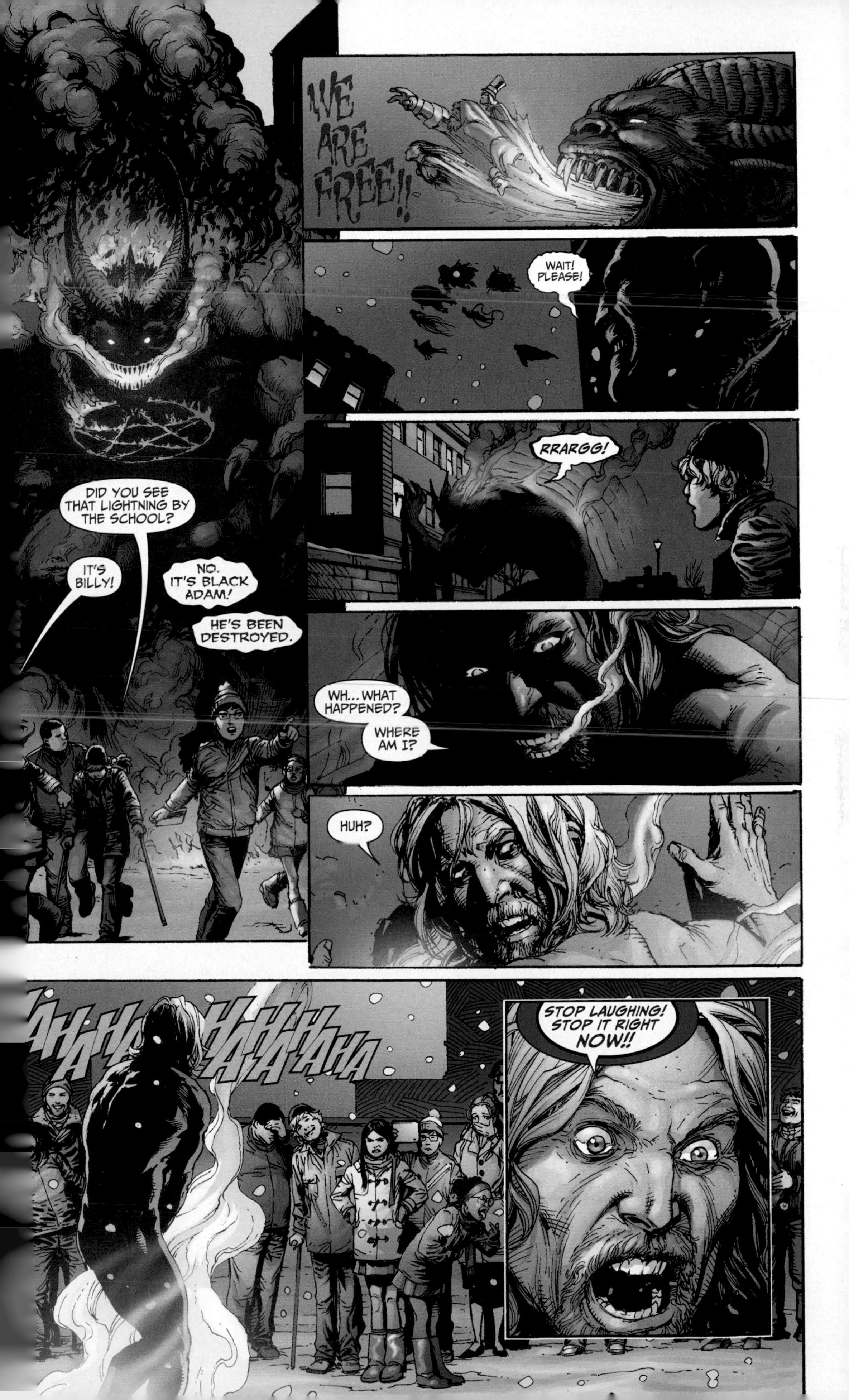
DID YOU SEE THAT LIGHTNING BY THE SCHOOL?
IT'S BILLY!
NO. IT'S BLACK ADAM!
HE'S BEEN DESTROYED.
WE ARE FREE!!
WAIT! PLEASE!
RRARGG!
WH... WHAT HAPPENED?
WHERE AM I?
HUH?
STOP LAUGHING! STOP IT RIGHT NOW!!

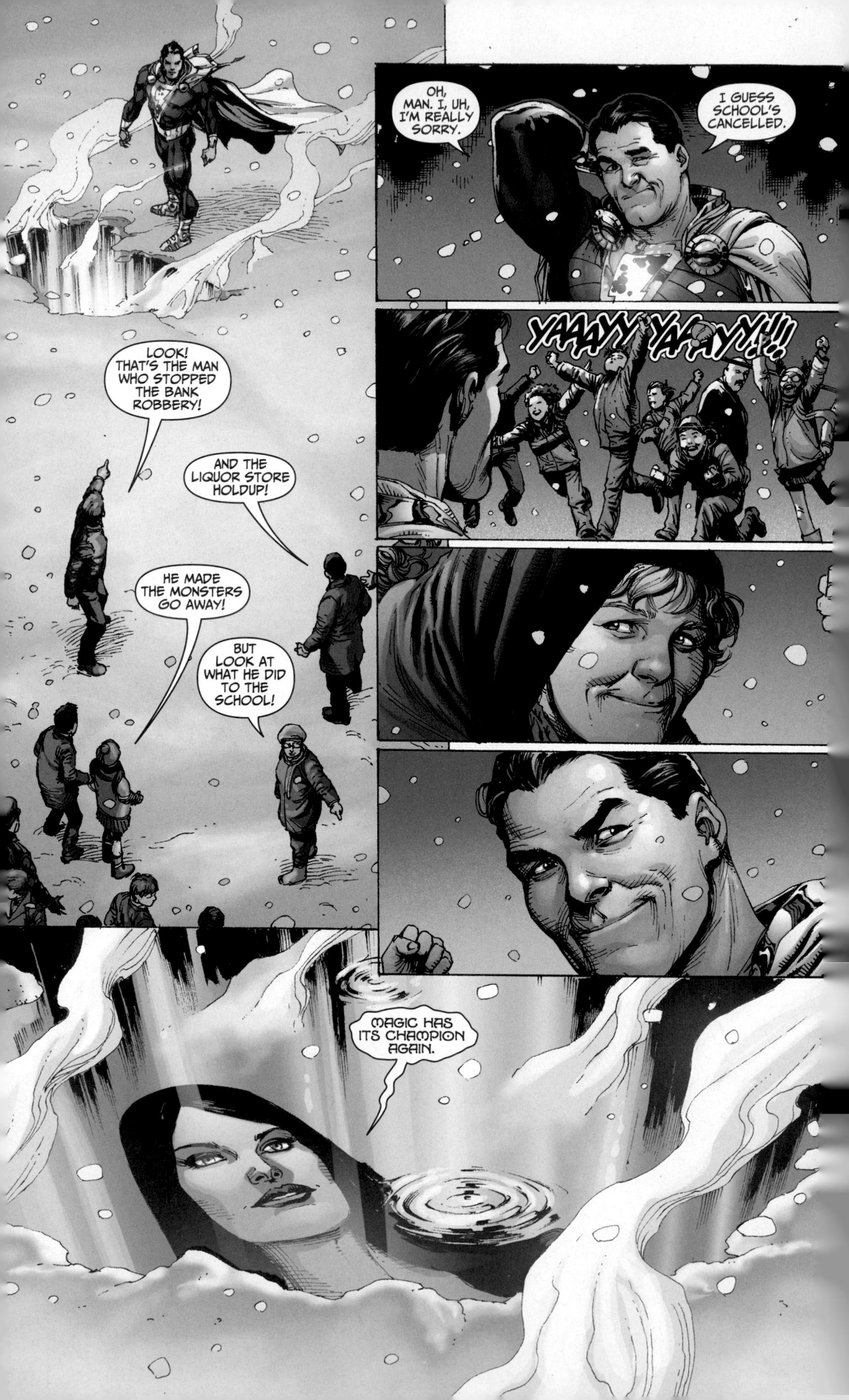
OH, MAN. I, UH, I'M REALLY SORRY.
I GUESS SCHOOL'S CANCELLED.
LOOK! THAT'S THE MAN WHO STOPPED THE BANK ROBBERY!
AND THE LIQUOR STORE HOLDUP!
HE MADE THE MONSTERS GO AWAY!
BUT LOOK AT WHAT HE DID TO THE SCHOOL!
YAAAYY YAAAYY!!!
MAGIC HAS ITS CHAMPION AGAIN.

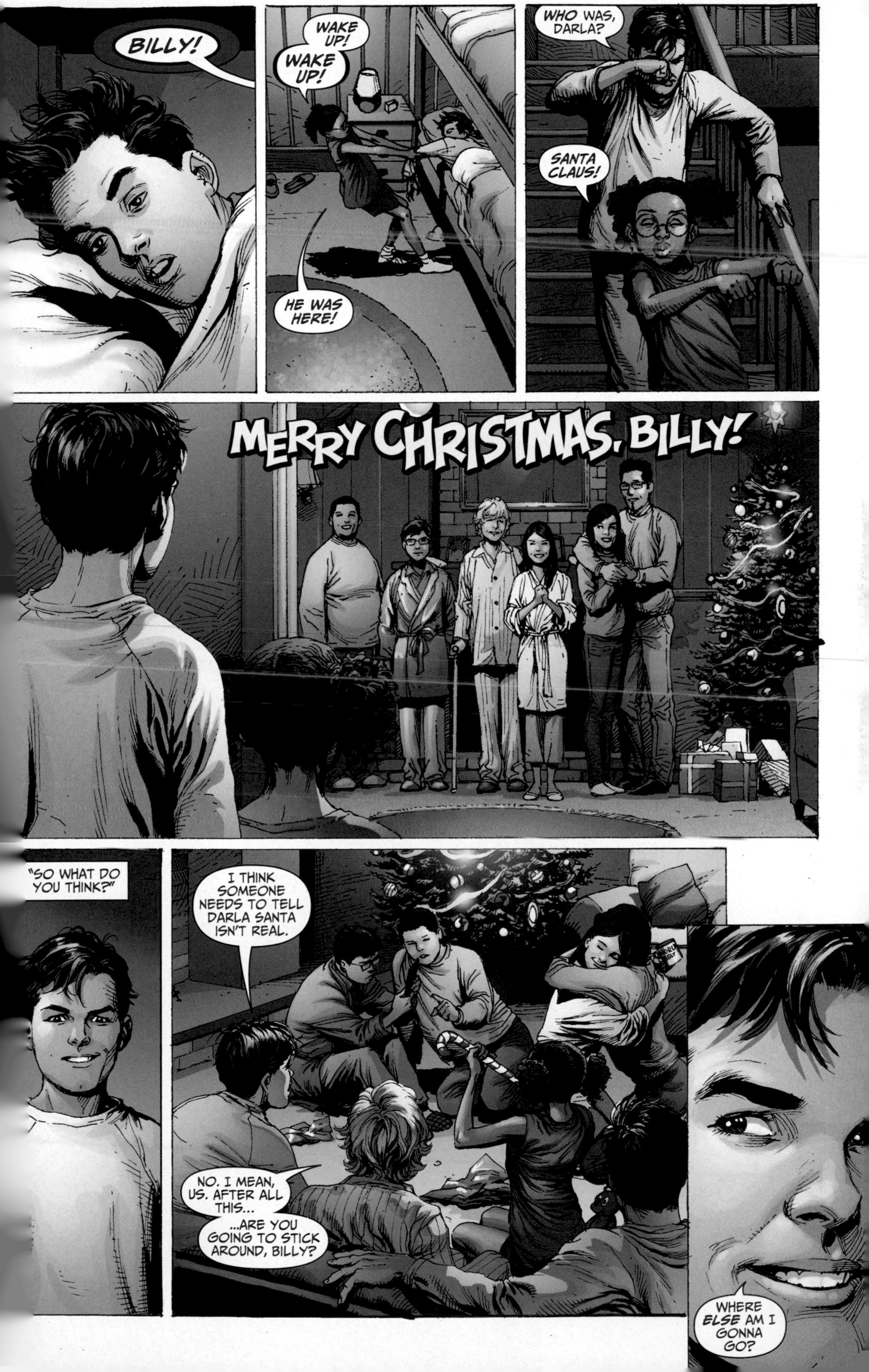
BILLY!
WAKE UP!
WAKE UP!
HE WAS HERE!
WHO WAS, DARLA?
SANTA CLAUS!
MERRY CHRISTMAS, BILLY!
"SO WHAT DO YOU THINK?"
I THINK SOMEONE NEEDS TO TELL DARLA SANTA ISN'T REAL.
NO. I MEAN, US. AFTER ALL THIS...
...ARE YOU GOING TO STICK AROUND, BILLY?
WHERE ELSE AM I GONNA GO?

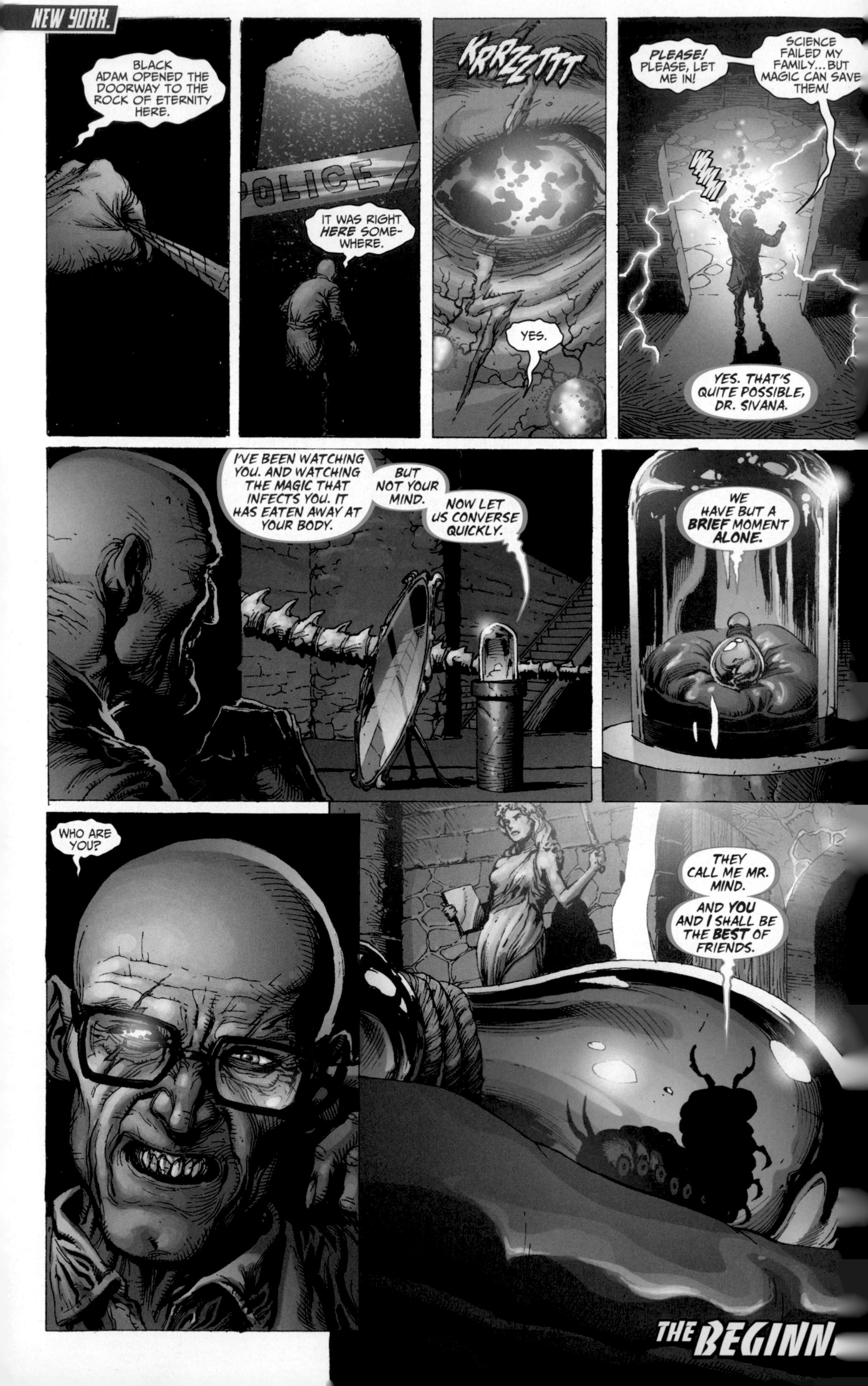
NEW YORK.
BLACK ADAM OPENED THE DOORWAY TO THE ROCK OF ETERNITY HERE.
POLICE
IT WAS RIGHT HERE SOME-WHERE.
KRRZZTTT
YES.
PLEASE! PLEASE, LET ME IN!
SCIENCE FAILED MY FAMILY...BUT MAGIC CAN SAVE THEM!
YES. THAT'S QUITE POSSIBLE, DR. SIVANA.
I'VE BEEN WATCHING YOU. AND WATCHING THE MAGIC THAT INFECTS YOU. IT HAS EATEN AWAY AT YOUR BODY.
BUT NOT YOUR MIND.
NOW LET US CONVERSE QUICKLY.
WE HAVE BUT A BRIEF MOMENT ALONE.
WHO ARE YOU?
THEY CALL ME MR. MIND.
AND YOU AND I SHALL BE THE BEST OF FRIENDS.
THE BEGINN

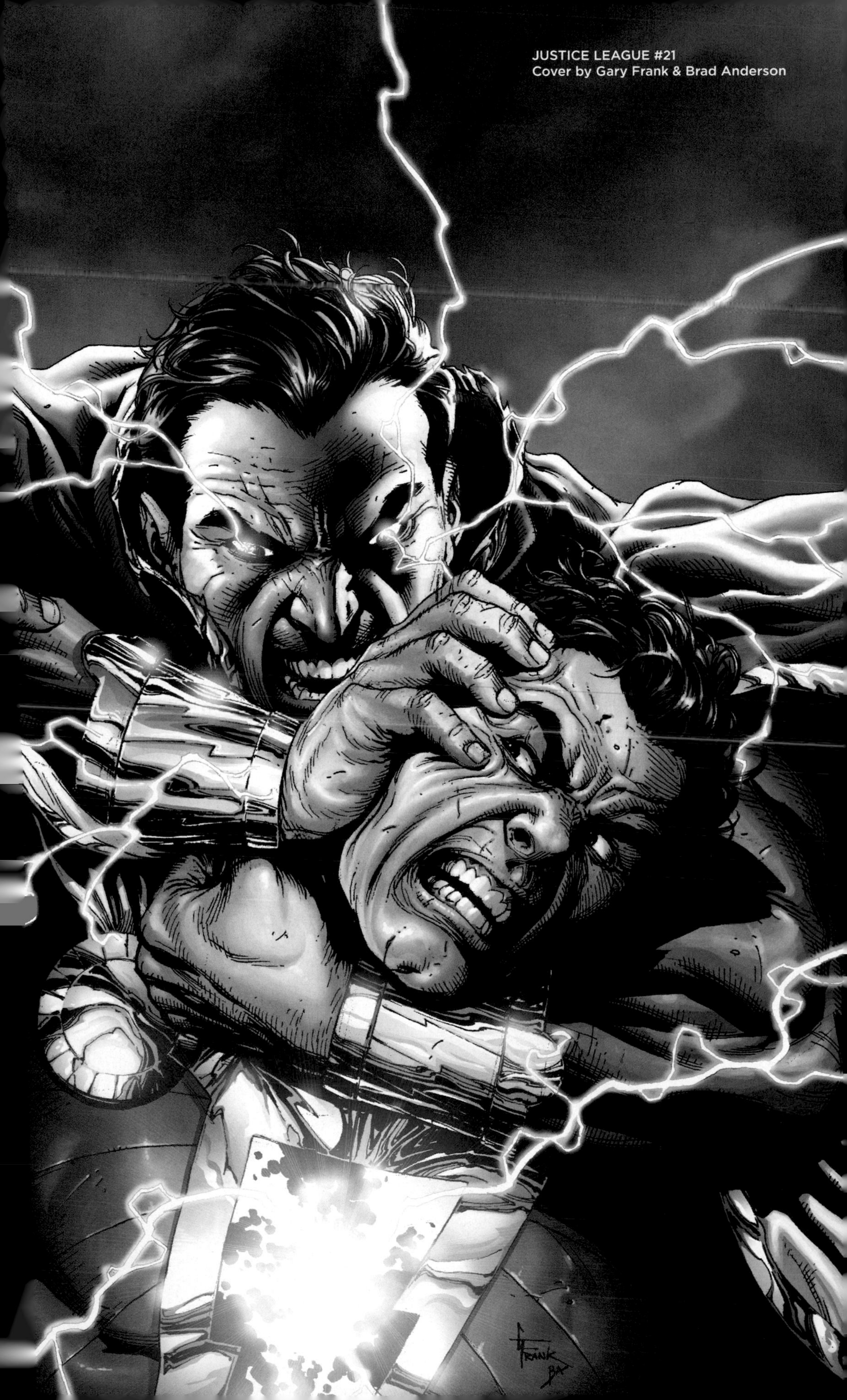

JUSTICE LEAGUE #21
Cover by Gary Frank & Brad Anderson

JUSTICE LEAGUE #21
Variant cover by Shane Davis, Michelle Delecki & Alex Sinclair

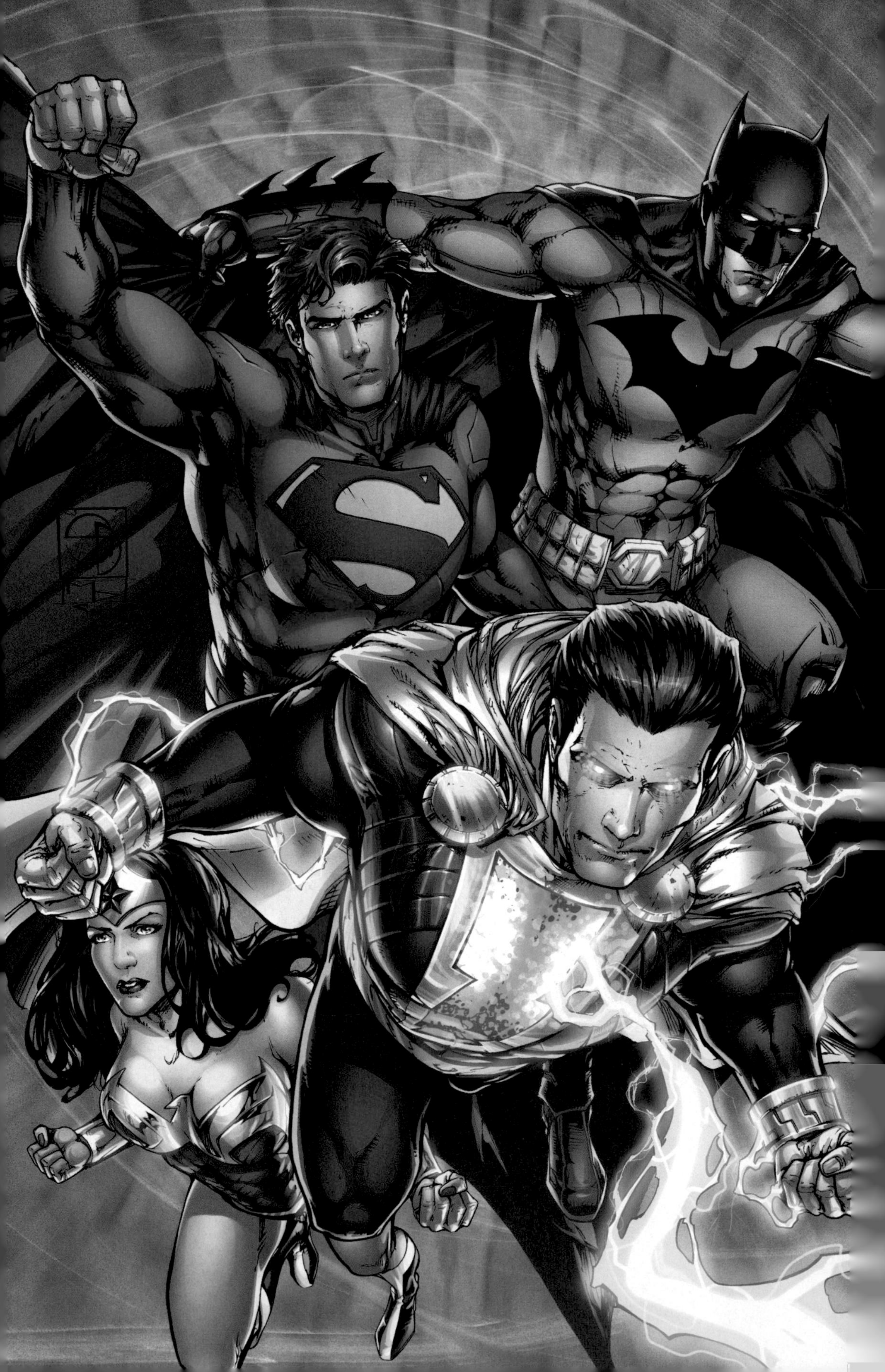

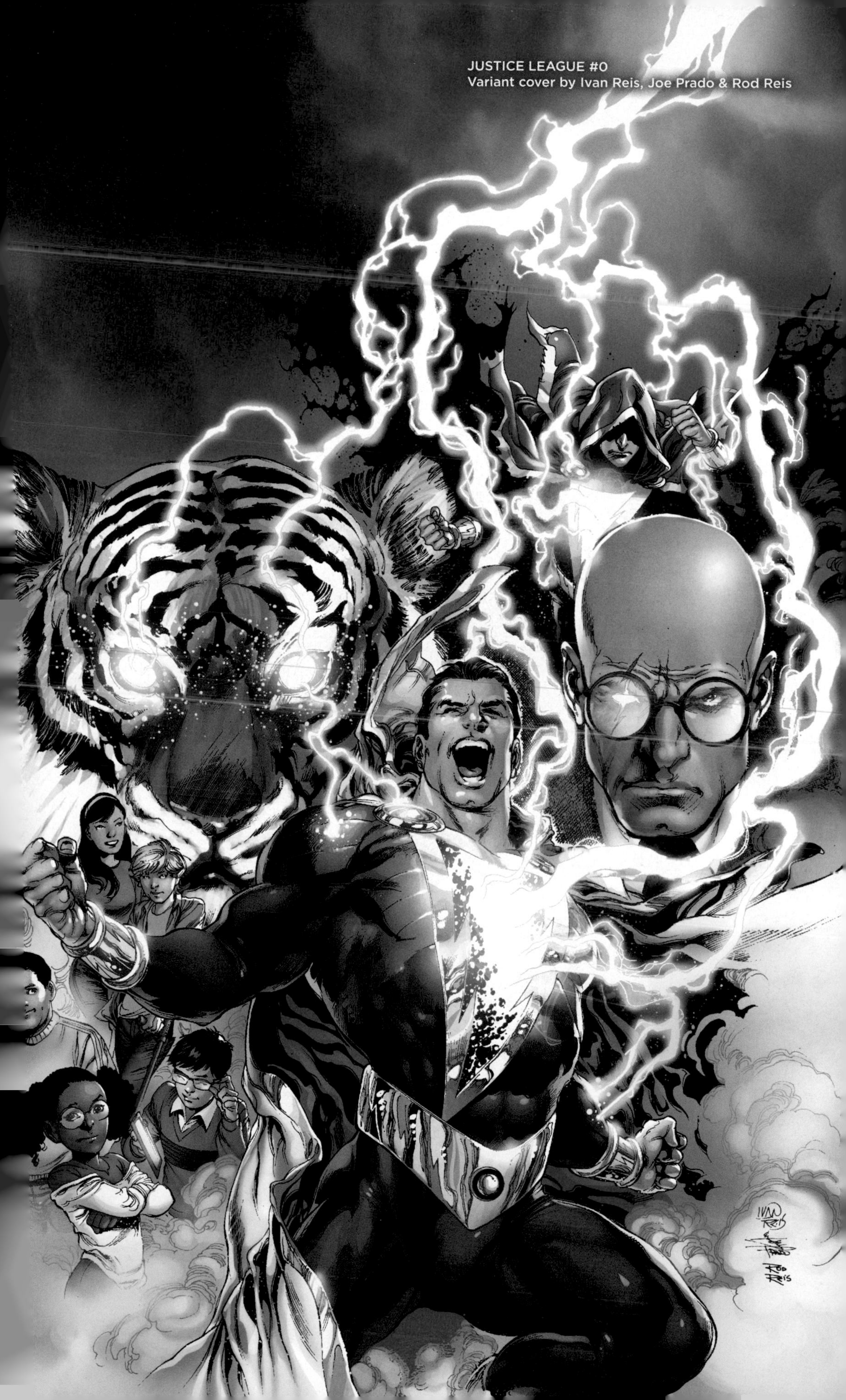

JUSTICE LEAGUE #0
Variant cover by Ivan Reis, Joe Prado & Rod Reis

SHAZAM!

CHARACTER DESIGNS BY GARY FRANK

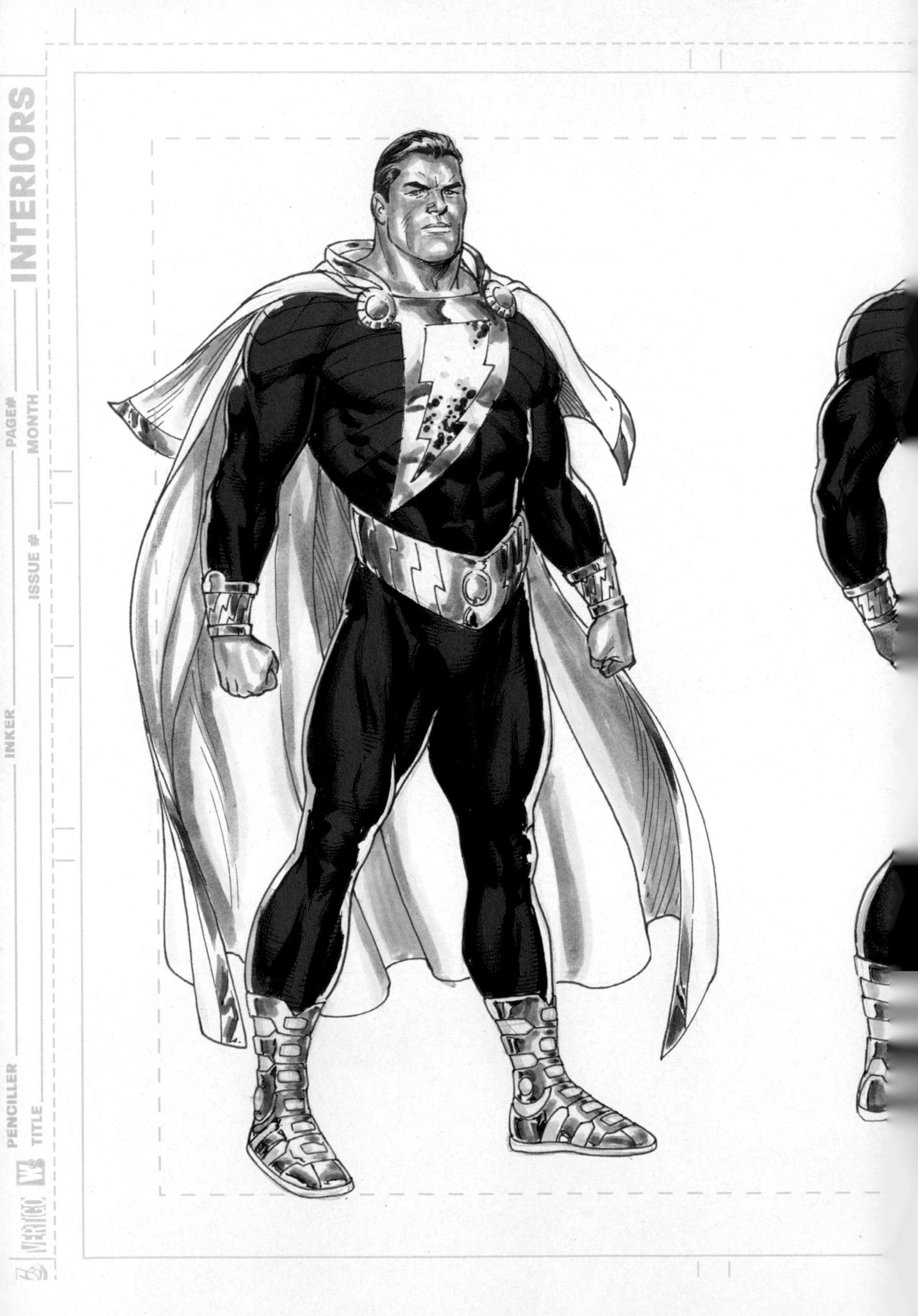
INTERIORS
PAGE#
MONTH
ISSUE #
INKER
PENCILLER
TITLE

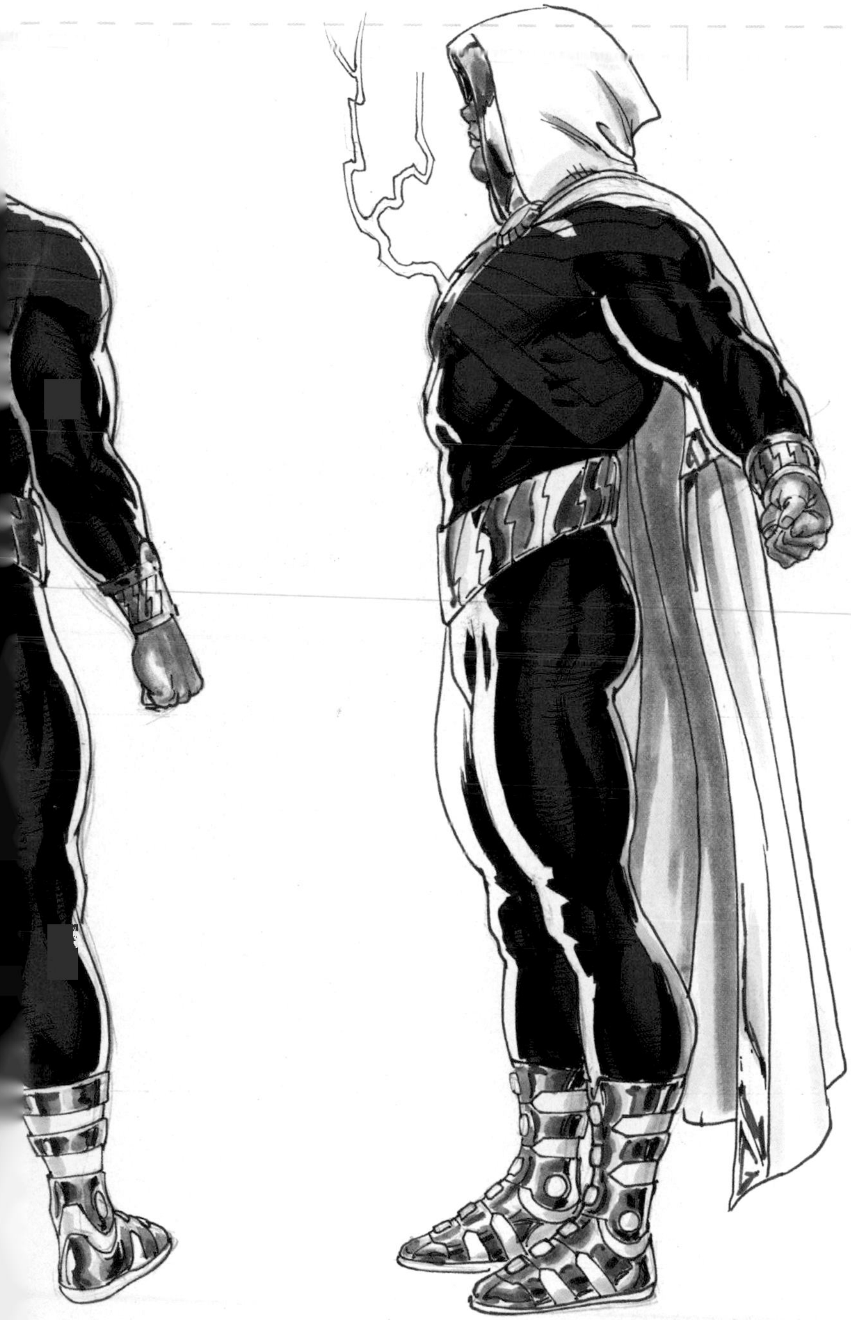

LIVE AREA

CROP

BLEED

CUT RIGHT-HAND PAGE AT THIS LINE

DOUBLE PAGE SPREAD: CUT AS SHOWN, ABUT PAGE EDGES, TAPE ON BACK, DO NOT OVERLAP

CUT LEFT HAND PAGE AT THIS LINE

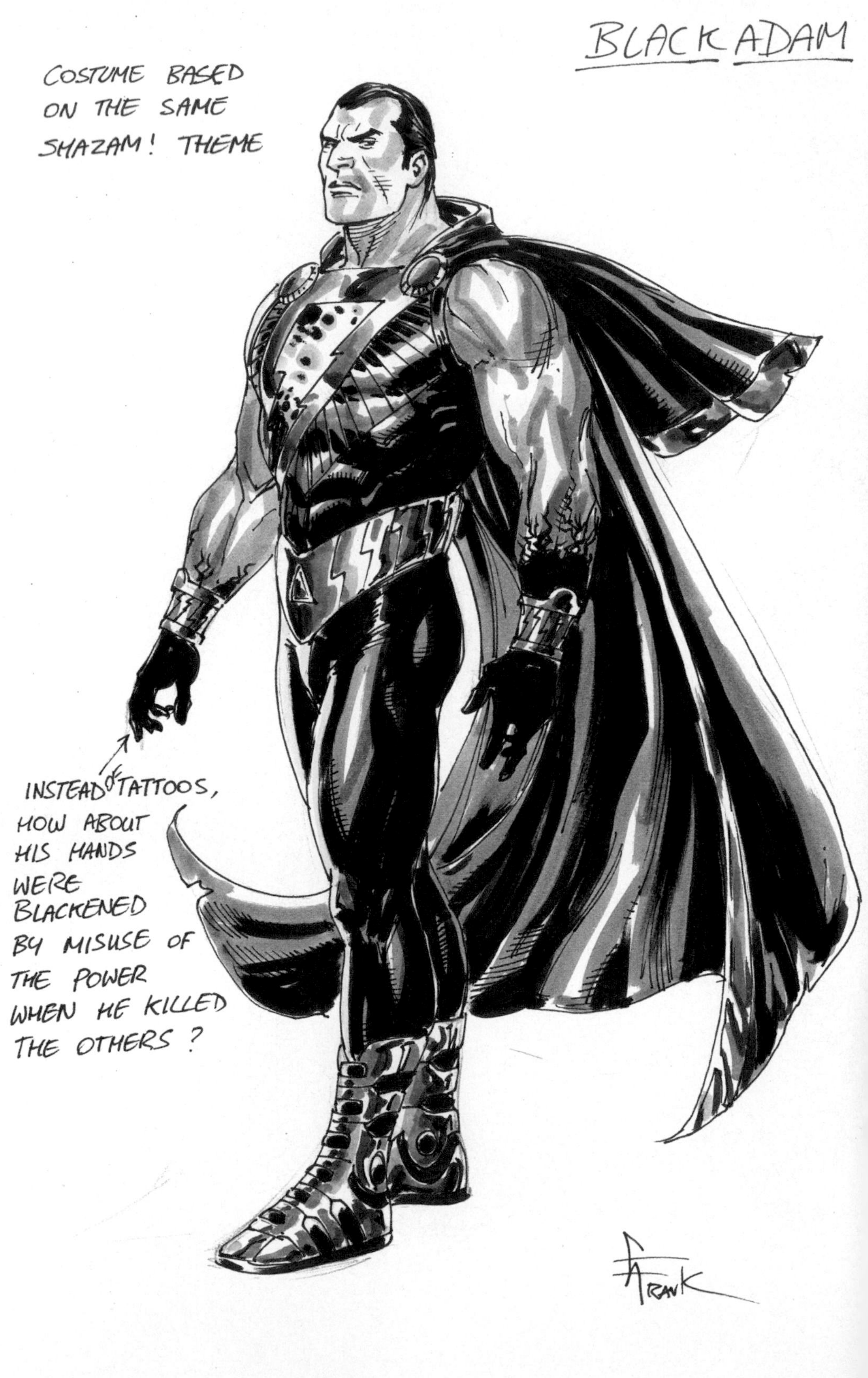
BLACK ADAM
COSTUME BASED
ON THE SAME
SHAZAM! THEME
INSTEAD OF TATTOOS,
HOW ABOUT
HIS HANDS
WERE
BLACKENED
BY MISUSE OF
THE POWER
WHEN HE KILLED
THE OTHERS ?
FRANK

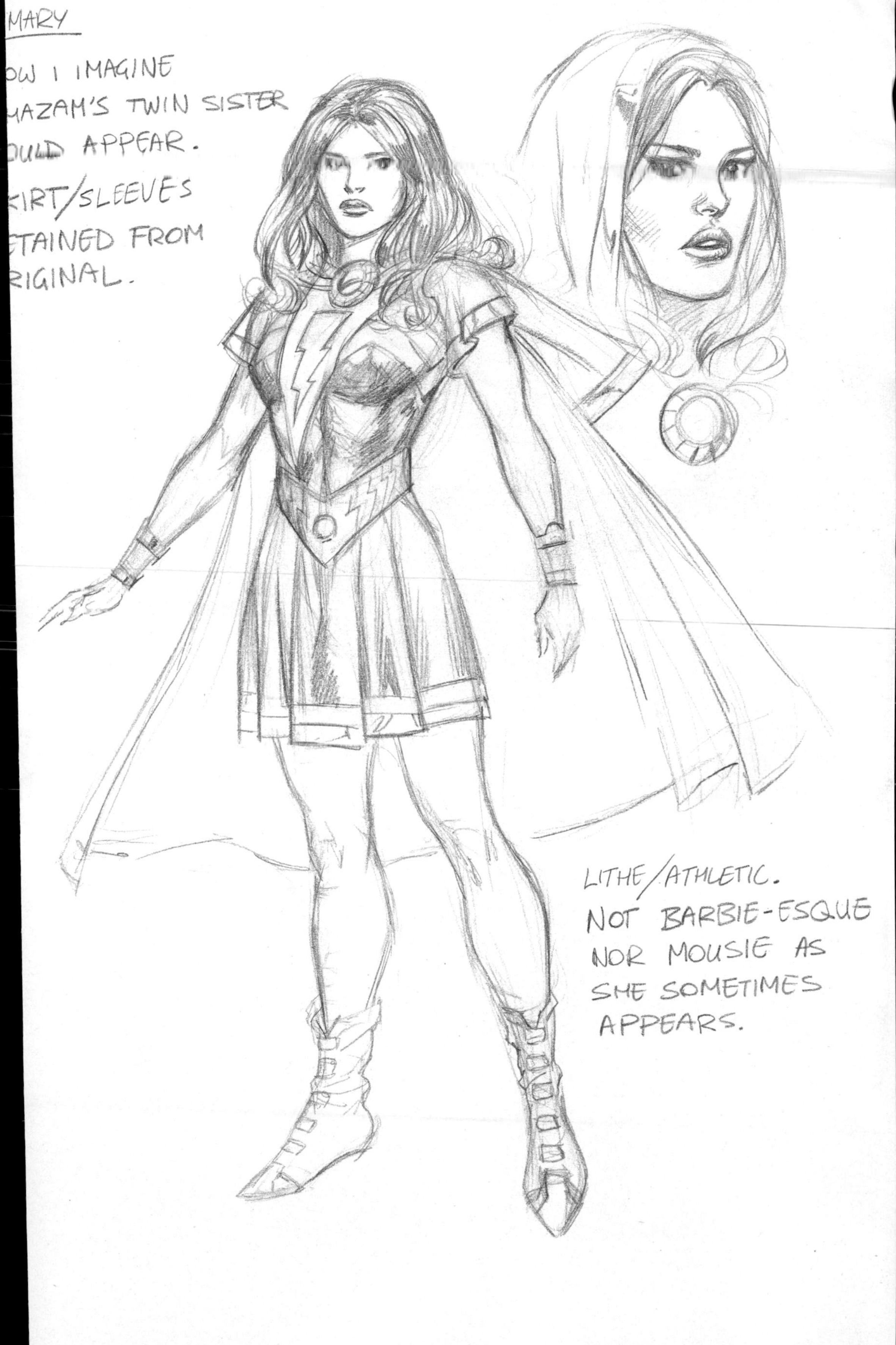
MARY
OW I IMAGINE
HAZAM'S TWIN SISTER
OULD APPEAR.
KIRT/SLEEVES
ETAINED FROM
RIGINAL.
LITHE/ATHLETIC.
NOT BARBIE-ESQUE
NOR MOUSIE AS
SHE SOMETIMES
APPEARS.

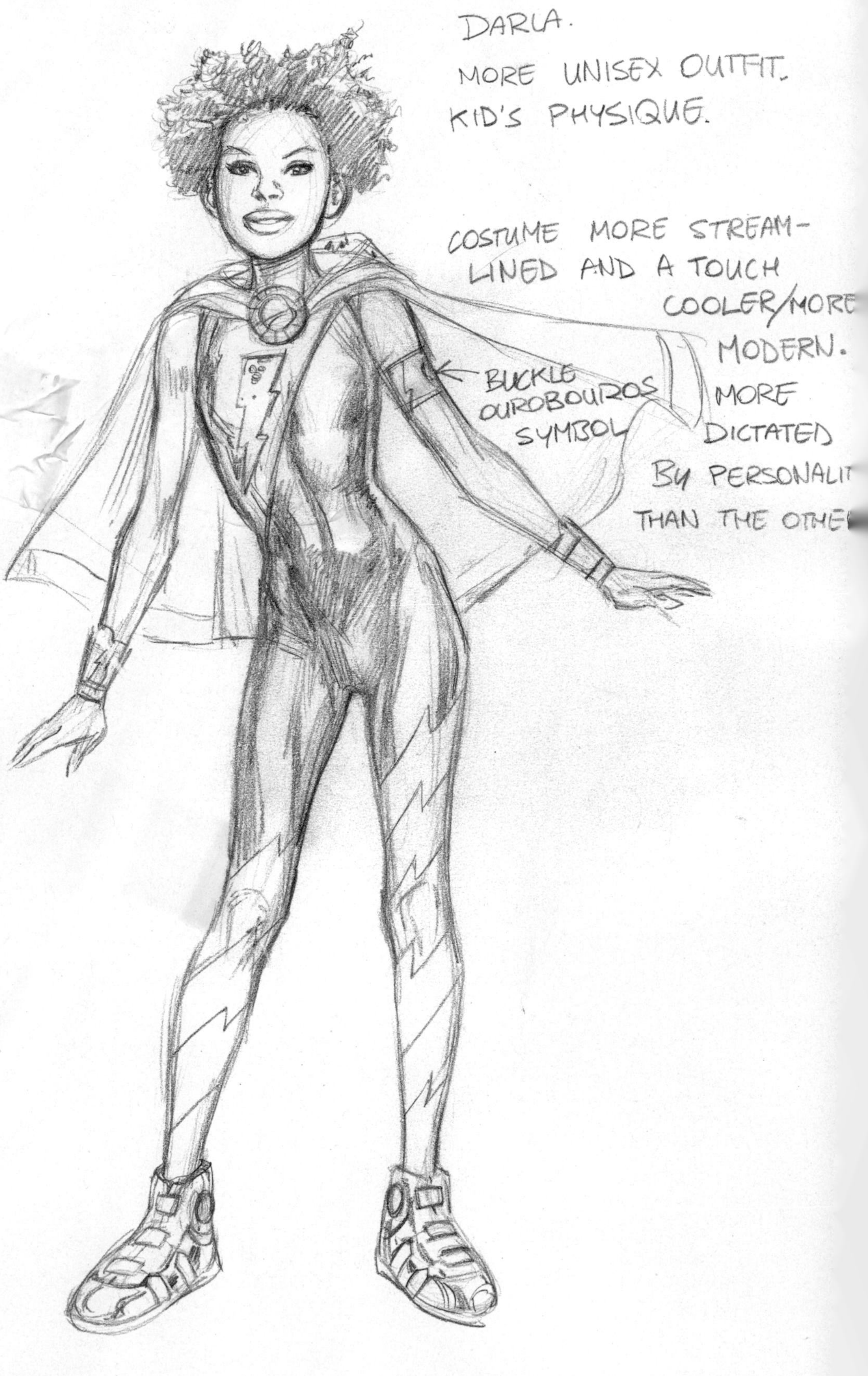
DARLA.
MORE UNISEX OUTFIT.
KID'S PHYSIQUE.
COSTUME MORE STREAM-
LINED AND A TOUCH
COOLER/MORE
MODERN.
MORE
DICTATED
BY PERSONALIT
THAN THE OTHE
BUCKLE
OUROBOUROS
SYMBOL

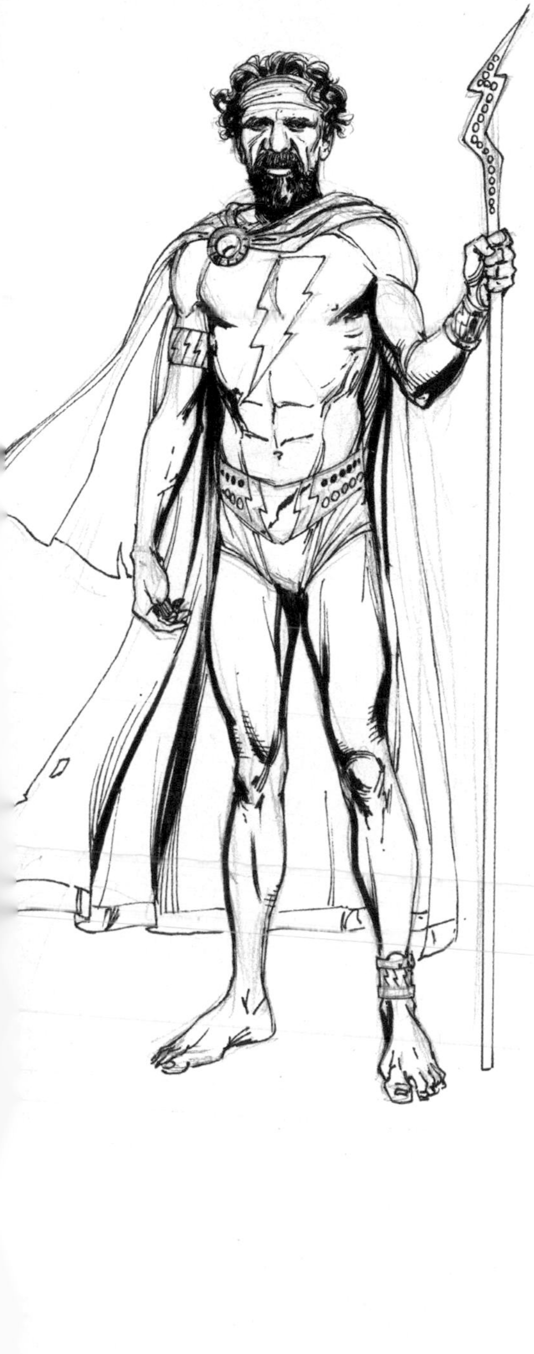

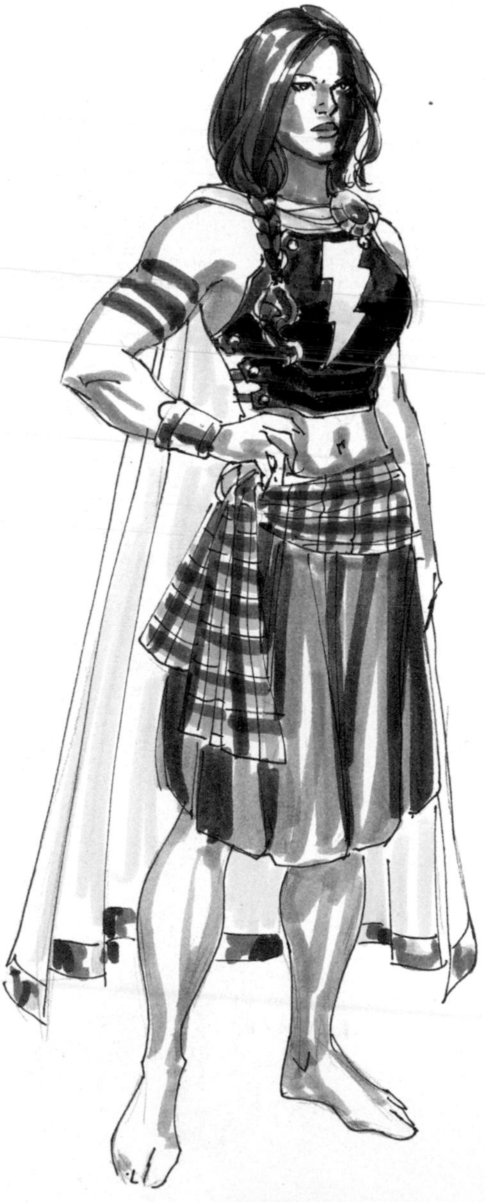

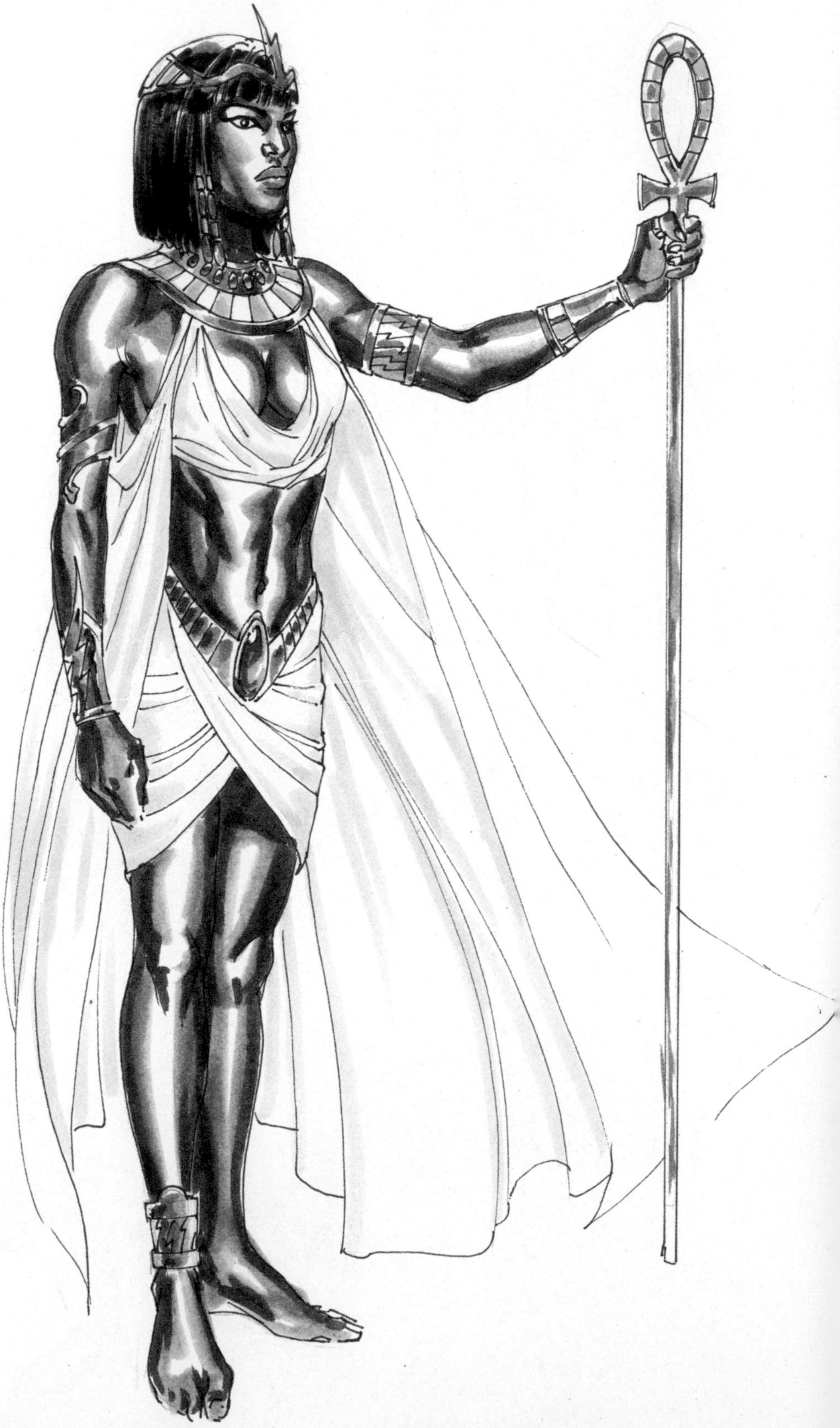

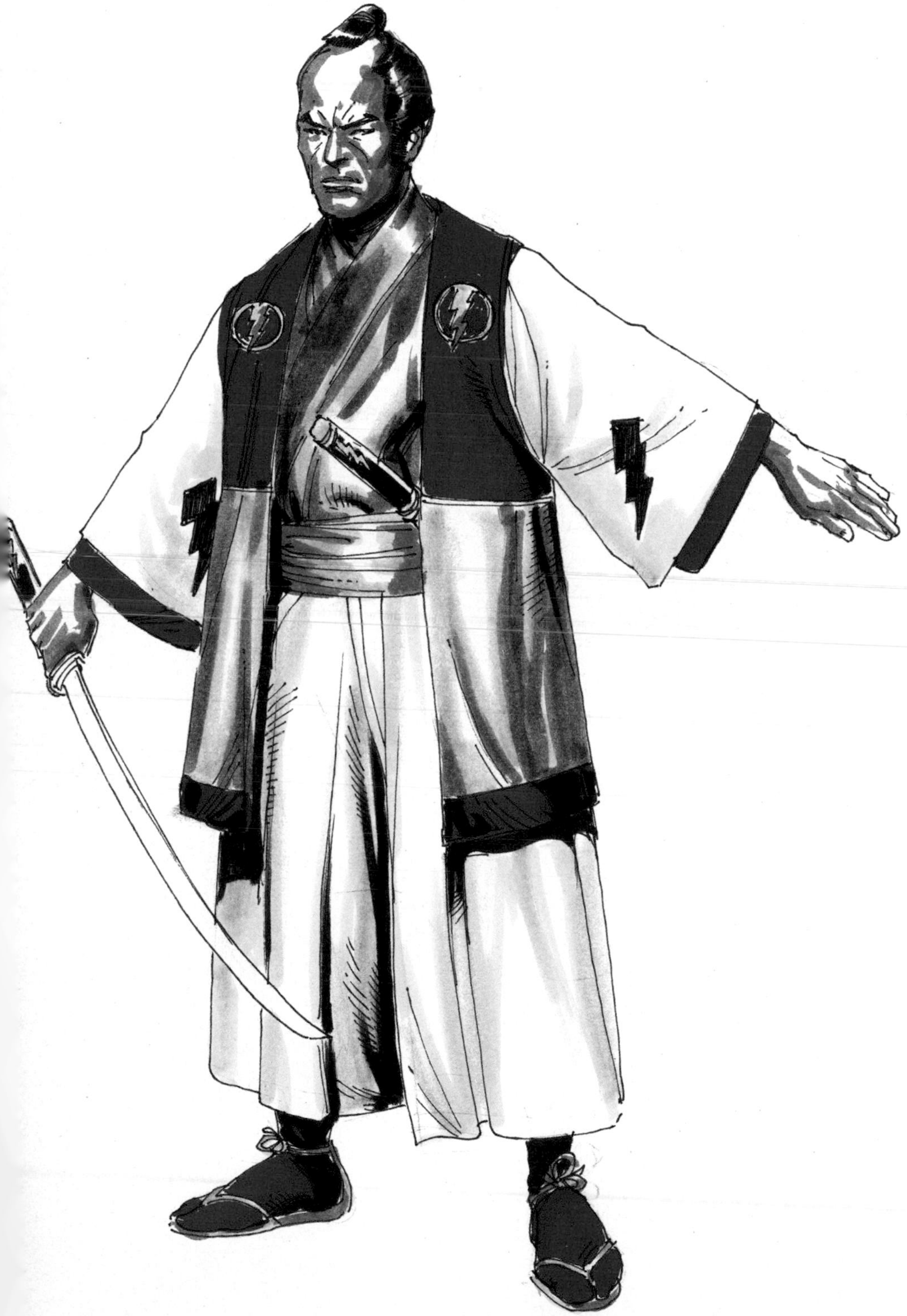

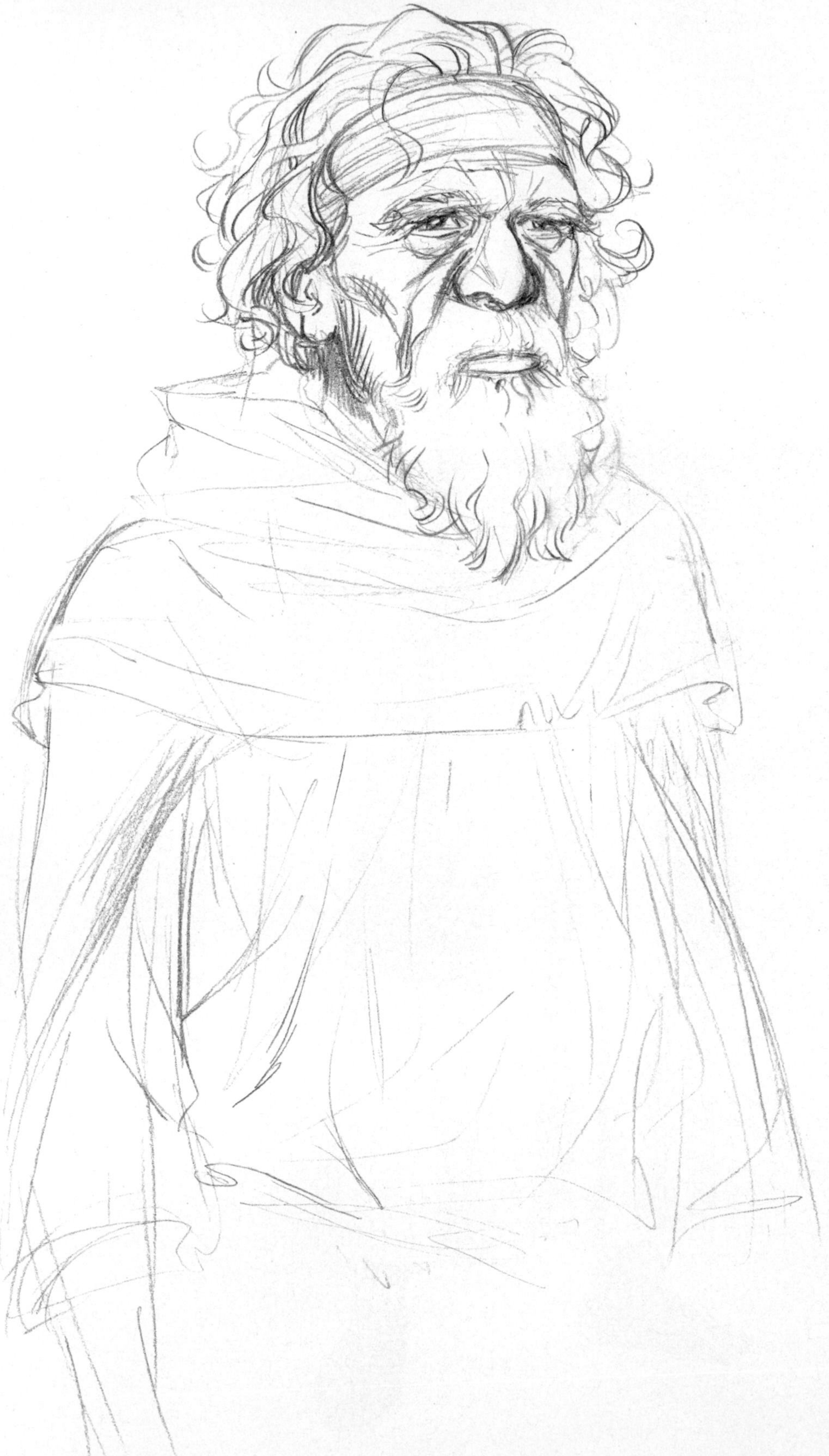

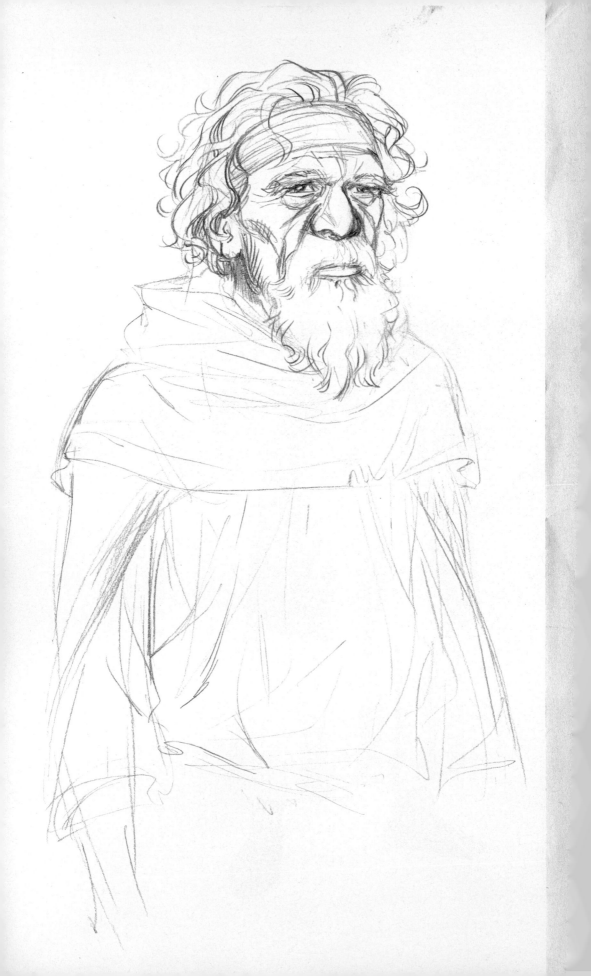

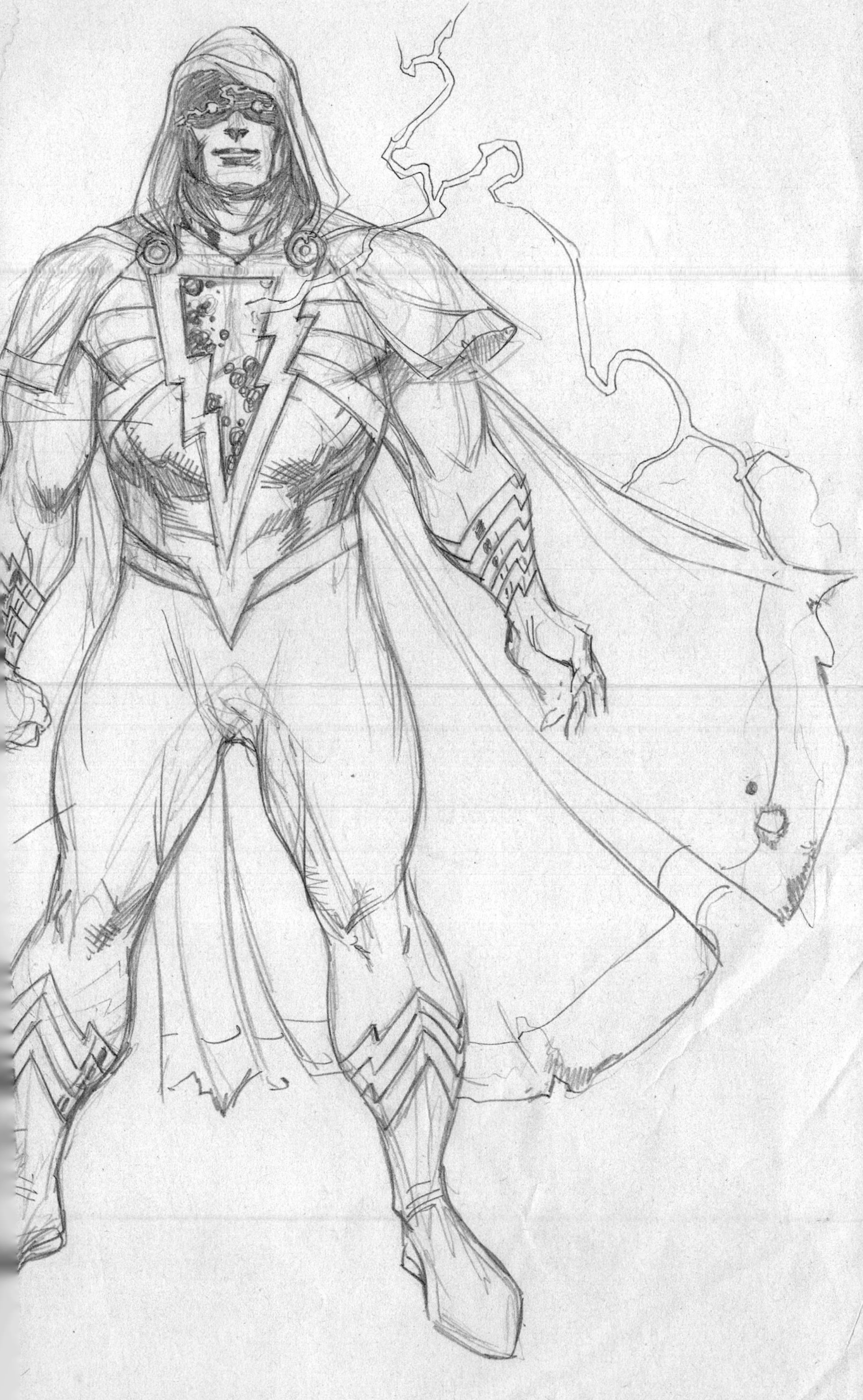

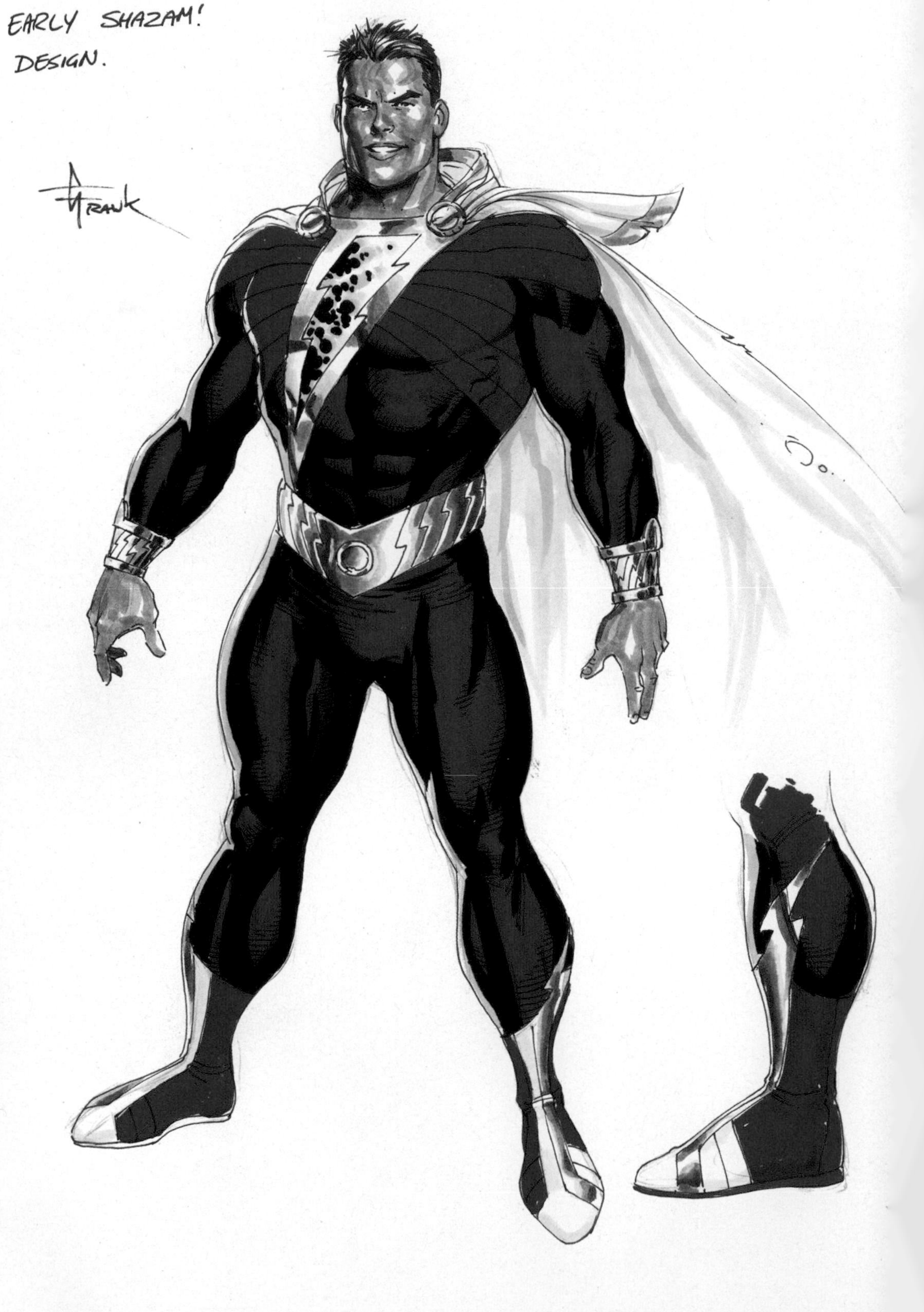
EARLY SHAZAM!
DESIGN.
FRANK